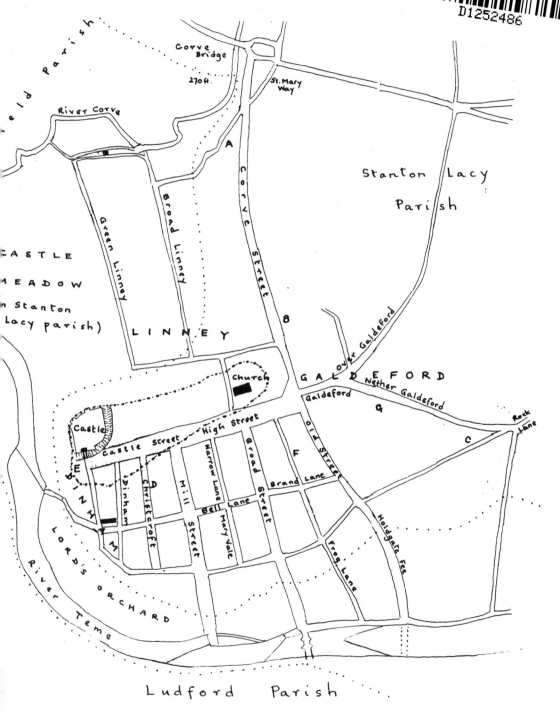

Corve Bridge

270ft

St. Mary Way

River Corve

...eld Parish

Stanton Lacy Parish

Green Linney

Broad Linney

Corve Street

A

B

CASTLE

MEADOW

n Stanton

Lacy parish)

LINNEY

Church

over Galdeford

GALDEFORD

Galdeford

Nether Galdeford

G

Rock Lane

Castle

High Street

Castle Street

Old Street

C

E

Dinham

Christcroft

Mill Street

Narrow Lane

Broad Street

F

Brand Lane

Bell Lane

Mary Vale

Holdgate Fee

Frog Lane

DINHAM

LORD'S ORCHARD

River Teme

Ludford Parish

LUDLOW
1085~1660

Ludlow from Whitcliffe, its common land since the early 13th century.

LUDLOW
1085~1660
A Social, Economic and Political History

Michael Faraday

Phillimore

1991

Published by
PHILLIMORE & CO. LTD.
Shopwyke Hall, Chichester, Sussex

ISBN 0 85033 804 2

Printed in England by
STAPLES PRINTERS ROCHESTER LIMITED
Love Lane, Rochester, Kent

For Janet

Without Whom Nothing

Contents

List of Illustrations

Frontispiece: Ludlow from Whitcliffe

Preface and Acknowledgements

Every age writes about the past to reflect its own preoccupations. Ludlow's history was written by Thomas Wright, father and son, in 1826 and 1852. The first was largely an account of Ludlow's contacts with great men and with great events, with some discussion of the castle, the church, the charities and the schools. The second, a more original work, since the son was a man of wide scholarly interests, was again essentially an account of Ludlow's contacts with national events, together with an idiosyncratic discussion of folk-culture and a very inaccurate list of Ludlow's post–1461 bailiffs. In 1857 was published the fifth volume of R. W. Eyton's great work *The Antiquities of Shropshire*. This volume took Ludlow history up to about 1200. Eyton's work, despite the occasional forgivable error, still stands; his skill with his sources, with detail, in an age when so few archives were properly catalogued, was first-class. Eyton was concerned chiefly with manorial history, which touched on the lives of the leading burgesses at least. Since then no one has attempted a full history of Ludlow. The work of Henry Weyman in a number of articles, based on a thorough knowledge of the borough archives, then still in Ludlow and for a long time in his custody, covers a great deal of Ludlow history. Unfortunately this did not reach the general reader, except in a small book *Ludlow in Bye-Gone Days*. Moreover the archives were uncatalogued, so that Weyman could not reference his writings. W. J. Sparrow wrote about the Palmers' Gild, suffering from the same handicaps as Weyman. Later published work covered specific subjects of research, like that of St John Hope on the castle and the town layout. There have also been articles on particular subjects in journals like the *Transactions of the Shropshire Archaeological Society*. Some of the best recent scholarship is to be found in the articles by Alec Gaydon and Marjorie Chibnall in the second volume of the *Victoria County History of Shropshire*. Peter Klein and Annette Roe's *The Carmelite Friary*, a recent work, is excellent. The various recent publications by David Lloyd have also added immeasurably to our understanding of Ludlow's origins and development.

Writing a history of Ludlow has in the past been hampered by the deficiencies of the archive material. Neither State nor municipal archives were at one time properly referenced and catalogued; even if relevant documents could be found, they could often not be referred to except in terms which scarcely allowed anyone else to find the same documents easily. The situation now, although better than it was, especially with State archives, is by no means perfect with municipal archives. The latter have been very roughly catalogued and much of the material has been differentiated no more than to a box of documents.

In recent years the Ludlow Historical Research Group, an amalgam of projects led by M. E. Speight and D. J. Lloyd, has done a great deal of work on Ludlow's history, generally with a bias towards architectural and topographical subjects. I joined my efforts to theirs in 1978, concentrating on documentary research in the various archive collections in London, Shrewsbury and Hereford, with a bias towards the period before 1660. This book springs from that tripartite collaboration and from the realisation that much that was new had been discovered and that the time was right for a fresh attempt to produce a conspectus of Ludlow history. The book has taken some years to write and some of the research for it has already been referred to in other publications more specific in their concerns, started later but produced sooner. Being overtaken is perhaps the penalty for attempting to be comprehensive.

The personal view upon which this book is based is that history is the story of communities, that is, the relationships between people – social, political, legal and economic. Human institutions are important manifestations of these arrangements, and their workings are particularly vital to a history of an ancient town. These, then, are the subjects which will be covered in this book. The planning of the original town, its development and architecture and the interiors of the buildings, along with the standard of living of the residents, are excluded as they will be the subject of Mr. Lloyd's forthcoming book.

I have adopted certain conventions which seem sensible, although they are not the practice of everyone. Individual people come into the picture only from the period from which records survive, that is, about 1250. This was the period when surnames were adopted by those below the rank of nobility. Often these surnames became hereditary, but it is not always possible to know which were. All references to them were in Latin or Norman-French; it was normal, therefore, for surnames of place to be preceded by *de*, but, unless the individual is usually known these days by the preposition, I have in all cases dropped it, because I believe that *Henricus de Chabbenovere* was called 'Henry Chabbenovere', not 'Henry of Chabbenovere', just as *Galfridus filius Andree* was called 'Geoffrey Andrew' and not 'Geoffrey son of Andrew'. I adopt the spelling of place-names as they are now (if known), but for surnames (even locative surnames) I have adopted the most typical spelling in use at the time in references to the person concerned; the great merchant, for instance, is referred to here as 'Lawrence de Ludelawe'.

I have always referred to the Corporation and the Community of Ludlow with capitals and have similarly treated the Gild and the Hospital. Certain officials, such as the Six Men, also need initial capitals.

Space constraints have affected the content of the book and the treatment of the topics covered. What is included here represents but a small proportion of the material now available for inclusion; a drastic selection has had to be undertaken, determined partly by the relative importance of the topics chosen for coverage, which is to some extent a matter of personal and subjective judgment. Some topics, such as population, are by their nature so complex that a whole book would be justified for each. It will have to be taken on trust that I have been through that complex process even though it is not all set out at length. This will not please everyone, but many would have regarded the detailed workings dry stuff.

The office holder lists are essential to a town history both to illuminate the text, to provide a permanent record, and to correct defective lists previously published.

I am grateful for help and advice freely given by several people. Miss M. Williams has generously made available some of her documentary transcripts. Dr. M. E. Speight and Mr. P. Klein have engaged in an exchange of the results of our respective researches, which has been especially valuable. Dr. Speight has kindly commented on drafts of the text and has allowed me to reproduce some photographs from his collection (Illustrations nos. 23, 26, 32 and 33). Mr. D. J. Lloyd has over the years been generous with his research material and in discussing the subject in great detail; without him the work would have been impossible. The archivists at Hereford and Shrewsbury, particularly, have been very helpful. Illustrations nos. 9, 10, 11, 12, 27 and 29 are included by permission of the Shropshire Record Office, and nos. 20 and 31 by permission of Hereford and Worcester Record Office. Much time in evenings and weekends, as well as family holidays for many years, has been taken up with this book; I owe my wife and family much for their tolerance.

M. A. FARADAY, 1990

Chronology of Ludlow History 1085–1660

1085	Death of Walter de Lacy I
c.1136–58	Castellany of Joce de Dinan
1169	Ludlow township paid royal tax
1171–86	Gift of 'Dinmore fee' in Corve Street to the Hospitallers
1186–1224	Ludlow in custody of royal constables for 23 years in this period
1199–1200	Reconstruction of the parish church
1228	Slaughter of the Welsh forces at Culmington
1231	Hospital of St John founded by Peter Undergod
1233	'Men of Ludlow' granted first royal licence to enclose the town
c.1243–48	Marriage of Margery Lacy to John de Verdun
1251–2	Marriage of Maud Lacy to Geoffrey de Genevile
1254	Foundation of Augustinian priory in Christcroft
c.1250–60	Foundation of the Palmers' Gild
1260	Partition of Ludlow between Genevile and Verdun
1267	Genevile gift of Ludlow rents and mills to Aconbury convent
1282	Genevile alienation of the Cotes rents
1283	Alternate advowson of Ludlow church agreed between Genevile and Verdun
1283–7	Ludlow a royal base for the Welsh campaigns
1294	Drowning of Lawrence de Ludelawe
1307	Marriage of Joan Genevile and Roger Mortimer whereby Mortimer became lord of Ludlow
1308	First definite record of 'The Twelve' and 'The Twenty Five'
1331	Earliest recorded Corpus Christi procession
1331	Murder of Thomas Marteley
1332	Edward III's second visit to Ludlow
1332	Ludlow represented at the parliament *pro stapulis ordinandis*
1335–67	The bailiffs, now merchants rather than clerks, became the executive authority of the borough
1350	Foundation of the Carmelite priory
1358	Ludlow re-united as a Mortimer possession
1398–1413	Ludlow in custody of royal constables
1405	Royal grant of privileges to Ludlow
c.1435–70	Major reconstruction of the church
1449	Duke of York's confirmation of Ludlow's form of government
1452	Ludlow held for York during Mulsho's rising; Henry VI's visit to Ludlow
1459	Sack of Ludlow after the Battle of Ludford Bridge
1461	First royal charter
1463	John Hosyer's legacy for founding the Almshouse
1493	Prince Edward's Council established in Ludlow
1525	Princess Mary's Council established in Ludlow
1538	Dissolution of the priories and the Hospital
1552	Dissolution of the Palmers' Gild
1582	Cloth-manufacture at its peak; thereafter decline.
1596	Presentation of Robert Horne, a puritan, as rector
1590–1601	Disputes over the Charters; failure of the attack on oligarchy
c.1610	Collapse of Ludlow's cloth-manufacture
1634	Borough lost Exchequer case over ownership of the town mills
1642	Abolition of the Council of the March
1646	Siege and capture of Ludlow by parliamentary army; destruction of the suburbs by royalists

1. Dinham, possibly one of the oldest settled streets in Ludlow.

2. Corve Street, looking towards Stanton Lacy. Ludlow formed the southern tip of the 11th-century lordship of Stanton.

Introduction

Ludlow is first recorded in the 12th century as *Ludeleya*, which may be distorted in trying to Latinise it. By 1177 it was *Ludelawe*. About 1270 the spelling had changed to *Ludelowe*. Towards the end of the 13th century the spelling *Lodelowe* came increasingly into use, becoming typical by about 1305. The 'e' represented a distinct syllable, but 'Lod' was probably pronounced 'Lud', just as 'Coventry' is often pronounced 'Cuventry'. This spelling was standard until about 1445 when Luddelowe and Ludlowe came into vogue.[1] At this time the old pronunciation 'Ludd-a-low-a' was giving way to 'Ludd-low'. By the 16th century the spelling Ludlowe was normal. By the end of my chosen period, 1660, some people were beginning to drop the final 'e', but the modern spelling of Ludlow was uncommon at that time.

Although the foundation of the town of Ludlow followed and was determined by the building of the castle on the ridge overlooking the River Teme, it is likely, to judge by place-names and the lay-out of roads, that there were two or three earlier settlements. Dinham may be a special case; if it acquired its name from the mid–12th century lord or castellan, Joce de Dinan, the settlement may have been founded no earlier than that, although the possibility of a re-named earlier settlement by a ford there should not be dismissed.

Galdeford, the eastern suburb of Ludlow, which gave its name to the three streets which converge on the crossroads outside what was Galdeford gate, may well have existed as a settlement or farmstead. The name is old in form and has never been recorded with the suffix 'street'. It is more likely to refer to pigs than to gallows and the element 'ford' implies that its centre was at the bottom of the hill close to the Teme, or possibly to the stream which used to run from the ridge of what is now Julian Avenue to the Teme. It may be that Galdeford was a township which encompassed all the land between Old Street, or further west, to Weeping Cross lane.

Linney is another old suburb name which has never had the suffix 'street'. The 'ey' element implies an island or marshy ground, which much of it certainly would have been in the 11th century. It is possible that a small settlement or farmstead existed here on the higher ground, perhaps even connected with the crossing of the Corve in the Lower Corve Street area where the old pattern of roads clearly pre-dates the planned grid of Ludlow.

Settlement in this part of south Shropshire, and especially in Stanton Lacy, in the 11th and 12th centuries was scattered. Beyond the periphery of Ludlow names like Henley and Wigley imply clearings in woods, while Fishmore and Dodmore, nearer to Ludlow, imply open land. A south-facing gentle slope may well have been partially cultivated open land, a more likely site for measuring and laying out a new town. Ludlow may even have been the name of an early farmstead occupying the land between Dinham and Galdeford.

Present-day Corve Street-Old Street represents part of the old north-south route, while Corve Bridge provided a crossroads with the main east-west route, a likely place for an early settlement, to the south and west of which was added the new planned town of Ludlow in the 12th century. The extent of the huge new borough was determined by the loop formed by the Corve and Teme rivers. There is no evidence that all the burgages formed were intended to be built on, or that they ever were.

The evidence of medieval property boundaries, still largely surviving, suggests that, before the outer bailey of the castle was added in the late 12th century, the drawbridge leading to the then gateway in the keep was the centre of the town. The nave of St. Thomas's chapel in Dinham was probably at right angles to a road running from below the chapel to the drawbridge. This, the narrow lane parallel to it on the other end of the chapel, together with a third parallel lane (or, more likely, ditch) 60 yards to the east, called Christcroft, may have been the first planned township of Dinham. The grid of the town of Ludlow between Dinham and Old Street was laid out within a few decades of this, with the High Street running from the drawbridge to Old Street along the ridge. Before the 12th century was out the outer bailey of the castle was built, expunging the upper parts of the Dinham streets.

Christcroft was enclosed and one or more of the minor north-south lanes in the new town grid seem to have ceased to be roads by the mid-13th century. The building of the town walls in the 13th century distorted existing roadways and property boundaries and must have involved the extinction of property-rights, probably compensated for by means of exchange.

Apart from certain areas of demesne land the whole of Ludlow seems to have been 'burgaged'. The plot-sizes varied from one part of the town to another, but it is not certain whether these variations signify chronological stages in the development of the town or merely attempts to produce plots of equivalent value; the latter seems more likely. It is clear that by the mid-13th century the pressure of population on the desirable parts of the town was such that very many burgages had been subdivided into two or three plots, just as there was encroachment of buildings on the edges and in the middle of the wide High Street.

I intend to say no more on the complex and fascinating subject of the planning and building of the town. This and other related topics will be covered in detail by Mr. D. J. Lloyd's forthcoming book which is in preparation and will be based on many years' research.

3. Castle Street, the only surviving section of the original wide street which ran from the Castle tower to Old Street. In the foreground was the medieval corn market.

Chapter One

The Lordship

The Lacy Family, 1085–1241

Ludlow is not in Domesday Book, notwithstanding Eyton's belief that it was.[1] It is hardly to be believed that an important settlement in that area would have been left out of Domesday, so it is reasonable to assume that it did not exist as a significant and separate entity. If one looks at the map of the parishes around Ludlow, whose borders seem to be those of the post-Conquest lordships, one can see that the ridge on which Ludlow stands is but the southern spur of the high ground which forms the mass of the parish of Stanton Lacy. There is a now isolated tract of that parish to the north-east of Ludlow and in the Middle Ages the vicar of Stanton Lacy claimed spiritual jurisdiction over Ludlow Castle.[2] All this suggests that the area now occupied by Ludlow was originally part of the lordship of Stanton Lacy and was hived off when it became more important, probably when the castle was built.

The first Norman lord of Stanton Lacy was Walter de Lacy, of Lassy in Normandy, who was granted estates in chief in Shropshire, Herefordshire, Gloucestershire and elsewhere.[3] Walter de Lacy died in 1085, before the Domesday record was compiled, and his son Roger appears there as lord of Stanton. Very early, but presumably after the building of the castle, Ludlow became the centre of an honor, although it was never named as such, always being referred to as part of the honor of Weobley. The building of the castle began shortly after this; at what point Ludlow was treated as a separate lordship we do not know, but it was probably when the town was created. Roger Lacy was succeeded by his brother, Hugh, and in 1115 by his own son, Gilbert Lacy.[4]

Eyton thought that Henry I ignored the claims of the Lacy heirs – although no reason was vouchsafed – and gave Ludlow, along with Weobley and Ewyas, to Payn fitz John. There is no direct evidence that the latter received Ludlow, but he did have Ewyas, and the two lordships usually went together. One may wonder why hereditary claims were ignored – if indeed they were – and a possible explanation is that when Hugh died Gilbert was still a minor. Payn may have had a claim of his own, through his wife, Sibil, a daughter or niece of Hugh Lacy. If these relationships are correct, Payn's claims to Ludlow, or at least parts of the Lacy estates, would have been strong. He was certainly powerful on the March from about 1121 until his death in 1136. He left two daughters by Sibil: Cecily, who married successively Roger, Earl of Hereford, William of Poitou and Walter de Mayenne, but died childless; and Agnes, who married Warin de Munchensy and had a son, William. In 1198 William and Cecily claimed their 'right' in Ludlow and Weobley; such right must have been derived from the previous title of Payn fitz John, although there is no evidence that they substantiated their claim. Wightman quotes Cecily as referring to Hugh de Lacy as her grandfather, which makes Sibil his daughter.[5]

Less open to doubt is the fact that, soon after 1136, the king put Ludlow in the hands of Joce de Dinan, who held the castle for about twenty years during and after the wars of Stephen and Matilda. The origin of his family seems to have been Dinant in Brittany; later generations, established in Berkshire, Devon, and elsewhere, were known as 'Dinham', perhaps an obvious anglicisation. What may be the oldest settled part of the town of Ludlow, immediately south of the castle and between it and the Teme, has, so far as we know, always been called 'Dinham' or, earlier, 'Dinane'. Although the name has a Welsh look, comparable with place-names like Dinmore and Dinedor, this is not necessarily evidence that the place-name antedates Joce de Dinan. It was certainly unusual in the mid-12th century for places to be named after their lords, other than as suffixes, as in 'Stanton Lacy', but the earlier examples of Montgomery and Richard's Castle do not permit us to exclude a later instance. Although there are some early 12th-century chronicle references to 'Ludelawe', there is no evidence that the chronicles themselves were written this early. If Joce de Dinan gave his name to the area, of which he was lord for only two decades, then it may be that he made some important change and the most likely would be to have founded a settlement there.

It is possible that during his lordship some form of proto-borough was laid out beside the castle along the western edge of the ridge. There is some circumstantial evidence to justify the view. The *Romance of Fulk FitzWarine* refers to Joce building a three-baileyed castle, which may have included the civil settlement since the castle has only two military baileys, the outer being later than the inner.[6] The existence of St Thomas's chapel may indicate an earlier parish chapel, turned over to other uses when the parish church was built on the ridge.[7] The position of the foundations of the nave of the chapel may also indicate a roadway at right angles to the nave and leading north to the drawbridge of the castle inner bailey where it would have met an earlier extension of Castle Street. Christcroft, a strip of demesne land running north-south between Dinham and the rest of Ludlow, may have been the eastern boundary of this proto-borough.[8]

Gilbert Lacy obtained the lordship of Ludlow in about 1156 and shortly afterwards 'retired', joining the Templars, becoming preceptor of Tripoli and dying in 1163. To join the Templars was to join a monastic order and involved giving up estates. His son, Hugh Lacy, may well have succeeded in 1158, but certainly no later than 1163.[9] In 1171 Hugh was sent to Ireland as Justiciar, Lord of Meath and of Dublin. It was shortly afterwards that many of the inhabitants of Dublin were expelled and replaced by English settlers; several of these came from Ludlow. So began Ludlow's medieval connections with Ireland; and so the concerns of Ludlow's lords began to shift well away from the town.[10] Hugh Lacy was murdered in Ireland in 1186. It was some time before this that he gave to the Hospitaller commandery of Dinmore part of the lordship of Ludlow which remained with Dinmore until the 16th century.[11] His successor was his eldest son, Walter Lacy, who received livery in 1189, therefore being at least 21, and who died in 1241 aged 73 or more. Much of his active life was also spent in Ireland, sometimes in the king's service, sometimes in opposition, but always promoting his own interests. Ludlow town was in the king's hands until 1189, when it was restored to Walter Lacy; the castle was restored in 1191, but by 1194 his estates were seized once more for his misconduct in Ireland. They were in the king's hands in 1197 and 1198. By 1206 Walter Lacy had Ludlow back, having paid 400 marks to the king, but his Irish disputes led to the re-seizure in 1207 when Philip Daubeny was put in charge. In 1208 Lacy was restored to favour, but in 1210 was in revolt again in Ireland, so Engelard de Cigogné was given custody of Ludlow, on behalf of the king. Not until 1215 did Lacy recover town and castle; he seems then to have lived in England until 1222 when Irish affairs recalled him. In 1224 Ludlow was surrendered to the custody of William de Gamages for the king as security for Lacy's good behaviour in Ireland; this lasted two years. He was still in Ireland in 1234 when he appointed William Lucy as constable of Ludlow.[12]

The Genevile-Mortimer Moiety, 1241–1358

The death of Walter Lacy in 1241 without a surviving male heir began a period of great complexity in the ownership of the lordship of Ludlow. Walter Lacy survived both his son and heir, Gilbert, and Gilbert's son and heir, Walter. After 1234 the heirs of Lacy were

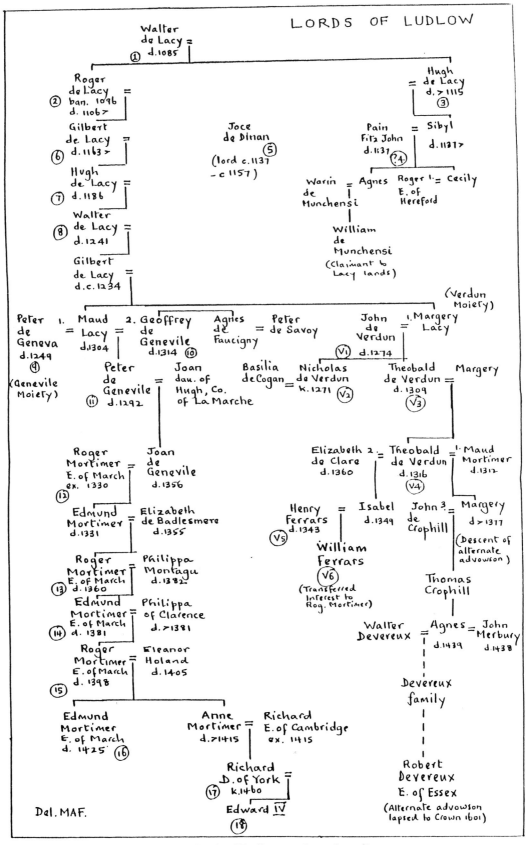

4. The Lords of Ludlow: a schematic pedigree.

Gilbert's two surviving daughters, Maud and Margery, who were apparently minors and unmarried at the time of their grandfather's death. Walter Lacy's widow, Margaret, was awarded part of her dower out of the issues of Ludlow, but it seems that Ludlow remained in the king's hands by right of wardship.[13]

In about 1244 Maud Lacy was married to Peter de Geneva, a son of Humbert, count of Geneva, and a connection of the new queen, Eleanor, whom Henry III married in 1236. Maud's marriage was an example of the king's generosity towards the queen's 'Savoyard' relatives. Ludlow was affected therefore by the Plantagenet attempts to extend their power in south-eastern France.[14]

As a consequence, or in contemplation, of Maud's marriage, the king ordered the sheriff of Herefordshire to value and divide into equal portions Walter Lacy's estates in that county; these included Ludlow, which was part of the honor of Weobley and Ewyas. One half, including the castle, was delivered to Peter de Geneva and Maud, while the other half was retained by the king, since Margery the co-heiress was as yet unmarried.[15]

Peter de Geneva died before 29 June 1249. About 1251–2 Maud was re-married to Geoffrey de Genevile (or Joinville), Lord of Vaucouleurs in Champagne. He was also brother of the Sire de Joinville, the biographer of St Louis, King of France.[16] Geoffrey de Genevile was also a member of the same Savoyard connection as Maud's previous husband; Geoffrey's half-sister, Agnes, was married to Peter de Savoy, since 1240 'earl' of Richmond, a first-cousin of Peter de Geneva and first-cousin once removed of Queen Eleanor.[17] The influence of the queen's relatives continued in Ludlow; indeed it is likely that Peter de Savoy had engineered both of Maud's marriages. An heiress would never have been permitted to choose her own husband; the fate of great estates could not be determined by personal caprice. An heiress whose father had died while she was still a minor would be married to a man whom the king considered (or could be persuaded) that it was in his own royal interests that he should be endowed with those estates.[18]

Before 1248, and probably after 1243, the other Lacy granddaughter, Margery, was married to John de Verdun, son of Theobald Butler by his second wife, Rohese, daughter and heir of Nicholas Verdun. John de Verdun was born about 1226 and in the summer of 1244 received Margery's share of the Lacy lands, which suggests that the marriage had either already taken place or was about to take place. Margery produced two sons for John de Verdun before she died in or about 1256.[19]

Although there was already in existence a partition of Ludlow between the husbands of Maud and Margery, on 10 June 1260 another formal partition took place when Geoffrey de Genevile and his wife, on the one hand, and John de Verdun, on the other, partitioned the barony of Weobley, of which Ludlow formed part.[20] We do not know if this partition merely confirmed the earlier partition in all particulars, but it is known that hitherto Geoffrey had had the castle and those things 'which pertained to the castle', that is, rents intended to finance the upkeep of the castle – rents of pepper and cumin and lands were mentioned – and after 1260 his family enjoyed all these. Although the Geneviles were assigned a 'moiety' of the town, strictly meaning a half, this does not mean that they did get a half. It is perhaps more likely that it was thought that the Genevile moiety, added to the castle, properly constituted an equal portion. This problem, which cannot be solved with certainty, has important implications for an understanding of the history of Ludlow throughout the Middle Ages.

Geoffrey de Genevile and his wife did not normally live in Ludlow; their main family interests were in Ireland, as had been those of the Lacys. It is, therefore, not surprising that in 1283 they gave all their lands in England to their son, Peter de Genevile; his name, similar to that of his mother's first husband, has in the past given rise to confusion.[21] On 11 October 1283 Peter received Ludlow castle and £10 13s. 4d. of Ludlow annual rents.

At about this time he married Joan, the widow of Bernard-Ezy I, sire d'Albret in Gascony, daughter of Hugh XII, Count of La Marche and Angoulême. Peter died in 1292 and his widow obtained the castle and his moiety of the town of Ludlow as her dower. Afterwards her lands were taken into the king's hands because she was an alien living in France, but they were restored in 1296. It is not known whether these included Ludlow, but they may not, since the moiety of Ludlow was in her lifetime given by Geoffrey de Genevile to her daughter's husband, Roger Mortimer, and in both 1294 and 1299 the king granted the murage of Ludlow (that is, the right to collect taxes for the purpose of repairing the walls) to Geoffrey.[22]

A further alienation of dominical rights occurred during Geoffrey de Genevile's ownership. In 1267 he granted to Aconbury convent (founded in 1216 by Walter Lacy's wife) the moiety of the four Ludlow mills, which had formed part of his share of Ludlow, together with 6s. 8d. rent from seven Ludlow burgages.[23] Rents from all of these were being paid in 1406 but apparently only from the mills in 1536.[24] The grant did not include pleas and perquisites of courts, so the alienation, while limiting the income of the lordship, did not fragment the manor in any other way. The grant provided a useful preliminary to an act which preserved the integrity of the rest of the Genevile interests – the placing of the two younger daughters of Peter de Genevile, Beatrice and Maud, in the convent at Aconbury. When Peter died his income from Ludlow had been £3 6s. 8d. from town rents, two thirds of two carucates of land worth £6 13s. 4d., and tolls, pleas and perquisites of courts worth £4. This totalled £10, fairly close to what he had been given nine years earlier.[25]

The dominical rights included the advowson of Ludlow church; this gave rise to disputes between the Geneviles and Verduns, settled in 1283 by an agreement between them that henceforth there would be an alternate exercise of the advowson by the two families.[26] This alternation was practised until 1596.

The marriage of Joan to Roger Mortimer presumably took place in 1307, for it was on 24 December 1307 that Geoffrey de Genevile had the king's licence to surrender to them lands in Ireland.[27] His own wife having already died, he shortly afterwards entered a Dominican friary in Ireland, dying seven years later. Mortimer was therefore his heir from 1307. For the first time for well over a century Ludlow had a lord who could be regarded as something of a local man. The Lacys and Geneviles had been extensively engaged in Ireland and rarely had occasion to visit the Welsh March, let alone Ludlow. The Verduns were based in Staffordshire and to them Ludlow was merely a source of income. The Mortimers, however, were based at Wigmore, only seven miles from Ludlow. Even so, we should not overestimate how often the Mortimers came to Ludlow. The earls of March, from Roger onwards, were magnates of the kingdom and their interests, obligations and ambitions usually kept them elsewhere, although occasionally they came to or passed through Ludlow, and Joan, the first earl's wife, is known to have made her home there. Her grandson, Roger, the second earl, was born in Ludlow on 11 November 1328. A later family event known to have taken place in Ludlow was the burial in 1432 of Anne, widow of Edmund Mortimer, the last Mortimer earl of March. The first earl cared enough about Ludlow, or at least its castle, to endow two chaplains for the chapel there, and he and his wife also obtained the king's licence to found St Catherine's Fair in the town. This last does not necessarily imply a close personal connection; it is possible that the town needed a fair and prevailed upon Mortimer, as its lord and a power in the land, to intercede on its behalf. In 1352 the second earl founded a chantry in Ludlow church, which suggests concern with, if not necessarily residence in, the town. In 1304 Roger Mortimer, on his way to Oswestry to help to settle a dispute, stopped overnight in Ludlow, staying at the house of Hugh Arblaster, and was there subjected to an attack by a mob. This took place

5. Ludlow Castle from the Teme. Built by the Lacy family, it dominated the north-south route and the way into Wales.

before he received a share in the lordship, but conceivably this would not have made the place more attractive to him.[28]

Although the castle and its associated moiety remained in the hands of the Mortimer family for over a century, during the lifetime of Roger the actual possession changed several times as a consequence of Roger's ambitions. In 1322 Roger Mortimer was brought to trial, along with others of the party of Thomas of Lancaster; although he escaped from the Tower and reached France, his lands were taken into the king's hands and between 1322 and 1326 were in the hands of royal nominees. In 1322 Ralph le Botiller was put in charge of the castle. John de Barewe followed him and was himself succeeded in about 1324 by John Inge, still keeper in 1326. In 1324 Richard Corve was described as farmer of the Mortimer moiety of the town, which was then worth £20 a year (compared with the value of the Verdun moiety – £30); Richard Corve delivered the town to John Inge at about this time.[29]

It was not until 1326 that Mortimer, now the queen's lover and leader of her party, was able to return to England, where he took part in the overthrow of his old enemies, the Despensers.[30] Mortimer, now the effective ruler of England, obtained his lands not later than 21 February 1326/7. In October 1328, he was created Earl of March. During the period of restoration to his estates he seems to have been active in the district. It is possible that Ludlow was more involved with its lord at this time than at any other.[31]

It did not last. On 18 October 1330, Edward III staged his coup d'état to take control of his kingdom; Mortimer was arrested, later to be impeached, attainted and executed. His estates were forfeited to the king. At the time of his fall Countess Joan was living in Ludlow castle, for the king at once gave orders that her wardrobe, jewels and other effects there were not to be interfered with by those sequestrating Mortimer's treasure.[32] Ten weeks later the king returned to her the castle, a third of the moiety of the town, a carucate of land, six acres of meadow and two watermills, because they were her own inheritance. It therefore seems that Joan continued to live at the castle for a while. The inquisition into her property, conducted after her death in 1356, showed that she still held the moiety of Ludlow.[33]

Roger Mortimer, her grandson, was her heir.[34] He came of age in 1349 and obtained an interest in Ludlow, for he gave £6 13s. 4d. in rents in 1352 to maintain two chaplains in St Peter's chapel in the castle.[35] Two years later Joan was given a licence to alienate in mortmain rents of lands and burgages in Ludlow to the Hospital of St John. By 1356 Roger, already Earl of March, had acquired the whole of the Mortimer interest in Ludlow.[36]

In 1358 the new earl succeeded in uniting in his hands the two moieties of the lordship, excepting only the earlier alienations to religious houses and the alternate right of presentation to Ludlow church. This he achieved by exchanging with William de Ferrars for Crondon.[37]

The Verdun Moiety, 1260–1358

The other moiety of Ludlow was in the hands of the Verdun family and its heirs from 1260 to 1358. Margery Lacy had died in 1256 and her husband went crusading in 1270, so her estates, including her share of Ludlow, were given to their son, Nicholas, and after his death in 1271, to their youngest son, Theobald de Verdun. As he was born about 1248, he was still a minor at the time of Nicholas's death, and it is likely that his share of Ludlow would have been in the king's hands until after his father's death in 1274; he received livery of both his parents' estates in November and December 1274. He did not succeed without difficulty; John's widow, his second wife Eleanor, claimed dower. To settle the matter she gave up her rights in Ludlow, Ewyas and Weobley in exchange for Irish rents.[38] The inquisition held on Nicholas's death declared him to have held in Ludlow £10 4s. of rents, rents of half a pound of pepper and two pounds of cumin, 80s. annual rents, a moiety of a garden, pleas and perquisites and fairs and a share of tolls, 7s. of foreign rents, 23 acres of land outside the town and half the issues of four mills worth £13.[39] When John died he was stated to have held in Ludlow £10 10s. of assise rents, 23 acres of demesne, a share of mills worth £13 and pleas, perquisites of courts and fairs worth £8, the whole totalling £31 17s. 8d. It is only clear that the latter included the former.[40]

The Verduns of each generation, like the Lacys and Genevilles, were more often in Ireland than England. Theobald, who claimed the title Constable of Ireland, was no exception. He was only exceptional in his family in that he seems to have died peacefully of natural causes at home; that home, however, was Alton. Ludlow was no more than a source of income. Theobald was succeeded in 1309 by his second son, also Theobald. He had married Maud, the daughter of Edmund Mortimer, Lord of Wigmore, in 1302. This marriage might easily, given the uncertainty of life, have reunited the manor fifty years before it was, had Maud been left an heiress and Theobald had a son. Neither event occurred and the alliance had no lasting effects. Maud, however, died in 1312 and Theobald remarried Elizabeth, the sister and co-heir of Gilbert de Clare, Earl of Gloucester, and widow of John de Burgh, heir of Richard, Earl of Ulster. The marriage took place without the king's assent and, as it united very great estates in England and Ireland, it earned the king's displeasure. Within six months of his second marriage Theobald died, and eight months after his death Isabel, his only child by Elizabeth, was born. A situation of extreme complexity was thus brought about. Theobald left four daughters, one posthumous, and all minors, and a widow who survived him by 44 years. Under the rules of inheritance of the time a widow had rights of dower and all daughters ranked equally; the latter could not, however, inherit until they came of age or married.[41]

Immediately the widow, Elizabeth, remarried. Her third husband was Roger Damory. To him was granted the wardship of the town of Ludlow during the minority of Theobald's heirs. He and his wife were also granted the Verdun alternate advowson of the church.[42]

Thereafter the sequence of events affecting the Verdun moiety of Ludlow became complex. In April 1317 the eldest daughter, Joan, married John Montagu, son of William Montagu, who, in 1316, had been granted her *maritagium* (the right to determine her marriage) as a reward for his services to the king. During this period William Montagu seems to have exercised some influence in Ludlow for it was he who sponsored the application for a grant of murage to the town on 16 June 1317. John Montagu died four months after his marriage and his widow then married Thomas de Furnival. As a result of her marriages Joan Verdun was freed from wardship and, with her, her estates.[43]

Roger Damory lost his lands to the king between 18 October and 2 December 1317, and this may have included his rights in Ludlow. He was restored to favour, however, and on 20 March, 1317/8 bought the *maritagium* of Margery and Isabel, then respectively aged seven and (almost) one. It is unclear what, if any, rights the younger daughters may have had in Ludlow at this time. The inquisition into Theobald Verdun's estates, held on 5 June 1317, stated that his heir was Joan Furnivall (by implication in relation to Ludlow), but it is known that Roger Damory sold the *maritagium* of Margery to Robert de Holand on 23 November 1318, and that this Robert was described in 1324 as having at some time in the past owned the Verdun moiety of Ludlow.[44] He was an adherent of the Earl of Lancaster and forfeited his lands after the Battle of Boroughbridge. Upon Holand's forfeiture Ludlow came into the king's hands and was put to farm. Roger Damory himself was a contrariant and an opponent of the Despensers. Late in 1321 his estates were taken into the king's hands and in the following March he died. His wife was imprisoned by the now triumphant Despensers, who extorted property and other concessions from her, but Ludlow may not have been included, although her dower still included the alternate advowson of Ludlow church. The fall of the Despensers in 1326 removed these disabilities.[45]

Thereafter the problems of the Verdun inheritance reflected, not so much politics, as the marriages of the heiresses. Margery married her first husband, William Blount, in February, 1326/7. Margery was married twice more, to Mark Husee in 1339 and to John Crophull in 1355. It seems that, owing to disputes among the co-heirs, the Verdun lands were taken into the king's hands early in 1328 and early in 1332, after which they were partitioned between the husbands. On 11 February 1328 William Blount was granted the Verdun rents and profits in Ludlow until a proper division of the inheritance could be made.[46] This grant appears not to have included the advowson, for on 3 May 1328 John Evesham, a Chancery clerk, was presented to Ludlow church by the king; in 1335 Elizabeth de Burgo, Theobald's widow. still held the alternate advowson in dower.[47] On 8 July 1331, the Verdun moiety was granted to Henry Ferrars, husband of the other daughter, Isabel, while a more permanent settlement was worked out.[48] Then, on 26 March 1332, Henry's fealty having been taken, the lands were granted to him permanently.[49]

After Henry's death in 1343, the Ludlow moiety was taken into the king's hands while the heir was established.[50] It was then accepted that Ludlow belonged to Isabel as part of her inheritance so it was restored to her until her own death in 1349, when it passed to her son, William Ferrars.[51] It was this William who exchanged it for Crondon.

The alternate advowson descended to Margery, Theobald Verdun's third daughter. It belonged to Elizabeth de Burgo in 1344, but by 1356 (in Elizabeth's lifetime) Margery had, without royal licence, granted the advowson to John Blount, presumably a relative of her first husband.[52] Her own title was not questioned and her third husband was allowed to keep it.[53] In practice the king was able to exercise the right four times during the 14th century, by reason of forfeitures and minorities.[54] The advowson then descended to Agnes Crophull, the daughter of Thomas Crophull, son of Agnes and John Crophull. Agnes married John Merbury, who subsequently had a successful official career in South Wales and the March in the service of the Lancastrian kings.[55] She had first married Walter

6. The *insula* bounded by Broad Street (on the left), Bell Lane, Raven Lane (formerly Narrow Lane) and Market Street (formerly Barons Row). The row in front – from the white corner building to the right – was developed later as an encroachment into the wide High Street. The site of the building encroaching into Broad Street, with exposed timbers, was part of the demesne in the Verdun moiety of the town.

Devereux and her grandson, Walter, married Merbury's daughter by his first marriage; the alternate advowson of Ludlow then descended through the Devereux family until 1601 when it came into Crown hands after Essex's rebellion. The Devereux right was last exercised on behalf of Robert Horne in 1596.[56]

March and York, 1358–1461

After 1358 the history of Ludlow lordship, if we leave aside lesser alienations of dominical rights, follows the history of the castle, which itself followed that of Wigmore, the *caput* of the earldom of March. Before his death – only two years after the merger of the two moieties – Roger Mortimer, the second earl, granted Ludlow and other manors to the bishop of Winchester and others, presumably acting as his feoffees, but this was partially revoked and readmitted by the king; Ludlow was then granted to Roger's widow, Philippa, as dower, along with the advowson of the castle chapel.[57] She was the daughter of William Montagu, Earl of Salisbury, son of the grantee of the murage in 1317; her father, an opponent of the first Earl of March, had been granted Roger's wardship in 1336 and this had enabled him to arrange his daughter's marriage.[58] The demise therefore effectively survived Roger's death so his son, Edmund, was to receive £1,000 a year from it after 1367. Advowsons were excepted from the grant in 1360, perhaps because the king found them so useful for rewarding his clerks. In 1367 the king granted Ludlow to Edmund, the heir, then aged only fifteen. In 1370, however, the king, rather than Edmund, licensed the brethren of St John's Hospital to elect a new warden, while in 1371 the king, by reason of his holding the lands of the earldom of March, presented Robert Faryngton to the Ludlow rectory.[59] Edmund should have succeeded to his estates *de jure* by 1373 and in fact received most of them in 1367.[60] He married Philippa, the king's granddaughter, in 1368 and they lived in Ludlow for a while. Their two younger children were born there in 1375 and 1376. At this time there was a growing practice of granting large family estates, like Ludlow, to feoffees for life with lease-backs to the current owner. Although of significance for the family they had virtually no effect on the actual custody of the town.[61]

Edmund Mortimer died in Ireland in 1381, his wife having predeceased him; his son Roger was seven years old. Although it was not until 1394 that Roger received his lands in England, it seems that his father's arrangements to some extent circumvented the effects of the minority. Ludlow and other places had been conveyed to William Latimer of Danby and others, who leased them back.[62] In 1388 Edmund's executors leased Ludlow and other places to Margaret, Countess of Norfolk, for eight years (that is, until Roger's majority and she leased them back to the use of Philippa, the daughter of Edmund, and her husband, the Earl of Pembroke. This may have come to an end with Pembroke's death. Philippa then married Richard FitzAlan, Earl of Arundel, who already had Roger Mortimer's wardship. FitzAlan's brother in law, Thomas Holand, Earl of Kent, had Roger's *maritagium* and, in 1388, arranged his marriage to his daughter, Eleanor. Roger received his estates in 1394 and was killed in Ireland in 1398, leaving a widow and four infant children.[63]

The heir, Edmund, did not receive his estates until 1413. Although his wardship was granted in 1405 to Richard, Lord Grey of Codnor, Ludlow was at all times in the king's hands. This was certainly true of the castle, which is not surprising, considering the turbulent state of the Welsh March in these years. There were five constables of Ludlow castle in this period: Sir John Lovell in 1402, followed by the king's half-brother, Sir Thomas Beaufort, Sir Hugh Cheyne in 1403 and Roger Acton in 1404.[64] The last of these deserted his post and was outlawed, being replaced by John Brigge in 1408. The patents of appointment make it clear that they included both town and castle.[65]

When Edmund Mortimer died in 1425, his widow, Anne, was allowed dower, which may not have included Ludlow. The heir was Richard, Duke of York, son of Edmund's sister, Anne, and then aged only 13, who was not granted livery until 1432. In 1449 York confirmed the ancient form of government of Ludlow. From Ludlow his estates in Wales and the Marches were administered. York himself often stayed at the castle.[66] After the debâcle at Ludford bridge in 1459 he suffered attainder, involving forfeiture, restored himself by force in October 1460, but was killed at the Battle of Wakefield in December. His son, Edward, Earl of March since 1445 (but not apparently proprietor of Ludlow), became king on 4 March 1460/1. Nine months later he granted Ludlow a new charter in which all the Mortimer rights of lordship, excepting only the alternate advowson, the castle, the Castle meadow and certain life-interests in particular properties, were vested in the Corporation in return for a fee farm rent. Ludlow had frequently been used by Richard, Duke of York, as a centre of his household; thereafter, perhaps as some form of continuation of this, its only personal connection with the Crown, it became the headquarters of the Council of the March.[67]

The Division of Ludlow 1244–1358

The earliest division was provisional and subsequent partitions were agreed, but it is not known whether all these involved revisions or confirmations. In 1261 John de Verdun gave Geoffrey de Genevile 68 acres of land in Ludlow in exchange for lands in Weobley.[68] There were later temporary divisions as each family made arrangements for the dower of widows.

When the Verdun line ended in a number of daughters a fresh series of divisions began, until finally the Verdun moiety of Ludlow came into the hands of William Ferrars.

The question of what precisely was divided between the two lines is a complex one. Each lord was entitled to half of each mill; this ensured that physical possession and control remained in the town, while the lords received a share of the rents. The Genevile half was given to Aconbury convent, which annually sent officials to collect them.[69] Perquisites of courts and other incidents were divided, but there was no division of the courts, markets or other aspects of borough life. The division of the demesne lands and the rights to receive burgage and other rents cannot be traced with certainty.

Several of the lords were active in endowing the church with Ludlow property. To do so, they had in the first place to own that property outright; that is, it was not enough to be entitled to a share of the town rents as collected by the bailiff; they had to be entitled to the rents of specific properties. In 1267 Geoffrey de Genevile gave the rents of specified properties, which included at least one in Pepper Lane, to Aconbury convent. In 1354 Joan Mortimer gave four acres of land in Ludlow to St John's Hospital.[70] Other gifts to the church came from various of the lords' tenants; the inquisitions which preceded these gifts generally made clear who were the lords. In 1292 Henry Pigin gave to the Gild a messuage in Ludlow held of Theobald de Verdun; this may well have been the one held by his father in 1272 of John de Verdun.[71] In 1341 a gift to the Hospital included two messuages held of Henry Ferrars.[72] In 1343 gifts to the Gild included a messuage held of Joan Mortimer, five held of Isabel Ferrars, five of Walter Circestre (holding of Countess Joan), one held of Ralph Lyngeyne (holding of Roger Mortimer), and six shops, a toft and a mill held jointly of Joan Mortimer and Isabel Ferrars, which demonstrates that some properties, at least, had no sole lord.[73] In 1350 the Hospital was given eight messuages held of Countess Joan.[74] In 1350 Lawrence Lodelowe gave eight burgages to his newly founded Carmelite priory, one of which he held of Dinmore and seven of Countess Joan.[75] In 1355 the Hospital was given three cottages held of Joan Mortimer and eight cottages held of William Ferrars.[76] In 1357, just before the reunion of the lordship, three messuages and 10s. rent in Ludlow given to the Gild were held of the Earl of March.[77] There are a few other minor indications of specific properties falling within one lord's moiety. The exchange between Verdun and Genevile in 1261, referred to above, gave the latter acreage lying 'towards Corve mill', more 'towards St Mary's way' and more in 'Hokenhulle' Field. As John Normand, the Genevile steward, witnessed a lease of Wenlock priory's shop in the period 1261–72, this probably fell within the Genevile moiety.[78] Peter de Genevile had 18d. rent from Narrow Lane in 1288.[79] In 1272 Roger Carter held a burgage of John de Verdun.[80]

While it is clear that specific properties were allocated to the respective moieties of the town, it is not clear precisely what the geographical allocations were, or, indeed, what the relative sizes of the two moieties were. 'Moiety' means 'half', but often is used to indicate any substantial fraction. The Verduns may have received the greater part of the town, perhaps to balance the fact that the castle went to the Geneviles. The earliest inquisitions *post mortem* are for the Verduns and, while they by no means each give the same figures, they give a strong impression that the rental income was greater than that accruing to the Geneviles. The burgage rents accruing to the Verduns imply a total of between 190 and 240 burgages, while the Genevile share seems to have been between sixty and seventy.[81] It may be that the parts of the town allocated to the Geneviles were thought to be sufficient to produce an income for the support of the castle. A further hint comes from a Common Pleas suit of 1274 when John de Verdun's widow, Alienora, sued Theobald de Verdun for her dower, which included a third of two parts of the manor of Ludlow. The implication is that the Verdun moiety was this two-thirds.[82] Within Ludlow there were demesne lands, as yet not built on, and these seem to have been divided fairly equally, with 20–23 acres

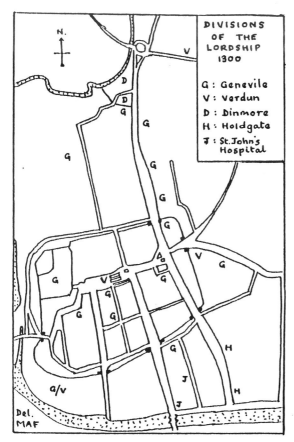

7. Map of the divisions of the lordship, 1300.

each. The mill rents were divided equally, as were the market tolls, fair rents and perquisites of courts. The Verduns obtained a garden, while the Geneviles had the Castle meadow. There were also cumin and pepper rents, the former for four tenements in Shoemakers' Row, two of which were allocated to Genevile and two to Verdun. The pepper rent arose from the Dodmore Fields and was also equally divided.

The Hundred Rolls provide evidence of tenements outside the borough but within the liberties, where the tenure was based on service to the castle; these remained with the 'lord of the castle'.

Alienations of Lordship Rights

Before his death in 1186 Hugh Lacy gave to the Hospitaller commandery of Dinmore part of the lordship of Ludlow.[83] The Hospitallers were a fairly centralised Order, particularly in the management of their estates, and the only records extant are later ones kept at the Clerkenwell headquarters. Nevertheless it seems likely that rents from Ludlow were paid directly to Dinmore. The part of Ludlow transferred to the Hospitallers was a block of 12 burgages at the northern end of Corve Street on the left, together with two virgates of land. The precise size and whereabouts of the two virgates is a matter of debate; it is not known whether this land was adjacent to the 12 burgages. A virgate at the time was about sixty acres, so it is unlikely that this land was all within the Ludlow boundaries.

After the 13th-century Hundred Rolls the only documentary evidence is from the mid-16th century. The 'Dinmore fee rental' lists 16 separate properties paying 13s. 4d. in freehold rents and 19s. 4d. in other rents.[84] The 'other rents' must derive from all or part of the two virgates. Although no court rolls relating to the 'Dinmore fee' have survived from the long period of Hospitaller lordship, a short series has survived for the period 1547–54 when the Dinmore estates were in Crown hands. We therefore cannot know whether Dinmore attempted to exercise jurisdiction in a full manorial capacity or whether it was only the Crown assuming that its property rights included jurisdiction and perquisites of courts. The court rolls, however, which include all or most of the Dinmore tenants, help to locate the whereabouts of the Dinmore fee, backing onto the River Corve, which some of the tenants were accused of fouling, while no street is mentioned but Corve Street. A close to the south of the chapel was included which establishes the approximate southern boundary.

The convent of Aconbury in Herefordshire had been founded by Margaret Lacy in 1216. There were later gifts when members of the family joined the house. In 1267 Geoffrey de

Genevile and Maud Lacy his wife gave it half of four mills in Ludlow, and 6s. 8d. rent from seven burgages, one at least of which, and perhaps some others, was in Pepper Lane, then called 'the lane leading to the Tailors' Gate'. The gift was intended to be temporary, until something more suitable and nearer to Aconbury could be substituted. No substitution in fact took place and the rents remained to Aconbury until at least the early 15th century;[85] at the Dissolution, however, only the mill rents were still in issue. The moiety of the mills then came into Crown hands and in the 16th and 17th centuries was the occasion of disputes with the Corporation, which in 1461 had acquired the other moiety of the mills from the Crown.[86]

The Lacys and their successors alienated parts of their dominical rights in the town, both to conventual houses and to laymen. The latter were generally the recipients of plots of demesne lands and of burgages or burgage rents. Few of the actual grants have survived, although there is subsequent evidence for them having been made before the statute *Quia Emptores* in 1290, probably as gifts or rewards for past or future expected service.

In 1291 Henry Pigin gave the Gild a shop which he held of William Moyl and three shops he held of Lawrence de Lodelowe and Peter Gilemin; the former suggests an earlier grant to William Moyl.[87] In 1344 among properties in Ludlow given to the Gild were five messuages held of Walter de Circestre (as mesne tenant of Joan Mortimer) and one held of Ralph de Lyngeyne (as mesne tenant of Roger Mortimer).[88] William Ocleye forfeited to the Crown, following his treason, a large tenement on the corner of Castle Street and Raven Lane, which he had been granted by Roger Mortimer, one in Lower Mill Street, which he acquired from John Lyney, and a shop in Butchers' Row, acquired from the daughter of Hugh Arblaster, who may have received it from the Mortimers as a reward for service. These properties were then granted to Stephen de Butterley and were the subject of a dispute with Robert Haukyns, who inherited Ocleye's claims.[89] Not all of the burgages of Ludlow can be identified in the later Corporation records, for the missing ones had been granted out of the Lacy, Genevile, Verdun and Mortimer demesnes.

At the southern end of Old Street is a part of Ludlow which was never part of the Lacy estates, but had originally belonged to the manor of Steventon, an outlier of the lordship of Castle Holdgate. This part of Ludlow has always been known as Holdgate Fee. It passed to Richard of Cornwall, king of the Romans, and, as mesne tenants, the Burnell family. Steventon was held in two portions in the mid-13th century, one by Nicholas Andrew with William Aldenham, the other by Nicholas Eylrich, all of them Ludlow residents. This part of Ludlow was never part of the lordship, although it shared the history of the town.

The devolution of self-government to the 'Community', as it was called, involved the devolution or abrogation of some aspects of lordship. The Lacys retained direct powers of lordship over a few people. In 1231 Walter Lacy transferred to Craswall priory his *nativum*, that is, his serf, Stephen *Saponarius*, with his lands and family.[90] As most property in Ludlow was held in free burgage, which ruled out serfdom, it is likely that Stephen and his family held their tenement on some older personal tenure which was not absorbed into the burgaged town.[91] Outside the town, in Steventon, William Abovethetowne, the serf of Reginald Eylrich, was transferred in 1308 with his lands to Thomas Foliot.[92] The Hundred Rolls demonstrate that the grant of part of the town to the Knights Hospitallers led to an abuse of a less usual aspect of lordship; the Order was exempt from taxes, so their tenants, Nicholas Savoner, Robert Brug, Thomas *de Capella* and Adam Cotele, claimed the same privilege to the detriment of both the king and the borough. As '*saponarius*' and '*savoner*' mean the same thing, it is possible that Nicholas was the son of Stephen. Reginald Eylrich or fitz Stephen claimed the same privilege in 1269 and the dispute between him and the Community of Burgesses was settled by Geoffrey de Genevile and others in a common sense way: he was to be free of taxes on property or trading within the Fee of Dinmore but not exempt for any other property or trade.[93]

The Lord of Cotes

In 1282 'Geoffrey de Genevile gave a rent which is called Cotes for other lands in Ireland'.[94] It is not known whether Cotes was the name of the parcel of rents before the exchange, or whether it only subsequently got the name, perhaps from the identity of its new proprietor, or perhaps from another manor he held. 'Cotes' is a common place-name, so this does not greatly help in identifying it. There were half a dozen manors of Cotes, all of which had some plausible connection with Ludlow or its lords; among these was Cotes in Rushbury parish, with its connections with Holdgate, itself connected with that part of Ludlow called 'Holdgate Fee'. If 'Cotes' was its name in 1282, it suggests that, for some reason unknown, a series of burgages throughout Ludlow had an identifying name of their own.

Genevile gave away the right to receive rents from burgages in Ludlow to a landowner in Ireland in return for property in Ireland, but he did not give away any other lordship rights, such as perquisites of courts, so a 'sub-manor' was not created. A good many English and Marcher lords also held lands in Ireland and this has hampered attempts to identify the 'lord of Cotes'. The best guess is based on the fact that in 1283 Geoffrey de Genevile bought from William de Valence the *maritagium* of Gerald Fitzgerald, Lord of Offaly in Ireland, and then married Gerald to his daughter, Joan de Genevile. If the rents called Cotes were part of either the consideration for the purchase of the *maritagium* or the marriage settlement itself an hypothesis is possible. Lands settled upon the marriage would have reverted to the Genevile family when Joan died for there were no children of the marriage.[95] The *Black Book of Wigmore* records a gift by Geoffrey de Genevile to his daughter, Joan, of the profits of Ludlow to endure for three years only; was this 'Cotes'?[96] If the payment were to William de Valence, Cotes would probably have followed his other estates, descending to his son Aymer and then through the Hastings family until the death, *sine prole*, in 1389 of John Hastings, Earl of Pembroke, or of his widow, Philippa Mortimer, in 1401; the Pembroke estates reverted to the Crown. If Cotes had been among them it could have been included in the grants associated with the charter of 1461.[97]

The Palmers' Gild rent collector's account for 1364–5 states that 15s. 8d. was paid at Michaelmas to the lord of Cotes for 'divers tenements in Lodelowe'.[98] In 1392 royal letters patent allowed the transfer to the Palmers' Gild of two messuages, five cottages, a shop and a toft which were held 'immediately' of the 'lord of Cotes', as distinct from the Earl of March.[99] This is admittedly hard to reconcile with the hypothesis (the 'Fitzgerald' route) that the Geneviles had resumed Cotes on Joan's death. An inquisition five years later on the same subject stated that these, as well as other properties, were held of Sir Richard Scrope, Hugh Boraston and Walter Colmyntone, who were certainly at this time feoffees for the March estates.[100] Either there had been some change in the intervening years or we have to conclude that the lordship of Cotes was also a Mortimer property by that time; if the latter were the case it would provide one explanation why the Cotes burgages eventually belonged to the Corporation; (the 'Fitzgerald' route perhaps). On the other hand it would not explain why the earl's bailiff in 1424 paid rents to the lord of Cotes, (the 'Pembroke' route perhaps). An implicit distinction was made between the Cotes rents and those given in 1267 by Geoffrey de Genevile to Aconbury convent, for the latter were in 1394 regarded, notwithstanding the gift, as being held of the earl of March as lord. Five of the Cotes properties tenanted by the Gild were in Corve Street outside the gate, one was in Galdeford, one at the top of Broad Street and the other in Dinham. We can assume that the Gild did not hold all the Cotes properties, but this does not indicate that the Cotes holding comprised a discrete part of the town, but only scattered properties.[101]

The fixed rents payable to the lord of Cotes were, by 1377–93, 23s. 4d.; the increase may represent the properties referred to above.[102] If so, it would suggest that by then the Gild had between 25 and 30 properties of the Cotes estate and that the whole Cotes estate comprised a substantial part of the town. The 1424 accounts of the bailiff of the earl of March show fixed rents of 2s. a year being paid to the lord of Cotes for two burgages in Castle meadow.[103]

In 1481–2 the Gild rent collector paid the Ludlow bailiffs 28s., called 'the Cotes rent'. Nine years earlier the same amount was paid to them and then called 'the chamberlain's rent'.[104] As the bailiffs did not pay the 28s. over to anyone else the properties concerned seem to have fallen into the hands of Ludlow Corporation. It is not clear what the mechanism was for the assumption of the other property rights, or when it took place. But this lack of certainty does not wholly invalidate either the 'Fitzgerald' or the 'Pembroke' hypothesis.

It may be significant that the Cotes rent was also called the chamberlain's rent, and that it arose wholly in the part of the town (chiefly on the east side) whose burgage rents were collected by the chamberlain. This may be evidence that the chamberlain was the successor of an official who collected rents from one of the historical 'moieties' of the borough.

A further puzzle remains. In 1536 the then Earl of Oxford and John Lyttleton sued the bailiffs for not paying over £6 13s. 4d. in burgage and other rents due by fealty to them as joint heirs of William Burley, the famous Speaker of the House of Commons *tempore* Henry VI.[105] This would have represented a large number of tenements, as many as 133 if all were burgages; was this Cotes? The result of the action is not known. Burley's antecedents are not well enough known to determine from whom he might have inherited such rents. As a friend, counsellor and sometime creditor of Richard, Duke of York, he may even have received Ludlow rents on his patron's behalf.

Ludlow and National Politics

With lords who, from the mid–12th century, were significant in national politics, it was inevitable that Ludlow and Ludlow people should be similarly caught up. Ludlow castle suffered siege during the wars of Stephen and Matilda, but we have no proof that the town itself existed then. However, it may safely be assumed that, if the castle was besieged, any town would have suffered severely.

The Lacy participation in the conquest and domination of Ireland widened Ludlow's horizons. Ludlow people settled in Ireland and Irishmen (probably of English descent) came over to Ludlow. Ludlow men frequently made their careers in the service of the lords of Ludlow; these careers often encompassed Ireland, for the lords held extensive Irish interests after 1171.

It was to Ludlow that the Lord Edward escaped in 1265; there he, the Clares and the Mortimers, planned the rising which led within three months to the Battle of Evesham and the overthrow and death of Simon de Montfort.[106]

Ludlow's raison d'être was as a fortress against the Welsh, so occasionally this function became apparent. The Ludlow annalist recorded two expeditions against the Welsh by Henry II, and seven in the 13th century; it is probable that Ludlow took part in the preliminaries for such campaigns. Whether the great carnage (*stragem magnam*) inflicted by the Welsh on England which the annalist recorded for 1262 harmed Ludlow we do not know, but the engagement in 1228 which resulted in the slaughter of the Welsh forces at Culmington was surely commanded from Ludlow.[107] Edward I's Welsh wars involved Ludlow as a forward base. In 1283 the town was obliged to send vendors of victuals to Montgomery to supply the army before its invasion of Merioneth. In 1287 vendors of victuals were ordered to go to Ludlow itself for a similar purpose, although they were then ordered to follow the army on to Brecon.[108]

Roger Mortimer's turbulent political career, together with deaths and marriages in the Verdun family, leading respectively to forfeitures, reinstatements and wardships, grants of dower and partitions, would have put considerable strain on corporate loyalties. The evidence is that the town authorities were prepared to bend with the wind. After Mortimer's arrest in 1330 Ludlow put a special watch on its gates; this can only have been to keep out his partisans.[109]

Ludlow was in the front line during the troubles of Henry IV's reign. In 1402 the bailiffs were required to victual the town quickly for military reasons.[110] Royal captains, such as Sir John Lovell and Thomas Beaufort, were placed in charge of the garrison.

The town was involved in the disintegration of Lancastrian England. For two months early in 1452 Ludlow was held for York during the short-lived uprising by Sir Edmund Mulsho, Roger Eyton and John Milewater, receiver general of the Duke of York's estates in the March; the ringleaders were tried at Bridgnorth and then at Westminster, but, having been convicted, were released 'by the king's grace'.[111] There then occurred another

8.   Ludford Bridge, the main route south and the site of the rout of the Yorkist forces in 1459.

outbreak in Ludlow, when on 30 April 1452, John Mason, John Mattys, John Preene, all tradesmen, led by John Sharp, gentleman, murdered Richard Fasackerley, a valet of the king's chamber. This again was part of a wider uprising, expressed as against a king who could not govern. At the trial Sharp was acquitted.[112] On 6 August 1452, John ap Richard, then rector of Ludlow, with Sir Walter Devereux of Weobley and 'other ill-doers to the number of 40', attacked and expelled Humfrey Blount from his manor of Ashton. Three years later John ap Richard was accused of further thefts from Blount; given the fact that both Devereux and John ap Richard were followers of York, these events have a political flavour, for national dynastic politics and local family feuds tended to coalesce.[113]

Whereas the political upheavals of 1310–30 seem to have consolidated the autonomy of Ludlow and distanced the town somewhat from its lords, the upheavals of the 1450s cemented the connection with the lord. It may be that the severity of the sack of 1459, which followed the rout of York at the battle of Ludford bridge, was a Lancastrian retribution for this close Yorkist affiliation. Edmund Delamere immediately took control of the castle and town and was rewarded in 1460 with the constableship of the castle.[114] Delamere was constable between 1473 and 1478, so he must have proved reliable to his new masters after 1461.[115] The sack of 1459 was bad enough to justify the grant of privileges to both St John's Hospital and to the Carmelite priory by the king and the pope respectively.[116] Earl Rivers's departure from Ludlow with the young Edward V in 1483, each going to his death, marked the end of Ludlow's special connection with national politics.[117]

Thereafter Ludlow's connections with national politics and policy were through the formal structures of Parliamentary representation and the Council of the March, in neither of which did Ludlow exert much influence. The increasing pressure of central government upon the localities over the next two centuries affected Ludlow considerably, but no more so than the rest of the country, with the dramatic exception of the Civil War.

Chapter Two

Government

The Early Borough

How Ludlow was governed before the mid–13th century has to be largely a matter of inference from the isolated contemporary documentary evidence which has survived, and from what is rather better evidenced from later periods.

The laws of Breteuil seem to have been granted to Ludlow by the Lacy family, probably not later than 1185. Walter Lacy, who was also Earl of Meath and Lord of Trim in Ireland after 1194 until his death in 1241, granted the laws of Breteuil to the borough of Drogheda, basing them on his borough of Ludlow. The Lacys did not bring the laws of Breteuil from their own estates in Normandy, but derived them by imitation from their use elsewhere on the Welsh March, particularly the old FitzOsbern borough of Hereford. The laws of the borough of Breteuil, in Normandy, had proved successful and were often imitated there and in England and, later, in Ireland, by lords founding boroughs.[1] Typically a borough operating under the laws of Breteuil enjoyed rules governing burgess-ships in case of sale or partition of burgages, the right of free marriage (that is, without the intervention of the lord), limited forfeiture of chattels to the lord (normal seigneurial incidents), freedom from wardship in minorities, exemption from distant military service for the lord (balanced by the local duty of 'watch and ward'), freedom within the borough from tolls, portage. passage, customs, heriots and reliefs – all seigneurial incidents and levies (although the first four were levied on non-burgesses using the town's facilities). Another right was that a vacant or demolished burgage would after a year fall to the 'Community' to answer for its rent to the lord; this is direct evidence that in some respects the burgesses in the borough were expected to act as a corporate body with some organisation to enable this. Other characteristics of the laws of Breteuil were annual chief rents of 12d. for burgages, with no other obligations attaching to the burgage, notwithstanding any attached to burgess-ship, and the right of burgage-holders to buy, sell and bequeath burgages and other real freehold (to use an anachronistic term) property, without restriction, provided title was good.[2] Several of these characteristics can be seen in Ludlow; it is reasonable to assume that most of them were established there.

When Ludlow became a borough is not recorded. In 1221 it was necessary to try in the king's courts a claim that the laws of Breteuil applied to bequests of property in Ludlow, which suggests that the foundation could not have been more than one or two generations further back.[3] The borough was laid out as a planned town and the 'burgaging' of the area of the borough inevitably followed the rules of Breteuil. It is unlikely that the grant of the laws could have followed the settlement of the burgaged town. Since it is similarly unlikely that the grant would have preceded by much the initial stage of the planning of the new town, we may assume that they were contemporary. Hugh Lacy's grant to Dinmore, which took place between 1158 and 1186, included burgaged land, so the burgaging process cannot have taken place later than 1186.[4]

In 1169 the township of Ludlow paid half a mark for a royal aid.[5] If the physical organisation of the town of Ludlow broadly coincided with the creation of the borough, it seems that the town, or a nucleus of it, existed in 1169. The Pipe Rolls contain sufficient evidence of organised and commercial activity in Ludlow in the following decades. In 1182 Roger de Ludelawe illegally exchanged 35s. 9d., and in 1184 Roger *Iuvenis*, apparently a different person, illegally transacted business in old money.[6] Then in 1187 Herebert, the reeve of Ludlow, rendered account for 100s. for not bringing a counterfeiter before the justices, and 'the men of Ludlow' rendered account for 20 marks – tallage for the maintenance of the castle.[7] This again is evidence of community responsibility. In 1199–1200 the church was either built or re-built.[8]

In 1221 Roger *Faber* of Stanton (Lacy) and Hawise his wife sued Wimund Fitz Wimund for a half messuage in Ludlow, being Hawise's right, because her father, Hugh Bum, gave it to her former husband, William Stantone, in marriage according to the laws of Breteuil. William Stantone, however, leased it out to her brother, Nicholas Bum, who then let it to Wimund.[9]

In a case heard before the justices in eyre at Shrewsbury in 1291, William Seynter claimed, on her death, his sister's tenement in Ludlow by right of *mort dancestor*. Presumably the tenement had belonged to their father. William Koke and his wife claimed that the tenement had been bought and was bequeathable and that the writ of *mort dancestor* did not run in Ludlow. The jury confirmed every detail of their case.[10] Where this writ ran the next heirs were entitled to succeed to property held *in dominico ut feodo* (broadly, freehold) at the time of death. In certain places however, Ludlow among them, the writ did not run and property could be bought, sold and bequeathed by will without the rights of next heirs automatically taking precedence. A trading borough, attracting its population from elsewhere, with a relatively free market in people as in goods, would need to be untrammelled by *mort dancestor*, and so it was with Ludlow.

The court had heard a similar case in 1288, when a tenement once purchased by William Milisent was held to have descended, not to his brothers, as his right heirs, but implicitly by will to William Ace, son of Thomas Ace and Isabel (presumably William Milisent's daughter), 'as is the custom in the town after purchase'.[11]

Even in 1318 the question was still being raised. Roger, son of William Wyggeley, sued for several free tenements in Ludlow. One of these was held by Margaret, wife of Hugh Tannour; she said that her husband had bought it by the custom of Ludlow by which 'time out of mind tenements which are bought anywhere in the town are heritable' and Hugh had left it by will to Margaret and others. The jury found for her, but Roger Wyggeley did not give up and was still engaged in actions at law as late as 1334.[12]

Although the principle was no longer in doubt, it had still to be called in aid in 1334 when Lawrence Lodelowe recovered seisin of tenements in the town in a dispute with William Doul and John Eylrich, the jury stating, 'land and tenements in Ludlow according to its use and custom time out of mind are bequeathable'.[13] Again in 1367 Margery Stretford defended herself against Roger Erslone and Joan, his wife, who claimed property as next heir of William Longe; she said that Ludlow was 'a walled town with a castle to which the town belonged and that all tenements in the town were burgages and ... since time out of mind and by custom all tenements in the town were buyable and bequeathable'. She then gave examples of people who had inherited previously purchased tenements. The jury found for her.[14]

Another early custom of the town was of a commonsense kind; it was recorded in 1302 that in Ludlow it was forbidden for one property to open into another once they had been built on, a necessary rule for a crowded built-up borough.[15]

The 'men of Ludlow' were mentioned in the late 12th century in contexts which emphasise their communal status. Burgesses as such appear in the 13th century, but the difference can only be one of nomenclature. In 1252 there was a dispute at Montgomery fair involving Ludlow men, one of whom, Peter Milysent, was described as a 'burgess of Ludlow'.[16]

In 1294 Theobald Verdun received 40s. 4d. from the farm of his part of Ludlow from the hands of 'the burgesses and community'.[17] In 1269 a dispute between Reginald fitz

9.   Bailiffs' account for 1287–8 (SRO 356/419).

Stephen, a resident of the Dinmore portion of the town, and 'the Community of the Burgesses of Ludlow' concerning his obligations to pay scot and lot in that part of Ludlow as well as in the rest of the town was referred to the arbitration of Geoffrey de Genevile and others.[18] Not only does this demonstrate the existence of the burgess community, but it shows that it was sufficiently autonomous of Genevile, one of its lords, for him to act as arbitrator. In 1287–8 lordship accounts refer to the £3 arrears of the Community, while the Community and borough were bounden to Theobald Verdun for £19 13s. 4d.[19] These seem to be the earliest references to the 'community' using that term. The earliest accounts for the Community relate to the first two decades of the 14th century; in them there is ample evidence of actions being undertaken on behalf of 'the community'. In 1313 the murage was collected by a leading townsman, the Community renting a shop for the purpose. The treasury of the Community is also referred to. Payments were made on behalf of the Community to its own and outside officials for work done or favours anticipated. In short, the Community was already developed as a broadly self-governing unit. Only Community ownership of real property is missing from this picture of a functioning corporation. This is a curiosity, for at this time the Palmers' Gild certainly had that character. Nevertheless the Community rented certain parts of the demesne, such as houses by the gates and meadows, from the lords and rented them out again at a profit which accrued to the Community treasury.[20]

     The degree of direct lordship control of the borough varied from time to time. The division of lordship rights after 1241 inevitably led to the borough being regarded as a source of rental income, particularly as the Verduns, the major proprietors, did not live there, while Geoffrey de Genevile spent most of his time in Ireland. Moreover, the early 14th century was a time of rapidly changing lordships. During these two periods the borough, or, more precisely, the moieties of the borough, were sometimes set to farm, that is, the lordship income was not directly collected for the lords entitled to it, but was collected by others who paid an agreed sum to the lords for the privilege. The accounts for the dominical income in 1287–9 do not identify the beneficiaries nor even the identities of the accountants, but they do distinguish the rights to that income belonging to Theobald de Verdun and Peter de Genevile. Since these are probably one surviving part of a three-part roll, originally consisting of lordship receipts, Community receipts and Community expenses, it is probable that the Community was responsible for all these receipts, but that does not prove that it held the sources of income at farm.[21] In 1291 Hugh Cleybury and Henry Pigin were farmers of Peter de Genevile's part of the town, paying 40 marks to John Vaucouleurs, who was both rector of Ludlow and a Genevile official.[22] In 1294 Theobald de Verdun's part was farmed by 'the burgesses and community', suggesting a communal rather than a personal devolution.[23] The 1299–1300 accounts include all three parts and make clear that the Community farmed at least the Verdun moiety and perhaps the whole. Income received from William Cachepol is there accounted *'de tempore domini G.'* (which, being written in abbreviated form as *'de tp'e d'ni G.'*, may be a transposition error for *'de p'te d'ni G.'*, that is, 'from the part of Lord Geoffrey'). This would be consistent with the following entries for income received from the same person *'de parte nostra'* and *'de tempore que tota villa erat in custodia nostra'*. Income arising from sources in different formal ownership or custody was collected by the same person who accounted directly to the Community. The revenue was farmed out and government was devolved.

During 1308–9 the Community paid 60 marks (£40) to Theobald Verdun for the farm of the town. As it did not pay for the farm of the Genevile-Mortimer moiety it seems that the arrangements with each lord were unconnected with each other, which implies that the Community was a unitary body which dealt with the lords as landlords rather than as governors.[24] The accounts for 1317–20, however, do not refer to payments in farm and do not include those sources of income which clearly derived from lordship, such as pleas and perquisites of courts, market dues and rents in kind. The farms were temporary and *ad hoc*, rather than perpetual, as the farm became after 1461. In 1324 Richard Corve was described as farmer of the Mortimer moiety of the town and 'John de Lodelowe' was farmer of Robert de Holand's moiety (that is, the Verdun part).[25] In 1326–7 William Waleyn accounted as farmer of the Holand moiety, then in the king's hands.[26] Some individual sources were individually farmed, for Richard Paunteley, the lord's bailiff, himself farmed the whole of the Sandpits demesne in 1367–8.[27] So these periods of farm were clearly temporary and not necessarily uniform in their conditions. The fee farm system which applied after 1461 was not a development of this.

Did the grant of a farm, that is, mediatising the collection of revenue, involve the devolution of other governmental functions? The only local expenditure charged upon the lordship revenues was upkeep of the castle and this could be met from the farm payments. When the Community held the farm it undertook no such obligation. The services of justice gave rise to income (the perquisites of courts), but no Community official ever presided over the lord's court; this was the task of the lord's steward. The perquisites of courts were certainly farmed with the bailiffs collecting the fines and paying the fees of clerks and steward. In a period of farm the farmer kept the fines, having only the duty to pay over a fixed sum; at other times the fines, after expenses, belonged directly to the lords. This is all entirely compatible with self-government, already substantial and not essentially altered in periods of farm.

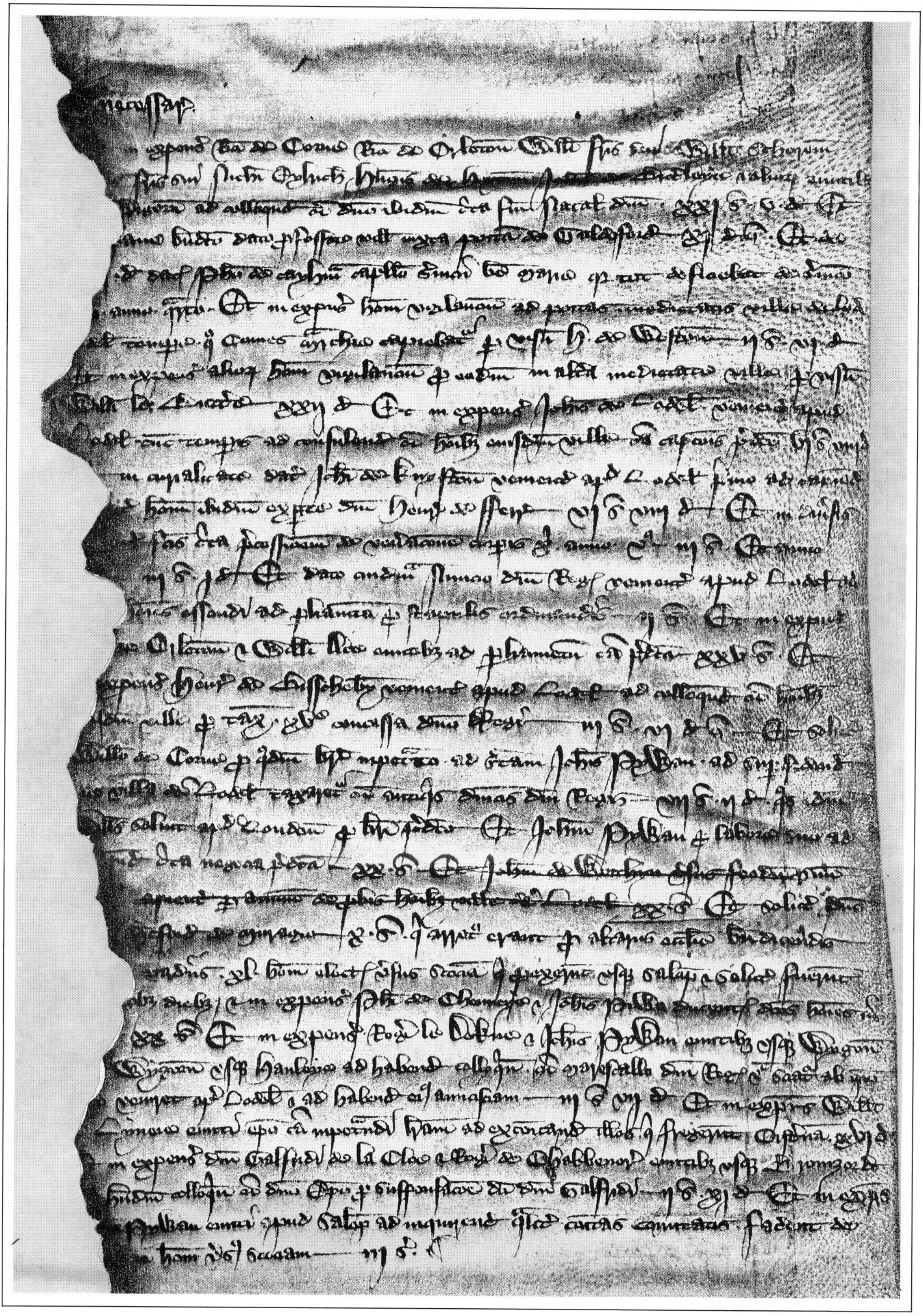

10. Community account for 1332–3 (SRO 356/419).

An early aspect of the dependence of the town and its environs on the castle is the existence of a small number of tenures for other than money rents. Robert Dovile held two virgates of land in Wigley in return for 15 days' service at the castle in time of war. The other tenures were for rents in kind, for the provision of luxuries for a noble household, like pepper, cumin, wax, spurs and tongs. These tenements included the castle fishpond, held of the castle for a pound of wax, a virgate of land held by William Clune for a pound of pepper, a plot in Ludlow held by Richard Canon for two pairs of tongs, a plot held by Hugh Moneur for a spur, two shops held by Nicholas Andrew and Maud de Home for a pound of cumin each. Such rents became common under King John.[28]

The Bailiffs before 1461

The most important officials in the borough were the bailiffs. As the earliest records were in Latin, we cannot be certain whether the first officials, apparently exercising similar functions, were called 'bailiffs', since they were described as *prepositi*, normally translated as 'reeve'. Not until the late 13th century did the word *ballivi* come into normal use. The evidence for the existence of such officials is so scarce that a great deal of guesswork is necessary to define their functions and offices.

Before 1461 it was usual for the bailiff to be described as 'bailiff of the town' or, less often but more formally, as 'bailiff of the lord of Ludlow' or 'the bailiff in Ludlow of the lord'. The last is the more accurate because in no case had the bailiff powers or responsibilities beyond the borough of Ludlow and its liberties. His chief function was to collect the revenues due to the lord from the borough, including burgage and demesne rents, profits from the mills, tolls, market dues and perquisites of courts, although in periods of farm all except the burgage rents were accounted for by the Community, even when the bailiffs collected them. Collecting the lord's revenues was a duty of private estate officials, but public duties were also laid upon them, for there were frequent royal orders to the bailiffs and the 'men' or Community of Ludlow to raise taxes, arrange musters, victual armies and otherwise carry out national policy. Such royal orders plainly saw the bailiffs as representative officials, although this may not imply their election.

If the bailiff were merely the lord's official a change of lord would sometimes mean a change of bailiff. Between 1292 and 1432 there were 20 changes of lord, other than where son succeeded father, but after only eight of these is there any sign of a possible change. There were a few coincident changes. When Geoffrey de Genevile resumed his moiety in 1295, John Tikelwardyne began his lifelong bailiwick, but he, however, may have represented the Verdun, rather than the Genevile, interests. Between 1320 and 1330, the most turbulent decade of the century, which ended in the execution of Roger Mortimer, none of the frequent changes of lord occasioned a change of bailiff. Many of the apparent changes of bailiff may be explicable otherwise than by the change of lord; death or illness may have played a part. In short, a change in the lord rarely, if ever, caused a change in the bailiff. Most bailiffs were their lord's accounting officers, but not necessarily their servants; they were equally the representatives of the Community.

For more than a century Ludlow had two lords. There is no evidence that hitherto there had been more than one bailiff at a time. From about 1288 there is abundant evidence of two bailiffs. But did one bailiff serve one lord and the other bailiff the other? In 1297 Robert Brun and Thomas Brid 'then bailiffs of Geoffrey de Genevile and Theobald de Verdun' distrained Ivo de Clinton's livestock within the precinct of the lordship (*precinctum dominii*) of these two lords after Clinton had been summoned to answer Roger Foliot in the court of Geoffrey and Theobald in Ludlow.[29] This implies one lordship and one court, rather than two of each; whether each bailiff served a single lord is uncertain. In 1272 William Radenovere was described as 'bailiff of Theobald de Verdun, chief lord of the fee'.[30] In 1291 both Henry Pigin and Hugh Cleybury were described as 'farmers' of the Genevile moiety.[31] When the two moieties of Ludlow were in the king's hands in 1324 his keeper of forfeited lands received £10 from Richard Corve, 'farmer of the moiety of the town which was Roger Mortimer's' and £30 from John de Lodelowe [32] 'farmer of the other moiety of the town which was Robert Hoillaunde's'.[33] In 1333 a borough murage account implies that the bailiffs, William Buttere and Hugh Westone, were each responsible for different gates in their respective moieties of the town.[34]

When the two moieties of the lordship were merged in 1358 the two bailiffs were not replaced by one bailiff for some time at least, although after 1390 there is very scanty evidence of two bailiffs serving simultaneously. After 1358, although it is not possible to discover precisely who was bailiff at all times, a succession in the office can be traced. Appointments were for indeterminate periods. Although the bailiffs accounted yearly at Michaelmas, their terms of office did not coincide with accounting periods. The 1461 charter referred to the rents and issues which had previously been 'in the charge of the bailiff' (singular), which may support the view that from 1390 at least there had been only one bailiff at a time, but the petition of 1405 sought powers of arrest for the 'bailiffs for the time being' and referred to the 'baillys in the Gildehall', which implies more than one bailiff at a time.[35]

From the mid-14th century the other officials received their stipends from, and in many cases paid over their revenues to, the bailiffs, who therefore had control of at least the greater part of the income of the Corporation.[36]

Most of the early bailiffs seem to have been south Shropshire or north Herefordshire men, although some, like Geoffrey Helyoun and Richard Dulverne, may have come from further afield in pursuit of careers in their lords' service. Many were very local men, like Nicholas Eylrich, Robert Broun and Henry Heytone of Stanton Lacy, and Matthew Agace, William Orletone, Richard Chabbenore and John Pywau, who came from long-established Ludlow families. At least six early bailiffs were described as 'clerks'; in 1241 the *prepositi* were Richard *Clericus* and Adam Cotele, clerk; Richard Momele, bailiff in 1271, was described as 'clerk', as was Henry Chabbenovere, bailiff in 1288. The long-serving John Tikelwardyne was also so described. Robert Moneter, bailiff in 1308, whose family were lords of Whitton, was called both 'clerk' and 'master'. They were all in some sense professional administrators. By the early 14th century, however, some of the bailiffs were Ludlow merchants; later in that century they were invariably merchants. Philip Glover, bailiff in 1315, was the first who was definitely a member of the Twelve. Thereafter this became common, if not invariable, a development demonstrating the increasing control of the burgesses over the town. The frequent changes of lord in the first three decades of the century may well have been a main cause. Nevertheless it is possible that the bailiffs were still appointed by the lords, even if their field of choice was greatly restricted.

The Twelve and the Twenty-Five to 1461

In 1593 it was stated that the Twelve and the Twenty-Five of Ludlow had been established by Lord Audley; which Lord Audley of very many was not stated. Some antiquity was implied.[37]

Twelve was the normal number of jurors on the panels of enquiries and trials. There are extant lists of 12 men called jurors in 1254, 1255, 1274 and 1291, but these may have been *ad hoc* panels rather than standing bodies. From 1308 there are surviving lists of the body known as 'the Twelve', later also called the aldermen of the borough. These lists survive for 1308, 1314, 1317, 1318, 1331 and 1448.[38] That for 1308 is accompanied by the names of the bailiffs, John Tikelwardyne and Matthew Agace, and also of the Twenty-Five – proof that the three chief institutions of town government, bailiffs, aldermen and common council (to use later names), were already in existence, although exactly what parts they played is not known.

The form of accounts for these years however indicates that it was the Twelve (*Duodena*) who ran the town. The 'Roll of the Community' for 1309 was noted as 'in the time of' the named Twelve. In 1317 and 1318 the Roll of the Community gives the names of 12 men who were 'at that time elected for the Twelve'. The roll for 1319–20 is more explicit: the roll of expenditure is headed 'expenses incurred by the aforesaid Twelve in the name of the whole Community'.[39]

In 1308 eight men were members of both the Twelve and the Twenty-Five, while neither bailiff was a member of either.[40] After 1461 the chief purpose of the distinction between the Twelve and the Twenty-Five was to perpetuate an oligarchic monopoly of municipal offices. This cannot have been the purpose in earlier days. Even so, the Twelve were accorded primacy; it was they who, in 1449, received the confirmation of the borough's privileges from Richard, Duke of York.[41] In 1339 it was all the members 'then of the Twelve of the Community of burgesses of Lodelowe' who witnessed the grant of a lease for life of the Mill Gate ditch.[42] Witnessing of Corporation grants was one of their functions, arising from their general supervision of the management of borough property.

Whereas in 1308 neither bailiff was a member of the Twelve, in 1317–19 two successive bailiffs, Philip Glover and William Sherman junior, were members.[43] After about 1336 both bailiffs were members of the Twelve.[44] Of the Twelve listed in 1448 four either had been or were to be bailiffs before 1461.

How did the men become members of the Twelve and the Twenty-Five? The words *electi erat* were used in 1318. Only five of the Twelve of 1317 were members again in 1319; this does not suggest co-optation but does imply election or nomination of the whole body annually from below.[45] This elective system seems to have changed well before 1461, when the town received its royal charter. In 1448 one of the Twelve, Thomas Whitegreve, was the Duke of York's receiver, that is, an important ducal administrator with responsibilities beyond Ludlow. In a co-optative system it would have been both understandable and practicable to seek influential friends for the Corporation by co-opting such people. The practice was still followed in the 17th century 'for good causes'. That such co-optations occurred suggests that the Twelve were not by that time elected by the votes of those below them. Whether it was the custom to choose the Twelve or the Twenty-Five to represent the four wards of the town is similarly not known. In 1593 the system agreed was for the bailiffs to choose a group of 17 men from all the wards who would submit three names from which the 'Company', that is, the council, would choose one to fill any vacancy in its ranks. As this was a compromise to go some way to meet the complaints of the objectors to the oligarchy, it is clear that hitherto unrestrained co-optation had applied, but it may have been a nod in the direction of a more ancient customary practice of choice by or consultation with the wards.[46]

The form of the accounts, however, shows that between 1335 and 1367 the main executive responsibility for government in the town shifted from the 'collegial' body of the Twelve to the bailiffs. The latter had always been important officials, but their financial responsibilities were restricted to collecting the burgage rents, which were excepted from the Community's own farms. The Community, through the Twelve, collected the perquisites of the courts, market tolls, certain demesne rents, rents from under-leases, profits from the mills (or the rents where the mills were under-leased), chenser rents and fines for liberties (that is, burgess-ships).[47] All these were usually obtained on farm from the lords. In addition the Community was entitled to collect the murage for its own benefit. The duties of government appear to have been carried out *ad hoc* by various members of the Twelve or by their town clerk. In 1367 the Corporation accounts presented by Richard Paunteley, the bailiff and keeper of the mills, comprehended all the sources of income previously accounted for by the Community, apart from murage, but including the burgage rents which had always been the bailiffs' charge. At this time the dominical revenues were not apparently farmed to the Corporation.[48] The murage was collected in 1361 by John Cachepol who also spent it on building repairs. If he were a bailiff this would indicate a division of responsibilities: murage under one, and other income under the other. Murage income became less important, not featuring as such in 16th-century accounts; it may be represented there by income from the town gates which was customarily set out at farm, the Community receiving only the rents therefrom. If so, the need for separate accounting would have disappeared; certainly by the 16th century the bailiffs presented joint accounts.

The Charters

Charters of corporate bodies are often assumed to be forms of constitution, final and comprehensive in respect of rights and obligations, within and without. Borough charters were rarely of this kind and those of Ludlow were no exception.

An interesting preliminary to the recorded charters of the Yorkist and Tudor periods is a grant made by the king in 1405 in response to a petition from the borough, reciting the town's loyalty and service during the Glyndwr rebellion.[49] During the minority of Edmund Mortimer the borough was in the king's hand and the grant was to apply for as long as it remained so. The town was given exemption from tallage, danegeld (that is, taxes on land), customs and tolls. The borough had sought a series of perpetual privileges, such as considerable freedom from the sheriff's interventions and power for the bailiffs to hear all pleas of debt and trespass in the town court in the Guildhall with powers of arrest in support, as well as control of the clerk of the market. The town was exempted from having 'foreigners', that is outsiders, on juries of any kind purely because they held property in the town. To what extent these privileges continued to be enjoyed, notwithstanding the precise terms of the grant, is not known; powers once devolved may not in practice have been easily resumed. The privileges recited in such detail in the petition all appeared in the royal charter of 1461, which gives the later charter a confirmatory as well as donative character.

The rights and powers of the borough before 1449 are therefore a matter of inference from circumstance. The Corporation has to be regarded as one of prescription only, although some form of charter granted in the 13th century once existed.[50] This may not have been the only one and what rights it allowed or confirmed is not known. In 1449 the borough received from its then lord, Richard, Duke of York, a general statement of its rights and powers which was thereafter treated as a form of charter. He guaranteed to the Twelve (who were named) and the Twenty-Five (who were not) that they should continue to govern the town as they and their predecessors had done 'time out of mind', except for the 'correction and governance that longeth and concerneth to oure Stuard there in holding our courtes and except also that that appertaineth to the constables for the king'. The exceptions were not restrictions of previous rights, but merely ensured that this was a confirmation of customary powers and not an extension of them.[51] It is not known why this confirmation was sought and given at this time. York had apparently already conferred the earldom of March on his son, Edward, and it might have been expected that the latter would properly have given Ludlow this confirmation. Three months later York went over to Ireland; his return a year later marked the beginning of the Wars of the Roses. It may be that Ludlow could see the way national politics were going and had sought some comfort before he went. In 1598 it was said that the town was run 'as it was under Richard II'.[52]

The charter of 1461 was presented as a reward for Ludlow's loyalty and sufferings during the first decade of the Wars of the Roses, but it is better seen as a means of bolstering

Yorkist support in Parliament. This charter did extend the liberties of the borough, but confined itself to the changes, to matters affecting relations with royal courts, taxes and privileges, to relations with outsiders and to specific exceptions. As it did not pronounce on unchanged aspects of internal administration which was largely based on custom, it left room for future internal dispute. The burgesses were henceforth each year to choose two bailiffs from among the 'foremost and fittest' of their number. For the first time, they were allowed to choose 'burgesses' (that is, Members) of Parliament 'of themselves' and were exempted from contributing towards the knights of the shire. They were granted all the lands and rents in Ludlow which had been in the charge of the bailiff (*sic.* singular) and for which he had to answer to the lord. All men resident in the town and its suburbs were to bear local and national taxation in the same way as the burgesses. There could be a merchant gild with a monopoly of trading in the town. There was to be elected a recorder or steward, and the recorder and bailiffs were to act as justices of the peace within the borough. A coroner was to be elected by the burgesses to carry out what had been the sheriff's duties there. They were also allowed to dye cloth as the burgesses of Bristol were.[53]

The Charter left it to the burgesses, implicitly to their existing representative institutions, the Twelve and the Twenty-Five, to make suitable arrangements for the election of bailiffs; nothing was specified, neither oligarchy nor democracy. Nevertheless the existing oligarchy used the opportunity to extend its hold on municipal power by monopolising both the choice and the candidatures of the bailiffs. Although the precise rules were altered as time passed, this basic principle never again changed.

The grant to the Corporation of the lands and rents, previously the lord's, did little for the town, except that, in addition to the redistribution of income involved, it ensured that the income remained in the town, instead of going to maintain the households and pretensions of usually non-resident lords. Like the later acquisition of the Palmers' Gild properties, it provided a source of enrichment for the oligarchy and, at times, the chief preoccupation of municipal politics. There is reason to suspect that Ludlow's economic performance in the next 150 years was adversely affected by this comfortable subsidy for lack of enterprise.

In 1478 a further charter was issued, confirming that of 1461 and requiring the fee farm rent to be paid to the receiver of the lordship, rather than to the Exchequer, and also granting the alnage of Ludlow (a tax or royalty on cloth manufacture) to the bailiffs.[54] This removed Ludlow permanently from the jurisdiction of the county or regional alnagers. It was under this power that the Corporation, rather than the bailiffs themselves, appointed an alnager to assess the levy.

An *Inspeximus* and confirmation of the charters followed in 1484 and 1509, as was usual at the start of a new reign.

A more important charter was that of 1552, which transferred the Palmers' Gild properties to the Corporation and specified responsibilities for the almshouse, a grammar school and a public preacher. As was customary, previous charters were ratified. Two fairs were now authorised.

Queen Mary's charter of 1554 addressed a practical problem of government. William Foxe, high bailiff, died during his term of office and the charter required the burgesses in such an instance to elect a replacement. The reason for the State's unwonted interest in such minutiae of appointments was simply that the bailiffs, under the 1461 charter, were justices of the peace and provision had to be made for the efficient conduct of the courts. To ensure that the courts carried on normally, it was also provided that until a new bailiff were elected the surviving one should be able to hold a court on his own. It is noteworthy that no attempt was made to specify precisely how a new bailiff was to be elected. The next charter, that of 1596, spelled out the procedure for the election and appointment of officials. This concern with detail stemmed from the municipal disputes of that decade; the government was anxious to quiet those disputes and to preserve a safe oligarchic regime. It also took the opportunity to ordain a Whitsun fair with a 'pie powder' court to resolve disputes between traders.[55] Eight years later, in 1604, a fresh charter extended the Whitsun fair to three days and another for 16 to 18 September. It defined some of the functions of the town clerk, an office long in existence.

The final charter in this series was that of 1627 dealing largely with the administration of the town court, still a concern of central government. In addition to the creation of the offices of capital masters, the charter required the recorder to be present before the court could sentence anyone to death or mutilation. The implication is that some irretrievable mistakes in this direction had been made by the essentially amateur bailiffs acting as magistrates. So that the normal working of the court should not be impeded, and notwithstanding the creation of the capital masters, it was thought necessary to allow bailiffs who were too sick to preside to appoint substitutes from among those in the common council who had been bailiffs.[56]

The Fee Farm Rent

An important provision of the 1461 charter was that the Corporation was bound in perpetuity to pay each year to the Crown a fee farm rent of £24 13s. 4d., a sum not very different from the burgage rents from the borough previously due to the lord. The rent excluded the Castle meadow, which the Crown leased directly. To start with, however, the Corporation was not required to pay the whole sum, as the 1461 charter temporarily excluded from the Corporation two properties already granted by the Crown to Master Jaakes and Maurice Porter for life; not until these life-interests were extinguished were the properties transferred to the Corporation and the latter required to pay over the full £24 13s. 4d.[57]

From the outset the fee farm rent was assigned in whole or part to annuities for pensioners and servants of the Crown. In 1461, £20 was granted to the king's physician, Master James Frirs, for life.[58] He was still receiving it in 1482.[59] In 1490, £10 a year from the rent was granted to Edward Haseley, the king's former tutor, then a clerk in royal service.[60] In that year Richard Sherman of Ludlow was granted the keepership of the new park at Oakley together with 51s. a year out of the Ludlow fee farm rent.[61] The 1478 charter required the fee farm rent to be paid, not to the Exchequer, but to the receiver of the lordship of Ludlow (an official of the earldom of March). The procedures for the disbursement of the fee farm rent and the annuities from it are unclear, however, although in 1638 it was paid directly to the then annuitant.[62]

From 1509 the annuitant was Ralph Egerton, a Gentleman of the Chamber and, later, keeper of Wigmore. He was succeeded in the latter office and as annuitant by Walter Walsh, a groom of the Chamber, in 1528.[63] Later annuitants were Edward Harman, a Privy Council page, Francis Cox and Griffith Jones, the castle janitor.[64] In 1620 the rent collector, Richard Edwards, declared however that the fee farm rent had for many years formed part of the jointure of James I's queen, Anne of Denmark.[65]

After 1552, as a consequence of the transfer to the Corporation of the property of the Palmers' Gild, the borough had to pay yearly to the Crown an additional £8 13s. 4d.,[66] which was assimilated to the original fee farm rent, for in 1638 the Corporation rent collector, Thomas Watkins, said that he paid £33 6s. 8d. from the rents to Richard Tomlins, who had it by the grant of James I, presumably after the death of Queen Anne in 1619.[67]

Richard Tomlins was a Ludlow M.P. when the grant was made to him. He bought the fee farm rent outright from the Crown and, it was claimed by the Corporation, in 1638 'being charitably disposed to Ludlowe because he was born there' he made a gift of a rent charge of £33 6s. 8d. to the Corporation for the 'good, benefit and relief of the poor'. In

1649, however, he left it in trust to his relatives to his own use for life, then to them for their lives and finally to the Corporation to the use of the churchwardens and the overseers of the poor of Ludlow. The relatives seem to have shown no sign of recognising the Corporation remainder, so, after his death, the Corporation sued for the entirety and there seems to have been an out-of-court settlement in 1652, followed in 1655 by a buy-out of the family life-interests. The rent charge continued thereafter to be paid to charitable purposes in the town.[68] A possible sale of the fee farm rent, described as a 'free rent of 32s. from customary tenements' in Ludlow, during the Commonwealth, was either abortive or cancelled, since the Tomlins' interest clearly survived unimpaired.[69] The castle meadow, exempted by the Crown from the fee farm, was leased until about 1475 to John Broke, then to Thomas Neville in 1476, and then to James Tewe for 26s. 8d. a year.[70] He was followed in 1480 by Richard Sherman and it may have remained in that family for, in 1540, it was leased to Edward Sherman for 32s. 4d. a year.[71]

The Bailiffs after 1461

After 1461 the position of the bailiffs becomes much clearer. The new charter allowed the burgesses to elect two, although, significantly, it did not state how this was to be done. By the early 16th century one of the bailiffs was called the high bailiff and the other the low bailiff, and by then the procedure for their election had been established. The high bailiff was chosen by the Twenty-Five from the ranks of the Twelve (that is, the aldermen), while the low bailiff was chosen from the Twenty-Five by the Twelve. As vacancies among the Twelve were apparently filled by co-optation from those members of the Twenty-Five who had already been low bailiffs, this effectively gave the Twelve considerable power over the choice of both bailiffs. This convention may not have obtained in the 1460s, only developing slowly over later decades, as at the outset there would not have been enough men of appropriate experience in the required offices. By 1549, however, the procedure had long been practised.[72] Oligarchy within oligarchy was an inevitable consequence of such a system and there were early complaints that the same people were taking office too often; in 1546 it was laid down that three years should elapse before a bailiff, chamberlain or alnager could serve in one of those offices again. This may have been aimed at John Morton, alnager for several years. In 1549 it was ordained that former high bailiffs should not be re-appointed while there was an alderman who had not so served; this restriction may have been aimed at William Langford, William Foxe, John Taylor and John Bradshaw, each of whom had served several times in the office; the immediate beneficiary was Thomas Blashfield, who became high bailiff only a year after joining the Twelve. The prohibition seems not to have worked, for later in his life Blashfield's own frequent tenure of office was to cause offence.[73] The prohibition was re-enacted in 1563, and extended to all offices in the Corporation, but in 1605 the rule was repealed. During the disputes of the 1590s the Bradford faction recited the words of the 1461 charter to justify direct election of bailiffs by the body of burgesses rather than by their supposed representatives, the Corporation. In the end they were not upheld, the Elizabethan government preferring safe municipal oligarchies to more populist arrangements.

The Twelve and the Twenty-Five after 1461

The 1461 charter did not explicitly alter the position of the Twelve and the Twenty-Five.[74] Apart from the changes engendered by now having control of the entire *cursus honorum*, the post–1461 Twelve and Twenty-Five were little different from what they had been earlier.

The complete membership of both bodies is known for 1469.[75] Among the Twelve were eight bailiffs, past and future, and five senior office-holders in the Palmers' Gild. Four

11. Part of a corporation rental for 1474–5 (SRO 356/420).

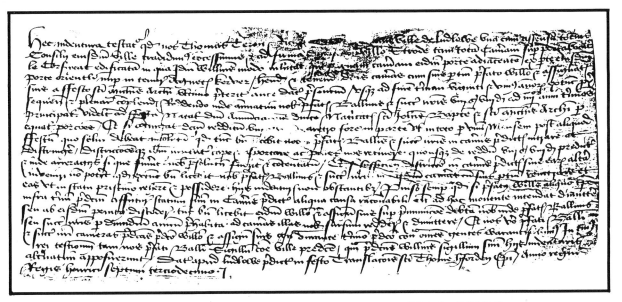

12. Corporation lease of a room over Corve Gate, 1497 (SRO 356/MT.614).

members, however, were never bailiffs before or after the charter. Fourteen of the Twenty-Five had been or were to be bailiff; only four are known definitely to have subsequently joined the Twelve, but it is probable that eight did so, leaving 17 who did not. As many as five men who joined the Twenty-Five after 1469 leap-frogged over them into the Twelve. Although early death played some part in this selection process, the chief factor was oligarchic co-optation.

The Twelve listed in 1541 between them held the high bailiffship 30 times, as well as providing four M.P.s. Of the Twenty-Five that year, five held no office and only eight eventually rose to high bailiff.[76] The same oligarchic selection as in 1469 can be seen. The dates of admission to burgess-ship are known for seven councillors. It took Lewis Phillips *alias* Capper 26 years between his admission and his first appointment as high bailiff, while Thomas Wheler, a well connected man, took only 13 years; 18 to 19 years was the average for this small sample of what were the successful men. The council of 1541 included 13 who were elders of the Palmers' Gild at its dissolution in 1551.

The records of council membership are full from the 1590s. The Twelve of that year held the high bailiffship 22 times between them and provided two M.P.s. Of the Twenty-Five, only four reached high bailiff, while nine achieved no senior office at all. Thomas Langford took 37 years from his admission as a burgess to appointment as high bailiff, while Robert Berry took only 12 years, 24 years being the average for those who got that far.

The high tide of oligarchy may have been reached in the 1590s, for, despite the political victory achieved in the Exchequer and the prerogative courts, which confirmed the oligarchy's centralised control of the borough, thereafter a widening of the circle of influence can be discerned. This may have been partly a consequence of the diminishing prosperity and importance of the town; the rewards of oligarchy may have diminished, too. The

Twelve of 1619 held the high bailiffship only 15 times between them; 17 of the Twenty-Five went through to become high bailiff, while only five held no senior office. Of the 84 petitioners in the 1596 'charter' dispute, 11 later became members of the common council.

The effects of mortality rates amongst the aldermen, which were the main factor in determining the rate of promotion from and to the Twenty-Five, should be recognised, but not exaggerated. From 1461 to 1660 the death rate amongst aldermen gradually rose. There were fluctuations; more than half the membership died in 1510–20, and again in 1550–60, 1580–90, 1610–20 and 1640–50; but the overall trend was upwards: 1461–1510, 2.4 per decade; 1510–1560, 5.2 per decade; 1560–1610, 5.8 per decade; 1610–1660, 6.4 per decade. The inevitable arithmetical result was that aldermen would on average tend to hold the high bailiffship less often than their predecessors had. It would have little bearing on the choice of replacements, the chances of individual members of the Twenty-Five reaching high bailiff, or of their being passed over in favour of newcomers. This was the more important factor.

In the period 1520 to 1660 only 50 per cent of those admitted to burgess-ship reached the first office in the *cursus honorum*, that is, churchwarden; 49 per cent of the churchwardens failed to reach the low bailiff's office (although 37 per cent of the churchwardens died too soon to do so); 39 per cent of the low bailiffs did not reach high bailiff (although 32 per cent of them died too soon); 49 per cent of high bailiffs served in that office only once (16 per cent being prevented by early death). About 15 per cent of burgesses rose to be high bailiff. In 1597 there were reckoned to be between 100 and 150 burgesses, so perhaps 3 per cent at most of the male population who lived most of their lives in Ludlow rose to that office. While the chances of reaching low bailiff were about the same in the 70 years before 1590 as in the 70 years after, chances of reaching high bailiff significantly improved after 1590.

Decade	Members who held no office	Average number of years in Corporation Before members held		
		Any office	Office of low bailiff	Office of high bailiff
1591–1600	10	4.4	5.8	13.5
1601–1610	9	4.7	7.4	14.8
1611–1620	5	5.3	7.2	15.7
1621–1630	4	5.9	7.1	16.8
1631–1640	3	5.7	8.3	16.9
1641–1650	4	3.7	9.6	22.9
1651–1660	0	3.5	8.4	21.3

The connections of bailiffs with former bailiffs or burgesses can be examined for the period 1560–1659. The following table looks at the antecedents of the low bailiffs appointed in each decade. Of the 100 appointments, 73 per cent are known to have been the sons or sons-in-law of burgesses; 47 per cent were the sons, grandsons or sons-in-law of former bailiffs. Indeed as many qualified by reason of being sons-in-law of former bailiffs or of burgesses as qualified by direct descent. Although there were fluctuations over the period, no long-term trend can be discerned.

Some burgesses qualified, not by kinship, but by special favour; in 1562 Simon Huddy, a 'sojourner', was admitted burgess at the instance of lord president Sidney.[76a]

Low Bailiffs with Ballival and Burgess Antecedents

Decade	Sons of former bailiffs	Sons-in-law of former bailiffs	Grandsons of former bailiffs	Sons, sons-in-law, grandsons of former bailiffs	Sons of known burgesses	Sons-in-law of known burgesses	Sons, Sons-in-law of known burgesses
1560–69	2	5	0	7	4	7	9
1570–79	1	5	1	5	2	5	5
1580–89	4	3	2	6	5	7	9
1590–99	2	3	0	5	4	5	6
1600–09	3	1	0	4	5	3	6
1610–19	4	2	2	5	6	3	7
1620–29	0	2	0	2	4	5	6
1630–39	5	1	3	6	10	3	10
1640–49	2	2	0	3	5	5	8
1650–59	1	2	1	4	6	4	7
Total	24	26	9	47	51	47	73

The Charter Disputes of the 1590s

The best documented disputes over Ludlow's government took place in the 1590s.[77] The bitter disputes began with a petition from a number of burgesses to the Council of the March alleging maladministration on the part of the council, particularly over Corporation property. Initially the Council of the March referred it to the Privy Council in London, which bounced it back quickly: 'but we have had no business in it. You are to end it according to justice and equities without any delaie or excuse'.[78] The view of the ruling oligarchy was expressed in the Corporation minute recording the disfranchisement of John Bradford and John Sutton who 'would overthrow the ancient government and bring all in common', demonstrating that the terror aroused by the rule of the 'saints' in Münster 60 years before was still real, even in Ludlow.[79] Sir Henry Townshend, who was both a member of the Council of the March and recorder of Ludlow, drew up a set of 27 articles, apparently commanding general assent and designed to settle the dispute. One article established a complex procedure for filling vacancies on the Twelve and Twenty-Five: the bailiffs to choose 17 burgesses at large representing the various wards; the 17 to draw up a short list of three names and the Twelve and Twenty-Five to choose from this the replacement; the crucial element of this was the choice of the 17. Another article limited leases of Corporation property to 21 years and prohibited accumulations of such leases by individuals. A third required leases to be granted with no fewer than 25 councillors present.

This did not settle things. Philip and John Bradford led fresh opposition to the council. Philip was ejected from his membership, but John Bradford and John Sutton instituted *Quo warranto* proceedings against the Corporation. The council reacted by depriving them not only of their council places but of their burgess-ships, too. While the *Quo warranto* proceedings were grinding on the ruling group applied for a new charter for the borough. The Bradford faction, now joined by John Crowther, then promoted a bill of complaint before the Council of the March, and followed it with an Exchequer suit. This was the most wide-ranging set of complaints against the ruling group as a whole and its individual members. *Ultra vires* actions, oppression, extortion, corruption, nepotism and misappropriation of funds were alleged in considerable detail. Before the case could be heard, however, there was a new charter.

The Bradford faction, now ineptly led by Crowther, then overreached itself. Prejudging the outcome of the lawsuits, a group forced locks to obtain the corporate seals, then dismissed the town clerk and ejected their leading opponents from the council, replacing them with their own supporters. Appeals to the Privy Council produced an order to the Council of the March referring to the 'great contention there concerning their government; for example's sake some such punishment should be shewed on some of the actors and ringleaders'. After four years the Privy Council had finally run out of patience.[80] Crowther made things worse by trying to rig the election of Ludlow's M.P.s, but the Commons overturned this. These acts were followed by a judgment in the Exchequer court which entirely upheld the former rulers. Crowther was expelled and the old oligarchy was restored with its assumed powers and accustomed practices now made explicit in a new charter. In the climate of the times, with a government anxious about religious and political dissent, no other outcome was likely.

The detailed allegations made in the course of these disputes provide a remarkable picture of contemporary Ludlow. Most of the statements made were *ex parte* and, after 400 years, neither provable nor disprovable. What can be demonstrated, however, is the fact that those complained against were closely connected by blood and marriage, as well as the tie created by their common enjoyment of the fruits of office and power.[81] Even public-spirited men did not think it dishonourable to take whatever advantage their public positions offered them. If God and the laws promoted men to office it was because they were deserving of honour and reward. It is unlikely therefore that the Ludlow 'masters' (as the leading burgesses were usually called) did not take such advantage.[82]

The articles of 'griffes' (grievances) presented to the Council of the March in 1593 by John Bradford and John Sutton alleged or implied the covert granting of leases and almshouse places and of illegal elections and appointments of Corporation officers, violations of prohibitions on repeated elections, the granting of leases to family and friends, misappropriation of fines, failure to pay stipends to those entitled to them, excessive fee-taking, extortionate rents, caucus decisions and bribe-taking.

Four years later the charges made in the Exchequer were even more explicit and detailed. Richard Bailey was alleged to have misappropriated or to have leased at undervalue 12 properties, market tolls and profits of two fairs. Richard Rascall justified the rents Bailey paid, but John Warde, Bailey's tenant, showed that one property for which Bailey paid the Corporation 8s. a year produced rents of 46s. to Bailey. Rascall claimed, probably correctly, that it was customary for the bailiffs for the time being to enjoy rents from the demesne lands along with the fair rents. Thomas Langford was charged similarly with more than 25 properties and the profits of fairs. Rascall again justified some of these. Richard Langford was alleged to have misappropriated part of the Corve Gate. Robert Berry was charged with at least eight properties and the fair rents. Rascall again obliged with a story of ruinous properties being done up by Berry and so paying higher rents, although Berry himself admitted getting a renewal of his lease for 41 years. Thomas Evans had misappropriated at least six properties and there were 'divers other lands etc'. Although Rascall duly defended him, it was shown that Evans acquired the headleases of properties occupied by Thomas Powell and had jacked up his rent 'to Powell's great hurt'. The Sherman family had 10 properties, paying entry fines on only part of them; Bradford was able to rebut Rascall by showing that the Shermans got the lands through the influence of their kinsman, Thomas Langford, and then sublet them at a large profit. William Pinner's misappropriations covered at least a dozen properties, for which Rascall's explanation was that some were later leased by Pinner while others had always been his own. This did not, however, dispose of the matter, since falsely claiming Corporation property as theirs by inheritance was central to the charges, and the fact that land was 'later' leased suggests that, earlier, Pinner had indeed made false claims. Richard Hoke obtained nine properties by means of 'kinred, affinitie and major voyce', in Bradford's words. At the very least it is incontrovertible that a small number of influential and closely related men accumulated a large number of Corporation properties and let them out at great profit. The charges against the oligarchy in substance were justified.[83]

William Comber said that before they would seal his lease, Bailey and John Clee, the bailiffs, demanded a 'reward' of 20s. each. Francis Jenks, the town clerk, by no means one of the petitioners, admitted that Thomas Langford, 19 years rent-collector, had presented only three or four rent-books in the whole time. With such casualness, very unlike the careful accounting of the Middle Ages, it is hardly surprising that Corporation officers found it difficult to distinguish between their public duty and their private interest.

The leading members of the council were indeed closely related.[84] There were two main dynasties or 'kindreds' in Ludlow: one consisted of the descendants and connections by marriage of Richard Handley, bailiff in 1541; the Farrs, Hokes, Bensons, Rascalls and Blashfields belonged to this group and all provided bailiffs. The other main kindred were the descendants and connections of Walter Rogers and William Langford, who died in 1546 and 1553 respectively, and who had not only been bailiffs, but were also the last two wardens of the Palmers' Gild; this group included the Sherman, Langford, Bailey, Pinner, Evans, Waties and Saunders families, as well as the Powys and Heath connections of Richard Bailey.

Although most of the opponents of the oligarchy were not in the first rank of the older Ludlow families, those who led them had that status; the Crowthers and Bradfords were related through a mutual connection with the Broughtons of Henley and with the Blashfields, Clungunwases and Mortons. Kindreds were not exclusive, however. The Blashfields were also connected with the Rascalls, but this did not inhibit them from joining the attack. The Heaths, despite their connection with Bailey, were of the Bradford faction, possibly because they were poorer relations. Francis Jenks, the town clerk, was connected through his wife with the Crowthers, but his office made him unavoidably one of the oligarchy.

Simon Blashfield shocked the town when he called Bailiff Benson 'a coore, a pottel . . . a cupp carryer, a raddleman, an asse . . . [and] a knavemaster', adding, ' I am as good a man as thou art'. The end of the charter disputes quietened faction, but it did not end the *ad hominem* vehemence with which public discussion was conducted, although it was nonetheless resented by those who came off worst. In 1630 Thomas Edwards was sequestered from the council for accusing Thomas Colerick, then bailiff, of being 'led home drunke Monday last'.[85]

Other Officials

The chamberlain is not found in the records until 1475–6.[86] He was originally called the catchpole, whose duties were chiefly regulatory and disciplinary, probably with charge of the town gaol, the gates and the administration of the town court. This official existed in the early 15th century, when John Ferrour and Walter Barbour, catchpoles apparently together in 1418–19, and a predecessor, Henry Bragot, each paid nearly £10 to the Earl of March's receiver.[87] Such sums look more than incidents of police functions and seem to be largely property income, a judgment reinforced by the fact that very similar sums were due to be paid by the chamberlains of the mid-16th century. We do not know why this office had attached to it more important financial and administrative duties, but the process clearly long preceded the change of name to chamberlain. In 1423 a valor of the lordship recorded payments to two catchpoles, who themselves paid over the perquisites of the courts to the bailiffs.[88] It is a puzzle, however, that two catchpoles apparently developed during the 15th century into one chamberlain and one or more sergeants (themselves numbering two sergeants-at-mace and one common sergeant in the early 16th century). It is tempting to think that the change may have taken place in 1461, although the new

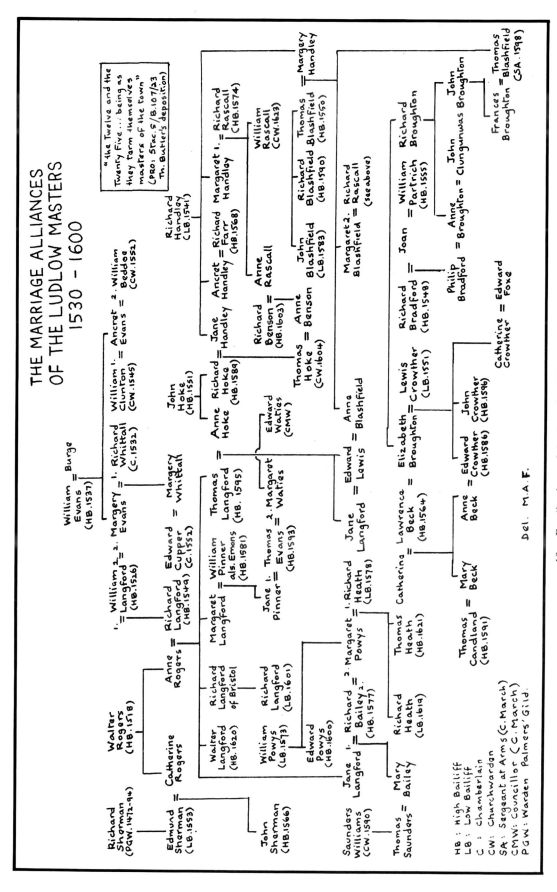

13. Family chart of the Masters of Ludlow.

charter was in most respects more a confirmation of existing institutions than a revolutionary change.

In the 17th century the chamberlain increased in importance; from at least the early 16th century the *cursus honorum* of Ludlow official life established the chamberlainship as the first office to be held by a man elected to the Twenty-Five, before he qualified to become low bailiff, but from about 1650 the chamberlainship was served after the low bailiffship, reflecting their changed relative importance.

The financial functions of the chamberlain are difficult to define. In the mid-16th century he was responsible for accounting for the receipt of burgage rents in Corve Street, Galdeford, Lower Old Street and parts of Linney. He also accounted for certain fixed rents, such as rents from the farm of Corve, Old, Broad and Galdeford gates, as well as properties which had formerly belonged to the dissolved religious houses of Ludlow. By 1562 the burgage rents had been transferred to the charge of the bailiffs.[89] At this time his annual account was for income of £9 10s. to £9 18s. 9d., very like the sums accounted for by the catchpoles of 140 years earlier. Since the burgage rents for which he was later responsible included all those we can identify as the burgages of the lord of Cotes, the possibility exists that by 1418 the earls of March were the lords of Cotes (by inheritance or exchange) and were receiving the income in that capacity but separately until the creation of the royal borough. The need at an early date to collect the Cotes rents separately may provide the clue to the origins of the catchpole/chamberlain's financial functions. By 1562, although the chamberlain was the receiver of minor sources of income, such as that from subscriptions paid by new councillors and officials, his main financial function was expenditure, chiefly repairs to Corporation property and to roads, walls and gates. Several chamberlains were brought before the Court Leet for neglect of such repairs (£6 18s. 2½d. in a half year in 1562).[90] There is a certain irony in this, as it was the chamberlains' duty to meet the expenses of holding these courts.

The chamberlain was also high constable of the town, generally responsible for the town gaol. He retained his police functions even into the 17th century. When William Sherwood was arrested in 1603 after the riot which followed his attempt to elope with Susan Blashfield, he was brought to the chamberlain and high constable of Ludlow, who committed him to gaol in Galdeford Tower to await trial.[91] Below were elected constables for each ward of the town. Not much is known of these officials, except that day-to-day policing seems to have fallen to them and that they were very minor in the hierarchy. These offices were not part of the *cursus honorum*.

Slightly more important than the constables, in that they reported directly to the Corporation, although they were not of it, were the two sergeants-at-mace and the common sergeant. The last seems to have been superior to the others in esteem, but their duties were similar and the holders of the offices sometimes exchanged with one another. Although annually appointed, most sergeants served for three or more years. The first recorded sergeant, in 1502, would have had predecessors.[92] They handled large sums (£132 altogether in 1562), mainly from fines imposed in the town court, which they collected. One of their duties was to keep the town gaol and also to help maintain discipline in the town. They did not always carry out their duties as expected: in 1625 Francis Hill, then sergeant-at-mace, was fined by the Council of the March for refusing to assist the chamberlain, William Lloyd, who was in trouble.[93] The sergeants were always burgesses ranking below the churchwardens in the town hierarchy of esteem and occasionally some went further, like John Bell, common sergeant in 1539, who reached high bailiff in 1573. This was unusual, however; most sergeants went no further.

Apart from the period 1641–5, the churchwardens served for one year and were appointed by the Corporation at the same time as the other Corporation officers. It was an office often filled by young men of some standing in the town for whom this was a necessary precursor to election to the Twenty-Five. In the period 1540 to 1660 approximately half the churchwardens went on to a higher office, while about five per cent died within five years and may have been out of the running for that reason.

A minor office, not in practice subject to annual appointment, was that of town crier, who summoned burgesses to meetings and the inhabitants at large to musters and other assemblies. Richard Job held the post from before 1587 until his death in 1603; as he was 66 when he died, he may well have held the post for many years. In 1637 his grandson, William Job, was town crier.[94] As the churchwardens' accounts for 1617–18 include 18d. 'for mendinge Jobs bell' and in 1606 John Jobbe, then aged 27, was a 'querrester' (and therefore in good voice) it seems likely that John, William's father, had also been town crier, perhaps until his death in 1630. It is not known when William died, but he was followed in the post by his aptly-named son, Jeremiah Job, until his death in 1661.[95]

The office, in principle appointive, was in practice hereditary, which may have been the consequence of its being closely associated with duties about the church, such as bellringing and odd jobs. Church posts were, apart from the churchwardens, not annual appointments, and sons often did follow their fathers. From about 1595 William Crump was sexton, bellringer and odd-jobman. (In 1608 he was accused in the ecclesiastical court of 'ringing extraordinarie peales at burialls'.)[96] He was succeeded in these duties, although possibly not in his level of devotion, by his son Thomas about 1611, who was paid for ringing the bells in celebration of the king's saint's day the following year. Thomas Crump died in 1624 and at some time was followed by Hugh Daniell, not apparently a relation, but Hugh was succeeded in 1646 by his own son, William Daniell, who retained the office until his death in 1674.[97]

The church was a relatively important employer of permanent jacks-of-all-trades. Thomas Higgs, father-in-law of William Crump and a centenarian when he died in 1606, had worked about the church, as deacon, chorister and odd-jobman for 50 years, along with members of his family, like Richard Higgs (who 'stopped the choughs out of the church' in 1586), John Higges (who cleared the churchyard in 1575) and the Thomas Higgs, 'querester', who died in 1567.[98] Perhaps William Higgs, one of the Austin friars who surrendered the friary in 1538, was a member of this family.[99] There were also John Roe, who did odd jobs there in 1577, and Thomas Roe, the church dog-catcher of 1607; Stephen Knight, who repaired the chimes in 1575, and John Knight who repaired the steeple in 1595; Richard Clench the elder and his son, Richard, clock-keepers, who carried out the same tasks for the Council of the March.

Each year were elected a group of experienced councillors, former office-holders, called the Six Men, to audit accounts, check the grant of leases and oversee the officials. These responsibilities were mostly exercised *ex post facto*. During the 1590s disputes, several former 'Six Men' gave evidence concerning the truth of the Bradford faction's allegations about abuses by bailiffs and others. The effect of such evidence is to lessen the guilt of individual officials but not to remove the impression of oligarchic abuse; that is, the auditing procedure was such that a generally exploitative system, provided it was run according to conventions accepted by the oligarchy, would remain untouched, even if individual breaches of those conventions were stopped.[100]

An important office, not an annual appointment, was that of rent-collector. From the start this was a permanent rather than an annual appointment; so expertise was brought to the task, but it may have resulted in lack of proper control by the council. Richard Langford held the office in 1562 and, as he had previously been for many years the Gild rent-collector, we may assume that he continued in office when the Corporation took over Gild properties in 1552. Hitherto the bailiffs and chamberlain had collected the much smaller Corporation rental income.[101] Richard Langford died in 1562 and was succeeded by his son Thomas who had just been elected to the Twenty-Five; he held the post in 1577 and was succeeded in 1597 by Edmund Lloyd. The Langfords had held the office for fifty years.[102]

Edmund Lloyd kept the post until his death in 1607 and was succeeded by Richard Edwards.[103] The existence of this office diminished the importance of the low bailiff, reflected in the relegation of that office in 1650. The rent-collector was responsible for a large proportion of Corporation income after 1551. On appointment Edwards had had to provide a bond to meet arrears of rent from his own pocket; he therefore began proceedings against various burgage-holders who were in arrears with their burgage rents; some of these were bailiffs and aldermen and he alleged that pressure was put on him to abandon these actions. By 1617 he himself was £18 16s. in arrear and the bailiffs sued him before the Council of the March. Evidence was given that Edwards had received some rents, and had not asked for other rent, while others coolly said that they would only pay if Edwards would depose before the court that they were in arrears. The court ordered Edwards to pay his bond and sue the defaulters privately.

An even more important non-annual office was that of town clerk, which had its origins in the late 13th-century clerks who are mentioned in the few surviving accounts and deeds of that time. Most described themselves briefly as 'clerks' (for they were witnesses because they were also the notaries who drew up the deeds), but some used the expression 'clerk of the town'. Indeed it would have been impossible for town business to have been carried on without at least one clerk with legal and accounting training. They may have had other professional work, too. As the town's business became more complex, it probably became full-time work. In the 1240s Adam Cotele *alias* Adam the chaplain *alias* Adam the clerk was also *prepositus*, but we do not know how this should be translated. *Henricus clericus de Ludelawe*, which may be translated either as 'Henry the clerk, of Ludlow' or as 'Henry the Ludlow Clerk' was also *ballivus*. It is not until 1341–57 that there is clear evidence of a town clerk as such, when William Uttoksacher (sc. Uttoxeter) was 'clerk of the town'.[104] Again in 1409 we find 'John, clerk of the town'.[105] In 1423 a clerk of the court is mentioned, who was very likely town clerk with a related duty.[106] Notwithstanding the town clerk's duty of maintaining the Corporation's records, it is impossible to trace a continuous succession of holders of the office from those very records.

Between 1546 and 1556 John Alsap served as town clerk; during this period he also served as low and high bailiff and as Member of Parliament. He was briefly recorder in 1569 and may have been town clerk until then.[107] Alsap was the only town clerk to hold elective offices at the same time. Francis Jenks held the office from 1587 to 1601 and was involved in the charter disputes of the time. He was followed by Thomas Tourneur (1602–6), Thomas Hill (1606–20) and Richard Mitton (1621–31).[108] Apart from the period after 1646, when he was briefly displaced by William Brayne, a Parliamentarian, John Rickards was town clerk for 39 years after 1631.[109] The town clerks provided a very important element of continuity and stability in town government, particularly after the institution of annual elections for most senior Corporation offices in 1461.

The office of alnager was created to administer the grant of alnage in the 1461 charter, so taking the place of the royal county alnagers. While the town was a significant producer of cloth, this office brought in a worthwhile income to the Corporation, even though it was effectively a tax on its own citizens. The revenue depended upon the state of trade and varied between under £3 and over £6. Throughout the 16th century the office of alnager was taken by a former low bailiff, usually of the previous year. The cloth trade declined substantially after 1600; from 1628 the alnager held office before he became low bailiff and retained that ranking after 1650 when that office was held before the chamberlainship. For long periods the duties were mainly carried out by a deputy alnager, who stayed in office for some years, as did John Holland from at least 1566 to 1592.[110] Offices which required deputies, particularly semi-permanent ones, were offices with onerous, time-consuming duties, as the inspection of manufactured cloth must have been.

Another royal office devolved to the borough in the 1461 charter was that of coroner, who oversaw and attended all executions in Ludlow, of which there were a great many.[111] Until 1627 the office was filled by the high bailiff of the year before, but thereafter the low bailiff of the year before was substituted. This was a consequence of the revision of the town charter in 1626 which permitted the annual appointment of two 'capital masters' (or chief magistrates) from the ranks of former high bailiffs. The men appointed to this new office frequently served several times, possibly where they displayed competence at the duties of sitting as judges in the town court. There may have been an increase in the volume of prosecutions and litigation which had proven a burden on the bailiffs sitting alone.

The recorder replaced the proprietorial steward, although there was some confusion over these titles at first. The stewards had presided at the lord's court in Ludlow; the recorders took their place, but were to be accompanied by the bailiffs, as *ex officio* justices of the peace, with the powers and responsibilities attaching to that office. The recorders often had another function – to act as the Corporation's protector and adviser in contentious matters.

The recorder was from the outset intended to be a man with legal training, and all or most incumbents were in fact lawyers, although most were also and primarily government officials, particularly as the judicial functions of the Council of the March developed from about 1540 and its judges and attorneys became available to fill the post. Only three recorders before 1660 could be said to be Ludlow men, rather than men who had made their careers elsewhere.[112] Sometimes the recorder performed another crucial function. Sir Henry Townshend, then recorder, used his legal skill and political judgment to produce a formula in an attempt to solve the disruptive charter disputes in the 1590s. His seems to have been the only attempt at compromise; it failed because none of the factions was interested in anything but victory; that kind of outcome could only come by the intervention of the forces of the State.[113] Nevertheless the episode demonstrates the value of the office as the last local means of defusing bitter confrontations. That a man of Townshend's ability and standing could not solve this dispute demonstrates both the gravity of the particular problem and the need for men of more than local standing to fill the office. It is likely that when there were other less grave issues requiring the recorders' advice or intervention this was obtained rather less publicly.

The market officials, although counting for little in the *cursus honorum* of the town, had important functions which impinged on its day-to-day life. There was a clerk of the market in 1405, but the office was probably very much older – at least as old as the earliest fair.[114] The market warden collected market dues for the bailiffs. Each year there were two of each kind of market official, including the wardens, the bread tasters, ale tasters, meat tasters, milk tasters and green tasters. Most were men of lower social standing than the officials discussed above, although Walter Cressett, market warden in 1479–80, was the brother of Nicholas Cressett, the bailiff, with whom he was often litigating.[115] The tasters tested the quality of the goods offered for sale in the retail market of the town. Both consumers' interests and Ludlow's reputation as a market needed protection. The fines levied for infringements provided a useful income for the Corporation.

The gatekeepers' duties included both security and the levying of tolls, an important source of income. During the Middle Ages it was common for the gates to be put out to farm, the tolls leviable at particular gates being collected by individuals who had paid for the privilege.

The Members of Parliament

Edward IV's charter of 1461 granted Ludlow the right to elect two burgesses to attend parliaments in the future. This was in the expectation that a Yorkist borough would support a Yorkist king. The grant was never revoked despite the fall of the House of York in 1485. Ludlow was represented continuously in parliament, not in its heyday as a commercial centre, but when this had passed and its importance was chiefly as the centre of a regional government – the Council of the March of Wales.

Ludlow was, however, represented in at least one of the earlier parliaments. In September 1332 William Ace and one of the Orletones, probably William, attended parliament *pro stapulis ordinandis* (for the ordaining of staples), that is, to consider the grant to the king of a tax on wool exports through the device of staple or regulated export ports.[116] In what precise capacity they attended, or the precise assembly, is not clear. The latter may have been the parliament itself or one of the connected assemblies of merchants convoked for the purpose of granting taxes out of mercantile wealth. Should Ace and Orletone properly be called Ludlow's first known M.P.s? The question is, however, unhistorical and otiose, since the forms of parliamentary assembly were then still various. It is not to the point that the merchant assemblies dropped out and did not feature in later parliaments; at that time they were a feature and Ludlow, as a leading commercial town, evidently participated.

The borough was allowed by the 1461 charter to choose its M.P.s 'of themselves or others', but for over 150 years it resolutely eschewed 'others', even claiming that it had no alternative. Not enough is known about the day-to-day business of parliament at the time to enable us to determine whether having two Members gave Ludlow any political influence, or, if it had, whether it was exercised in its own interest. Nevertheless, being exempted from maintaining the Shropshire knights of the shire saved Ludlow the expense of supporting persons who might not be favourably disposed to them.

From 1461 Ludlow's Members of Parliament (itself an anachronistic expression) have been the subject of articles by Henry Weyman and the editors of the *History of Parliament*.[117] Neither is wholly satisfactory, however. No list is complete, and before the reign of Henry VIII only a minority of the M.P.s are in fact known; there were 15 parliaments but M.P.s (seven) for only four of these are known. Of these, five were Ludlow men, of whom three also served as bailiffs, while one other, recorded as Thomas Pratte, may in fact have been John Pratte, the bailiff. Richard Sherman has been included in some traditional lists of bailiffs, but there is no corroboration for this. Two served as wardens of the Palmers' Gild. The other two M.P.s were men of political influence; Piers Beaupie, a Montgomeryshire man, was a royal official, holding such offices as clerk to the controller of the Household and clerk of the Greencloth. Richard Littleton was a lawyer and a son of Thomas Littleton, the judge.

During the reign of Henry VIII the M.P.s can be better traced. The Foxe family dominated the representation throughout much of the reign; this was the period when that family, minor gentry, aggrandised itself through the marriage of William Foxe with the heiress of Richard Downe, the warden of the Gild, providing several M.P.s for Ludlow, and by acquiring conventual estates. The other M.P.s at this time were John Cother, member of a Ludlow family resident there for a century, Thomas Wheler, whose second wife was William Foxe's daughter. John Bradshawe, although not Ludlow-born, was a Ludlow resident until he transferred his interests to Radnorshire. Robert Blount, a Derbyshire man and servant of the earls of Shrewsbury, was a sergeant-at-arms in the Council of the March.

Mary's reign began with a dispute before the Council of the March, when 13 burgesses of the second rank obtained a ruling that M.P.s were to be chosen by the Twelve and the Twenty-Five, the implication being that, hitherto, some smaller group had chosen them. This may have been an anti-Foxe tactic, since previously that family had provided M.P.s at every occasion, and this ceased after the Council's decision.[118]

During Mary's reign, of earlier M.P.s only Wheler was elected. The 10 M.P.s were about equally local men and connections of the Council of the March, some being both. Four were bailiffs; only one, William Heath, was a known Catholic, while one, Sir John Price, was a reformer. Those who had earlier done well out of the dissolution of local conventual houses were absent.

In Elizabeth's reign there were 20 M.P.s elected and a further three replacements for deceased or irregularly elected M.P.s, but these terms were filled by only nine men. William Poughnill was elected to four parliaments; Robert Mason to three;[119] Philip Sidney briefly took Mason's place; Robert Berry had a long incumbency, lasting from 1581 to 1614, with a brief intermission during the charter dispute in 1597, finally losing his place in 1614 after returning himself as M.P., being bailiff at the time; Thomas Candland served on five occasions. Apart from the very brief terms of Sidney, Hugh Sandford and Thomas Butler, all the Elizabethan M.P.s were townsmen, although Berry doubtless owed his election to his position as an official (first castle porter and then clerk of fines) of the Council of the March, while William Poughnill was clerk to the Signet. During all this time Ludlow's only active part in parliament was, with one exception, to incur the expulsions of its returned members for irregularities.[120] The one exception was when Berry, alone of the Shropshire M.P.s, voted to include Shropshire in the Bill to convert pasture back to tillage; he was 'greatly frowned at for it'.[121]

In 1596 a blatant irregularity occurred when John Crowther, then bailiff, intercepted the sheriff's writ and returned Hugh Sandford, the Earl of Pembroke's secretary, and Thomas Butler, having them made burgesses of the town immediately beforehand to qualify them. The House of Commons declared this void and a new election was held, by which time the bailiffs had changed.[122] It is significant that, when it suited the 'popular' faction, they were prepared to be even more exclusive in their actions than the oligarchy itself.

The 17th century saw the rapid erosion of Ludlow's parliamentary independence, (never as absolute as afterwards claimed for it). In 1605 the council refused Salisbury's nominee, declaring that statute prevented them 'electing one who was not a burgess resident among us'.[123] In 1609 the Corporation refused to elect a government nominee, John Leveson, on the grounds that they were bound to elect their own burgesses, and elected Richard Fisher, a townsman, instead. Thereafter the most important criterion seemed to be the willingness of candidates to pay their own expenses; on each occasion the council declared its own standing orders to be 'for this time void'.[124] Richard Tomlins, M.P. from 1621 to 1628, was the last with a claim to be a townsman, apart from John Aston in 1654–6, but even Tomlins had made his career elsewhere. Ralph Goodwin, an official of the Council of the March, was elected six times in a row. Tomlins was succeeded by Charles Baldwyn, a country gentleman, who was to be the type for more than 300 years. After the capture of Ludlow in the summer of 1646, two Parliamentarians from outside, Thomas Mackworth and Thomas More, were imposed on the borough. In 1659 the pattern for the future was set with the election of Job Charlton and Samuel Baldwyn. Thenceforth Ludlow subordinated itself politically to the gentry of the county in return for being relieved of the expense of representing itself; this pusillanimity was typical of a good many boroughs in England, but it was a sad end to Ludlow's political independence, for the consequence was that the town's interests were to be served only by the grace of its supposed representatives and then more outside parliament than within. Deference replaced independence.

Municipal Government in Action

Before the 16th century, evidence of Corporation activities is sporadic and largely inferential. Murage had been granted to the 'good men' of Ludlow, that is, the leading citizens who ran things. It is not known to what extent murage and pavage were in fact disbursed on walls and roads. In 1352 James Wottenhulle, John Gour and Hugh Monynton were appointed to enquire into allegations that the men of Ludlow had collected the murage and retained it for their own use.[125]

Before the 1461 charter the aldermen and common council played a part in municipal government distinct from that of the bailiffs. The former represented 'the Community', whereas the latter represented the lords. The Community had its own sources of income – the murage collections, the issues of the mills rented from the prioress of Aconbury, fines for burgess-ships (or 'liberty'), rents of gates and other property rented from the lords; of these the first two were overwhelmingly important.[126] The bailiffs looked after the revenues arising from burgage rents, demesne rents and perquisites of the courts. Municipal expenses, including repairs of the walls, were met from the Community's funds; what the bailiff collected, after his expenses, belonged to the lord.

From early days the Corporation sought to protect Ludlow's trade, especially within the town at its markets and fairs, keeping these as monopolies for their own burgesses. The appointment of two merchants to attend the parliament of 1332, even though the initiative may have come from the government, reflects the town's concern to protect its own interests.

In the 16th century the records are better and continuous. In 1590 the council barred strangers from selling bread in the town because of the 'impoverishment' of its own bakers. So far as we can tell, there was only one baker on the council at that time.[127] In 1596 the council petitioned the Earl of Essex against his iron mills in Bringewood and Mocktree and against the destruction of timber these brought about; it is not known what the motive for the petition was, unless the price of timber had been forced up; there were no builders on the council, but council members were typically men who commissioned house-building.

Increasingly the officials of the town were used to assess and collect national taxes and were particularly so engaged during Charles I's reign. During the civil wars the council seems to have been subservient to the requirements of the various military governors, but when the wars were over, in 1647, the council sought to improve the blasted economic fortunes of the town when it resolved to relieve Alexander Nelme of all extraordinary taxes and charges if he came to Ludlow to set up cloth manufacture.[128] From this time the council actively promoted rebuilding by means of building leases of empty sites.

Defence of the town's privileges and the administration of those privileges formed the chief activity of the council at all times. There was a great deal of deferential activity – gifts to eminent persons and their wives when visiting the town, arrangements of celebrations, bell-ringing, banquets, on such occasions – all with the purpose of forging and maintaining relationships which could be used whenever the council needed direct access to government or influential friends of any kind. This went on at all times, but the long periods of minorities and forfeitures affecting the lordship were notable for such activity; friends in high places were necessary at these times. When the Council of the March was in being, Ludlow was well placed to take advantage and did so. John Devawe, then bailiff, tried through his contacts in the Council of the March, of which he was a lower official, to compound provision money for a lump sum; this was an example of the value of appointing Conciliar officers to Corporation office. Gifts and celebrations were frequent. Even when the borough was still independent electorally, it did not stint these acts of deference. Costly though they were, they were under control and capable of direction where they might achieve results. Giving up electoral independence, by contrast, meant never ceasing to pay a price for temporary short-term favour.

An economic privilege which required constant defence was the right of commons on Whitcliffe, to the south of the Teme, opposite the town. This had been acquired (or probably confirmed) in the early 13th century from Jordan de Ludeford.[129] Four hundred years later, in 1603–5, the council had to authorise research on the Corporation right of commons there and to seek counsel's opinion on a Ludford man's cattle-grazing there. In 1605 they had to confront Sir Charles Foxe about his stone-digging on Whitcliffe.[130]

The Mechanics of Town Government

The division of responsibilities within town government is fairly clear only for the 16th century. The nature of institutions is such that considerable earlier elaboration of function can be assumed to have taken place. The 1562 accounts enable the structure of town finance to be delineated. A few years before then nearly £10 of rents had been collected by the chamberlain while the far larger proportion had been collected by the bailiffs. These sources were now combined. The change may have been connected with the appointment of a Corporation rent-collector. As the bailiffs became increasingly executive rather than financial officers of the Corporation, so the chamberlain's importance increased. The town treasury seems to have been in his day-to-day charge. The collecting officers paid into the treasury, the 'chamber', the surpluses of income over their proper expenditures, or received subventions from the chamber to meet legitimate deficits. Each officer rendered half-yearly accounts audited by the Six Men who authorised quittances and allowances or ordered adjustments. The officer most likely to incur deficits was in fact the chamberlain, since it was he who became responsible for major expenditures on the maintenance of streets, walls, gates, bridges and other public buildings. Surpluses on other accounts went to finance this type of municipal expenditure.

Although the responsibility of Corporation officers, there were other sources of revenue earmarked for particular expenditures which were not, so far as we can tell, mixed with 'chamber' finance. These include the churchwardens' revenues and expenses (chiefly on the upkeep of the church); the overseers of the poor, who raised the poor rates and spent them on the poor; national taxation, collected by the Corporation officials, but paid over to county or national authorities as required.

The following is a summary of the accounts for the half-year to Michaelmas, 1562. Some figures are unreadable and in minor ways do not reconcile precisely, but nevertheless this is the best picture we have for Corporation finances in the mid-16th century.[131]

Payments & Allowances				Receipts			
Receiver of Rents Accounts:							
Fee farm rent for ½ year	£12	6s.	8d.	Assize rent	£14	17s.	11d.
'Aconbury' mill rent ½ year	£2	3s.	4d.	Burgage rents	£8	13s.	10d.
Attorney's fees		10s.	0d.	Foreign rents	£1	6s.	5½d.
Burgesses & overcharges	£2	12s.	11d.	Tolls & murage	£6	6s.	8d.
				Chamberlain's burg. rents	£3	4s.	7d.
Surplus payable to Bailiffs	£17	7s.	5½d.	Other	£3	5s.	0d.
	£35	0s.	4½d.		£35	0s.	4½d.

....

Chamberlain's Account:							
Repairs	£6	7s.	2½d.	Entry fines burgesses, etc		13s.	0d.

Payments & Allowances				Receipts		
Wax for lord of Bromfield		2s.	8d.	Mortgages		5s.	6d.
Two Views of frankpledge	£1	10s.	0d.	Deficit payable by Bailiffs	£6	18s.	2½d.
	£7	19s.	2½d.		£7	19s.	2½d.

Alnager's Account:

Payable to bailiffs	£6	1s.	2d.	Alnage fees	£6	1s.	2d

Sergeants at Mace 3 Accounts Totalled:

Allowances	£116	11s.	5d.	Fines etc.	£131	17s.	0d.
Mortages in Tower		14s.	7d.				
Sergeants' fees	£1	10s.	0d.				
Payable to bailiffs	£12	10s.	0d.				
	£131	17s.	0d.		£131	17s.	0d.

Bailiffs' Account:

Recorder's fee	£1	6s.	8d.	Fines & Amercements	£2	19s.	3d.
Bailiffs' fee	£10	0s.	0d.	Two Fairs	£1	6s.	8d.
25 petty courts	£3	2s.	6d.	Chenser rents		15s.	0d.
Repairs	£2	0s.	3d.	Clerk of the Market's fines		12s.	4d.
Own sustenance	£18	11s.	4d.	Other fines		12s.	6d.
Cloaks for sergeants at mace	£1	0s.	0d.				
Other		5s.	0d.	Deficit	£30	0s.	0d.
	£36	5s.	9d.		£36	5s.	9d.

Payments out of the Chamber:

To bailiffs	£30	0s.	0d.				
To chamberlain	£6	18s.	2½d.				
To John Alsap	£3	3s.	1d.				
Building Corve Gate	£5	0s.	0d.				
Previous over-charged accounts		16s.	6d.	Total paid out of chamber	£50	4s.	1d.
Plumber, pavior, clockwinder	£2	4s.	8d.				
Ric: Hall calling court		5s.	0d.				
Six Men sessions		16s.	0d.				
Sergeants for prisoners	£1	0s.	0d.				

Taxation and Levies

Until 1461 Ludlow was subjected to both its own taxes and to national taxes, for which it had to account to county or other authorities on behalf of the Exchequer or its nominees. In early days national taxes were infrequent and scarcely distinguishable from feudal aids of various kinds.

In 1169 the township of Ludlow paid a half-mark to the king's aid. Then in 1187 the 'men of Ludlow' accounted for £7 18s. 4d. for tallage, specifically for the maintenance of the castle.[132] In 1218 the 'men of Ludlow' paid tallage, but in the following year it was Walter Lacy who paid it.[133] Then 83 years passed before the next record; in 1270 a tax of one-twentieth of the value of goods was levied in Ludlow.[134]

Ludlow would not have escaped its share of the charges levied increasingly from 1295 onwards by Edward I and his successors.[135] This series began with a tax on boroughs of one-seventh of the value of goods, followed by a one-eighth tax in 1297. These taxes were initially charged to finance the Welsh and Scottish wars, from the first of which Ludlow did well enough, so there may have been rough justice.

Until 1332 the rates of taxes varied. Ludlow was assessed with the county, at the lower rate, rather than as 'ancient demesne' or as a borough, which attracted the higher rate. In 1332 the rates were fixed at a fifteenth and a tenth. There was an attempt that year to charge Ludlow at a tenth, for William Corve was paid to plead the town's case, taken on the point that it had never been 'ancient demesne', that is, a former Crown estate.[136] That it was plainly a borough was overlooked, which is strange considering the town's evident prosperity. In 1327 the rate was one twentieth and 105 persons paid £10 0s. 8d. or on average just under 2s. each; four people paid the highest charge of 6s. each, while 19 paid the lowest charge of 6d. In Shrewsbury 137 persons were charged and 17 of these paid 6s. or more, often considerably more, for Shrewsbury was much wealthier than Ludlow, itself at the height of its prosperity at this time.[137]

From 1334 the 'fifteenth and tenth' became standardised; what each place paid under the old rules in that year became the amount it was expected to pay in the future each time the tax was voted in Parliament; each place, including Ludlow, allocated shares of its charge to inhabitants. Ludlow's charge of 320s. was less than a third of Shrewsbury's.[138] In addition, however, there was often another subsidy on lands and goods for which few records remain. The poll taxes of 1377 and 1379 applied to Ludlow; for the former year the records remain and are here discussed under 'Population', for which they have more significance. Numbers of other taxes of temporary significance were levied in the next 190 years, such as taxes on burgesses without tenements – in c.1450 this raised £6 from 121 persons in Ludlow.[139]

The 1461 charter exempted Ludlow from the oppressions of purveyance,[140] but at a later date purveyance was nonetheless exacted, for in 1594 John Devawe was asked by the Corporation to use his contacts in the Council of the March, of which he was sergeant-at-arms, to compound 'provision money' for ever for £3 4s.[141]

Ludlow was specifically exempted from the new subsidy tax of 1525 by the final section of the Act which recited the 1478 borough charter granting exemption from all tenths and fifteenths.[142] The exemption was recited in the Subsidy Act in regard to 'the towne of Ludlowe, its burgesses, inhabitants and reseaunts and in its suburbs'. This is a good early example of the superiority of parliamentary acts over royal charters; the exemption was in fact valid because the Act stated it to be so, not because the charter declared it. No later taxing act mentioned an exemption and none was enjoyed, the charter notwithstanding.

Local taxation bore more heavily on individuals, although, since it was mostly spent again locally, its effect was not so damaging for the town. In 1233 the 'men of Ludlow' (rather than the lord) received a royal licence to enclose the town.[143] Thereafter the town was regularly granted permission to raise murage (literally, 'wall-dues'), ostensibly to maintain the walls. A five-year murage grant to Geoffrey de Genevile in 1260 was followed in 1266 and 1271 by similar grants to the Verduns.[144] The two families each owned part of the town; it is inconceivable that the grants to them related only to their parts however, so it seems that the grants in fact were made, at these lords' request, to the Community itself. In 1280 Genevile was the supposed recipient, and in 1285 and 1290 his son, Peter.[145] Geoffrey de Genevile again received the grant in 1294, after a petition from 'the liege people of the town', who claimed that the town was no longer a safe haven in time of Welsh risings.[146] In 1299 the grant was expressed as being, at Genevile's instance, 'to the bailiff and good men of Ludlow for 5 years'. The intercessor in 1304 was Master John Kenles, a king's clerk, followed in 1309 by Ludlow's new lord, Roger Mortimer. In 1312 and 1317 the grant was made directly to the 'good men' of the town. Roger Mortimer, briefly back in favour, was intercessor again in 1327 for an extended grant of six years.[147]

After this the grants were always made to the bailiffs and men of Ludlow for varying periods of between one and 12 years. The longer periods were to take account of the ruinous condition of the walls; any shorter period was insufficient to finance the repairs. There was an almost unbroken succession of grants between at least as early as 1260 and about 1446. Only in 1352 was there a suggestion that the funds so gathered were being diverted from their proper destination by the bailiffs who retained the murage and pavage for their own use.[148]

Murage was collected by the Community, which remained responsible for town defences. In September 1317, William Cordwaner, a burgess, had the farm of the murage, paying over £5 for it, but as the Community also received £9 2s. 4d. from the murage between June and February, collected by Robert Sarote, murage may have been dealt with differently in one part of the town from another. Murage was usually charged on goods and traffic coming into a town. A tax on the incidents of trading, rather than a rate, its product would have been hard to forecast. This encouraged the authorities to farm it out to someone who would pay for the right to collect it. In 1317, 49s. 4d. was spent on work on the walls and gates and a few shillings on administration; as this money was accounted for along with mill receipts and other Community income and the disbursements for all municipal purposes came from the same pool, the impression is that murage was not spent solely on walls and gates.[149] The levy did not keep this name after the mid-15th century, but tolls and other charges on trade goods remained and the borough's right to collect them was regularised in 1461.

In the 16th and 17th centuries Ludlow participated in national taxation. In 1571 Ludlow produced £18 13s. from 76 people, 12 of whom were assessed on lands rather than goods.[150] In 1626, 69 people contributed £78 13s. 9d. to the 'Voluntary Loan' (with five persons refusing, and another nine thinking better of their initial complaisant generosity).[151] By the 17th century the stereotyped subsidies no longer sufficed and rated taxes, more closely based on actual wealth, were levied. Ludlow suffered coat and conduct money, levies for various *ad hoc* purposes, like the rebuilding of St Paul's, forced loans and benevolences.

Ludlow entered the period of shipmoney no more co-operative than many other parts of the country. The sheriff was required to allocate the county quota between the various hundreds of the county. Ludlow was allocated £102, compared with £456 10s. for Shrewsbury, £302 for Wenlock and £51 10s. for Bridgnorth. The bailiffs and Corporation petitioned the sheriff against both this and his relieving Shrewsbury at Ludlow's expense. The Privy Council intervened and the assessment was reduced. Ludlow was later acquitted for its £102 charge on the shipmoney writ of August 1637, but it is noteworthy that the town did pay its whole assessment, and, such was its distrust in these matters of the county authorities, Adam Acton, the bailiff, arranged for it to be paid directly in London by the hand of his agent. This changed; in October 1638 the sheriff claimed to the Privy Council that Ludlow had paid nothing of its charge of £102 under the 1637 writ 'and is the worst in the county'.[152] Otherwise Ludlow's shipmoney record was in line with that of the county; 97 per cent of the 1635 county charge was paid within 12 months; 90 per cent of the 1636 charge within 12 months, 97 per cent within 16 months; 60 per cent of the 1637 charge paid within 14 months, 97 per cent within 31 months; none of the 1638 charge within twelve months, 86 per cent within 30 months; 2.5 per cent of the 1639 charge paid after 18 months when the arrears were written off.[153] Ludlow seems not to have taken a constitutional objection to shipmoney, but it distrusted the sheriff's willingness to be fair in allocating the county quota. The borough regarded shipmoney as infringing its autonomy, but showed

14. Remains of Mill Street gate. The gates and walls were financed from murage, a toll levied on goods entering the town.

15. Part of Old Street Ward, now regarded as part of Corve Street; these properties backed onto the town wall, little of which is left.

no signs of sharing the views of Hampden. Towards the end of the shipmoney quinquennium Ludlow, like Shropshire and much of the country, became unwilling to pay a tax which showed some likelihood of being abolished and arrears remitted, as eventually happened.

In May 1640, Ludlow was reported to the Council of the March by the deputy lieutenants for being £30 short in its coat and conduct money (the local tax for the support of the county militia); this levy was unpopular when it looked as if it would be spent in Scotland, rather than Shropshire.[154]

Chapter Three

The Church

The Medieval Church

The chief activities of the medieval Church were the relief of need, prayer, the promotion of orthodox belief, social control and the management of property, which hindsight suggests to be in ascending order of importance. In Ludlow these functions were carried out through the parish church, the church court, four extra-mural chapels and three conventual houses, requiring many clergy and religious. There may have been a cleric or a religious for every burgess family in the town. Few of these enjoyed benefices, normally reserved for the rich or well-connected. In the 14th-century deeds of the Palmers' Gild 86 clergy are named. Although participating in prayer and religious ceremony formed a large part of the life of many clergy and religious, many other tasks fell to them.

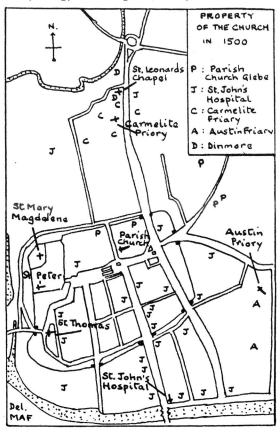

16. Map showing the property of the Church in 1500.

Clerks who did not proceed beyond minor orders often became administrators, lawyers and men of business. Between 1300 and 1400 nine Ludlow men, and several others from neighbouring places, acted as attorneys for Ludlow litigants in the Common Pleas and King's Bench. In the 14th century the most important local attorneys, whose clientèles were solely from the district, were Richard Estham of Ludford, practising 1328–59, William Orm (1322–5), William Rutone (1311–26) and John Pusselowe (1359–70). Many clergy, especially the Gild-chaplains, acted as feoffees for townsmen. Others went into service with magnates, as Thomas Ace served Roger Mortimer, Earl of March.

Apart from the men of business, they were all connected with the ecclesiastical institutions of the town which are the subjects of the following narrative. Considerable parts of the endowments of these institutions came from the lords of Ludlow, from whom a continual flow of gifts and payments could also be expected in return for general spiritual support. In 1378, for instance, Roger Nasshe, receiver of Wigmore and Ludlow for the Earl of March, paid 18s. to the clergy of the parish church and 40s. each to six priories, including the three in Ludlow.[1]

Piety was more characteristic of the laity than the clergy and leaves few records, other than bequests in wills for the high altar of the parish church or to local conventual houses. Ludlow wills displayed this kind of formal piety, although some testators were more generous than others. Piety requiring more effort included pilgrimages, few of which would have left a record. John Ace, who went to the shrine of Santiago de Compostela in Spain in 1332, and Henry Herdeley, who went there in 1358, would not have been alone. In 1469 Joan Taylor, an adulteress, was sentenced to make a pilgrimage to the shrine of St Thomas (probably at Hereford, rather than at Canterbury.[2]

The Parish Church

The site of Ludlow's parish church, on the ridge of the town in the centre of the planned area to the west of the Old Street- Corve Street through-road, suggests that it formed part of the original layout of the town. If an earlier settlement in Dinham had its own church or chapel, the site of which may have been where St Thomas's chapel was later built, then the location of St Lawrence's parish church would have been part of a grand design in urban planning by the Lacy family. Of this early stage we know nothing and may never know anything as archaeological examination of the site of the existing church may never be possible.

In 1199 (or 1200) considerable work was done on the church, the nature of which is described differently in two sources. One chronicle suggests that in 1199, because it was too small for the congregation, the church was extended into a tumulus where the entombed bodies of three Irish saints were found. The other source states that in 1200 the bell-tower of the church and the body of the church were rebuilt from their foundations in which were found the entombed bodies of the same Irish saints.[3] Each source gives the precise date as the third of the Ides of April (11 April). The two descriptions of the building work are sufficiently different for us to conclude that they are not based on each other, although the accounts of the discovery and what was found are so close that minor differences can be put down to one being a more corrupt version of a lost third source. The implication of both accounts is that a church was already on the site, although if the relics were found in the foundations, there are two possibilities – the first that the new building work required deeper foundations in whose digging the relics were found at a deeper level than the footings of the old church; the second that the relics had been placed in the old church. The saints, Fercher, Corona (otherwise, Ona) and Cochel, according to an inscription *in verbis Anglice* (which Eyton translated as 'in the British tongue') were alleged to have lived in Britain for 15 years. Eyton dismissed the whole thing as a fraudulent attempt to provide Ludlow with holy relics. Irish immigration into Wales, even into the upper Wye valley, had occurred centuries before, but it is unlikely that an elaborate funerary inscription would have been engraved, let alone survived, in the Teme valley. Given that the only early settlement possible in the Ludlow area was not on the ridge of the hill, but around Dinham, Eyton's scepticism may be well-founded. The Lacy connection with Ireland since 1171 affords a link if not an explanation. Relics of some sort may well have been brought back at any time between 1171 and 1199; why they were not subsequently exploited is a mystery; conceivably Irish saints ceased to be fashionable.[4]

Other major building took place in 1295 when a chapel dedicated to St James was built. This seems subsequently to have been re-dedicated. In 1299–1300 Nicholas Leech (*medicus*) was paid 30s. by the Community for church repairs. Then in 1305–6 the north side of the church was built.[5] Even where information is lacking, it is certain that repairs and rebuilding work must have gone on continually. In 1327–8 the Community of the town paid Matthew Hoptone, keeper of the works of the church, to repair the church porch (*portacum*).[6] The building and maintenance costs of the parish church clearly were assumed by the Community of the town, helped out by gifts from the faithful and occasionally other receipts. St Edmund's chapel was built in 1348 when William Pirefeld left money for it.[7] The north transept was built before 1400.[8]

17.   The church from the east, its physical and spiritual dominance emphasised by the 15th-century bell tower.

The next major building work on the church took place in the mid-15th century when, *inter alia*, the new bell-tower was put up. The work was preceded in 1433 by a petition from the town to the pope against the neglect of the church fabric by the rector, John Donwode; this was referred to the bishop and settled by Donwode taking a pension of 16 marks and leaving the rest of the church income to be administered by a chaplain and two parishioners.[9] The work may have begun soon afterwards and was going on in 1454 when a 20s. fine levied in the church court was commuted to work on the bell-tower, and in 1466 when Richard Knyghtone left money for the new building.[10] The bell-tower may have been completed shortly afterwards, for the church-wardens' accounts for 1469 onwards show lead being laid on the steeple and repairs to the bell-wheels. A great deal of internal building work was financed by bequests and by the Palmers' Gild and the craft gilds. These massive and protracted works fortunately coincided with a period of economic prosperity and religious piety, expressed in corporate and personal liberality towards the church. The ordinary income of the church would never have been enough.

The spiritual functions of the church seem to have been conducted largely by chaplains attached to the chantries, particularly those maintained by the Palmers' Gild. Before the Reformation the rectors rarely showed themselves as pastors, teachers or celebrants. Medieval rectors figure more commonly in the records for their secular interests, some unedifying, than for their spiritual or pastoral concerns. A laudable exception arose in 1322 when the rector and burgesses of Ludlow asked the bishop for advice when the Austin prior in Ludlow refused to bury in the priory cemetery a lapsed and runaway friar, Richard Moyl, who had repented before he died. The bishop ordered absolution and burial, as required by 'pity and humanity'.[11]

The parish church was probably built when the Lacy borough was laid out. Since the origin of rural parish churches is generally to be found in proprietory estate chapels, the Lacy family may have provided both the land and the initial funds. The church which was substantially extended and rebuilt in 1199–1200 was probably the first church on the site. It had stone foundations and probably stone walls. The church was dedicated to SS Philip and James and to St Laurence, but the first pair of patron saints was eventually dropped. Although a chapel in honour of St James was built in 1295, already by 1284, according to a document which now exists only in a version of 1389, the church itself was called that of the Blessed Laurence.[12] In the mid-15th century the dedication of the parish church to

St Laurence was celebrated yearly on 13 February.[13] St Laurence's Day, 10 August, also marked the town's major fair from at least 1274, although, as the fairs were much older, it is likely that one was held on St Laurence's Day as early as 1200.[14]

The church has remained the formal centre of civic life to the present day. Although there were other centres of activity – the Guildhall, the Gild College and the market-house – none of these had the universal or emotional appeal of the church. It was also the largest place of assembly in the town and the place where formal and informal social hierarchies were recognised in seating, ceremony and monuments. The incumbent, a rector, was in charge. A few medieval rectors were absentees; those who were held the benefice for only short periods, incidents in administrative careers elsewhere, usually as king's clerks. William Beverley (c.1288–90), John Wottenhulle (1326), William Humberstane (1369–71) and Robert Faryngton (1371–2), may have been the only ones, apart from those who obtained study leave, like Hugh Tyler, granted eight years leave in 1274 to attend university.[15] John de Vaucouleurs was commended by the king in 1295 for having resided in his church for seven or more years (although he had been presented in 1290).[16]

Nevertheless, there are sufficient hints available that much of the burden of spiritual and pastoral work was borne, not by the rector, but by another priest, like Thomas Routone, who had celebrated divine service in the parish church, but in 1321, aged and sick, was allowed by the bishop to carry on doing so in his own home; in the same year he was remembered in John Ace's will.[17] In 1375 Roger Nasshe, the rector, sued Reginald 'That Was Pareshprest of Lodelowe'.[18] John Stowe was the parish chaplain in 1407 and John Heyer was 'parish chaplain of Lodelowe' in 1427, being still in office in 1436.[19] Lewis Shobdone, described as 'parish priest of the parish church of Lodelowe' in John Parys's will (1449), was 'curate there' in Richard Dylowe's will of 1453.[20] The existence of a 'parish priest' or 'curate' is well-attested thereafter. 'The curate of my parish church of Ludelowe' appears in Richard Sparcheforde's 1480 will, while Richard Shepherd was described as 'curate of St Laurence' in 1487.[21] The close connection of the curate with the parishioners is later emphasised by references in wills to 'my gostely fader', as Robert Toy called Edward Stirop in 1498 and Walter Hubolde called James Pyser in 1500.[22] Other chaplains, like William Wiatt, William Mappe, Thomas Cherme and Richard Sutton, witnessed and oversaw wills and it is likely that these, too, were the parish curates of their day.[23] None held a benefice.

The origin of the office may have lain in the second (non-Gild) priest of the Lady Chapel, whose stipend of 16s. 6d. had been paid by the Community of the borough in 1299–1300. In 1308 arrears of 8s. 3d. were similarly paid by the borough to Nicholas, the chaplain of the Blessed Mary, while in 1330 payments were made to Philip Cayham, who held the same office. Between 1362 and 1393 William Toggeford held the post. Payments to John Buterleye 'our clerk' in 1319–20 may indicate that the Corporation-sponsored priest was expected to carry out borough administrative duties. Richard Ewyas was presented to the Lady Chapel in 1410.[24] After 1551 the duties (duly Reformed) seem to have been undertaken by the Corporation-appointed lecturer and 'reader'.

By the late 13th century the development of chapels and chantries in the church, each with its endowed chaplains, became increasingly important in the religious life of the town. The late 15th century saw further chantry foundations. Piers Beaupie, a royal official and recorder and M.P. for Ludlow, left funds in his will which were used to found a chantry in 1484. Although important in terms of its value, this had a comparatively short life, being dissolved 63 years later. At that time the chantry-priest, Richard Benson, had an income of £6 9s. 3d. from it and only a tiny sum went to the poor. John Hosyer left money for a chantry-priest to pray for him at the Holy Trinity altar; his gift was for the life of a particular chaplain and the chantry seems not to have existed in 1547.[25]

The craft gilds also used particular parts of the church in their own ceremonies and devotions; some gilds held their normal meetings there. Both the Palmers' Gild and the craft gilds devoted a growing proportion of their income to repair, building and decorative work about the church. The devotional, and even social, life of the town was centred there, but by the early 16th century much of the devotional and institutional life of the parish church had been devolved to these corporate groups. The numbers of chantry-priests could never have been wholly taken up with their endowed services and were doubtless available for many other kinds of duties, as men of business, scriveners, and schoolmasters.

In the parish church the impact of the Reformation may have been felt most strongly, not in terms of changed theology, but in the reversal of this devolution. Thereafter the incumbent himself became an important, if not sole, spiritual authority in Ludlow, although the Corporation largely controlled ways and means and, through its power and duty to appoint a preacher, could influence the religious character of the town.

The Chapels

The first and oldest of the two chapels in the castle was the round chapel in the inner bailey, dedicated to St Mary Magdalene, and built in the early 12th century. Its shape suggests Templar influence, but it may precede the lordship of Gilbert Lacy, the first lord of Ludlow known to have been a Templar. Always described as 'the free chapel', it served the spiritual needs of the castle household, not an onerous function. John Piers, the rector of Ludlow, held this chaplaincy at his death in 1404, but it was then granted to William Lochard, a king's clerk, the advowson being in the king's hands during the minority of Edmund, Earl of March.[26] In 1458 the chapel was united to St John's Hospital by Richard, Duke of York, on condition that the Hospital arranged masses there for his family. When Prince Edward's household was at Ludlow the prior of the Hospital said mass in this chapel when asked to do so by the Cofferer or clerk of the Kitchen.[27]

The other chapel, dedicated to St Peter, was founded by Roger Mortimer. A licence was granted in 1328 for him to alienate 10 marks rent to endow it. In 1354 Countess Joan and her son, the second earl, gave rents to the Hospital to find a chaplain for this chapel.[28] An independent existence for the chapel and its chaplain was no longer contemplated. The expense of maintenance, however, fell upon the castle authorities; extensive roof-repairs were undertaken there in 1317–18.[29] Richard, Duke of Gloucester (later Richard III), promoted William, his chaplain, to be prior of St John's Hospital in about 1478; every day for three or four years this William, or one of the brethren of the Hospital, attended St Peter's chapel to say mass for Prince Edward's household. It was at this time that the vicar of Stanton Lacy claimed unsuccessfully that Ludlow castle fell within his parish and so the oblations of the chapel were rightfully his.[30] It was also used for diocesan administration; in 1475 institutions to various Shropshire benefices were ordained there.[31] Later still it was used as a courtroom by the Council of the Marches.

The chapel of St Thomas of Canterbury in Dinham is the oldest separate building in Ludlow, although greatly altered to more profane uses. Since the impetus for disseminating the cult of Thomas à Becket in England came from Henry II himself, the chapel may have been founded between 1177, when Ludlow was taken into that king's hands, and 1189, when he died. This would have been within a generation of the building of the parish church and it is conceivable that an earlier settlement of Dinham may have previously enjoyed a simple chapel on the same site, part of the lord's demesne.

This chapel thereafter seldom featured in the recorded history of Ludlow, but it was kept in repair and use until the early 15th century. Agnes Orm left a small legacy to 'the chapel of Dynan' in 1304, and in 1349 Henry Weolere left a 30 gallon leaden vessel to the chapel.[32] In 1386 Isold Galus left 40d. towards the fabric of the chapel, as did John

18. Roger Mortimer's chapel of St Peter, founded in 1328; it later became a courthouse for the Council of the March.

19. St Thomas's chapel, the oldest surviving building in the town outside the castle.

Marsshetone, chaplain, in 1410.[33] Had Marsshetone celebrated masses there? St Thomas's chapel was referred to in a deed of 1483 and in a Gild lease of 1492 and, in 1519, 40 days' indulgence was offered to those who contributed towards its repair, implying its contemporary use as a chapel. The chapel altar was briefly restored in 1556–7.[34] There is no record of it in use as a chapel after this date.

The chapel was not a benefice; no endowments can be traced; nor were there any appointments to it. It was probably an outpost of the parish church whose clergy officiated there. That so few donations can be traced suggests that its appeal may have been very local within Ludlow and, without resident clergy, it was unable to participate in the lucrative obituary business enjoyed by the other religious institutions of the town.

A small chapel was built on Ludford bridge before 1406 when Bishop Mascall granted 40 days' indulgence to those who contributed to its repair. It was then in the custody of Thomas Shelve of Leintwardine, a resident hermit, who received a royal pardon for felonies of various kinds in 1410.[35] Another indulgence was granted for the repairs in 1464.[36] In 1487 Richard Dodmore left a candlestick to the chapel of St Catherine on Ludford bridge. Leland mentions the chapel in his *Itineraries* (*c*.1540) and the building was there in 1722.

The chapel of St Leonard on the western side of lower Corve Street may have been founded in the time of Hugh Lacy (d.1186) who gave 12 burgages and two virgates of land to the Hospitaller commandery of Dinmore. The two virgates were assigned by the commandery to support a chaplain in the chapel of St Leonard, an assignment which probably reflected Lacy's wishes.[37] Dedications to St Leonard are often associated with the monastic military orders.[38] Geoffrey Andrew (d.1284) donated the ephemeral benefit of part of the rent for an easement of a shop-front to the St Leonard's chaplain *pro tempore*.[39] The chapel had a chequered history and has generally come to notice only when in need of repair. Richard Toresdone left 6d. in 1342 and William Pope 10s. in 1381 for repair work.[40] The chapel's income was sequestrated in 1453. Was there a vacancy in the chaplaincy or had the chapel ceased to be used? No other sequestration has come to light.[41] By 1550 dereliction was order of things; the chapel graveyard was rented to John Taylor *alias* Barker for 8d. Three years later he and Richard Bingham stole a chalice worth £5 6s. 8d. from the chapel, while John Weldyng removed the tiles from the roof.[42] This was a time when the townspeople had shown themselves very ready to rob the parish church of its fabric and treasures. It was Weldyng's initiative rather than his sacrilege which was frowned upon. In 1562 the Corporation itself removed 1,000 tiles from the chapel to roof the house on Corve Gate.[43] What was then the 'ruinous' chapel was granted by the Crown to the Earl of Leicester in 1574.[44] By 1598 the building was being used to 'in' the town corn.[45] In 1603 the chapel yard was Frances Blashfield's garden, while the chapel building was used as a school-room by Richard Heynes, a young schoolmaster.[46] The sad story of St Leonard's ended in its total destruction after 1760, an act leading to a lawsuit in the early 19th century which nearly ruined the Corporation.[47]

Moral and Social Control Before the Reformation

People were subject to considerable social control through the various institutions of society, chiefly courts of every kind. The resident of Ludlow was subject to his lord's court (the view of frankpledge), the town court, the assizes, even the King's Bench in London. Personal conduct was also subject to quite intense supervision by the ecclesiastical courts, claiming jurisdiction over faith and morals, extending to oversight of oaths and their consequences, such as unpaid debt. Sexual morals, widely defined, formed the chief business of these courts. It was an unruly society – not from lack of jurisdiction, but from the sporadic nature of its exercise. The well-off were more likely to find themselves in court

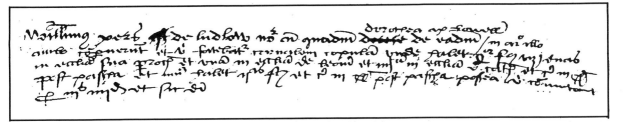

20. Prosecution before the bishops' court of William Pers and Dorothy ap Howel of Ludlow for 'carnal copulation', for which they were to be whipped around Ludlow and Leominster churches and Hereford cathedral, 1535. (HWRO: Dioc. Rec. AO 1534–5 f.131)

for correction or redress, perhaps because they, unlike the poor, could pay fines. Hundreds of them are recorded as being charged with virtually every possible offence.

For business the medieval church courts relied on delation by the apparitors (of whom Chaucer's 'summoner' was an example) and others, motivated by spite and the prospect of fees. Men were accused of adultery who had married elsewhere, like Richard Broune, carpenter, accused in 1446 of fornication with and maintenance of a woman he claimed to have married in Beaumaris. John Peper and Agnes, his wife, similarly accused in 1446, claimed prior marriage in St Albans. Others were accused of fornication, but, having proved prior marriage, were then charged with 'clandestine marriage' (an offence because the banns or licence system formed the church's only means of control of morals, marriage, legitimacy and inheritance of property); John ap Griffith and Lusot verch Jenkyn, his wife, were sentenced to three whippings each for this in 1445.[48]

Sexual offences predominated in the 15th century, but the numbers of prosecutions fluctuated from year to year which, given the constancy of human inclinations, suggests a sporadic purge on sin. Although the average number of prosecutions of Ludlow people for sexual offences each year was over 13, in six years, mostly in the period 1474–82, fewer than 10 prosecutions took place each year, while there were 20 in 1453–4, 24 in 1499–1500 and 46 in 1445–6. No trend can be discerned. Some of the accused confessed: Nicholas Mylward was a married man, and his adultery could hardly be justified, so he was fined 100s. in 1445, half payable to the fabric of the parish church and half to Hereford Cathedral, and sentenced to be whipped six times around Ludlow market carrying a candle.[49]

Such conduct and consequent punishment involved the well-to-do. Nicholas Cresset, later bailiff of the town, was accused in 1446 of adultery with William Collys's wife and (along with others) of fornication with Alice Cokks.[50] The clergy and religious were, if anything, worse behaved in sexual matters than most people; on average, in the 15th century, one chaplain or friar was prosecuted each year. Before the Reformation Ludlow people were seldom charged with anything else. There were in the surviving records only three cases of clandestine marriages, one of Sunday trading (in 1447–8) and one of practising magic (in 1502).[51]

The church courts, which normally met in the chancel of the parish church on up to eight occasions in a year, were the means of exerting ecclesiastical jurisdiction. In defending the privileges of the Church they were successful. In improving behaviour they were not, but to expect improvement would be to mistake the Church's objectives. The Church did not expect to eradicate sin; indeed sin was the justification for the existence of the Church. The numbers of Ludlow people who were punished annually were an advertisement, not for the value of virtue, but for the power of the Church.

The Austin Friars

There were three conventual houses in Ludlow. One was the Augustinian (or Austin) friary. Although the order was regularised by Pope Alexander IV in 1256,[52] houses of 'hermits' were being founded in England before this. The Ludlow friary were founded in 1254.[53] The original premises used by the Austins was at Christcroft in Dinham, which was part of the demesne. In 1256 the friars *'dimisso habitaculo eorum in Cristescroft primo habitabant in Galdeford quorum primus frater Albanus erat'*.[54] That they occupied demesne land within the town implies that one of the lords of Ludlow sponsored their arrival. Austin friaries were usually established, not on prime central sites, but on the outskirts of towns, where they could minister to travellers, and so those of Ludlow were very quickly transferred to a large open space at the eastern end of Lower Galdeford, where a priory was subsequently built. This move and the naming of Friar Alban as the first prior coincides with Alexander IV's ruling. The Ludlow house was now properly organised.

Thereafter the Austins of Ludlow played a peripheral role in Ludlow's life, for it was an order which did not amass riches and ministered chiefly to the poor. Ludlow was one of the most important houses within the order in England, being the chief one among the group which included Shrewsbury, Woodhouse, Droitwich and Newport.[55] A provincial chapter is thought to have been held in Ludlow in 1426.[56] Austin friars frequently moved between different houses, which ensured that normally they did not have or form strong local connections. Over two-thirds of the 14th-century Ludlow Austin friars whose names are known bore names apparently unconnected with Ludlow.[57] Considerable numbers of friars were sponsored for ordination; in the years 1327–39, 54 men from Ludlow were ordained and of these at least 30 were Austins; 22 were of unknown affiliation and may have included Austins. In 1340–9 there were 31 Ludlow ordinands, of whom at least 14 were Austins, while 10 were of unknown affiliation. In the 1350s the numbers were 22, 10 and eight. After 1355 the Austin ordinations declined rapidly, being overtaken first by the Carmelites and, after 1370, by St John's Hospital.[58] In the period 1517–35 only five Austin friars from Ludlow were ordained.[59]

During the priory's first half-century significant building and development took place. In 1278 the king ordered six oak trunks from his Forest of 'Havelehurst' to be given to the priory.[60] In 1279 Brian de Brampton was remembered for his help in enlarging the building.[61] In 1284 the priory enclosed a lane, still known as 'Friars' Walk'; this enclosure represents the diversion northwards of part of a lane which ran from Old Street, through the priory grounds, to the lower end of Rock Lane.[62] The priory had a church in 1299, for in that year Bishop Swinfield complained to the king that the townsmen had violated sanctuary when they arrested John Berner in it.[63] In 1326 the priory acquired land from Richard Dobyn, parson of Bitterley, to enable the extension to the south of the existing building. This was in Holdgate Fee, for Dobyn held of John de Hanlo, its lord.[64] The building was not completed until about 1340.[65] The priory grounds straddled the course of the stream running from the Sandpits area to the Teme; it provided a water supply and, after the friars had dammed it in places, fishpools.

The Austins may have had small gifts from the living, but they enjoyed few testamentary bequests. Between 1300 and 1350 only six small bequests can be traced and in the next half-century only four. In the 15th century only five, although one from Robert Toy was a substantial gift, after his wife's death, of an acre of land by St Mary's Lane and the Little Field.[66] This property was not in the post-Dissolution accounts but appears in the parish church glebe terriers in 1615 and 1736, so it may be that it never came to the Austin friars.[67] Four gifts in the 16th century included 3s. 4d. from John Browne in 1509 to repair the buildings.[68] The foundation of the Carmelite house in 1350 must have deprived the Austins of potential gifts. Later bequests were increasingly conditional upon the celebration of obituary masses. Some donors, like Eleanor Eye in 1517, appointed the Austin friars as 'back-up' or third choice for the observance of obits lest the Gild or the Carmelites defaulted.[69]

In 1355–6 several of the friars were licensed by the bishop to hear confessions in the diocese.[70] The surviving references to the house are few, suggesting that the Austins concerned themselves either with the order's affairs elsewhere or with Ludlow's poor. After Friar Alban only nine priors are known, three of them by their Christian names only. The prior in 1407 was 'William'. In 1442 a papal indult was granted to William Musselwyk, 'an Augustinian friar of the house of Ludloe', to choose his confessor; conceivably he was then prior. Between 1468 and 1469 a Prior William was succeeded by Prior Hugh and he, within two years, by John Tylowe. Richard Staunton was prior in 1480; like his three predecessors he is remembered only for trivial litigation in the town court.[71] The Austin friars had their share of 'criminous clerks'.[72] In the early 16th century the friars were involved in the massive papal fund-raising campaign for the rebuilding of St Peter's in Rome, for Prior Robert Stevenson was licensed in 1520 to collect alms for the purpose; by 1530 the campaign was put on a more systematic footing when two professional fund-raisers were similarly licensed as the Ludlow friary's 'proctors'.[73] As this fund-raising, promoted through the sale of indulgences, was one of the causes of the Reformation, the Ludlow friars may be said to have contributed towards their own dissolution.

The Ludlow Austins were often called the 'Black Friars'; Piers Beaupie left them a legacy under this name in 1480.[74] Thomas Cookes named them as back-up should the Carmelite White Friars default on his obit, and the bailiffs' accounts for 1534–5 include expenses on the occasion of the then new prior's inaugural sermon.[75] At the Dissolution their possessions included vestments of black worsted and blue damask.[76]

The priory surrendered its possessions to the king on 23 August 1538. The document of surrender was signed by Prior Giles Pickering, and three brothers, John Pratt, William Higgs and Christopher Hogeson.[77] As the friars held their property communally, this was the full complement at the time. All received dispensations in 1538 to hold benefices with change of habit, that is, to become secular priests able to hold benefices.[78] The priory property, all in Lower Galdeford around the priory itself, was partly let by this time for rents totalling £4 9s. 8d. from four tenants.[79] After the Dissolution the site of the house and its Inward Yard and Outward Yard were let to the farmer, Richard Palmer, for 6s. 8d. After expense on repairs, the buildings or materials therefrom were sold off for £17 18s. 4d. to Robert Hode, who was also a creditor for supplies to the former priory. The lead from the roof and the bells, the most valuable items, were melted down and sold.[80] In 1547 a 21-year lease of the site, together with some of the properties (Nether and Over Orchard, Hill Close and half of Friars' Meadow) was granted by the court of Augmentations to Sir Robert Townshend.[81] The rest (Barley Close and Broad Meadow and half of Friars' Meadow) were leased to Robert Hode. Then in 1554 all these lands were granted to Sir Edmund Peckham, but, as the Townshend family remained owners of the site into the 17th century, this may have been the equivalent of a freehold subsequently subsumed in the lease.[82]

The Carmelite Friars

The Carmelite priory was the last of the conventual houses to be founded in Ludlow.[83] It was the only one founded other than by a chief lord of the town; Sir Lawrence Ludelowe was licensed in 1350 to alienate in mortmain to the prior provincial of the order a messuage, held of the commandery of Dinmore, on which to build a habitation for the friars.[84] That the foundation came within about eighteen months of the Black Death striking the Welsh Borders may not have been a coincidence.[85] Five years later it was alleged that the friars had illicitly used the licence to acquire seven burgages, held of the Countess of March, and to pull down the existing buildings there; the king, however, formalised the gift provided the friars prayed for him.[86] All this property was at the bottom of Corve Street on the west side.

The Carmelites' chapel was intended to be Lawrence Ludelowe's family chapel and mausoleum; it was the founder's funeral which gave rise to the first dispute involving the priory, for the rector, John Evesham, demanded the offerings as of right and by the custom of the town. The bishop solved the problem by allowing the rector the offerings and the right to hold a quasi-funeral in the parish church when the burial itself took place elsewhere.[87]

Although the site was cleared quickly building work seems to have gone on for some time. The friars re-used the materials from the demolished original buildings. In 1381 William Pope left 20d. to the building of the 'new church' there[88] and in 1399 James Burley left £4 to build a new chapel, so that his family's remains could be held there.[89] In the 15th century building seems to have begun anew, for a papal relaxation of enjoined penance was granted to those who contributed to the fabric of the church of the Carmelite house 'which has lately begun to be built'.[90] The priory seems to have been unfortunate, for in 1465 it was found necessary to obtain, through the good offices of Edward IV, another papal indulgence for those who contributed towards the completion and restoration of the buildings which 'need very great outlay' beyond the resources of the friars, after the sack in 1459, although no damage to the buildings was alleged. It seems that earlier building projects were still unfinished.[91] The priory was not very well-endowed with land and depended on gifts of money, which accounted for the time its building projects took.

The bequests came in fairly steadily, to judge by the small sample of wills which have survived.[92] David Chirbury, a former prior, left his library. In 1509 John Browne left 40d. for building and glazing the west window of the chapel, an existing project[93]. During the late 15th and early 16th centuries bequests were increasingly tied to requests for obituary services.[94] John Hosyer, in 1463, was the most liberal, leaving 20s. to the priory, 40d. to the prior and 10s. to two other members of the house, without any conditions.[95]

The first known prior was Stephen Oxford, who was permitted to hear confessions in the diocese in 1358, along with two other Ludlow friars.[96] The surnames of religious cannot always be assumed to be hereditary and it is likely that he was an Oxford scholar. The Carmelite order was then notable for scholarship and preaching, and the Ludlow house was no exception. Walter Teukesbury was prior in 1387, when his chamber was robbed by a friar and an accomplice of gold and silver worth £34 and £10-worth of other things – large sums for a house dedicated to poverty.[97] His successor seems to have been Robert Mascall, an Oxford scholar and an energetic builder while prior, later Bishop of Hereford, and confessor to Henry IV. When he died in 1416 he wished to be buried in the *arcum ecclesie* of the Ludlow house but, notwithstanding his wish, he was buried instead in London.[98] He was immediately followed as prior in 1404 by Richard Auger, whom he also appointed penitentiary-general of the diocese of Hereford in 1405.[99]

The next known prior was David Chirbury, also an Oxford scholar, well-qualified as a preacher and theologian, who held office from about 1422 until 1430. Despite his reputation

21.   The site of the gate of the carmelite priory. Parts of the priory foundations have been excavated in recent years.

as a man of exemplary life his priorate records only court cases; for instance, his prosecution of William Money, a London tailor, for breaking into the priory in 1422 to take away Hugh Money.[100] In 1430 Chirbury accused eight Ludlow men of wounding him; had he provoked them? In 1431 he sued three men for £8 owed him when he was prior. Shortly after giving up the office he 'despoiled' his successor, Thomas Dyne, for which in 1436 he spent a short time in the Marshalsea prison, until he received a royal pardon. For all his scholarly capacities, Chirbury seems to have been a hard man.[101] While holding the priorate he was an absentee bishop of Dromore in Ireland; he was a suffragan of St David's and Archdeacon of Brecon from 1437 to 1451.[102]

Subsequent priors were shadowy figures, perhaps a reflection of a decline in the priory's standing, particularly after the sack of 1459. After 1430 nine priors are known who, if the only ones, served an average of 12 years each. In 1438 Thomas Dyne sued John Howe, a barker, for trespass; Ludlow's barkers and tanners were congregated at the northern end of Corve Street, close to the priory, so this looks like a boundary dispute.[103] Prior Nicholas appears in 1467. In 1480 Prior Walter Dier was given a papal dispensation to hold a benefice.[104] There is then a 40-year interval before the records disclose the names of what may be a complete series of six priors between 1520 and 1538, indicating a very rapid turnover, which does not say much for the importance or morale of the Ludlow Carmelites at the time.[105] Thomas Capper was prior in 1537, but no prior was recorded in 1538 at the time of the surrender by five friars, who included Richard Wyllett, a former prior who had stepped down.[106]

Like the other Ludlow conventual houses, the Carmelites sponsored considerable numbers of ordinands (at least 79), although the numbers before 1450 were nearly double those in the period to 1538. Enthusiasm, perhaps finance too, seemingly was much diminished and remained so.[107] The ordinands were augmented by at least 25 known friars who had not been ordained from the priory; 25 may greatly understate their numbers, as friars from elsewhere would rarely leave a record in Ludlow. The Carmelites frequently moved between houses; many Ludlow ordinands were sponsored by other houses for one or more of the orders and many must have moved on after ordination. Few of the priors seem to have been local men in origin. None of the five friars who surrendered the priory in 1538 had been ordained there, while Klein has traced two former Ludlow friars who were among those who surrendered Denbigh Priory, and former Ludlow friars a surrenderer at each of Gloucester, Chester, Oxford, Hitchin, London, Stamford, Coventry and, possibly, Northampton.[108]

Although not wealthy in land, the surrender-inventory of 1538 shows that the priory possessed quite sumptuous furnishings and vestments.[109] The building (of which only small parts of the footings remain) seems to have been large and imposing.[110] On 12/13 August 1452, Henry VI and his household stayed in Ludlow; although the purpose was to overawe York's supporters, they chose to stay, not in the Duke of York's castle, but at the Carmelite priory, for which hospitality the keeper of the wardrobe made small payments.[111] It is strange therefore that the one place in Ludlow with a record of assisting Henry VI should have so suffered after his forces' victory at Ludford bridge seven years later.

The Dissolution came swiftly. The priory was surrendered to the king on 23 August 1538. The resident friars later received dispensations for a change of habit. Already Thomas Vernon, descendant and heir of the founder, Sir Lawrence Ludelowe, had reported to the authorities a bungled attempt by the friars to hide some of the priory valuables in a ditch and he seized his chance to ask for the priory for himself.[112] The lead from the roof and guttering was stripped at once and the bells taken away; the valuations were £19 6s. 2d. and £10 13s. 4d. respectively. Despite the haste to take the metal, it is not clear what in fact happened to it; some of the lead, for instance, was in the hands of John Scudamore, the king's commissioner, in 1555, while Vernon still had the bells in 1540: for a full account of the demolition and a careful analysis of the fate and values of the materials see Klein and Roe, pp. 25–7. Vernon obtained a 21-year lease of the greater part of the site in 1539, for which he paid £65.[113] He then demolished the buildings for their materials, completing the work by 1542. He also obtained a head-lease of land already let to Richard Cleobury. A third piece of land was let by the Crown to William Clungunwas. Vernon's lease ran out in 1561, but the land eventually finished up in Ludlow hands again. Thomas Blashfield was the occupier of a part of it, having built a house, 'The Friers', there. Clungunwas's plot was void after his death in 1544 and found its way, via Edward Fiennes, Lord Clinton, into the hands of Charles Foxe, already the owner of the old St Leonard's chapel. In 1590 the two latter sites formed the endowment and site of Foxe's almshouses.[114]

St John's Hospital

The oldest conventual house in Ludlow was the Hospital of St John the Baptist, founded in the early 13th century by a rich Ludlow merchant, Peter Undergod, who was not a Ludlow burgess, but a bondsman of Walter Lacy. He endowed it with lands bought from Walter de Lacy, his son, Gilbert, and from others in Ludlow, Rock and Ludford.[115] The site of the Hospital itself, on the northern side of the Teme from Ludford, was also bought, as was the Ludlow fulling mill, from Gilbert Lacy with the valuable monopoly of Ludlow fulling.[116] In 1233 Walter Lacy confirmed the foundation with the assent of the rector of Ludlow. In addition Lacy remitted all rents and other services due. Undergod was also the first master – the only layman known to have filled that office, for his successors were all secular clergy.[117] Three years later papal approval was received. The Lacy confirmation stated 'we in charity have taken into our protection and defence the master and brethren of the religious hospital . . . their lands, liberties etc . . . without service being made'.[118] The special protection so accorded may well have been the justification for later royal intervention in the process of electing masters when the lordship of Ludlow was in royal hands. Lacy made other gifts of land and rights before his death in 1241. A royal confirmation was granted in 1266 and further confirmations from the earls of March followed in 1379 and 1417.

The Hospital endowment may have been threatened by the lengthy disputes between Walter Lacy and Warin de Munchensy when the latter, who had bought up Jewish moneylenders' claims on Lacy, sought some of Lacy's lands. Peter Undergod was himself involved over one carucate of land in 1237–8. The Hospital seems not to have lost, however.[119] In 1246 the sheriff of Shropshire was ordered by the king to prevent Moses, son of Hamo, a Hereford Jew, distraining upon Hospital property to recover Lacy's debts.[120]

The Hospital was dedicated in 1233 to the Holy Trinity, the Blessed Mary and St John the Baptist, but it was generally known only by the last of these, although in 1246 (see above) and in 1292 it was called St Mary's Hospital only.[121] By 1301, however, Prior John called himself 'master of the Hospital of the Blessed Mary', but an assize held that his correct title was 'prior of the Hospital of St John the Baptist', presumably echoing the popular appellation, and this was established.[122]

The first endowments made the Hospital fairly well off. Property continued to be acquired through the 13th and 14th centuries in Corfham, Richard's Castle and Overton, including the manor itself.[123] There were many gifts of property in Ludlow.[124]

One of the most generous benefactors was Joan, Countess of March and daughter of Peter de Geneville, who, in 1354, gave the Hospital land in Hawkbatch in Worcestershire and land and burgages in Ludlow, provided prayers were said in the castle chapel of St Peter.[125] In the following year property in Ludlow, Rock, Steventon and Sheet was acquired from the feoffees of the Earl of March, who had already licensed the Hospital to acquire 40 acres in these places in return for a relief after the death of each prior.[126]

In 1364 Richard Estham gave the Hospital a mill and other property in Ludford and Ludlow to endow perpetual prayers for himself in the Hospital church.[127] That so much property was acquired in southern Ludlow and in Ludford and neighbouring townships suggests that a deliberate policy of aggrandisement in the area was in operation; that gifts were solicited. The Hospital estates were by this time substantially as they were in the 16th century, although in 1466 Edward IV granted view of frankpledge over all its estates and immunity from other courts as compensation for the depredations suffered by the Hospital, presumably after the Battle of Ludford bridge.[128] In the same year an indulgence was published for benefactors of the Hospital.[129]

The Hospital, particularly in the persons of its masters, wardens or priors, played an important part in Ludlow life. Much of this was in pursuit of its property claims, for all Hospital lands were leased out. Master Stephen sued Roger Westone in 1284 for a Ludlow messuage; eight years later he failed to dislodge from her house Geoffrey Andrew's daughter, Yvette.[130] The next prior, John, successfully defended a disseisin suit by Roger Pywau over common pasture in Rock.[131] In 1358 Prior William Onibury successfully defended a suit begun by Agnes Paris over a tenement in Ludlow,[132] and he later sued Walter Hopton for waste of houses leased to him.[133] Prior Richard Wotton conducted litigation in 1377 to recover rights, suing for the wardship and *maritagium* of the daughter of John Cheyney, whom he claimed held of the Hospital by knight service; he, too, sued a tenant for waste of property leased to him by the previous warden.[134] Onibury had been quite ready to resort to armed robbery in his quarrels, as was alleged in 1352.[135] Actions at law against

22.   Lower Broad Street, including a house on the site of St John's Hospital. The arch is part of the Hospital.

tenants for 'waste' seem to have been settled Hospital policy, for Prior Hugh Ferrour lost no time in 1398 suing Thomas Paunteley for abusing his life-tenancy of property in Ludlow.[136]

It was Prior Onibury, with the then bailiff of Ludlow, who oversaw the resolution of the dispute between the craft-gilds over the Corpus Christi procession in 1368, doubtless a consequence of his influence rather than his diplomatic ability. [137] In the 14th and 15th centuries the Hospital became involved in the obituary arrangements of prominent Ludlow burgesses. William Pyrefeld gave 100s. for masses in 1348 as well as a donation towards work on the Hospital church.[138] In 1405 it became the guarantor of John Hawkins's obit, in the case of default by the Palmers' Gild.[139] William Russell required the brethren of the Hospital to join all the friars at his *dirige* and mass in 1519.[140]

After the mid-14th century the Hospital was seldom a recipient of gifts or bequests from ordinary people but relied on gifts from the great. Only three bequests can be traced from the 14th century and two from each of the 15th and 16th centuries.[141] In 1411 an indulgence was issued by the bishop for those who helped pay for the repair of the Hospital's bells, and in 1418 there was another for those who came to make offerings and to pray for the Lancastrian king's, Henry V's, success in battle.[142] A close association inevitably developed with the Mortimers and the House of York; property and privileges were received at the price of greater intervention in the affairs of the Hospital, particularly over the appointment of priors. The Hospital had had its own church as early as 1241, but this may have been rebuilt, for in 1328 it was dedicated by the bishop.[143]

The original object of the Hospital was to care for the poor and sick, but it rapidly acquired the functions of arranging obituary masses for those who could afford it and, later, responsibilities for services in the two castle chapels, which became the chief purposes of the house. Alms were a minor charge on income. The Hospital's complement was never large, and became so small that ministering to the needy would have been difficult, yet in 1504 Thomas Eyton of Aylesbury left a bequest to 'the poor men of the Hospital of the Poor' in Ludlow; perhaps they managed better than now seems possible.[144] Considerable numbers of ordinations of the Hospital clerks took place from the 1370s onwards; there were 15 in the decade 1380–9, and 27 in 1505–27, for instance. In the last 10 years of the Hospital's existence, however, no ordinations took place. The Hospital was usually a stage in a career, which would take men, if they were lucky, to benefices elsewhere or to curacies if they were not. The charter laid down that the brethren should live communally under a rule and by 1384 they were explicitly following the Augustinian rule.[145] They disputed the authority of the bishop of Hereford over them; in 1435 the bishop collated John Thorpe as prior, but the brethren would not accept it as a precedent. The king gave the right of presentation to laymen in 1529, but the bishop himself was successful in imposing his own conditions. Broadly, however, it suited the brethren until the 15th century to claim on occasion that they were regulars. As late as 1512 Prior Holland admitted to being 'a religious'.[146] Most of the priests ordained from the Hospital, however, went on without difficulty to benefices and curacies. When the court of Augmentations inquired in 1542 into the Foxe-Leighton lease it was in the Crown's interest to claim that it was not a house of secular priests and so should fall into Crown hands, but a witness described it as a house of secular priests who wore no habit but special robes at burials and processions; moreover they owed obedience 'only to the bishop'.[147]

The dress of the brethren was described in 1542, five years after the closure, which may explain inconsistencies. They normally wore secular priests' loose gowns; over these, on ceremonial occasions only, they wore long blue or dark violet mantles to the ground. These had canons' hoods always worn back. On the left breast of both gown and mantle was a white crescent- or half-moon under a cross variously described as red, blue or white, the last being most likely. One witness, looking back 60 years, said that the prior then had worn a murrey (red) habit.[148]

The foundation deed intended masters to be elected by the brethren of the Hospital.[149] So, in 1349, William Onibury *alias* Chirchemon, who had been a brother there since ordination as an acolyte in 1334, was unanimously elected by the brethren and admitted by the bishop.[150] In 1369, on the novel footing that the priorate of the Hospital was then in his hands, owing to the minority of Edmund Mortimer, the king granted the office to William Irelonde.[151] Irelonde was never instituted and in January 1369/70 the brethren were allowed to elect a prior. The brethren then elected Richard Wotton, whose name suggests a local origin.[152] The next prior, Philip Kymley, a brother, but not apparently a local man, was elected in 1384 by all the brethren, numbering four, including himself. The qualification was that he should profess the rule of St Augustine and be in priestly orders. 1391 saw another attempt by the Crown to impose a prior, this time John Wyche, a royal clerk.[153] This also failed, for by 1392 the prior was Nicholas Stevenes, a great-grandson of Philip Stevenes, a 13th-century burgess. He had been ordained from Wigmore abbey (a house of Augustinian canons) and had previously been a Gild chaplain.[154]

The next prior, Hugh Ferrour, was in his early thirties when elected prior in c.1398, having been ordained from the Hospital of which he was doubtless a brother.[155] Local connections and a long tenure of office gave him a standing few of the other priors could match and he was given several important commissions, such as collecting clerical taxation in 1407 and a visitation of Limebrook priory in 1435.[156] In some ways his priorate from 1398 to 1435 was the high point of Hospital influence in the town.[157]

His successor, John Thorpe, a brother, had been ordained from the Hospital and had received a dispensation for illegitimacy in 1408.[158] He was appointed prior by the bishop in 1435 with the licence of the Duke of York, rather than elected by the brethren 'at this turn only', for there was only one other brother.[159] In 1457 Thomas Oteley was elected prior by three brethren; he had been a brother since before his ordination in 1446.[160] On this occasion the brethren elected the prior and the Duke of York, as patron, asked the bishop to confirm it. This was done after a public opportunity was given for rival candidates or objectors to give voice. The duke then presented Oteley. Afterwards the Hospital became subject to outside influence. In about 1480, William, one of the chaplains of the household of Richard, Duke of Gloucester, was appointed prior. Prince Edward's council was then established at Ludlow and the most obvious function of the priors of the Hospital was to see to its spiritual needs, particularly in arranging masses in the two castle chapels.[161]

Prior John Holland claimed in 1512 to have been elected by the brethren. He was prosecuted in the church court in October 1501 for sexual incontinence with four women, two of them married. As an unnamed prior of the Hospital was said on 6 October 1499 to have committed adultery with another woman, we may assume, from this consistency of conduct, that Holland had been prior then.[162] He was distrained upon by the town-sergeant in 1502 for the recovery of 10 marks owed to a widow.[163] In 1512 Holland claimed exemption from any obedience to the bishop but, being unable to prove it, had to submit.[164] There were three brethren during Holland's time, until he expelled Thomas Holland in 1517, receiving him back when the bishop enjoined brotherly love (the shared surname suggests a family quarrel rather than conventual discipline and the brotherly love to be meant literally).[165] There were also novices.[166] During the period 1505–1527 at least one Hospital candidate a year was ordained. As Thomas Holland's expulsion occurred two years before he was ordained acolyte, it seems that novices remained there some time before the four stages of ordination, which they passed through in about twelve months. Some obtained benefices; others remained as curates; only a few remained at the Hospital. Novices were not full brethren and had no vote.

John Holland died in 1528.[167] There was then an interval while Edward Leighton, an Oxford scholar, touted to both Wolsey and Cromwell for the office. The presentation, now apparently assumed as a royal right, was given to two of Leighton's relatives, one a Crown servant, who appointed him.[168] Leighton then sought the approval of the bishop of Hereford who assessed the quality of the man pretty accurately and refused, unless he first became a resident brother in Ludlow. 'Many displeasant words passed' between them, but Leighton did as he was told and was instituted in 1530. No formal election seems to have taken place, for the bishop explicitly confirmed Leighton on the grounds that the brethren had failed to elect a prior within three months of the vacancy occurring.[169] Such a failure could only have been the result of outside pressure.

The scene was now set for the dissolution of the Hospital. If Holland had been a disgrace, Leighton was a disaster. During his priorate no ordinations took place and only two brethren were admitted, John Hughes and Richard Bawdewyn. The former had to profess poverty, chastity and obedience to Leighton, while the latter claimed never to have made any profession but to have been admitted on Leighton's sufferance. Leighton began to make unprofitable leases of Hospital lands, resisted by Bishop Bothe. But, when Bothe died in 1535, Leighton promptly put pressure on Bawdewyn and Hughes to seal a 99-year lease of the entire Hospital estates to William Foxe and his son, Edmund, reserving only a rent of £6, payable to Leighton, and 40s. to each of two priests; the traditional hospitality was to be maintained by Foxe. When the two friaries in the town were dissolved in 1538, William Foxe required Bawdewyn and Thomas Baker, the two remaining brethren, 'to put away their cloaks' and leave. The 1536 Dissolution Act suppressed only the smaller religious houses; the 1539 Act covered all other religious and ecclesiastical houses, but did not suppress them, supposing that other means would have induced their surrender, merely vesting their property in the king. If the Court of Augmentations accepted the Hospital as a secular house, it escaped the only compulsory dissolution provisions. The Foxe-Leighton scheme ensured that there was then nothing to surrender 'voluntarily'.[170]

By 1542 John Cragg, the rector, had the Hospital's brass seal, there were no brethren there and religion had 'utterly cessed'. Bawdewyn gave up his Hospital cloak and 16 years later received the bequest of Foxe's gown.[171] He died in Ludlow in 1565, having been a curate there. In 1539 Leighton surrendered the mastership to Charles, a son of William Foxe, in return for a £6 pension and by 1533 was a royal chaplain and was accumulating ecclesiastical benefices.[172] Thomas Baker remained in Ludlow; in 1546 William Foxe, his executor, may have acceded to his wish for obituary masses in the former Hospital.[173]

The Hospital had owned property in Broad Street, Castle Street, Corve Street, Old Street, Frog Lane, Mill Street and Galdeford, as well as substantial property in Ludford, Overton, Rock, Ashford, Cainham and Bennett's End. In 1536 it was worth £17 a year clear. The Ludlow and Ludford rents alone amounted to over £34 in the hands of Edward Foxe in 1583.[174] The Foxes claimed in 1546 to be paying alms and clerical stipends for the castle chapels amounting to £13, but it is likely that this outlay ceased soon after.[175]

Charles Foxe married a Leighton. One of his father's feoffees was the Ralph Leighton who presented Edward Leighton to Eastham; it is therefore probable that it was these family connections with the Foxes which lay behind the series of transactions which provided Leighton with an unearned income and the Foxes with one of the most valuable estates in and about Ludlow.[176] Even after 400 years this still has the appearance of a corrupt bargain, which founded a powerful local dynasty on the ruin of a Ludlow charity.

This take-over, along with their acquisition of the estates of Bromfield priory, had one ironical consequence. The king was chief lord of the possessions of St John's upon two grounds: as heir to the earldom of March and under the 1547 Chantries Act. In 1547 the site of the Hospital was granted to the Earl of Warwick who promptly transferred it to the Foxes, who now had the freehold of the 'manor of St John's'. The Foxes were later regarded as holding all their estates by knight service from the king, which made them liable for feudal dues.[177]

The Reformation

For Ludlow the Reformation was a revolution imposed from above. There was no tradition of heresy or dissent. Lollardy, which existed around Kington in Herefordshire in the early 15th century, seems not to have affected Ludlow, although the Ludlow bailiffs, amongst others, were required by the government in 1407 to enquire into 'any preaching against the Catholic faith' and to imprison them. What they found is not known.[178]

In 1529 Henry Clee was accused of having said 'in the presens of mony peple' in Ralph Bradshawe's house at nine o'clock one morning that 'hytt was nott the good lorde that the preeste dyd heve over hys hedd at masse'. He denied saying it and was eventually acquitted of heresy.[179] But what were many people doing in Bradshawe's house at nine in the morning? Could there have been some kind of religious gathering at which heretical sentiments were uttered and overheard by an informer, perhaps a servant? No other cases have come to light, however, at any time in the 16th century. Most Ludlow people believed what they were told to believe and accommodated the many changes in official theology over the next half-century with great ease of spirit and some material profit.

In Ludlow the Reformation concerned property as much as belief. The dissolution of the conventual houses benefited a few speculators and local landed families, who were quick to take advantage. There were prolonged disputes in Ludlow over the estates of Wigmore abbey involving Thomas Wheler, Charles Foxe, John Bradshaw, Bishop Lee and Thomas Croft; of these Croft was regarded as a Catholic but the others were neutral in religion.[180] The dissolution of chantries led to further large transfers of property, chiefly that of the Palmers' Gild. Ludlow men were also prepared to take quick profits from chantry lands; those of the Holy Trinity chantry of Welshpool passed to Thomas Meysey, then successively to two other Ludlow men, passing finally to a Londoner. Ludlow chantries, however, seem to have escaped quickly into the hands of Londoners, although one of the two recipients of Beaupie's chantry lands, John Cupper, bore a Ludlow name.[181] St Leonard's chapel was merely looted.

The lands of the Knights Hospitallers fell into Crown hands in 1539, and remained Crown property until 1558. Until then the Crown exercised dominical rights, including that of holding a court for the Dinmore Fee, at which were exacted reliefs on succession to burgages. The rents themselves amounted in 1542 to 32s. 8d., including 5s. from the former Carmelite priory.[182] There was a short-lived attempt in 1558 to revive the Hospital and to place the Ludlow property of Dinmore in the hands of Sir Thomas Trentham.[183] There was no further attempt to hive off part of the jurisdiction of the town court.

Aconbury convent surrendered its rights in the Ludlow mills to the Crown which, as we have seen elsewhere, continued sporadically to exploit them for a century or more.[184] Of the rents it had been granted, nothing is known after 1406.[185] Beaupie's chantry lands in Ludlow and Wigley were granted to John Cupper and Richard Turnour of London in 1549, doubtless to find their way into other ownership. There were other minor properties, such as rents accruing to Wigmore abbey or to a chantry in Richard's Castle church, which also found their way into lay hands.

The effect of the Dissolution was the enrichment of the already rich and the creation of spoils for the oligarchy which had socially corrupting consequences. The Foxes were aggrandised most spectacularly; they became the richest and most powerful family in Ludlow, playing a part in the later decline in the independence of the borough.

The willingness of the people of Ludlow to abandon the old forms of religion is best evidenced by the removal and selling of the ornaments of the church, many of which had been provided or piously maintained by their fellow-citizens but a few years before. In 1549 the 'images' of Jesus, St George and the Dragon, and St Anne's tabernacle were sold off by the churchwardens at their first opportunity under the law. Within the year pews were set up and rented out where Beaupie's chantry and Cooke's chancel had been. In 1550 more 'images' were sold to Richard Lloyd, the old service books were sold off and the frescoes were replaced with whiteliming. All this came to an abrupt end with the accession of Queen Mary in 1553, when expenditure on candles resumed and the Rood was regilded. The previous depredations, however, were not put right. In 1559, on Elizabeth's accession, after a few months' interval to see which way the wind blew, the dismantling of Catholic emblems began again with the removal of the Rood, the dismantling of altars and the plinth on which the image of the Virgin Mary had stood.[186]

Other signs of change are more formulaic, but nonetheless significant. In 1538 Henry Yong's will commended his soul to 'Almighty God and Our Lady Mary and the holy company of heaven'.[187] This was a typical commendation of the time which was revived under Mary; Adam Stephens used it in 1556, as did seven others in Mary's reign.[188] Peter Ford and Thomas Dobles, notwithstanding the change to a Catholic government, in 1555 trusted 'by the meryts of Christ's passion to be among the elect number in the kingdom of heaven'.[189] Among the latter's witnesses were William Bradshaw and Ansell Clee, perhaps providing a link with the Henry Clee case of 1529. In 1560 William Phillips, clothier, trusted 'to die in the Catholic Christian faith', a man too old to change his beliefs, but nonetheless unusual in holding out.[190] John Bufton of Burway, in a spirit of uncommitted ecumenism, declared in 1574: 'I hope to be one of the elect number and to be in the company of the blessed angels, saints and the holy company of heaven by the intercession and prayer of the most glorious virgin and blessed lady mother of Christ'.[191] For the most part, however, the people of Ludlow carefully followed the religious courses laid down by the government. After 1558 pious formulae were rarer, sometimes perfunctory, often absent. Catholic formulae disappeared; moderate Anglican and, increasingly, Calvinist formulae only were used. So, in 1589, Edward Phipson trusted 'to be of the number of the elect and to be saved'.[192] Hugh Bevan, in 1579, had adopted the formula 'Trusting in the merits of Christ to be one of the children of salvation'.[193] These two themes, sometimes mixtures of the two, prevailed thereafter. References to the 'kingdom of heaven' became much rarer after 1560. Towards the end of the 16th century an emphasis on the testator's sins, his unworthiness and his penitence, along with references to Christ as 'Redeemer', is noticeable. John Waties described himself as an 'unprofitable servant of God'. This self-abasement before God is paralleled in other wills by firm statements stressing a belief in salvation solely through the merits of Christ's passion.[194] Wills proven in the prerogative court, rather than at the bishop of Hereford's court, were often those of well-off persons and these indicate a high proportion of believers in the predestinarian doctrine of the 'elect'. One only displays both humility and a firm attachment to Anglican belief; in 1621 William Lane wished to be buried 'without any pompe or chardge with coffin, sermon, singing, mourning apparel or extraordinary ringing, but only as yt is set downe in our holy communion book'.[195]

The Protestant Church

By the late 16th century the parish church was largely under the control of the Corporation of the town, which appointed the churchwardens and the preacher and controlled most of the church finances, other than the glebe lands. The rectors were appointed by the lay patrons still and seem to have reflected their views. Thomas Hopkins, a former monk of Hailes, was appointed in 1551 but presided without difficulty through the reigns of Edward VI, Mary and Elizabeth.[196] By 1575 he held three benefices against the law but, because he had been a good preacher and was now blind, the Privy Council ordered that he was not to be 'molested'.[197] In 1582 a dispute between John Buste, the rector, and parishioners was investigated by Bishop Whitgift, who reported to Burghley that 'trulie they are a good people and lovers of Godes worde . . . have zeale without discretion', although 'manie things were alledged against the townsmen but few proved'.[198]

Religious politics came to Ludlow when Robert Horne was presented in 1596 by Robert Devereux, Earl of Essex, a notable supporter of Puritans.[199] Horne was a Puritan, as it was understood in the 1590s. Very soon he was before the church court for not wearing a surplice. In 1601 the same charge was made against him, together with not making the sign of the cross when baptising children and not publishing names required every Sunday.[200] In 1605 five leading burgesses, led by Richard Bailey and Edward Crowther, were charged with wearing their hats during divine service; if this were a sign of Puritan attitudes it proves that the Charter disputes of the 1590s had no religious significance, for then Bailey and Crowther had been on opposite sides. There may have been a subsequent shift in opinion, for in 1622 the churchwardens, Samuel Lloyd and John Brasier, were charged with wearing surplices at sacraments.[201] In 1637, however, the then rector, Thomas Colbach, was prosecuted by the High Commission for not wearing a surplice, not bowing at the name of Jesus, not standing to read the creed and allowing communicants not to kneel.[202] These were isolated instances of dissenting attitudes. The post-Reformation church put much more effort into the control of religious observance and social behaviour, especially in promoting sabbatarianism.

From the 1570s an increasing proportion of church court prosecutions involved non-sexual offences, particularly non-attendance at church, disturbing divine service, trading and gaming on Sundays, and cursing. These prosecutions reflected the church's growing insistence that orthodox belief and reverent conduct went together. Such misdemeanours had not usually been committed in order to make a religious point; non-attendance at church, however, may have been more often a matter of conscience than of unconcern. In 1563 three people were punished for non-attendance at church and two others for not taking communion. Joan Jones was whipped in 1570 for not going to church. That Christopher Hollond was let off for not attending church in 1583 because he was poor may suggest that sometimes the church's interest in punishing non-attendance was less the reformation of the flock than making money out of them. Minor persecution of Catholics occurred, but as the only Catholics were the powerful Townshend family and their servants, the persecution was limited and easily borne, confined to penal rates of taxation and fines for non-attendance at church.[203]

Playing games in the churchyard or anywhere on Sunday was frowned on in the late 16th century. In 1596 three boys were charged with playing ball in the church porch. In 1604 Richard Goughe was playing 'coites' in the time of vespers. The next year Edward Evans was charged before both the church court and before the town court with playing at 'tables' during divine service; the bailiffs imprisoned him. 1606 was a good year for punishing games-players; Charles Amyas played unlawful games during divine service, while six others played bowls. Francis Baule was accused of the socially subversive act of encouraging apprentices and servants to play cards. Two men played cards during service-time in 1612, while in 1620 Joan Sutton was said to have held shovel-board parties at home in service-time. There was no private life in the face of a watchful Church.[204].

Sunday trading also invited punishment. In 1599 John Jennings was accused of working as a barber on the sabbath and Robert Hill for working as a fletcher. Roger Bebbe was selling his butcher's meat on Sunday in 1605, but that year 12 others were charged with Sunday trading and the churchwardens stated that when the market was held on 'holidays', 'most sort of all tradesmen and vitulers doe use their trades and victualing'. The would-be regulators were fighting a losing battle, for the wardens said again in 1622 that all the shops remained open on feast days. Feast days were treated by the church in the same way as Sundays, but they were so frequent that the practice must have seriously inconvenienced traders and their customers; it is not, therefore, surprising that the rules were disobeyed. In 1613 William Lloyd, a cordwainer, opened his shop at Candlemas and put his employees 'to working as at any day at his trade'.[205]

Unseemly conduct in church was next to invite correction. In 1556 Anne Bellymy obstructed divine service.[206] William Glover and Joan Rogers were swearing during a church service in 1562. Griffin Lloyd threw Abraham Gretton from his seat in church in 1621 and that year William Gregory and five others were accused of 'striving and struggling' in church. All were later involved in the later litigation over the town's mills.[207]

It is likely that the church saw such behaviour as misconduct rather than a matter of principle. Puritanism, however, did exist in Ludlow among a minority who lived until the Civil War without undue hostility from the dominant conforming groups. The Harleys at Brampton Bryan, notable Puritans in the 1630s, had their followers in Ludlow. The foremost was John Aston, elected to the Corporation in 1631 and low bailiff in 1639, one of the leading men in the town during the Interregnum. The religious gulf was fairly narrow, however; John Aston was related to the Catholic Townshends and during the Interregnum tutored Robert Townshend's daughters.[208]

Catholic recusants may have existed during Elizabeth's reign but, if so, they kept their heads down. It is doubtful whether many of those prosecuted for not attending church at that time were Catholics. By the 17th century, however, things were changing. In 1603 an informer recommended to the government an investigation into a meeting at the *Sign of the Crown*, a Ludlow inn, to which Robert Townshend had sent his servant to meet William Watson, a wanted Jesuit. Townshend, along with Charles Foxe and Richard Broughton, was alleged to have attended meetings with notable papists, were 'enemies to the Stait . . .' and were 'known to be the greatest receyvers, mayntayners and releavers of Jesuitts . . . Questionles if Watson shall be examined rigourouslie itt will appear thatt these gentts are as traitorous as Wattson himselfe'. There is no evidence that this was acted upon, or that the allegation was untrue.[209] In 1619 John Hodges was excommunicated for refusing to take the oath of supremacy.[210]

23. Tomb of Sir Robert Townshend, Chief Justice of Chester, the first member of this Catholic family to live in Ludlow. The tomb is situated in the parish church.

The religious and political affiliations of most Ludlow people became apparent only during the Civil War, when some of them suffered for being on the losing side for the time being.

Protestant 'Reformation of Manners'

The Church authorities exercised a close supervision over sexual morals and many other areas of behaviour before the Reformation, being concerned to punish misconduct but unable to reform it. The Protestant Church maintained this concern, but made a more determined effort to achieve reformation of manners. It was an uphill struggle, but slowly manners and conduct did improve. This may, however, have been the consequence of the spread of education and the general development of secular taste and sensibility rather than ecclesiastical repression. In the 16th century to the church courts were added the prerogative courts of the State (such as Star Chamber, the court of the Council of the Marches) and the ecclesiastical court of High Commission, all interested in the correction of conduct.

Until the 1570s the medieval pattern continued; nine out of ten prosecutions of Ludlow people before the church courts concerned sexual misconduct: adultery,   fornication,   fostering

24.   The Preacher's House in Old Street, the residence of the Corporation appointed preacher in the church.

immoral persons and prostitution.[211] Thereafter these offences continued to be 'corrected', but 'Sabbath' offences for the first time became an increasing concern of the courts.

Accusations of clandestine marriage were still levelled indiscriminately; William Gregory was accused in 1570 of so marrying his wife Anne, but was able to produce a marriage licence from the dean of Leintwardine. In 1571 Thomas Butler confessed to clandestine marriage in Richard's Castle church, while William Bebbe was accused of the same in 1579 after marrying in Stowe church; some of the animus for these prosecutions must surely have been resentment at loss of surplice fees to the Ludlow clergy.[212]

Bigamy was not unknown. William Jones, a tailor, dismissed Maud, his wife, and in her lifetime married again, for which he was whipped thrice in 1576. Thomas Jones, a sojourner in Broad Street, was accused in 1596 of having two wives. Just as men were prosecuted for living with other men's wives, so, on occasion, could they be prosecuted for not living with their own; in 1613 John Lloyd of Ludlow was accused of living apart from his wife in Worthen, which may have been the Worthen churchwardens' apprehension that their parish would be left to maintain her.[213]

Incest continued to be punished, but the net was cast less wide than by the medieval Church. John Price, a tailor, was accused in 1566 of incest with his wife's sister, an offence which Thomas Phillippes, *alias* Capper, and Juliana, his deceased wife's sister, were also accused of committing.[214]

The post-Reformation clergy were little better behaved than their predecessors; in 1576 William Harris, the curate, fornicated with Juliana Capper, but escaped punishment.[215] By the early 17th century the clergy seemed to be behaving better, as indeed we might hope from those engaged in a general reformation of morals.

Accusations of fostering immorality were also frequent and probably difficult to rebut, given the shaky evidential procedures of the church courts; in 1544 John Tempulle was charged with fostering immorality between his brother, Thomas Tempull, and Margery Wyllde, his concubine. The mid–16th century was as concerned about illegitimate births for economic reasons as much as for moral ones and the church courts co-operated in taking a severe line against unhallowed pregnancies and births. In 1546 Richard Tyler, servant of William Partryge, made Agnes ap (sic) Thomas pregnant; but it was Agnes who was whipped twice. That year Margery Wyllde, mentioned above, was made pregnant by Roger Daicus of Richard's Castle; her punishment was to stand in the pillory holding a white stick. If the Church viewed illegitimate births with disapproval, it abominated abortions; in 1548 Margaret Baugh was prosecuted for drinking a savin preparation, an abortifacient, and Margaret Hyll was charged with supplying it.[216]

At this time, and for three centuries more, men were open to suspicion, often with justification, of immoral liaison with their servants. So William Powes impregnated his servant, Margery Daves, in 1548; William Poughnill committed adultery with his servant, Elizabeth Dolphin, in 1565; and Thomas Canland was 'noted' with his servant, Margery Smyth, in 1571. That year William Frenche was whipped thrice – the usual tariff – for making his servant pregnant, and John Tyther only escaped punishment for a liaison with his servant in 1576 by leaving the diocese. It is surprising, however, that quite a few servants were apparently made pregnant by 'unknown men', like Margaret Baghe, servant of John Carpynter, in 1548, and Margaret Coneway, servant of Thomas Becke, in 1579. William Jones, a surgeon, in 1579 fostered Mary Barckley, his housemaid, who had been 'made big with child by an unknown father'. Were these girls merely shielding their employers?[217]

Other misbehaviour began to excite the church courts' interest, reflecting a new ecclesiastical willingness to oversee and regulate every aspect of life. Prosecutions for swearing and drunkenness abounded; the same names often cropped up. In 1605 Ferdinando Dey and several others were charged with 'common swearing and [being] drunkards', a woman among them with being 'a common ribald and filthie speaking to the bad example of others'.[218] This was the first of very many such convictions for Dey, who seems to have been one of the worst-behaved Ludlow people ever. Swearing, cursing and defamation became frequently-punished offences, in which Dey and his friends often participated.

In 1608 Elizabeth Webb reviled the minister, saying 'I pray God that you and your children may not be worth 2d. before you die'. When accused, she was quick-witted enough to claim that she had in fact said 'may not want 2d. before you die'. In 1609 William Crump, accused of habitually leaving the church during the sermon, explained that he left for his 'smale occasions'; he was given a warning nonetheless.[219] It is not surprising that the clergy of so censorious a church should themselves invite the kind of verbal abuse which Edmund Leigh shouted at the rector in 1619: 'Go, goose-cap fool. A fart for you!'

A sentence of excommunication required everyone to avoid contact with the excommunicate but, as the church courts used this sentence for minor offences, such as not attending the court to exhibit an inventory of a deceased person's possessions, it was very common. Life could become difficult in a small town if everyone obeyed an excommunication; in most cases we may suspect that most people did not obey and the sentenced person was not too worried. Occasionally the court pursued those who did associate with an excommunicate; in 1596 Richard Cooke was charged with visiting Ellis Beddow and his wife, both being excommunicate, and in 1619 John Lloyd, a fisherman, had to do penance for walking the streets with an excommunicate.[220]

Elizabeth Evans, administrator of Thomas Evans's estate in 1612, lent his money widely; she was the only person convicted of usury after the Reformation.[221] The prosecution may have been aimed less at interest-taking than at lending money to avoid paying administration fees.

The church court records provide a picture of Ludlow people at their worst; it does not show the town in a better light if accusations were untrue, for it was spite and greed which gave rise to them. Ludlow was typical of most towns. Prurience was institutionalised, but vice was never reformed. Men who cared deeply about honour and dignity nevertheless constantly disregarded both.

Chapter Four

The Palmers' Gild

Foundation and Early History

The original stimulus for the formation of religious gilds, of which the Palmers' Gild of Ludlow was an example, may have been the need in towns and even some villages, but particularly in towns of a particular size and prosperity, for a social focus. Urban government was in essence regulatory rather than aspirational; even self-governing boroughs could not provide an adequate outlet for their citizens' ambitions for influence and esteem, nor could they provide for all the social needs of the people. To cater for such various needs in Ludlow the Palmers' Gild was founded. Other important towns developed similar institutions; in the Midlands Coventry had its Corpus Christi Gild and, after 1364, the Holy Trinity Gild, while Stratford-upon-Avon had its Gild of the Holy Cross, and Wolverhampton its St Catherine's Gild. The Palmers' Gild of Ludlow was an earlier example. It was not only one of the most important institutions in Ludlow for nearly three centuries, but is also one of the best documented, for it was a large property owner, and its records were maintained by its successor, the town Corporation.

These quasi-religious gilds, although existing even in villages, were often founded in mercantile towns at the height of their prosperity. They provided an outlet for piety and display for men who had accumulated wealth without recognised position, and who wished to participate in affairs in a manner similar to landed families. It is, therefore, no coincidence that the Palmers' Gild came into being in the mid–13th century when the wool trade in the March was at its height.

What led to the foundation at that time? This may be connected with the problem of the name of the Gild. Eight undated deeds of the time of Geoffrey Andrew's 'gildaldernemanship' were in favour of 'the Blessed Mary and the Brotherhood of the Palmers' Gild', so it may have borne this name from its inception, even though the list of rent charges, compiled later, referred only to the service of the Blessed Mary. A 'palmer' was one who had been on a pilgrimage to the Holy Land, as thousands from western Europe did yearly in the early 13th century. Hugh Lacy (d.1186) and Philip Daubeney (*de Albini*), governor of Ludlow under King John, had both been crusaders and we may be sure that someone from Ludlow made the journey, just as in the next century Ludlow men went to Santiago de Compostela. The most likely person to be a pilgrim would have been someone with family wealth, especially land, producing rents in his absence. Geoffrey Andrew came from such a family; his father, Andrew fitz Miles, invested his commercial fortune in property in Ludlow and Stokesay; the other son, Nicholas, owned Clee St Margaret and a moiety of Steventon. Geoffrey became the first gildalderneman, doubtless because he had been the prime mover in founding the Gild.[1] Possibly he made the pilgrimage and, with the fall of Jerusalem to Sultan as-Salih Ayyub in 1244 and the failure of Louis IX's subsequent crusade in 1254, may have thought the time ripe to commemorate at home what could not be celebrated in Jerusalem. One of Louis IX's crusading companions was his biographer, Jean de Joinville, elder brother of Geoffrey de Genevile, lord of Ludlow. That Ludlow was interested in this crusade is clear from the details recorded by the Ludlow annalist in 1248–9.[2] By 1525 a legend was established that pilgrims from the Holy Land had brought a ring back as a token from St John the Evangelist and had given it to Edward the Confessor and that these men were from Ludlow, who, implicitly, then founded the Gild.

Robert Watkynson, a carver from Lilleshall, contracted with the Gild in 1525 to depict this story, among other general religious themes, in the chapel of St John the Evangelist in the parish church.[3] Leland published the story in 1533.

The earliest surviving dated document records an assembly of the leading burgesses at Pentecost, 1284, which promulgated the objectives and ordinances of the Gild. This, however, is not conclusive evidence that the Gild was in fact founded then. That meeting was a later stage in the formalisation of its corporate development. Incorporation was a necessary protection for pious or charitable bodies which owned property against the provisions of the Statute of Mortmain of 1279, which was intended to prevent the diminution of the king's revenue from feudal incidents which followed from the alienation of property by laymen in favour of religious uses. Corporations, perpetual persons in law, did not die, so the feudal incidents due to the king upon the death of a tenant-in-chief could not arise. The next stage would be to apply for a specific royal licence to alienate or acquire property. The 1284 document, coming within five years of the Statute, may have been a response. Indeed it includes a statement that the Gild had received 43s. 6d. in rents before the Statute of Mortmain, so the Gild existed in some form before 1279. It was not until 1329 that royal sanction to acquire property was sought for the first time and this, along with a request for a licence in 1344, was cited in a further petition in 1379.

The 1284 ordinances were not cited in Chancery until 1389, when gilds were required to make returns of their ordinances and property.[4] The final sentences of the 1284 ordinances then cited include the date of that reference, which suggests it would be rash to assume that these were the *ipsissima verba* of 1284, although one scholar resolved this by taking the date to be the date of the ordinances themselves – mistakenly, I think. Dating the documents has caused successive scholars difficulty and the solutions proposed in the more recent studies are still flawed.[5] At best the 1284 document is a set of rules and objectives for the Gild drawn up in 1284, but not sanctioned, in truth, by the king; at worst it is a 'back-projection' of the ordinances of the Gild from the 14th century into the 13th century, an act of anachronistic wishful thinking by no means unusual at that time. The ordinances probably applied in much of the 14th century and, in substance if not in detail, the same objectives and the broad structure of the Gild obtained in 1284. The Gild's officers, as described in the ordinances, were a *rector* and *procuratores*, who were the officers later known as the stewards or *seneschalli*. The return into the Chancery in 1389, which recited the 1284 document, was in the name of the warden and the stewards. By that time the Gild was a considerable property owner, had many members in many places and a consequent need for officers other than the warden. In 1284 most of its income was in the form of annual rent charges rather than rents from tenants and there were fewer members. Would there then have been a need for two stewards? The first stewards' accounts we know of are those for 1344–5.[6]

The specific objectives of the Gild were to help men and women members impoverished by robbery, fire, shipwreck, house collapse or other misfortune. If a member were arrested or his goods unjustly seized, the Gild was to help him. Members impoverished through sickness, blindness or injury were also to be helped from the Gild's funds. Honest and marriageable girls without dowries were to be endowed to enable them to marry or to take religious vows. All members in the town were to attend services for the dead. Night-watches for the dead could be held by men only, provided it were done reverently. A healthy and suitable chaplain had to be chosen to celebrate divine service; this was connected with the final provision linking the ordinances with rent in Ludlow totalling 43s. 6d. *before* the Statute of Mortmain. This may refer to the grant of a licence by letters patent in 1292 to Henry Pigin, then 'gildalderneman' or rector of the Gild (although the grant did not mention the Gild), so that he could alienate in mortmain rents of 53s. 4d. to support a chaplain in the parish church. As this gift cannot be traced in the Gild records this could have been a way of retrospectively rendering more secure a series of previous grants to the Gild for that purpose.[7] If so, the surviving '1284 ordinances' may represent a rewriting of those ordinances at a later date.

Retrospectively writing a document to reflect facts thought to have been established much earlier, for which actual contemporary evidence may have been wanting, was common in the Middle Ages. There exists an undated document which, from its contents, purports to be the earliest evidence of gifts of rent charges to the Gild.[8] It is a list which begins:

> To all Christ's faithful who will see or hear this present writing, Geoffrey fitz Andrew of Lodelauwe everlasting salvation in the Lord: let our community know that, for the sake of charity, I have given and granted and by this present writing confirmed for the salvation of my soul and of the souls of all my ancestors and successors, in pure, free and perpetual alms for the perpetual maintenance of a chaplain to God and the blessed Mary serving in the church of Lodelauwe, an annual rent of 12 pence for ever to be obtained from [the house] which is opposite the house which Andrew Macy once held.[9]

There follow 250 other gifts from other persons, all in this form: 'I, Hugh le Masun, 3d. annual rent from my house ...'. Comparison with other records shows that it was not compiled all at one time. It suggests a list, drawn up as an original multiple deed of gift from many individuals, but detailing many gifts made at various times, some possibly unevidenced. There is no reason to doubt the facts given, however, particularly as the spelling and form of the names – *Galfridus filius Andre, Johannes de Breconia, Willielmus de Radenovere* and Thomas Haranc – are typical of the late 13th century rather than the 14th century.[10]

It is the only evidence for dating the Gild's foundation. Geoffrey Andrew, who heads the list, was the first recorded warden or, as he was then entitled, 'gildaldernemon', of the Gild; he was alive in 1280 and probably dead by 1284.[11] In undated deeds of gift to the Gild – which seem to come after the listed rent charges – he generally appears as a witness along with Richard Momele, then bailiff or constable of Ludlow, which places those deeds into the period between about 1270 and about 1280. The date can be narrowed down further; donors like Andrew Pire, John *de Breconia* and Henry fitz Melede were dead by 1272 at the latest.[12] Henry Marescall, the husband of Rose, was dead before 1267, when rent from their house was given to Aconbury convent.[13] John Capin may have been dead by 1266, when his son, Roger, was prosecuted by Hugh Mortimer.[14] Hugh Dublur was dead by 1260, when his wife, Isabel, sued for her dower.[15] One donor, William *Monetarius*, may have been the one of that name who died before 1272[16] or another – the first of his line to be lord of Whitton – who died before 1255.[17] Several of the donors, including Geoffrey Andrew himself, can be shown to have been living in the period 1255–7. The Gild was therefore founded in the late 1250s.

Administration of the Gild

During Geoffrey Andrew's term of office, lasting 20 or 25 years, the character of the Gild was established. The 1284 ordinances may have applied then, except that some of the provisions seem to have become dead letters. On the other hand, it is possible that some of the provisions were already long established. It may be that, if Andrew were the founder, provisions for the elections of wardens or gildaldernemen would have fallen into desuetude. He would have remained in office for life as a matter of esteem.

The ordinances laid down 'that each year the power of electing may be committed to five or seven suitable men of our aforesaid Brotherhood, who, on behalf of all and singular, may elect a *rector* on the day after Michaelmas and two *procuratores* at two terms of each

year, that is, on the next day above-mentioned and on the day after Easter Sunday . . . '.
This is the only statement we have for any period of how the officers of the Gild were to
be chosen; moreover, there is no evidence from any period that this was how they were in
fact chosen. Wardens generally stayed in office for long periods, mostly until they died,
although between 1393 and 1440 William Broke served twice (1393–4 and 1404), as did
William Parys (1401–2 and 1422–40). An undated rental, which internal evidence enables
to be dated shortly after 1284, states that 'the steward (*seneschallus*) received 4s.' from
Denise Kynwe of Old Street.[18] Two stewards are known only from 1344 onwards and the
evidence is that they normally served in pairs for five years. These apparently ineffective
provisions may be the best evidence that they applied early on, possibly written (before
Geoffrey Andrew's death) in the vain hope that in future no one else would exercise a
similarly permanent dominance.

The 'five or seven' to whom the power of election was committed must be the men
subsequently called 'the elders' or 'the council' of the Gild. Who elected them is unknown;
rather than assume election by the members at large, a form of indirect representation, we
would be on surer ground if we assume that the elders were co-opted into vacancies, a
method more typical of the age. The elders may have numbered seven and at least five
had to vote for a candidate before he could be elected.[19] The Gild was ruled by a self-
perpetuating oligarchy, operating rules for minimising faction.

The usual formula used in deeds and other instruments to express the corporate identity
of the Gild was 'the Warden and Brotherhood of the Palmers' Gild of the Blessed Mary
and of St John the Evangelist' of Ludlow. During the wardenship of Richard Corve, which
spanned the second quarter of the 13th century, however, the formula was usually 'the
Warden and Community of the Palmers' Gild of the Blessed Mary and of St John the
Evangelist of Ludlow'. The expression, the 'community' of the Gild, first appeared in the
1329 petition for a royal licence to incorporate, which was promoted by Richard Corve.[20]
This temporary formulaic change may indicate that Richard Corve saw the Gild as more
of a public, even secular, body, a *communitas*, than the private, semi-religious body implied
by the word *fraternitas*.[21]

From its inception the Gild was known as 'the Palmers' Gild of the Brotherhood of the
Blessed Mary'. During the 14th century the dedication was extended to include St John
the Evangelist, presumably to reinforce the connection between the Gild and the legend of
that saint. The first reference to St John was in the grant of 1329.[22] The will of William
Vilde in 1377 refers, however, to the 'Fraternity of St Andrew of Ludlow called the
Palmersgylde', which may reflect the support given by the Gild to the service at St Andrew's
chantry in the parish church. Gild accounts in the 16th century were produced on St
Andrew's day *'coram fratribus . . . in collegio latus et auditus'*.[23]

The elders remained a shadowy group, although they had a continuous existence. In
1359 a lease of Gild property in Broad Linney was effected by the warden and five others,
'then the elders of the Gild'. Did the elders now number only five or was five the required
quorum from a larger number, such as seven? None of them held any office afterwards, so
it may be that the elders were generally former stewards; choosing governing bodies from
former office-holders was a common medieval practice and, indeed, was practised in the
16th century by Ludlow Corporation itself.[24] In 1383 a property agreement was effected in
the names of the then warden, the two stewards and 12 other men, described as 'aldermen
and brethren' of the Gild; the numbers of the ruling group had increased, but the change
of name was only temporary.[25] In 1386 another lease in Linney was made in the name of
'the warden, the elders and the brethren' of the Gild; in 1460 the formula included just
the warden and the elders.[26] Papal permission was obtained in 1400 for the Gild to
have its own confessor who was to be chosen by 'the warden and four superiors called

Gildaldernemen'. Allowing for the misunderstandings inevitably created by distance, this is so factual that it must have emanated from the Gild itself; by implication there was, within the elders, a smaller group exercising power, but we hear no more of them.[27] In the 1420s the 'masters and elders' of the Gild were given hoods at Gild expense.[28] The warden and 12 brethren 'of the council' were appointed overseers of Geoffrey Baugh's will in 1500, and about that time the warden, Walter Morton, and 12 named 'brethren and councillors of the Gild' received a gift of an annual rent. The elders or aldermen were a formal council, not merely a group of individuals of higher status. Several of them, perhaps all, had been stewards previously, which supports the conclusions drawn above in relation to 1359. A similar list of the elders exists for 1503, in which at least seven can also be shown to have been former stewards.[29] In about 1508 the stewards paid for new robes, at 16s. each, for each of the *nine* members of the council of the Gild; such changes in the numbers suggest that fixed numbers had lapsed; all surviving previous stewards may now have automatically become councillors or aldermen.[30]

The administration of the Gild was elaborate. The chief executive was the warden; perhaps by 1284 there were two stewards. By 1344 the collection of rents was in the separate hands of a rent collector, an office filled until the early 15th century by one of the Gild chaplains. This duty was given to a chaplain because the gifts of property to the Gild were generally for the support of Gild chaplains in the parish church; when the Gild bought property the revenues were in theory used in the same way and so were collected along with the others. When property was left to fund particular obits, it was the rent collector who collected the rents, although he accounted for them separately. The last clerical rent collector recorded was Walter Russhe in 1437–8, although he had been preceded by a layman, Richard Kynstone, in 1424–8.[31] Thereafter the rent collectors were always laymen who served for one year at a time, occasionally coming back to the office after a spell of years. The net rents were paid over to the stewards.

The stewards from this time were responsible for collecting the members' dues, a duty which gradually led them into itineraries around the country, the results of which were recorded in 'riding books'. As they recruited members further afield, the itineraries took longer. In 1505–6 the stewards, Richard Bragott and John Brown, each with a helper, were travelling on Gild business for 127 and 163 days respectively. In that year, two men referred to as the 'selesters' were given cloaks, as were the senior men of the Gild; By 1534–5 there were 'selesters' in Kingsland, Wigmore, Yarpole and Hanley. It may be that these local representatives (who also bought supplies for the Pentecost feasts) saved the stewards from including the villages around Ludlow in their itineraries.[32] The stewards also oversaw the maintenance of the growing number of Gild properties, organised the annual Pentecost feast, bought supplies and paid stipends. Although property was acquired in the name of the warden and the Gild, it was generally leased out by the warden and stewards.

Although there is a risk that undue significance may be given to the Gild administration only because its records are relatively good, an impression is gained that the Gild was from the outset more efficiently run than the town itself. The Gild did not farm out its revenues, as did the town, to save itself the trouble of collecting and administering them. There was a kind of ordered hierarchical career in the Gild's offices, which may have formed the model for the *cursus honorum* which operated in Corporation offices, certainly in the 16th century. Many of the Gild's functions in estate management, education, almshouses, and auxiliary activities in the parish church, were taken over by the Corporation after 1551. It is only in the last decade or so of the Gild's existence that it seemed to have become less well-run.

The Gild employed others. In 1364 Hugh Ewyas was paid 6s. 8d. as Gild janitor,[33] but his successors are not known until John Shrawley, who served from 1506 to 1537 and was

25.   The Guildhall: the Gild headquarters from the late 13th century, although by the 16th century much of the administration was conducted from the Gild college.

given a lease of a tenement as a reward.[34] The Gild employed a bellman, who had to ring the Gild bell at requiems and to walk the town calling for prayers for the deceased 'according to the laudable custom of the Yeld', as the terms of Elinor Eye's obit put it.[35] Attorneys were also engaged for various legal business; Howell Goyke was paid as 'the Gild attorney' in 1424–5 and was followed by others, not all Ludlow men.

The Gild's document of surrender was signed on 1 June 1551 by the warden, William Langford, and 21 brethren, more than the customary membership of the Gild council, but presumably the men of most standing in the Gild, the entire Gild membership being much larger. At least 14 of them were members of Ludlow Corporation at the time. One, Charles Foxe, was at no time a member of the Corporation, but may have been there purely because of his influence in the town as well as his avaricious interest in the estates of moribund religious institutions.[36]

The Gild was incorporated on 17 November 1329, when its petition to the king was followed by the grant of community, a common seal, power to admit members and to choose a warden. A day later the Gild was allowed to acquire lands and rents of £20 a year in mortmain, in practice a retrospective exemption for the acquisitions of decades.[37] Many of the Gild's acquisitions of property evaded the need to obtain (and pay for) a royal licence by the device of employing leading members of the Gild, or its chaplains, as feoffees to uses – that is, in modern terms, putting property into trust.[38] The Gild was in this practice copying the landed nobility who used the same device to escape feudal dues falling on their estates in case of premature deaths.

In 1330 a group of six, the Orletone brothers and others, were recipients of a large donation of property, intended for the Gild, from the estate of John Brompfeld. The group, leading members of the Gild, were acting as its feoffees, although the Gild was not mentioned. The Gild records include many of these, although it became more common to employ the Gild's chaplains for the purpose, particularly as most acquisitions were for their support, even for the performance of particular obits. In the early 15th century John Hory, John Assheford and John Hoper often so acted; it may be that the Gild chaplains' willingness to act as 'men of business' was as important to the town as their spiritual services.[39]

The Gild already occupied its 'Gildhalle' in 1283 on the site in Mill Street where the Guildhall is today, leasing it for a further six years from the widow of William Bradestone, but it was implicit that they had been doing so for some time already.[40]

Although the majority of the Gild's early endowments were rent charges, even in Geoffrey Andrew's time it was acquiring properties. A house in Corve Street was let for two lives to William Ledewys and his wife in return for 3d. annual rent.[41] Rent charges were perhaps less welcome than capital, for a rent charge of 11d. a year from a house in Old Street was sold to Robert Brun for 11s.[42] Many of the original listed rent charges cannot be identified in the Gild's muniments of title or in the rentals. Some may have been for short periods or for lives, others may have been subsumed in later larger gifts or acquisitions, while some may have been sold off.

The Chaplains of the Gild

The main specific purpose of the Gild was the support of chaplains for the chantries in the church. This was the destination of funds derived from the Gild's properties, while money raised from members' entry fines and annual dues was devoted to the repair of property and to the mutual insurance and social objectives of the Gild. As property repairs also supported the flow of funds from rents to the chaplains, it is plain that this was the chief end of the Gild's financial administration. To 20th-century eyes such colossal expenditure on unproductive religious ritual may seem strange, but in the 13th, 14th and 15th centuries most people were in no doubt that what kept mankind from both spiritual perdition and temporal catastrophe was an incessant flow of prayers to God from the priesthood and from religious orders. It was more vital expenditure than commercial investment or relief of poverty.

In the 13th century the Gild chaplains' spiritual duties in the parish church seem to have been for the general benefit, but in the more individualistic atmosphere of the 15th and 16th centuries donors became more selfish and more frequently endowed obits for themselves and their own families, sometimes laying down elaborate rules for checking that the services they were paying for were carried out upon pain of forfeiture of the endowments. In 1427 the warden had to enter into an agreement with the prior of St John's Hospital that the Gild would pay the Hospital an annual rent of 100s. secured on Gild property, if a chaplain were not maintained at Gild expense to pray at the altar of St John for the souls of Thomas Paas and Isold his wife, or if they did not hold a very elaborate annual obit for them and keep candles permanently burning.[43] From this time private chantries and obits, administered by the Gild, multiplied; the Gild provided a popular service and made a good business out of it.

Not all endowments of obits were made over directly to the Gild; it was usually left to executors to find a chaplain to carry out the tasks. Perhaps because the Gild was a well-organised and continuing body with an establishment of chaplains attached to the chantries in the church, it appears that such duties, along with the endowments, quickly accrued to the Gild chaplains. John Ace, who died in 1321, provided for masses for his and his wife's souls, to be arranged by his son, William; the will found its way into the Gild archives, probably because William paid the Gild to take on the duty.[44] William himself left the reversion of much of his estate to the Gild for its general purposes (that is, to 'sustain the charity of the Gild'), while his son, Hugh, left property to three chaplains and three leading members of the Gild in return for annual obits.[45] Some at least of these obits were kept up faithfully; Henry Pigin's obit was being observed in 1344–5, 30 years after his death, and the stewards were still paying chaplains for the obits of both Hugh Ace and his brother, Philip, in 1472–3.[46] The Gild chaplains were able to provide other services arising from the administration and performance of obits. They often acted as feoffees to lay people, so, in 1436, John Hory, John Assheford and John Hoper acted for William Mersshetone, overseeing aspects of his will and various term interests within it, as well as twice-yearly services for Mersshetone's, his wife's and his family's souls in the All Saints' chancel of the church, and finally the endowment of two chaplains for 20 years after the reversions.[47] The Gild provided an institutional continuity and, in its chaplains, administrative experience which enabled it to offer unrivalled spiritual and administrative services; inevitably it attracted business in the form of endowments. Over 30 private endowments of obits have been traced from the last 150 years of the Gild's existence, some of these for daily masses.[48]

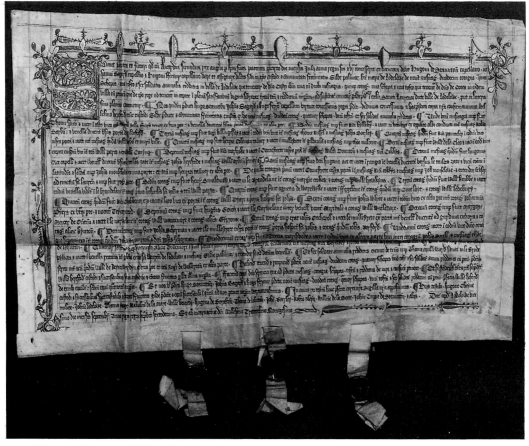

26.   Richard III's licence of 1392 to allow the Gild to receive property in mortmain. This illustrates the function of the Gild chaplains to act as feoffees.

The numbers of chaplains maintained by the Gild increased over the years, no doubt in response to the demands for their services. In 1284 the ordinances referred to three chaplains, but the rental of that year shows four. During the next century their numbers varied between four and five, reflecting their indeterminate status; strictly they served the altars within the church, which were supported by, but were not exclusive to, the Gild. In 1344–5 four priests were maintained, including Hugh Wystanstowe, who was also Gild rent collector; their stipends amounted to 44s. 8d., plus 10s. for rent collecting.[49] There were other sources of support for more priests, including one in the Lady Chapel provided by the Corporation. William Toggeford, although much involved in Gild business in the late 14th century, was not maintained by the Gild. William Andrew had endowed the chantry of St Andrew and vested patronage in the Community of Ludlow, but as one testator, William Vilde, referred in 1377 to 'the Fraternity of St Andrew, called the Palmers' Gild', one of the Gild chaplains may have been involved there.[50] The rents for both chantries were collected by the Gild renter in the 15th century, although he accounted for them separately.[51] The Gild chaplains were housed together; in 1364 the rent collector paid 5s. for expenses on a house 'set to the chaplains of the Gild by the church for half a year'.[52] In 1393 the Gild acquired land, possibly the same site, for it was opposite the church in what is now College Street, upon which, in the following year, it built a college for the chaplains which was extended in 1446–7. This is the first confirmation of a corporate existence for the chaplains, distinct from membership of the Gild itself. By this time eight chaplains may have been accommodated.[53] Numbers still varied but there were ten in 1472–3 and in 1540.[54] By the 16th century the college seems to have replaced the Guildhall as the Gild headquarters, for this was where the officials presented their annual accounts to the assembled brethren.

Only one of the wardens of the Gild was not a layman. John Hawkins, warden c.1361–71, during this time and afterwards was also rector of Whitchurch, later vicar of St Michael's, Coventry, until his death in 1406.[55] His father, Robert Haukyns, had been an elder of the Gild, and he himself was the heir of his aunt, Joan, widow of William Ocley, for whose block of tenements on the corner of Narrow Lane and Castle Street he successfully sued Stephen de Butterleye.[56] He seems also to have been related to Geoffrey Warewyk, an elder of the Gild. His brother, William, was steward in 1383–5. In 1367 his wardenship 'of the chantry of St Mary and of St John the Evangelist in the church of St Laurence of Ludlow' was ratified by the king, although he had been warden since at least 29 September 1365, and probably since the death of Richard Orletone on 13 October 1361.[57] The Mortimer lordship of Ludlow was in the king's hands during that time and the royal Chancery liked to exercise rights of ecclesiastical patronage on these occasions, even when strictly there was no patronage to exercise.[58] Usually, however, such patronage was exercised in favour of royal clerks. Perhaps John Hawkins himself sought to protect himself against internal opposition by obtaining an unprecedented royal grant of a post for which the members of the Gild had the right and powers of election. He did not remain there long, being replaced about 1372 by William Orletone, probably the son of Hawkins's predecessor. After Hawkins's death in about 1406 an obit was established for him in Ludlow.[59] His wardenship may not have been a success, for William Orletone, admittedly a litigious man, at once embarked upon a flurry of law suits against the Gild's debtors, often explicitly in his capacity of warden suing for moneys due to his predecessor, particularly against John Pusselowe, a previous steward.[60]

Just as the Gild gradually assumed the patronage and maintenance of the priests of the various services within the church, so it began to assume responsibilities for – and influence over – the ornamentation of the church. In 1446–7, at the time the College was extended, the Gild bought the materials for the new choir stalls and may have paid the craftsmen's wages. In 1469 it is known to have paid for the carriage of stone to the church.[61] In 1538–9 the Gild provided iron to repair the vestry door,[62] and in 1525 the Gild contracted for expensive carving at various places in the church. Its influence extended to musical arrangements; in 1486 a Gild chaplain was paid to supervise the choir, possibly to ensure that it sang well before John Hosyer's tomb, as required by his will. By 1492 two Gild chaplains acted as 'singing men' in the Lady chapel; the Gild porter was paid to serve there. The Gild had been paying the organist since the early 13th century; during 1344–5 there was recorded a payment of 3d. to the *minstrallum organorum*[63] and in 1492 Thomas Sherman was paid for the job.[64] The Gild probably bought the organ, for in 1533–4 John Hoskyns was paid 40s. 'for mending the Gild's organ'.[65] At the dissolution of the Gild the stipend of the then organist, Morris Phillips *alias* Morris *Cantator*, may have become a £4 charge on the Corporation, for later in the century it was the Corporation which appointed all the organists.[66]

Along with this, the Gild became involved in general social good works. In the early 15th century it started a school near the churchyard. In 1446–7 the stewards paid for bars on the window of the Master of the Scholars' house.[67] Around 1527 this was moved to Mill Street. The schoolmasters, of whom there was only one at a time, were varied; some were Gild chaplains, one was Thomas Sherman, the organist, others were clerics employed only as schoolmasters. By the time of the Dissolution the school was an established charge on the Gild, so that the Corporation had to support the school as a condition of taking over the Gild endowments. This became Ludlow Grammar School, which for centuries was a lasting and valued legacy of the old Palmers' Gild.[68]

Provision for members in distress never became a heavy charge on Gild funds, although a few cases of relief occurred in most years.[69] The Gild's involvement in general charity was not of its own initiative, but occurred in 1486 when the endowments provided during his lifetime by John Hosyer for his almshouse were transferred to the Gild to continue the work. During the next 65 years only Gild members could qualify as inmates; after the Dissolution this qualification was necessarily removed.

The Brethren of the Gild

The Gild began as an expression of the needs and aspirations of the people of Ludlow. So in 1329 the king's grant of incorporation was to 'the good men of the town of Lodelowe'.[70] None of the 13th-century donors of rent charges seem to have been outsiders. By 1377–8, however, the Gild was accepting members from outside, like Richard Mulleward of Edgton and Henry Taverner of Bristol; the former was from only 10 miles away, while the latter may well have been related to the Ludlow family of Taverner *alias* Colemon.[71] It recruited among those to whom Ludlow was a natural local place of business and among emigrants; there were brethren in Bridgnorth, Bishop's Castle, Leominster, Pembridge, Shrewsbury and Chester during Richard II's reign.[72] In 1425–6 the Gild gave relief to a member, Reginald Draper of 'la Pole' (Welshpool), who had been plundered by thieves, as was another member in Chester in 1427–8. In 1426–7 the Gild received 6s. 4d. from 'Brother' John ap Llewelyn of Alcester and Dothgy his wife.[73]

The patronage of the Mortimer family was natural in the early 14th century, and in 1437–8 their successors, Richard, Duke of York and his wife, joined, paying a large entrance fee of £16 13s. 4d.[74] In 1433–4 the stewards were taking admission fines from men and women throughout Shropshire and all the neighbouring counties, as well as London, Gloucestershire and Bristol. The accession of the House of York to the throne in 1461 brought fresh opportunities. Ludlow had been a centre of the Yorkist household and the Gild exploited the connection when most had moved to London; the Gild registers for the early part of Edward IV's reign contain over 50 royal servants and office-holders, along

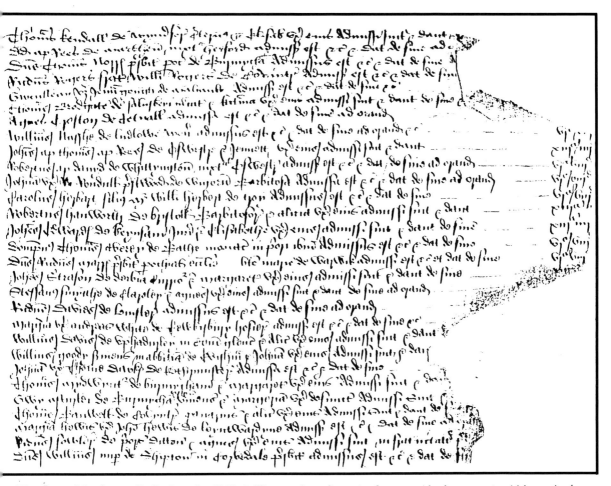

27.   Part of the Steward's Register for 1505–6. The number of recruits from outside the town should be noticed.

with the Duke of Suffolk and two other noblemen and their families.[75] To a lesser extent this continued; 10 members of Prince Henry's household joined in 1502–3.[76] The royal connection brought other favours; Edward IV made a donation of £5 to the Gild in 1472–3.[77] The nobility were also recruited and included Richard Woodville, third Earl Rivers, in 1488–9, and the Duchess of Buckingham in 1507–8.[78]

To collect the substantial annual income which arose from admission fines, the two stewards had to embark on several 'rides' a year in various parts of the country. These began in Lent and were repeated at intervals during the summer months. They were extensive, but no longer included London, Reading, Lincoln or Lancashire, in all of which former members were to be found. It can only be conjectured how the stewards came by members, but it is likely that they maintained contact with former residents of Ludlow, enrolled some of them and used these groups of members as nuclei for further admissions. In 1507–8 several clergymen in Lincoln were admitted, but we do not know if the stewards were exploiting some connection with Ludlow or had gone there speculatively to drum up business.[79]

The stewards were selling a form of insurance; for members living far from Ludlow the social benefits of the Gild may have been less compelling, although members from outside Ludlow did attend the annual Pentecost feasts. The large number of people who enrolled their deceased spouses as members, along with themselves, demonstrates that it was the spiritual benefits of having prayers said for them by the Gild's chaplains which were most highly regarded. A well-established institution like the Gild could offer a reasonable certainty that prayers paid for would continue to be said as long as necessary; such things mattered. The income from this source varied from year to year, consisting of single lifetime payments, part-payments, *post mortem* enrolments and arrears from previous years. In 1377–8 a total of £27 came in; in the 1420s an average of £20 a year was collected. By 1446–7 the total had risen to £34, a level maintained in the late 1480s when an average of £35 a year was achieved. In 1508–9 admission fines reached about £81, but had fallen to £43 by 1538–9; in 1544 the warden's accounts show a total of only £16.[80] The sudden fall in recruits in the late 1530s, after two decades of slow decline, may represent not only the spread of Protestant ideas, but growing doubts about the Gild's chances of survival and being able to keep its promises in the political climate of the day.[81]

The annual Gild feast held in the Guildhall at Pentecost was the main social event of the year in Ludlow for two-and-a-half centuries. Some members of the Gild came from afar to attend. A great deal of bread was baked and beer brewed; cheese, bacon, fish and venison were usually bought, as was wine, from Bristol. Candles to light the feast, rushes for the floor and actors to entertain also formed charges on the accounts. Every year the officers and elders of the Gild were given robes which were worn for the first time at the annual feast, whose cost they often exceeded. Responsibility for organising and paying for the feast fell upon the stewards. The annual costs of the feast, although dependent upon corn prices, provide some kind of index of the health and popularity of the Gild. In 1345 it cost £2 12s. 8½d., rising rapidly to £5 3s. 6½d. in 1378, to an average of more than £10 a year in the 1420s and an average of £17 in the late 1430s. In 1447 the cost was £11 15s. 11d., while at a feast in the period 1505–8 the warden and stewards together spent £17.[82] These levels can be compared with the costs in 1533–4 of £3 0s. 8d.; in 1539, £1 6s. 3d.; and in 1541, £1 13s. 4d.[83]

Estates

The largest number of gifts, mostly of rent charges, was made to the Gild in the first three or four decades of its existence. These were generally small, typically 4d., which was equivalent to two or three days' wages for a craftsman or, in an easy year, a bushel of wheat. One hundred and thirteen gifts are reckoned to have been received by the 1270s when the first list was drawn up and 41 were later added. This is consistent with the claim, made in 1389, that before 1279 rents of 43s. 6d. had already been received. This was enough to support two chaplains, but not much more. Thereafter there were fewer gifts, but more munificent when made; often properties inside and outside the town were given, increasingly, as we have noted, less out of pure altruism than from the desire to look after the donor's spiritual interests. The Gild itself, when it acquired or accumulated capital, sometimes by converting rent charges, went in for property purchase. Gradually the Gild properties increased until they formed the largest estate in Ludlow. Until the 1380s the Gild typically leased its properties 'for lives'. Thereafter leases for terms of years became the norm; the lease in 1389 of a house and garden in Old Street to Henry Snoudone for 40 years at a 20s. rent was one of the first.

In 1439 the Gild owned 167 rent charges, 96 tenements, 30 shops and 18 other properties

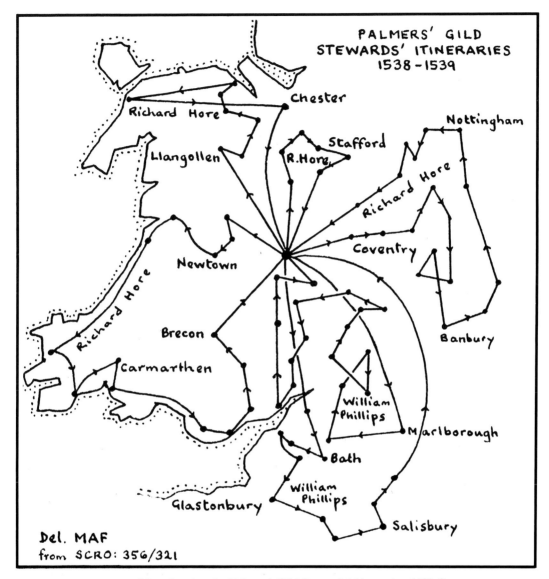

28.   Map showing the Palmers' Gild Stewards' itineraries, 1538–9.

in the town, producing rents of about £84; another 19s. 8d. arose outside the town. Gross rents increased dramatically in the early 16th century to £122 in 1546–51.[84] By this time more than half the rent charges had disappeared, probably by desuetude, but in the town tenements had increased to 152 and shops decreased to 14, while other properties rose to 75; rents of about £20 a year arose outside Ludlow, mostly from places around Ludlow – Ashford Carbonell, Hopton Wafers, Cleobury North, Richard's Castle, Eastham and Stanton Lacy, with an accumulation at Marlborough. These 'foreign rents' mostly arose from careful investment of surplus funds in the years 1517–26.[85] Gross rents, the rents which ought to have been received, were diminished by 'decays and allowances', which included

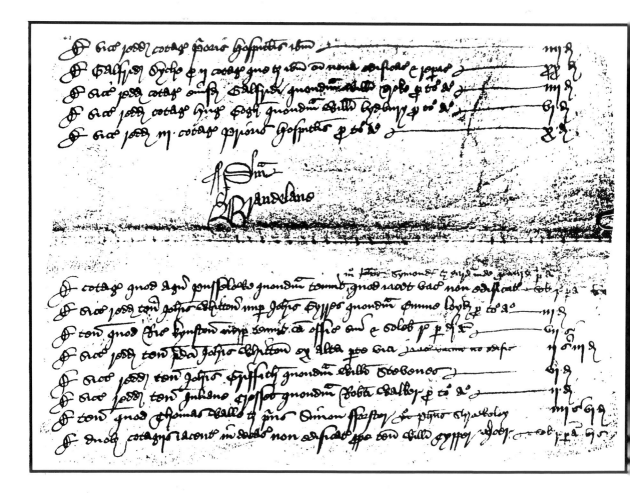

29. Part of the Gild rental for 1439, covering rents and small rent charges from Brand Lane. The name may derive from a bad fire as early as 1200 (SRO: 356/322).

empty properties, those in a state of ruin and those let rent free. In 1364–5 at £7 1s. 11d. they amounted to 19 per cent of gross rents; in 1472–3, £9 14s. 2d. was over 12 per cent; by 1546 they were £19 14s. 2½d., or 16 per cent of gross rents. In 1551 many Gild tenements in Ludlow were described as being 'very ruinous and far out of repair', void and uninhabited, producing no rent.

The growth of the Gild's property produced increasing rental income. In 1284 gross rents of £5 11s. were received; they had grown to £24 8s. 7½d by 1345 and £37 3s. 11d. by 1365. They had risen to £78 2s. 7d. by 1472–3; £95 16s. 7½d by 1502–3; £106 3s. 2½d by 1525–6; and £122 7s. 11½d by 1546, from which peak they declined slightly before the dissolution of the Gild in 1551. The first account for building costs shows that £4 14s. 1½d was spent in 1377–8, which was more than a quarter of the net rents that year. Building work, which included repairs as well as new work, averaged over £13 a year in 1437–40, similar to the amount of the net rents. In 1505–8 nearly £31 a year was spent on building work, equivalent to a third of gross rents. Gross rents amounted to £122 in 1546, while repairs, which had run at a rate of £24 a year between 1521 and 1545 (over £23 in 1538–9), had suddenly declined to £10 18s. in 1544 and £5 2s. in 1546, perhaps reflecting current uncertainties.[86]

The Gild seems to have suffered from bad luck or maladministration in its final years. In 1546, out of gross rents of £122, £20 could not be collected because tenements were either empty or ruined. Rent charges totalling 72s. in 1551 had not been collected for 12 years. By 1551 the gross rents had fallen to £119. Expenditure had not fallen, however. After about 1540 the stewards seem to have played no major part in the administration of the Gild, which had fallen largely into the hands of the warden and the rent collector, who were William Langford and his son, Richard. Property repairs, a charge on admission fines, were administered by the stewards in the 15th century, but were now overseen by the warden himself. In 1546 an excess of such repairs, amounting to £5, was charged to the rent account. There are no stewards' accounts after 1538–9; the warden's accounts for 1540–1 include several receipts, transfers *a stauro*, and charges, such as building repairs, stipends and expenses as had customarily appeared in the stewards' accounts. Admission fines were shown in the stewards' accounts, which had reached a peak of £156 in 1515 and fell to £120 in 1533–4 and £43 in 1538–9.[87] The warden accounted for less than £3 of such fines in 1450–1.

Without having any accounts for the Gild treasury we cannot be sure whether the stewards were receiving and accounting for more, but the impression is that the source of income, brethren's dues, was falling catastrophically, perhaps as Protestant objections to paying for prayers gathered force in the community at large. As admission fines customarily provided the funding for property repairs, the stewards' dual function of receiving the income and paying for the repairs rapidly dwindled. Property repairs and the payment of stipends and expenses seem then to have been transferred to the warden, who financed them from both income and transfers *a stauro*. The very large numbers of properties in disrepair, even ruin, at the time of the dissolution in 1551 may well have been a result of the fall in brethren's dues, and the semi-moribundity of the Gild the consequence of a change in religious attitudes.

The Surrender of the Gild

The Chantries Act of 1547 dissolved chantries and religious gilds, and set up commissioners to certify their properties which were put under the administration of the court of Augmentations.[88] The Palmers' Gild was included, although it put up a fight to thwart it, applying to the court itself for a declaration that the Act did not apply to the Gild, as it came within the exception added to the Act whereby foundations confirmed by Henry VIII or Edward VI were to be excluded. Behind this struggle seems to have been the objective of ensuring that the possessions of the Gild came into the hands of the Corporation of Ludlow. The Gild's officers were at pains to emphasise their maintenance of the almshouse (not, however, stressing that they used it to retire their own members in need), the grammar school and the organist in the church. The Gild had a good case in law for their exemption, but political prudence suggested compromise, that is, Corporation control of the Gild endowments at the price of the Gild's abolition; the Crown, for its part, was fearful that, if Ludlow won in open court, other towns would be encouraged similarly to resist, so in 1551 the Crown acceded to Ludlow's petitions and granted the Gild's possessions to the Corporation in return for an annual fee farm rent of £8 13s. 4d. payable into the Court of Augmentations, and upon condition that the Corporation continued to maintain the almshouse, the grammar school and the organist and also maintained a preacher in the church.[89]

We have seen that the last two decades of the Gild's existence seem to have been years of diminishing piety and popularity, but equally years of growing rent-rolls. There is reason

30. The Grammar School, supported by Gild endowments, was transferred to the Corporation after the surrender in 1551.

to think, however, that the estates were not all that well managed. The proportion of ruined property was very high and the gross figures had never been higher. Most of the 'sack rents', the annual rent charges, had not been collected for 12 years; this was particularly reprehensible as half of those unpaid were due from elders of the Gild. A quarter of the Gild's Ludlow property, taking closes and burgages together, was let to senior members who signed the instrument of surrender in 1551 – nearly 10 per cent of it to the warden, William Langford, and his son, Richard, the Gild rent collector. The latter held a life-tenancy of one property, worth 20s. a year, for which he paid one red rose; he paid 4s. rent for 12 acres in Halton field under a 21-year lease granted to him by his father in 1547 a few months before the new Chantry Act, but when it was known that the days of chantries and gilds were numbered.[90] Father and son were aldermen of the town and could be confident that these doubtless beneficial leases would be protected by the transfer. It was alleged in 1552 by John Barkeley in a suit before the Court of Augmentations that William Langford and his son, Richard, together with John Alsoppe and John Taylor *alias* Barker (who may have been the last stewards), had misappropriated rents of £300 over the last three years, as well as taking the Gild plate worth £150; Gild lands had been leased out between 1548 and 1551. Two of those supporting Barkeley were signatories to the surrender, Thomas Cother and Lewis Phillips, the latter, strangely, claiming never to have been a Gild-brother.[91] Most of the pre-dissolution leases which have survived were saved by being in force at the time of surrender. There may have been favouritism in leasing Gild property hitherto; in 1507 Walter Morton, the warden, had granted a 41-year lease of land in Halton field to his son, John, at a 2s. 6d. rent.[92]

The Palmers' Gild and the Corporation

The Gild had played a major part in town life for 350 years. Its officers and elders were generally members of the Twelve and Twenty-Five. The wardens, first to last, were men of standing in the town. Of the nine 13th- and 14th-century wardens only four served as bailiffs of the town: Henry Pigin, in 1291, and William Orletone in 1378–92, doing both jobs at once. Of the 13 wardens in the 15th and 16th centuries only two did not serve as bailiffs.[93]

Between 1364 and 1460 only 22 stewards can be identified; of these only five became bailiff at any time. The first, John Cachepol, was steward during a long spell as bailiff (1352–69); the others' stewardships did not coincide in this way. If there were a Corporation *cursus honorum* at this time there is insufficient evidence to substantiate it or to link it with that of the Gild.

After 1461 Gild office was somewhat loosely linked to the *cursus honorum* of Corporation offices. Limited evidence suggests that being churchwarden may have formed the first qualification for Gild office, as it was for Corporation office. The low bailiffship was of roughly equal seniority with the stewardship, the offices being held in no accepted order. The Gild rentership was usually held after the stewardship, while the Corporation high bailiffship usually came after both these Gild offices. Richard Langford, however, was high bailiff in 1549 while he was Gild renter, another reflection of his family's dominance over both Corporation and Gild affairs at this time. With the apparent exception of Richard Sherman (warden 1472–94), wardens were always appointed from the ranks of former high bailiffs. So the wardenship became the peak of a burgess's public career during which he was freed from being bailiff and probably from any other onerous Corporation office.

Some of the procedural practices of the Gild may have influenced town government. It would be going well beyond the evidence, however, to assume, as is often assumed with gilds of this kind, that the Palmers' Gild was in some way the 'real' government of the town, that the economic interests of merchants who dominated the town were chiefly furthered by the Gild. The municipal ruling body seems to have shown itself, whatever its comparative lack of sophistication, quite capable of looking after the town's interests in general and the merchant class's interests in particular. What we cannot know is whether policies to be promoted in the Corporation's deliberations were first formulated in private within the Gild, but where the town's own council filled its own vacancies and deliberated in secret, another private caucus hardly seems necessary.

31. Will of Richard Downe, warden of the Palmers' Gild, 1535. His period of office (c.1509–c.1535) was probably the most prosperous in the Gild's history.

Palmers' Gild Finances

Gross Rents				Decays and Allowances				Building Costs				Admission Fines				Pentecost Feasts			
Year	£	s.	d.	Year	£	s.	d.	Year	£	s.	d.	Year	£	s.	d.	Year	£	s.	d
1284	5	11	0																
1344–5	24	8	7½													1344–5	2	12	8½
1364–5	37	3	11½	1364–5	7	1	11												
								1377–8	4	14	5½	1377–8	27	10	8	1377–8	5	3	6½
								1423–8	13	17	0	1423–8	22	15	6	1423–8	10	11	7
1439–40	37	0	8½					1437–40	13	8	0	1438–9	9	2	10	1437–40	17	1	2
												1446–7	33	17	0	1446–7	11	15	11
1472–3	78	2	7	1472–3	9	14	2					1472–3	31	0	5				
												1485–9	35	5	8				
1502–3	95	16	7½																
								1505–6	30	16	6					1505–8	17	3	8
1525–6	106	3	2½									1507–9	49	2	0				
								1521–45	24	0	0								
																1534–5	3	0	8
								1538–9	23	4	2½	1538–9	43	2	11	1538–9	1	6	3
								1540–1	3	1	4					1540–1	1	16	4
								1544–5	10	18	6½	1544–5	16	6	8				
1546–7	122	7	11½	1546–7	19	14	2½	1546–7	5	2	1½								
1551	119	0	0	1551	17	0	0												

References: Palmers' Gild rentals and rent-collectors accounts; stewards' accounts; stewards' registers; wardens' accounts for 1540–1, 1544–5.[94] Accounts years were normally Michaelmas to Michaelmas, represented here '1472–3'; where a span of years is given the figures are the yearly average for that period.

Chapter Five

The Council of the March

The Council of the March of Wales existed in some form from 1473 until 1689, apart from 1483–93 and 1641–61.[1] Ludlow provided it from the outset with an important centre and, after 1501, with its main seat. Since Ludlow had become the normal residence of the earls of March in the early 14th century, it had enjoyed the presence of a large noble household, comprising family, retainers, servants, chaplains and officials; the Mortimers, like most magnates, had their councils of advisers and administrators. When the earldom of March descended to Richard, Duke of York, he kept on a larger scale much the same arrangements.

The household and council set up in 1473 for Prince Edward were essentially like this, with public functions added. In 1493 Prince Arthur's household and council was similar, and remained so after his death when the presidency of the council was given to a succession of bishops. Public functions gradually increased as family functions disappeared. Princess Mary's establishment after 1525 was a magnate household and council, with public functions, but without the care of estates. The executive president, however, remained, notwithstanding the royal figurehead. The Council of the March was now permanently established, but its transformation into a form of devolved regional government took place in 1534 with the appointment of Bishop Rowland Lee as president. Not until the late 16th and early 17th centuries did more noble presidents maintain splendid households reminiscent of the earlier royal households. It was the high level of domestic consumption which accompanied them, rather than their administrative or judicial powers, which made them important to Ludlow.

Although the Council developed a permanent establishment which spent most of its time in Ludlow Castle, it did not at any time supplant the autonomous government of the Corporation, nor did it often interfere in the business of the town; such intervention as did take place followed petitions from townsmen either to it or to the Privy Council in London, which usually referred them back to the Council of the March. Members of the Council occasionally adjudicated when interpretation of the town charter was in issue. The Council would have ensured that the politics of Ludlow never got so out of hand that national policy would be either threatened or contravened; apart from that it did not interfere.

A much more pervasive influence, however, came through personal connections. Some important members of the Council became members of the Corporation or M.P.s for Ludlow, Charles Foxe and Sir Henry Townshend among them. For Foxe this was an incident in his lifetime of aggrandisement of offices and property, but Townshend's membership was a mere technicality to qualify him as M.P. Lesser officials of the Council also became members of the Corporation; John Devawe (?Devaux), sergeant-at-arms in the Council of the March, although not by origin a Ludlow man, married the widow of a former bailiff and himself rose to low bailiff in 1593.[2] Another sergeant-at-arms, Thomas Blashfield, was a Ludlow man and, although he did not hold municipal office, he attempted to use his conciliar office in the interests of the Bradford faction by trying to prevent Robert Berry taking his seat in the Commons in 1596, for which he was hauled before the bar of the House.[3] The precise duties of the sergeant-at-arms can only be surmised, but they were neither so onerous nor so well rewarded as to exempt the incumbent from more gainful activity. Blashfield, for instance, was a rich man. There must have been many sergeants-at-arms, but the identities of only three are known. Unlike most, it was not a post funded

32. Tomb of Edward Waties, a local man who became a member of the Council of the March. The tomb is situated in the parish church.

33. Tomb of Edmund Walter, Chief Justice of Chester, a senior judge on the Council of the March (in the parish church).

from fines imposed by the Council. Richard Jones was sergeant-at-arms in 1617 and in 1620 when he was given permission to absent himself in London.[4]

The porter (or keeper) of the castle usually held the keepership of the *spheristerium* or 'Tennis Play'. It seems that this post replaced that of constable of the castle, for there is no distinct reference to the latter post after Edmund Delamare in the 1470s, although Griffith Jones was variously described as 'porter', 'keeper' and 'constable'.[5] The portership was commonly granted as a reversion for life after the current life interest, implying that the post was significant more for its income than its duties. The first porter to play any known part in Ludlow life was Richard Pulton or Pooton (1558–62) who at the same time worked his way up to join the Twenty-Five. His successor may have been briefly Edmund Larkyn, who kept the *Crown* Inn, but he was succeeded in 1564 by Thomas Singleton who kept the office until 1596, and then by the reversionist (since 1572), Robert Berry, who gave up a year later. Berry seems to have lived in Castle Lodge, an obvious place for the castle porter, so it is possible that he had acted as Singleton's deputy for some time, although there is no evidence for it and Singleton certainly drew the pay.[6] Berry was the first porter to be of any significance in the town, being bailiff and M.P. several times. John Hartgill then held the office for 11 years, but neither he nor his successor, Griffith Jones, played much part in the official life of the Corporation. Richard Edwards, the rent collector and bailiff, held the reversion in 1616, but never carried out any duties. Jones was succeeded first in 1623 by Greville Gibbs and then by Arthur Winwood, who did carry out the duties, not wholly to the satisfaction of either the Council of the March or of the Privy Council, being hauled before both for his derelictions.[7]

In general, however, apart from the officials referred to above, most of the officials of the Council of the March played no part in the official life of Ludlow. They were either not present at all and discharged their duties by delegating them to lesser-paid hacks or they were kept busy enough by conciliar duties. The attorneys who practised both officially and privately before the court were more likely to play some such part. Thomas Evans, for instance, practised law and was integrated into Ludlow society by marriage and interest, becoming bailiff himself in 1588.

The Council of the March was often riven by factions, reflecting those which pervaded both the Privy Council and many of the commissions of the Peace throughout the country. There are some hints that these factions had their connections in Ludlow. It would have been surprising had they not, since faction in 16th-century England was a mixture of policy difference and private interest, linked by a network of personal alliances.

In Bishop Lee's time rival personal connections came to the fore in disputes over former monastic property. John Bradshaw, three times bailiff of Ludlow and three times its M.P., married Lee's niece. He obtained some of the property of Wigmore Abbey and was in dispute with Thomas Croft of Croft, a member of the Council of the March, over this. His link with Lee would have been useful to him. Charles Foxe was an opponent of Lee and in 1542 was brought before the Privy Council for slandering him. Foxe, however, was a great survivor who was no one's follower for long; his strength came by maintaining connections wherever he could, and so he outlived accusations of corruption and abuse during a long and successful life.

An important local official of the Council was Richard Broughton, who had family connections with the Crowthers, the Blashfields and Bradfords of Ludlow. These, however, were not allied with faction in the Council, since Broughton was notoriously unfit for his office and his position was undermined by Lord President Pembroke's enquiries into the fitness of officials. In fact, these were the very families who led the opposition to the Ludlow oligarchy and who were ultimately to be blocked by the Privy Council, acting through the Council of the March. Broughton was one of Essex's party and lost his official position

34. Castle Lodge, where prisoners convicted by the Council were kept. Later it became the residence of the Castle Porter.

when Essex was brought to the block.[8] Broughton was a prime mover in the feud with William Sherwood, one of Pembroke's servants, which led in 1603 to a riot and thence to proceedings in Star Chamber, from which Broughton emerged much poorer.[9]

The real impact of the Council upon Ludlow was social and economic. The leading officials of the Council, whether local gentry or career men from afar, were the social superiors of most Ludlow families. Nevertheless the former class generally centred their lives on their country estates, while the latter hoped, sometimes with justification, for their careers to take them back to higher things in London; full integration for these people was impossible. The most minor officials and servants were either locals by origin or became locals by adoption and circumstance; these included pursuivants, clock keepers, clerks, servants, artisans, sempstresses, laundrywomen and ushers. The total salary bill of the Council varied from year to year; in 1580 it was £568; in 1603, £520; in 1607, £399; and in 1615, £687.[10] A large part of this must have been spent in Ludlow on the maintenance of the household of the Council, administrative support and repair of buildings, chiefly Ludlow Castle.

The chief source of income for the Council was the fines levied by its court. Between 1576 and 1582 these averaged £1,118 a year.[11] The level rose at the turn of the century with £3,910 being levied in 1600 and £2,139 the following year; this was a temporary surge and fines fell to £1,186 levied (of which £421 was subsequently discharged) in 1614 and

35.   The *Angel* Inn, one of the inns which catered for officials, lawyers and litigants attending the Council.

36.   The house of Rees Jones, an attorney at the Council. Built *c.*1620, it later became the *Feathers* inn and hotel.

£800 in 1615.[12] More of these sums were spent in Ludlow than had been levied on Ludlow people.

As early as 1464 £30 13s. 4d. was provided by John Milewater, receiver general for castles, to pay for repairs on Ludlow Castle.[13] In 1510–11 the chapel was re-roofed and major repairs were carried out between 1518 and 1525 when Princess Mary took up residence.[14] This programme was in the hands of Ludlow men, like Walter Rogers and Ralph Bradshaw. A period of neglect followed. In 1534–5 it was left to the receiver-general of the earldom of March to pay £10 1s. 10d. for castle repairs.[15] Bishop Lee, then president, thought the castle to be unfit for use. Considerable repairs were carried out in 1537–9, when timber from the 'Friary House' became available. Lee claimed to have spent over £100 at this time. Nevertheless in 1535 Sir Thomas Englefield thought that there was such decay that it was not possible to reside there.[16] The Porter's Lodge, which played some part in the Council's later disciplinary activities, was built in 1552–3 at the order of William Herbert, Earl of Pembroke.[17] From the 1580s the maintenance of the buildings formed a main charge on the funds of the receiver of fines. This reflected the development of a stable and continuous jurisdiction, the income from which was ample and steady. In 1582–3, £487 was spent[18] and in 1596–7 a new stable in the outer bailey cost £574.[19] This was the period when the chapel of St Peter was converted into a court house for the Council.

Expenditure averaged about £420 a year in the early 17th century, much of which would have been spent in Ludlow. In 1615–16 the expenses which the Council incurred to the benefit of Ludlow residents included 10s. paid to William Pingle for cleaning the castle walls, 15s. to Thomas Gruffith for 'killing noysome vermin as ratts and mices in Ludlow

37.   Corve Street: the riot which followed the attempt in 1603 to abduct Susan Blashfield took place here.

castle', 12s. to Richard Adams for renewing the arms on the Castle gate and in the garden house, £1 16s. 6d. for repairing furniture and wooden fixtures in the residential quarters, 4s. to a goldsmith for mending plate, 18s. to Francis Bosley, a Ludlow carrier, for bringing linen from London, and £1 5s. 4d. to the *Bull* Inn for lodging a preacher.[20] There was some expenditure outside Ludlow; luxury goods were brought from afar, as were many foodstuffs, to judge from the 1615 accounts of the clerk of the kitchen.[21]

To this must be added the need of the Council's staff, the attorneys practising there and litigants for accommodation and victualling. This supported several lodging houses and inns. Overall the Council may have been worth in income to Ludlow as much as, or more than, the cloth trade itself. Whether this was a good thing in the long term may be doubted; like the windfall of the Palmers' Gild estates, which provided great opportunities for private exploitation, the profits from the Council's presence may have come too easily and so blunted the commercial enterprise of Ludlow's residents. A chill wind blew when the Council was eventually abolished.

The Council also brought benefits to Ludlow of a less tangible nature, although we do not know how much ordinary Ludlow residents participated in them. On 5 November 1615 and again on 18 March 1615/16 the Council was entertained at a cost of 20s. and 30s. by 'The Queen's Players' (presumably a London company); but musicians were apparently more to hand, for a group was present from 18 November 1615 to 16 January 1615/16, and cost £3 6s. 8d. In 1614 players and musicians were paid a total of £6 3s. and the year before that 20s.[22]

The town certainly regarded the Council as a benefit, for, when Parliament prepared to abolish it along with the other prerogative courts in 1642, the bailiffs petitioned Parliament against abolition, citing the 'great conflux of people [who] did resort to the said Town to have justice administered unto them', declaring that 'the inhabitants . . . for the entertainment of such suitors did dispose and make fit their homes and laid out their stocks in making provision . . . and by that means they maintained their families, relieved the poor and paid all taxes laid upon the town', and claiming that the town, having no 'means of trading', would 'fall into great poverty and misery'. Given the state of the cloth trade at the time, this may not have been an exaggeration.[23]

Chapter Six

The Economy

Agriculture

The early growth of a semi-urban settlement outside the castle walls seems very likely. Not only was it within a few hundred yards of an ancient north-south route, crossing the River Teme at the best ford for some miles, but it would itself have had needs to be met; it would have attracted visitors itself, also needing supplies.

Manorial lords founded boroughs for the rents and other perquisites arising to them from trade and the concentration of people and wealth. Boroughs failed which, like Richard's Castle, were too artificial and dependent upon lordly favour or could not overcome competition from rivals. Ludlow was able to exploit existing advantages. A semi-urban settlement may well have preceded the formal enfranchisement as a borough.

The earliest development may have taken this form. The castle itself was the largest institution for a long way in any direction; it depended upon supplies and labour from much of that area, some bought and hired, and some taken as dues from the manorial estates owned by the same lords. Later some holdings in the district were held on condition of support services; earlier there may have been more of them.[1] The castle developed as the administrative centre of the Lacy estates in south Shropshire; it was where surpluses there gathered.[2] Ludlow became a participator in this agricultural distribution and control system, so its people had standing opportunities to profit from supplying the castle with produce and manufactures and perhaps from disposing of surpluses. This would have been the basis of a market economy of sorts. A market for agricultural produce for local farmers would have grown naturally along with this.

Ludlow began as an agricultural centre and remained a local market for 900 years; it was the business which occupied most of its inhabitants directly or indirectly. Apart from consumption trades and support services for the lords and, later, the Council of the March, all based at the castle, Ludlow's business was agriculture, distribution of produce and livestock, agricultural support trades and trades based on agricultural produce, wool, cloth, and tanning and leather work.

The boundaries of the borough were wide, stretching from the Corve in the north to the Teme in the south, from the Teme in the west to the ends of the Galdefords in the east.[3] Ludlow's boundaries have been dictated to a large extent by the area of land encompassed by the Corve-Teme loop and so they included a great deal of agricultural land, some of which has remained agricultural until now. Some was 'burgaged', that is, laid out in plots of regular dimensions and subject to the rights and obligations of burgage tenure throughout the town, but this does not imply that it was built on, although it is possible that in an early access of enthusiasm it was hoped that building would take place. Occasional references in medieval records to 'tofts' imply that some of these plots had at one time been built on but were no longer. This does not, however, seem to have been general and we need not suppose that large areas of Ludlow had been first built up and later reverted to agricultural land.

Linney was burgaged even where the River Teme floods every year, an unlikely place to contemplate building. Whether it was flooded before the weir was built is not known, but it is unlikely that the burgage-holders would have accepted a weir if it did not and there were buildings there. That, however, would have depended on the degree to which

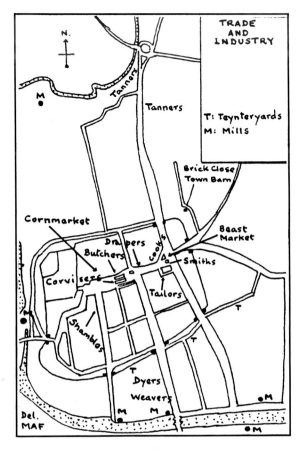

38.   Trade and industry.

the lords, who built the weir to serve the castle mill, could extinguish the property rights of burgage-holders. Attentive though the times were to property rights, both the extension of the castle's outer bailey and the building of the town walls must have involved the destruction of buildings and the extinction of private property. Nevertheless, throughout our period significant areas of land within the borough were cultivated by the inhabitants, much for direct domestic consumption, that is, food crops, animal fodder, mostly hay, and probably flax, although growing for the town markets was probably very profitable.[4] By the late 13th century many of the cultivators rented these meadows, pastures and closes. Owners of property were already less numerous than occupiers.

There were also wide areas of town lands in Stanton Lacy, but within the liberties of Ludlow, which were also farmed by Ludlow residents. The origin of these fields and liberties is unknown, but probably date from the settlement of the town itself. These were originally rented from the lords, but formally from 1461 (and informally much earlier) the Corporation became the landlord. Obtaining favourable leases of town lands became a preoccupation of Ludlow politics. The Lord's meadow was let to Richard Bailey for 18s. a year, but he let it out at £4 a year, perceived as an unacceptable profit achieved through political influence.[5] The town's liberties also extended into the Halton fields in Bromfield parish and into Overton township in Ludford.

When the borough was established, the demesne lands within and without the town remained in the lords' hands for direct exploitation. By the late 13th century they were generally administered by the bailiffs who collected the rents on behalf of the lords, although they may have frequently formed part of the 'farm' of the borough, whereby the Community enjoyed the profits and paid for it through an overall rent for all borough rents. In 1288–9 the demesnes were rented out to 'Lawrence' (who was known outside the town as 'Lawrence de Ludelowe'), Thomas Eylrihc, Geoffrey Goldsmith, Henry Furbet and Peter Gilemin, paying over 68s. a year. For 28s. 3d. Thomas Eylrihc (and in the following year Adam Caynham) rented the castle meadow, lordship land always associated with the castle rather than with the borough. Although there was considerable continuity in tenancies, the lettings were renewable annually, ensuring that the lordship derived the full benefit of rack-rents and kept full control over the land. Evidence of direct cultivation of the demesne lands is limited to a reference in William Leynthale's account for 1328 in which he set out payments for seed for Visepolesmedwe and Dodmore fields, but such conditions for tenancies would have made switching from letting to cultivation quite easy.[6]

Parts of the demesne lands were later let rent-free to the bailiffs as perquisites of office; in the 16th century the bailiffs took farming this land very seriously. Many of the disputes over misgovernment in the town centred on the use and misuse of these rights; many parts of the demesne lands, for instance, were treated as common each year 'after sickle and scythe', although the Corporation frequently attempted to alienate these common rights by exempting one of their senior members from his obligations or by permitting enclosure and cultivation. By the 16th century there were several 'closes' (that is, usually fenced or hedged enclosures) within the town fields, the work on which implies the application of private capital.[7] St John's Hospital had particularly extensive holdings in each of the town fields. In the late 16th century the bailiffs had the right to one-third of the corn grown on the demesne lands, which had to be delivered to the town barn; they also took 20 loads of hay from Corve and Hucklemarsh meadows. In September 1597 Richard Benson, then bailiff, found his *ex officio* corn and hay from Corve Meadow and Hucklemarsh Field forcibly removed by his opponents while it was waiting to be 'inned', that is, gathered in.[8] These may have been ancient lordship rights which devolved upon the Corporation's officials after 1461. The demesne lands were an important part of the Ludlow economy and provided a substantial part of the income of residents over many centuries.

Ludlow, therefore, like many towns, had a class of resident farmers who lived in the town and went out to farm their lands in the countryside. At harvest time they would bring the crops back into the town to their private barns. Any empty building would do; in 1598 the town corn was 'inned' in St Leonard's chapel.[9] Several barns were built in Galdeford, being closest to the town fields. There were few full-time farmers of this sort; most Ludlow agriculturalists combined the activity with other trades and interests, presumably mostly relying on members of their families and on servants to do much of the time-consuming work. William Beck (*c.*1533–1613), high bailiff in 1597, was one of the minority of full-time farmers, always described as 'yeoman' or 'husbandman', who seems to have had no other trade. Because of the intricate pattern of demesne rights, common rights and tenant rights, there were frequent disputes over entitlements to crops, and from these disputes we get a picture of well-to-do Ludlow bourgeois visiting their fields, checking on their servants and watching their rivals, sometimes engaging in altercations and brawls with the latter. In 1439 Edmund Morys accused William Tranter and Walter Howe of stealing six cartloads of grass and hay from his close;[10] in 1610 John Passey accused Francis Smalman of taking his corn from Talltree Close – an old dispute since in 1587 he had prosecuted Gilbert Smalman and Philip Bradford in the Council of the Marches over a land dispute in which Bradford set a mastiff onto Passey's servants.[11] Over the centuries these agriculturalists increasingly rented their land to local farmers, but some always preferred to take the crops for their own account.

In addition to the demesne and burgaged lands within the borough and its liberties there were quite extensive gardens behind most of the houses and shops in the town. Burgages were typically narrow on the street, but usually very long back from the street, 200 ft. not being unusual. Although outhouses of various kinds were built in the back this still left a great deal of space for growing garden produce and, probably, flax and hemp, and there is little doubt that it was so used. At least half the 'built-up' area of Ludlow consisted of cultivable land throughout the period. The Corporation rental of 1592 also lists 130 gardens as separate properties.[12] Orchards were common in the town, the largest and oldest of which may have been the Lord's Orchard, a stretch of demesne land between the town wall and the Teme from Dinham to Mill Street. This may have been the garden of which half was owned by Nicholas de Verdun in 1271 and by Theobald de Verdun in 1309. The value of the whole of this garden rose between 1271 and 1329 from 16s. to 20s. a year, which may be some evidence of the rising value of agricultural land and possibly a clue to rising population.[13] In 1368 the Lord's Orchard was farmed out for 13s. and in 1423 it was rented to John Rokeley for 13s. 4d.[14] After 1461 it was let by the Corporation. There were at least six other orchards rented out by the Corporation and there may have been others wholly in private hands. In 1558 Richard Hanley left an orchard in the Narrow Lane; Thomas Wheler died in 1568 owning an orchard in Old Street; William Bedowe held one on the west side of Corve Street in 1590.[15] The chief crop was apples, mostly used in cider-making.

Ludlow was a natural centre of the livestock trade. Ludlow people also kept animals both within the town and on the common lands outside. This was economically important as is shown by a 1221 dispute over pasture with the Abbot of Gloucester, who, through the priory of Bromfield, owned much of Whitcliffe over the Teme from Ludlow.[16] Subsequently the burgesses bought the grazing rights on Whitcliffe in perpetuity from the abbot and from Jordan, lord of Ludford, in return for rights of toll-free trading in Ludlow and other considerations. The quarrying rights there remained with the abbot.[17] The castle meadow, running below the castle along the Teme to its confluence with the Corve, was never part of the original borough but remained in Stanton Lacy parish, still part of the lordship of Ludlow. Its exclusion may have been because it was once used for grazing the castle's horses. In practice it was rented out as grazing to Ludlow residents by the bailiffs acting for the lords. After 1461 the rights were generally leased out by the Crown. Horses provided transport and in a town like Ludlow might well have numbered 500; a great deal of grazing and hay would have been required close at hand and found in the pastures and meadows in Ludlow. Horses, being necessary and comparatively valuable beasts, would not have been left unattended, so the gathering of hay from the further fields was essential. Hay was as important a local crop as corn; disputes, thefts and brawls over hay were frequent as late as the early 17th century.

Every household of substance would have owned a horse, while most would have owned other livestock. Even comparatively poor people would have kept a pig or a cow in their backyards. Between 1540 and 1659, 52 Ludlow wills include specific bequests of animals, with totals of over 200 cattle and 730 sheep, but this would greatly understate their numbers, as they would need to be mentioned only where there were to be specific bequests. Lawrence Beck, a weaver (d. 1579), left 69 cattle, 80 sheep and a number of horses, kept in Ludlow and on three farms he owned in surrounding counties.[18] The shortage of grazing close to the town is evidenced by the distance at which livestock was put out to graze in the keeping of relatives, friends and tenants, usually as a matter of business. In this Ludlow was typical of all the towns of the March. Stock owned in Ludlow could be kept at Henley, a few miles away, like William Mershetone's two oxen in the keeping of Hugh Pole and John Edwards in 1436 and Philip Hibbins's sheep in the keeping of Thomas Nicholls of Farlow in 1584.[19] Provided a trustworthy keeper could be found, it was worth putting cattle and horses bred for sale to graze in central Wales, where grazing was abundant and cheap; many did this. They would expect to see their stock only when it came to market to be sold, if indeed it came to Ludlow for this. In 1551 John Clee, a cordwainer, rented out a farm in Overton to his brother, but kept cattle and sheep in Llandyssil and Kerry in Montgomeryshire.[20]

Although sheep provided meat, it was mostly tough meat, for in Shropshire the flocks were kept chiefly for their wool used in the wool export trade of the 13th and 14th centuries and in the cloth-weaving trade throughout. When these trades were at their most prosperous Ludlow-owned flocks would not have supplied more than a fraction of the wool needed. The latter were, however, a profitable side-line, possibly achieving better returns than the flocks owned by people unconnected with the entrepreneurs of the wool and cloth trades. In 1573 William Harrys owned 60 sheep at Llanbadarn Vynydd whose wool he sold to Richard Hoke who would have made cloth from it. In 1617 Thomas Candland had 180 sheep as well as other livestock which he probably kept on his lands at Bettws-y-Crwyn and Beguildy.[21]

After 1600 the numbers of Ludlow people who owned substantial numbers of livestock at a distance greatly declined, although farming property held at a distance did not. Wills mentioning cattle owned far away were much less numerous after 1600; sheep-owning at a distance was at a high level between 1570 and 1620, declining thereafter. The numbers of testators owning land outside Ludlow, often in central Wales, remained at a high level throughout the period 1540–1660; it is no more than an impression, however, that it was only earlier in this period that such lands represented reinvested commercial fortunes rather than inherited family estates or fortunes acquired through government office. This may be evidence of a lessening of entrepreneurship in favour of property-owning, as happened in Ludlow's manufacturing trades, particularly after the collapse of the cloth trade.

Pigs were kept all over the town and the obnoxious conditions they created led to frequent prosecutions, like that in 1553 of Elinor Huckisley of Corve Street whose 'piggescote' was held to be to the hurt of her neighbours.[22] In 1476 the town court issued an order forbidding pigs within the town walls under pain of confiscation; this probably had no more effect than most contemporary general prohibitions, whether national or municipal. Poultry were probably kept everywhere, but the records are few, apart from the interesting fact that the Townshends kept turkeys at The Friars in Lower Galdeford as early as 1626.[23] In 1291 John Durant had to seek sanctuary after stealing a beehive in Ludlow.[24] Richard Swanson, an ironmonger (d. 1577), kept bees, perhaps on the close in Linney rented from the Corporation.[25] Pigeons were also kept, despite their depredations upon cultivators. Culver-house Close, next to the Corve at the north end of Linney, was an early dovecote or pigeonhouse. There were others, like Ellis Evans's pigeonhouse in Corve Street.[26]

Fish was an important part of diet, partly for religious reasons, both before and after the Reformation, and partly because it was for many people the only opportunity to eat protein which was not already going bad. Fishing was a gratuitous resource until the weir-ponds were created. The mill-sluice under the castle was a source of income for the Corporation as early as 1367, when it was rented out for 5s.; in 1423 it was stated that it used to be let for 13s. 4d. but by then was let along with the mill. This may have been the mill-sluice which the Community was letting out in 1317 to Robert Sarote and others.[27] The Palmers' Gild owned the Linney fulling mill and reserved the fishing there to its chaplains (1439 Rental). The mill-sluices, although artificial, were created for purposes other than fishing; elsewhere, however, artificial ponds were created at least as early as 1313 at Fishpool meadow and Fishpool Lane.[28] Others were created by the Austin Friars in the Whitebrook flowing from St. Julian's Well to the Teme.[29] The 1846 tithe map shows a Fishcage meadow, which implies the use of this method of trapping fish in running water, probably a long way back. The frequent prosecutions before the town court for pollution of the rivers were probably in the interests of saving the fishing; more positive concern is shown by the order of the town court in 1468 regulating the size of mesh to be used.[30]

Not only freshwater fish were eaten. Henry Kyngeslone was accused by the Abbot of Reading of seizing a six-horse cart loaded with wine and salted herrings in 1372 while it passed through Ludlow; the implication is that the herrings came from a northern fishing port and were going to Leominster Priory of which the abbot was the superior.[31] In 1428 the Palmers' Gild bought one barrel of herrings from Bristol, the carriage of which cost 22d.; it was a luxury still.[32]

The numbers of animals kept in or passing through Ludlow must have produced great

39.   St Julian's Well, one of the sources of Ludlow's water in the Middle Ages.

amounts of dung, in the right place a valuable commodity, used both to manure fields and in the tanning trade. Unsurprisingly, however, it comes to notice only when a cause for complaint. For several years in the early 1550s Alice Sankey was accused of keeping a dungheap in Lower Corve street and latterly for polluting the Corve with it. The dung was probably intended for use in the tanning trade centred in that street.[33]

The Mills

The original town mills were built on demesne land – probably paid for by the Lacys. Mills, serving a prosperous town, would have been a steady source of seigneurial income. There were nine mill sites in or close to Ludlow, six on the River Teme. Domesday Book records a mill worth 6s. in Ludford and two mills worth 26s. in Stanton Lacy. As the Teme, then without the weirs, was a turbulent stream in 1086, it is unlikely that the very small community of Ludford could have built a mill on its banks; it was probably on the brook which joins the river downstream from Steventon, where an adjoining field was called Mill Field in 1846.

Weirs were later built to exploit the fall of the Teme. Occasionally even the gradient could not prevent the river freezing and the mills coming to a halt; this may have happened in December 1325.[34]

The earliest mills on the Teme were at the ends of Mill Street and Broad Street, where the bed-slope gradient is steeper than on any other section.[35] On the Ludlow bank they were all Lacy mills. The Mill Street site may be the earliest (12th century) and may have given the street its name. The Broad Street mill was the fulling mill on the Teme given by Peter Undergod to St John's Hospital as part of its original endowment in about 1231. All cloth made in Ludlow had to be fulled there for a fee – a seigneurial right of very great value. The Old Street mill was of later building; as late as 1331 it was known as the 'New Mill', presumably to distinguish it from the Mill Street mill known as the Old Mill in 1346.

The first record of any of the mills within the borough boundaries is from 1241. Ludlow being in the hands of the king, John Lestrange was ordered to rebuild the Corve mill if it seemed to him more profitable to do so than to let the site.[36] As the Corve, a less strongly flowing river than the Teme, was likely therefore to have had a mill later than the Teme, and as its mill was in need of rebuilding, it suggests that, not only was the first building of a Corve mill some time in the past, but the other mills were even older, probably mid-12th century in origin. We do not know what Lestrange did, but the mill must have been rebuilt by 1261 as it was mentioned in the charter by which John de Verdun and Geoffrey de Genevile exchanged property in Ludlow and Weobley.[37] In 1274 Wigmore foresters were said to have abducted the lord's miller from the Corve mill.[38]

While the lordship was in single ownership before 1241 it is possible that the mills were managed for the lord by a bailiff, rather than leased to a tenant.

When the lordship of Ludlow was divided between the Geneviles and Verduns, the coheirs received, not two mills each, but a half of all four mills. This hints at how Ludlow was administered for the next two or three centuries. If each proprietor had to share each mill, it was impossible for him either to manage the mill himself or to appoint his own tenant. There had to be intermediaries whose task it was to make or receive the profits and pay over the shares to the respective proprietors; the intermediaries were the officials who ran the borough.

The Verdun moiety of the four mills remained with that family and its heirs until 1358 when it passed to the earls of March along with the Verdun moiety of the borough. This moiety remained part of the earldom of March until Edward IV's charter, under which the moiety of the mills passed to the Corporation.[39] The Genevile moiety of the mills, however, was given by Geoffrey de Genevile to Aconbury Priory in 1267.[40] Aconbury continued to collect the rents due from borough officials until the priory was dissolved in 1536.[41] Before 1535 the division of rights to the profits of the mills was administered amicably but, when the Aconbury moiety came into Crown hands, there followed long and bitter litigation between the Corporation and the Crown, ending in a costly defeat for the Corporation.[42]

Another ambitious undertaking was at Ludford near the bridge. This shared a weir with the Old Street mills on the north bank and can therefore be dated to before 1241. There were two fulling mills here in 1349 and 1350, when they were given to the Gild in an access of post-Black Death piety.[43]

In 1270 the Verdun moiety was declared to be worth £13 a year but in 1327 only £10.[44] One of the mills may have been demolished. From the early 14th century three, rather than four, jointly-owned mills are recorded; two at the foot of Mill Street and one at the foot of Old Street.[45]

In 1406 Aconbury convent received 66s. 8d. from the mills there; the same amount was received in 1535 by the king's receiver, then comprising 40s. from two mills at the end of Mill Street, leased to Thomas Talbott and Richard Milwarde and 26s. 8d. from one old mill leased to Thomas Rascall; the 'old mill' must surely be the one so described at the foot of Old Street. The three mills in 1535 were identical with those existing in 1406. This is supported by the bailiff's account of 1368, that is, after the Mortimer-Ferrars exchange, where three mills are described as 'formerly William de Ferrars'.[46] Independent descriptions of the two shares of the same mills agree that there were now only three.

The latest mill site to be developed was that of the castle mill or mills. This did not exist when the mills of Ludlow were divided between the Lacy heiresses, for it would surely have been subjected to the same division. In 1331, however, Joan Mortimer was granted two mills along with a third of the moiety of the town as her dower. These had, therefore, to be new mills, so the building of the castle mills can be ascribed to the early 14th century. The castle mill appears in the account of 1368 as being far more important than the other three mills, requiring more expense, handling more grain and producing more income.[47] It was built below the castle, but was not part of the castle; the division of the borough, apart from the other three mills, was a territorial one rather than merely a financial one. The Mortimers could not have built a new mill for themselves unless the site belonged to them entirely.

A mill, particularly a water mill, was the largest and most valuable piece of industrial plant in a medieval town. When buttressed by a seigneurial monopoly, even one that had been leased out, it would, if a corn mill, have affected the lives of all the inhabitants by influencing the cost of their daily bread and beer, or, if a fulling mill, have dominated the town's cloth manufacturing trade, being more important than a dye plant (although the fullers and dyers were often connected). Capital expenditure was often considerable. Corporations were the only persons, apart from the nobility, capable of financing such enterprises.

About 1505 the Gild carried out work on its Ludford fulling mill which extended over several weeks and involved several workmen.[48] Not enough accounts have survived for us to know whether this was typical for annual repairs, but the impression is gained that this society did not maintain property and machinery so much as repair or replace it when it had fallen into 'decay', which would have been a costly and wasteful policy when the pace of technological innovation alone would seldom have justified replacement.

The mills experienced many changes of fortune between 1350 and 1500. The Corve mill was described as a fulling mill in 1444, as was the Linney mill in 1439.[49] The two mills on the south bank at Ludford bridge seem always to have been fulling mills, but in 1417 the Hospital was licensed to convert its fulling mills into corn mills, although that in Broad Street later reverted to fulling. The Sheet mill was a corn or grist mill in 1494, although that, too, later became a fulling mill.[50] The seigneurial mills were always corn mills.

That there was an economic need for another and larger mill in the early 14th century suggests that Ludlow was at the height of its prosperity – or at least that its population had reached an historically high level.

The division of ownership of three mills determined the manner in which the lords took their income from them. Few conventual houses, other than the Cistercians, involved themselves directly in productive processes, preferring to take rents. Aconbury did just this with its interest in the Ludlow mills. The Verduns did the same. In 1286–7 the receipts from the mills for the quarter ending at Michaelmas were £3 17s. 11d. and for the following 12 months £5 7s. 9d., the harvest period producing most of the income, which came from running, rather than leasing, the mills. In 1312 John Routone accounted to the Community for the mills.[51] The Community ran the mills at this time for its own profit, paying 11 marks rent to Aconbury. The Verduns' dues came through the farm of the moiety of the borough.

The account for 1368 includes the bailiffs' expenses for repairing and running the mills as well as their profits therefrom.[52] Richard Paunteley was described both as bailiff and as keeper of the mill, that is, on behalf of the Community. In the 14th century the involvement of the Community in the mills was much more entrepreneurial than it was to become two centuries later when leasing out was usual. In 33 weeks in 1368 Paunteley sold the produce of the mills for £24 10s. 11½d. His expenditure included the cost of three horses and half the cost of four others (the other half being borne by Aconbury or its tenant), totalling £5 3s. 10d., less 7s. from the sale of old horses. This account shows that the cost in hay of the castle mill was half as much again as the total cost of hay for the two moieties of the Old Street and Mill Street mills, although the number of horses used in the period was two at the castle mill and one each at Mill Street and Old Street. The hay cost, however, overstates the relative dominance of the castle mill, for sales of the output of the mills (after adding back an estimate for tithes and doubling up the other mills' figures for the Aconbury share) shows that in the 33 weeks the castle mill produced 335 bushels of wheat, mixtal and malted wheat and oats, while the other three mills sold 362 bushels. Nevertheless it is plain that the castle mill was at this time by far the most important of the four mills in the town. Repairs on this mill cost as much as those on the other three.[53]

In 1406 Aconbury received a rent of 66s. 8d. for its moiety (with several years' arrears of rent) from the constable. The 1424 bailiffs' accounts show that they were receiving on behalf of the lord the same sum from their moiety. The valor of 1443 shows the Duke of York to have been due to receive 53s. 4d. from the old mill (?Mill Street), 40s. from the Old Street mill and £8 6s. 8d. from the castle mills. There was in addition 6s. 8d. from the fulling mill on the Corve in Linney.[54] In that year 75s. 8d. was spent on repairs of an unspecified mill or mills. Repairs were not the lessee's responsibility at this time, although at the end of the next century tenants were expected to repair and develop the mills at their own expense. This may be another sign of the lack of entrepreneurial spirit which the chartered borough displayed compared with the economic vigour of its proprietorial predecessor. By 1427 the tenants were named for the first time – Henry and Thomas Milward.[55] The former was still a tenant in 1482 and paying the same rent, although Alice Milward and John a Corte were respectively named as tenants – perhaps sub-tenants – of the Old Street mill in those years. In 1512 the borough and Aconbury collaborated in paying for the repair of the Old Street mill.

In the 16th and early 17th centuries the mills declined. The Gild fulling mills at Ludford were added to the Corporation estates in 1552. In 1619 they brought in a gross income of £18 13s. 8d., although expenses were continual and high. There were two fulling mills in lower Broad Street in 1619, while there were two fulling mills and a corn mill at Steventon in 1603.[56]

The castle mills remained the dominant mills of the town. In 1424 they brought in a rent of £8 6s. 8d. which still obtained in 1482 when William Croket had been the tenant for some years. The rent had fallen to £7 13s. 4d. by 1540, remaining at this level until at least 1619. In that year the tenants of the two castle mills were Jones and Norncott.[57]

Although the castle mills had been included in the borough estates in the charter of 1461, so that in return for the Crown's fee farm rent the profits of the mills accrued to the Corporation, the position was less clear with the other mills. The lord's moiety fell to the Corporation, but the Aconbury moiety did not, so when the convent was dissolved in 1536 its moiety fell to the Crown. The Corporation regarded the power to lease out the whole as its own and in 1537 let the old mill to John Bowland for 31 years; this lease was either assigned or sub-let.[58] Doubtless the Corporation's view of its right to choose the tenants for both moieties sprang from centuries of complaisance in the matter by Aconbury. The Old Street mill was leased from 1528 to 1545 to Thomas Rascall, father of Richard Rascall, and he and his successors continued to pay a rent of 53s. 4d. in all to the two landlords until about 1567. In 1535 the tenants of the Mill Street mills were Thomas Talbot and Richard Milward, who were still paying £4 rent. By 1540, however, the Mill Street rents had risen to £6, according to the borough accounts.[59] It was in about 1567 that disputes arose; in that year the Crown leased its moiety to Ellis Wynn and Robert Newman for 21 years at a total rent of £4 6s. 8d.; when this lease expired a 21-year lease was granted to Edward Lewis. It is apparent that these were head-leases, for the actual occupiers seem to have been townsmen who paid their rents in the first instance to the Corporation. The Crown and its grantees seemed equally complacent until the early 17th century, when the Corporation nominees began to demolish and replace the mills and add to the number on the same sites; this effectively 'watered down' the relative interest of the Crown tenants, possibly even displaced it. Neither these tenants nor the Crown were ultimately disposed to accept the position.

The rapid decline of cloth manufacture in the early 17th century brought changes to the mills. The larger of the Ludford bridge fulling mills was pulled down about 1600 and replaced by a small corn mill, but the smaller fulling mill survived until the 1620s. Both mills were then demolished by the new lessee, Thomas Colerick, a butcher, who built three new corn mills. The fulling mills at Steventon were left to deteriorate, but the corn mill was repaired by Rees Jones, and it was then used by Ludlow people to the detriment of the Ludlow mills.[60] The Broad Street fulling mills continued to work until 1659 and thereafter intermittently until the late 19th century.

The Old Street mill was occupied by the Gregory family, John, his son, William, and his son, Edmund. In 1610 William Gregory obtained a lease at the old rent of 53s. 4d.; he rebuilt the mill and built a second mill by its side in 1620. The two Mill Street mills were leased to William Huck and later to Edmund Walter and his son, James. Their under-tenants were Thomas Bedo and, later, his widow, Edith. By this time the annual rent had increased to £6. Richard Edwards held one of the Mill Street mills in 1615 and built another beside it in 1628.[61] In 1621 the newer of the two Mill Street mills was tenanted by Samuel Lloyd, who had acquired the lease from Thomas Fowler of Bitterley for £30 and who rebuilt it in 1631. Lloyd had first to sue Bonham Norton and Thomas Bayton of Church Stretton to whom Fowler had previously mortgaged the mill.[62] The tenurial interests in the mills in the early 17th century were a complex series of short leases and sub-leases which proved difficult to unravel in evidence given in the various court proceedings.

Now the Corporation and its tenants ran into trouble. In 1634 Alexander Gretton, clerk of the spicery in the royal Household, was granted a Crown lease of the moiety of all five mills. The Corporation claimed that both moieties now belonged to it, and the case, in various specific forms, came before the Court of Exchequer. In 1634 judgement was given against the Corporation which was required to hand over the mills on the old sites and to pull down new mills on new sites.[63] A new Crown lease for 99 years at £6 13s. 4d. was made to Gretton in 1636.[64] The Corporation tenants, the Gregorys, Lloyds and Edwardses, were dispossessed, which, after their considerable capital outlays in the recent past, must have nearly ruined them; William Gregory, described as 'an ancient alderman fallen into want', had to apply to the Corporation for a handout in 1638. The court case was followed by an agreement between the Corporation and Gretton, whereby the former was to pay the latter £900 for his past losses and to convey in perpetuity to him their own moiety of the mills in return for a rent of £4 6s. 8d.[65] Gretton later claimed that the Corporation had not kept its side of the bargain.[66] Nevertheless the Corporation was forced to borrow £936, secured on the demesne lands, to pay legal costs and Gretton's damages.[67] Gretton left the mills to his heirs in 1673.[68]

Although there were no 'private' water mills in the borough, there were competing mills in neighbouring parishes. There was a fulling mill in Ludford in the mid-13th century, which was given by John, lord of Ludford, to Richard Boys, lord of Sheet, *tempore* Henry III.[69] It was probably that owned by Nicholas Andrew and later by his son, William, lords of that manor.[70] In 1349–50 Richard Stone gave an annual rent from a Ludford fulling mill to the Palmers' Gild. John Brune gave the Gild his interest in the mill by the bridge. The Gild acquired a powerful stake in the mills of the area, for it also owned the mill in Linney by 1397, when it leased it on a 60-year lease for 20s. a year. Such a rent implies large potential profits.[71]

Peter Undergod was a party to a charter in the mid–13th century which referred to a Ludford mill.[72] This was probably not the Ludlow fulling mill which Undergod obtained from the Lacys.[73] Thomas Ludeford sued William son of Hugh Deghere in 1306 for building a mill to the harm of his own free tenement in Ludford, perhaps his own mill, for in 1316 William Waterledare gave a mill in Ludford, held of Thomas Ludeford's widow, Juliana, to St John's Hospital. The Hospital is recorded as leasing it in 1350 to Roger Smyth and Adam Meuryk.[74] The Hospital acquired another mill in Ludford from Richard Estham in 1364.[75] Although the water mill in Steventon which John de la More, lord of Steventon, granted for life to John Munetone, a miller, in 1330 was probably a corn mill, before the dissolution of religious houses in 1536 it seems that most of the mills around Ludlow found their way into the hands of secular or religious corporations whose attitude to their property was not so much entrepreneurial as increasingly seigneurial, even monopolistic.[76]

The only water mills surviving within the borough by the 17th century were corn mills. Further down the Teme, however, were fulling mills, usually owned by Ludlow people. There were three mills in Ludford on the north bank of the river in 1639; by then they were all corn mills, but previously there had been only two fulling mills. One of these had been pulled down c.1600 and the other c.1627. These demolitions reflect the sudden and disastrous decline in Ludlow cloth-manufacture at that time.[77]

It was worth building corn mills in Ludford at this time; that tenants were also rebuilding and adding to the Old Street and Mill Street mills suggests that the markets and profits were there to be had. In 1632 the castle mills, also called 'the Lord's mills', were described as decayed and it may be that it was as much a substitution of supply as absolute increase in the demand which supported these new buildings.[78]

The mill at the northern end of Broad Linney on the Corve was given to the Palmers' Gild in 1330 by the executors of John Bromfild and leased at once to William Leintwardine. The site had been sold in 1292 with no mention of the mill. It was a fulling mill in 1351 and in 1439, but it had fallen out of use by 1462 and was never used again. At the end of the 16th century Philip Bradford said he could not remember it in existence, although he knew that it had been there.[79] In the 15th century the Gild began to receive a rent from two fulling mills in Ludford, perhaps supplanting the Linney mill. The faster-flowing Teme may have provided more power and profit.

In the early 17th century the Corporation monopoly was threatened, not only by litigation by the Crown's grantees, but also by competition from other mills. In an attempt to defeat this they themselves went to law, not apparently to any effect. Thomas Lewkenor of Stanton Lacy built a malt mill near the northern end of Corve Street which replaced an earlier one in Stanton Lacy which had been destroyed by flooding; Lewkenor's mill, operated by manual labour rather than by water power, could grind malt at the rate of 200 bushels a month and attracted trade from the Corporation's Ludlow mills. A corn mill and a fulling mill, on the site of a fulling mill, were built on the Teme c.1600 only 80 yards from the Old Street mills. These were in turn replaced by three mills in 1629 for which a wider mill race was dug by the entrepreneur, Thomas Colericke. By 1629 they were all in the hands of Thomas Aldwell, Colericke's widow's second husband. Another competitor was the corn mill called Chapman's mill in Steventon, which was at that time owned by Rees Jones, a Ludlow attorney, who reconstructed the weir in 1628; his mill was much used by Ludlow people to the detriment of the Corporation mills.[80]

40.   The Tolsey House (where markets were administered and dues levied) and the Bull Ring
('Butchers' Row' in the Middle Ages).

Markets, Fairs and Trade Regulation

Ludlow's markets and fairs were not restricted to agricultural produce and livestock, although these were the most important goods sold there. Agricultural prices would have dominated the economy; low prices would reduce the cost of supplies of food and materials to Ludlow consumers and manufacturers, but would also reduce Ludlow incomes, both because many inhabitants were directly involved in farming and because low agricultural incomes inevitably reduced the money available to spend in Ludlow. On balance the upper classes would have preferred high prices and the lower classes low prices until low prices put them out of work. Quantitative evidence is very limited, so it is impossible to estimate the volumes and values turned over in the markets or to compare them with other towns, like Shrewsbury and Leominster.[81] Ludlow held specialised markets in different parts of the town; the beast market, the corn market, the apple market. Of these the beast market, held in the area of the present-day Bull Ring, was doubtless the largest, noisiest, most noxious and dangerous.

The establishment of a market was a reason for the establishment of the borough; market dues were a good source of income to the lords. Receipts from market tolls on 9 August 1287 were 14s. 1d., and from market tolls and stallage on 13 August 40s. 11d. During the rest of the year they totalled another 84s. The same level was maintained in 1299 when £6 14s. 8¾d. was brought in. In 1308 it was £14 9s. 9d., a very substantial income.[82] Another major source of lordly income, perquisites of the courts (fines levied in the town court), was also greatly augmented by the numbers of outsiders trading at the markets.

Markets must have been held in the 12th century, but there is no record of them until the 13th century. In 1255 Philip le Lou of Stokesay murdered Walter Schyre of Clinton while they were on their way from the marketplace of Ludlow.[83] Markets were held on one day a week. The form of the 1287 accounts implies that this was so then. The theft of a side of bacon from Roger Wygele took place in the market on Tuesday after Easter 1274, which implies that this was market day.[84] In 1368 the day was Monday; in 1429 it was Thursday and was changed back to Monday in 1552 by royal charter after a local petition.[85]

Markets were intended to serve the locality, which certainly extended as far as the hamlet of Rock, two miles to the north-east, for on Monday, 22 February 1283, Adam Hubert killed a man, having been *ad ferum* in Ludlow.[86] Fairs were more important and were intended to attract trade from further afield. The St Lawrence fair (9 to 11 August) certainly existed in 1274; in that year two Cleobury men imprisoned the Galdeford gatekeeper for not letting them out of the gate without paying a toll on oxen bought at the fair.[87] The fair existed before 1241, possibly at the turn of the century, for Walter Lacy granted land in Upper Heyton to Gerard le Angevin for an annual rent of a pair of gold slippers to be paid at the yearly Ludlow fair; Lacy died in 1241 and he, Gerard and at least some witnesses were alive several decades earlier.[88] This was the only fair of the year; Geoffrey Andrew, who died not later than 1284, gave someone the use of three windows of his shop on all market days except on the days of the fair.[89]

In 1328 Roger Mortimer and his wife obtained a royal licence to establish a second fair, this time on St Catherine's Day (24–26 November).[90] It became the custom to farm the two fairs to the bailiffs for £11 a year but this ceased with the grant of the 1461 charter when the tolls became the Corporation's and were included in the fee farm rent paid to the Crown.[91] The tolls leviable at the gates were also farmed out to individuals in return for a lump sum and an annual rent; so in 1599 John Becke obtained the lease of Galdeford gate tolls and was succeeded in 1612 by his son, William, who renewed the lease 'according to the custom of the town' for 21 years, paying £8 and £6 1s. 8d. a year.[92]

The 1461 Charter granted one fair a year to be held at St Philip and St James. This must have been an additional fair, for in 1462 the Palmers' Gild received 7d. rent for a standing let to 'men of Gloucester' at the St Catherine's fair.[93] The accounts for 1472–82, however, refer only to two fairs, and the 1552 charter made no reference to the St Philip and St James fair, which may have had a short life only. The foundation of the Whitsun week fair by letters patent in 1597 gave rise to opposition during the charter disputes of that time.[94] As Ludlow became relatively less prosperous the income from the existing fairs may have declined and the solution desired was to add another one; the effect would have been to have rendered all three fairs, as well as the new St Lambert fair added in 1604, less important still, until they became local events only. Local needs were increasingly met by retail trading from permanent shops and, as Ludlow's control over its sources of supply and its markets diminished, so did the importance of periodical fairs.

Markets and fairs were closely regulated, being sources of income from tolls and stall dues; it was also important to the town to maintain its reputation for fair dealing in matters of weights and measures and, indeed, judicial procedures for settling disputes. On one occasion, in 1604, the St Catherine's fair was cancelled because of plague.[95]

Market tolls and stallage were collected for the Community in 1287–9 and in 1308.[96] By 1442 they were normally put to farm, yielding, with fairs and chenser rents, £21 a year.[97] In 1368, £13 came in from the weekly markets and the St Lawrence fair; in 1424 market tolls and two fairs brought in £11 6s. 8d. In 1429 £10 was set as the income from Thursday markets and the St Lawrence fair; although neither the accounts nor the valor say as much, these round sums suggest that this was already a farmed source.[98] Farming continued until after the grant of the 1461 charter. Thereafter it seems the Corporation collected the dues of the market for its own account, but left the fairs in farm. In 1482 the two fairs produced 29s. 8d. and the markets 20s., while from 1539 to 1562 the two fairs yielded a round 2 marks. In 1562 market fines yielded a non-round sum of 12s. 4d., suggesting a considerable decrease in trading prosperity.[99] After 1461, at least, the town court met fortnightly, hearing on average about fifty cases a session; extra sessions were held on the days of the two annual fairs, although, on the evidence of 1476, these did not throw up a significant amount of extra business, the lists being shorter than for the fortnightly sessions.[100] Although the Corporation was entitled to various dues, on occasion unwarranted dues were demanded. In about 1597 Richard Nightingale, a burgess and glover, refused to pay the so-called 'picking penny', demanded by the then bailiffs for his standing at the town fair, so they seized his stock of gloves. The Council of the March upheld, with costs, his appeal against the illegal demand.[101]

Various officials, ranking quite low in the town's hierarchy – low rank doubtless correlating with burdensome duties – were appointed to supervise the markets, checking for bad meat and ale, false weights, short measures and other irregularities. Above them there was also a clerk of the market to collect the dues and generally administer the markets and account financially. Although the titles of the offices are not recorded before the late 15th century, the functions were carried out long before; the officials certainly existed in the late 13th century.

Standard weights and measures were maintained. These included the 'strike' in which oats were measured as late as 1598, when the price was given as 24d. a strike; as barley, normally not priced much above oats, was 60d. a bushel, this suggests that the Ludlow strike was equivalent to two bushels, in which case it was an unusual local measurement. The 'Guildhall weight' of 40 stones of tallow specified in Anne Achelley's will in 1606 was probably the national standard, but so-called in Ludlow because it was kept at the Guildhall.[102] The day-to-day administration of the markets was carried out in the 16th and 17th centuries at the Tolsey in the Bull Ring. The origins of the tolls were in the original lordship rights and the many grants of murage to the town between the 13th and 15th centuries, whereby all goods brought into the town for sale were subjected to toll; the funds so raised rapidly became general purpose funds. The 1461 charter embodied a scale of charges and these continued to be applied.

While the cloth industry was so important to the town, outside competition was restrained by the use of these tolls and other regulations. Outsiders paid heavily for the privilege of access to the town's markets. In 1554 John Dawson, an outsider, sued the bailiffs for seizing his pewterware for being unmarked.[103] Administration became lax in later decades and became one of the issues in the charter disputes of the 1590s; the articles drafted by Sir Henry Townshend indicate the abuses intended to be reformed. Townshend himself summarily resolved one dispute in 1597 when a Shrewsbury upholsterer at Ludlow fair had his stall demolished by a crowd led by Charles Amyas; Bailiff Crowther then refused to let him sell at the fair. Only Townshend's warning to Amyas ('What hast thow to doe with hit? Gett thee home or ells I will cause boults to be putt on thy heeles and thow shalt weare them untyll the fayre be done') allowed the Shrewsbury man to trade undisturbed.[104] Outsiders could have a hard time. Thereafter only burgesses were now to be allowed to 'brew and vittle' and no outsider could sell bread and food other than at the Monday markets. Linen, doubtless an important local product, should be sold from market stalls and not private houses. Burgesses were to have free standings at markets and fairs, while chensers were to be constrained in starting up in trade. This was an attempt to prolong the medieval arrangements protecting the 'smaller' burgesses against outsiders, newcomers and the rich; as burgesses were by now a small minority of the residents of the town this was highly restrictive and may not have been in the long-term interests of the town.[105] Ludlow was equally anxious to dissuade its shopkeepers from trading in other nearby towns. In 1609 Samuel Parker was in trouble with the town authorities for opening shop in Leintwardine, although his motive was only a desire to escape the plague then raging in Ludlow.[106]

The Wool Trade

The English wool export trade to Flanders began before 1100; by 1200 it was vital to both countries. Eastern England participated early, followed later by Wales and the March. Until 1270, and the outbreak of the war with Flanders, Flemish merchants dominated the trade.

The earliest evidence of the involvement of Ludlow merchants in the wool trade was in 1271 when Thomas Eylrich was granted the king's licence to export 20 sacks of wool.[107] In 1272 Philip Wyggemor, otherwise Philip fitz Stephen, and William Orletone, Ludlow merchants, were granted similar licences. At the same time Nicholas, Lawrence and Thomas 'de Ludelawe' were granted licences, In 1273 Eylrich and Wyggemor again received licences, as did Thomas Langeford, another Ludlow merchant. The following year Nicholas Alriche (sc. Eylrich) and Nicholas Gour were licensed to trade in wool within the realm.[108] Although the amounts of wool involved do not rank Ludlow among the leading wool towns, they do suggest a considerable trade and possibly one of some standing.

Nicholas de Ludelawe, the founder of the Ludelawe family, was a Ludlow man, as was his more famous son, Lawrence, but he is described as a Shrewsbury merchant in the Patent Roll grant of 1273. It is possible that he began his commercial career in his home town, Ludlow, but moved to Shrewsbury, which was, and remained, far more important in the wool trade than Ludlow. In the 1260s he was already one of the greatest merchants in the country. Lawrence, his son, became the greatest merchant in England, adviser to the king and commander of the wool fleet to Flanders in 1294, a voyage never completed by him as he went down with his ship off Aldeburgh. His personal connection with Ludlow was maintained, as he was buried there.[109] In Ludlow Lawrence was referred to merely by his Christian name at a time when other men were called by both Christian and surnames.[110] In 1277 Nicholas and Lawrence were granted licences for 250 and 200 sacks respectively (108,000 fleeces), figures which show the family's relative superiority over their fellow merchants in Ludlow.[111]

In 1273 five Ludlow merchants exported 113 sacks through London, that is, about 27,000 fleeces, so ranking after Shrewsbury and Dunstable in the London export market. Some of the northern towns, exporting through Boston and other ports, were, however, more important. Nationally there were nine towns ranking above Shrewsbury in 1271–2 and 11 in 1273–4.[112] Trading was by no means all towards exports; in 1287 William fitz Baldwyn of Montgomery owed £16 to Geoffrey Goldsmith of Ludlow for four sacks of wool. Although this may represent an advance payment, it is more likely that a Ludlow merchant was selling wool back into Wales.[113]

Ludlow remained a middle-ranking wool town into the 14th century. In 1332 several Ludlow merchants, Nicholas Eylrich, Richard and William Orletone and Richard Goldsmith, with others from Yorkshire and the Midlands, were accused by the Duke of Brabant of seizing the wool of a Bridgnorth merchant at Bruges on the pretext of his trying to export wool to Brabant without their permission. They were operating an illegal staple, that is, a monopoly export market, subject to control, of the kind which the English kings were using to control the trade in the interests of revenue and public policy. The king's order to return the wool was ignored, so sheriffs were told to distrain on the offenders' goods in England.[114] In 1332 Ludlow was one of the mercantile towns required to send two merchant representatives to the parliament *pro stapulis ordinandis* summoned to establish the wool trade staples in England, which may have been a consequence of the Bruges trouble.[115]

William Ace, Nicholas Eylrich, Richard Corve and Philip Cheyne the younger, all of Ludlow, were granted royal protections while engaged in buying wool for the king in 1337.[116] In 1338 the merchant assemblies agreed to sell to the king 30,000 sacks of wool at a valuation with the prospect of being repaid in instalments. Richard Orletone, with others, was made responsible for the wool of Shropshire being taken to London, valued at 10 marks a sack.[117] The wool was taken to Durdrecht in the Netherlands and sold there. The figures provided in 1338–43 by the royal repayment warrants indicate the relative importance of the towns of England engaged in the wool trade. The merchants of the main ports, that is, London, Hull and Boston, were accorded the most, but much of this represented wool bought from merchants inland. Apart from Shrewsbury, the Marches towns were relatively unimportant, compared with towns like Melton Mowbray, Coventry, York and Beverley. Within the March, Ludlow was less important than either Shrewsbury or Bridgnorth.[118]

Warrants to Repay Loans of Wool to the King at Durdrecht 1338–1343

	1338	1343
Ludlow	£ 456	£ 838
Shrewsbury	£ 542	£3015
Bridgnorth	£ 647	£2832
Wenlock	£ 141	£ 141
Hereford	£ 383	£ 162
Worcester	£1298	£1228
Chester	£ 365	£ 540
Stafford	£ 260	£ 200
Coventry	£3068	£3273
Melton Mowbray	£2655	£4041

The administration of the so-called 'confiscations' of Durdrecht led to the recording of details of the pattern of the trade, which enable us to see fairly exactly the hinterlands of the wool ports. London exported wool from a wide area of southern and midland England, stretching up the Thames valley into Warwickshire, Worcestershire, Shropshire and as far as Chester. Stafford and Wenlock exported through both London and Boston; Shrewsbury, Bridgnorth and Ludlow were firmly within London's hinterland.[119]

In this period Richard Orletone was credited for wool worth £200 and £344, William Ace for £148, John Ace for £92, John Schrosbury for £109, Thomas Pirefeld for £74, Nicholas Eylrich for £63, John Corve for £34 and Philip Cheyne for £24,[120] considerable sums, which were to be individually recovered from the customs collected at specified ports, a tedious and not always successful process, for Eylrich seems not to have recovered all of his money by the time he died about 1349.[121]

The 10 men named in the royal warrants dominated Ludlow's wool trade, but there were other Ludlow wool merchants whose stocks of wool at the time escaped appropriation. In 1349 Isabel, the widow of John Lyney, claimed to have been robbed by other Ludlow merchants of 33 sacks of wool, worth £100, which, with almost 8,000 fleeces involved, could hardly have been a clandestine act.[122] Ludlow merchants often invested in sheep kept by friends or relatives elsewhere, exemplified by William Pope, who died in 1381 and left all his sheep in his sister's keeping.[123] Ludlow merchants had access to the wool from the large flocks kept on the estates of the earls of March. Wool collecting was a mobile trade; merchants could quite easily establish themselves elsewhere, as the history of the Ludelawe family proves. The great Nicholas de Ludelawe also bought his wool from a wide area, including Oxfordshire, and presumably took it straight to London; not all the wool handled by Ludlow's merchants passed through Ludlow.[124] What benefit Ludlow gained from the trade is unknown, except that the merchants themselves would have had the profits to spend in Ludlow, where they lived and acquired or built houses. Only one member of a related occupation has come to light before 1400 – Walter Rede, a woolpacker, in 1363. Humbler occupations do not figure much in records, but they would have existed.[125]

The English wool export trade began to decline in the 1360s. This was hastened by internal strife in Flanders 1379–85. The establishment of staples, particularly that at Calais, would have tended to reduce the participation in the export trade of the merchants of non-staple provincial towns like Ludlow. There is some evidence that merchants operating from London became more dominant in the collecting of wool from Wales and the March; this would have reduced Ludlow merchants to local gatherers. In 1358 Richard Malmeshulle and others bought a large quantity of wool from Richard Toggeford (on credit, for they entered into a bond for 100 marks) important enough to them to remember it 23 years after.[126] Such circumstances could, however, have encouraged gathering for local weaving, a trade which preceded the wool export trade and long outlasted it. William Parys, 'wolmonger', was engaged in this trade in 1404–13, during which time he was later accused of having cheated people around Shropshire of over 2,000 fleeces by using the prohibited measures called auncels – hand-held balances very open to the use of false weights.[127] Parys was also a draper, that is, a dealer in cloth, and exemplifies the transition from wool exporting to cloth selling. Thereafter the wool trade did not have more than local significance and was chiefly the first stage in cloth manufacture.

The Cloth Trade

Cloth manufacture existed in Ludlow from at least the early 13th century. When Peter Undergod founded St John's Hospital (1220–30) he bought from Gilbert Lacy a fulling mill on the Teme with a monopoly of fulling all Ludlow cloth.[128] The existence of cloth manufacture does not in itself imply trade in cloth beyond the town. We know little about habits of dress, how much cloth was worn and how often worn out. Did Ludlow serve only its own district? A better knowledge of the distribution of fulling mills might answer this. The fulling mill at Ludford was there in the mid–13th century.[129] Fulling mills remained in operation throughout the following centuries; in 1343 the Sheet mill was given to the Gild.[130] In 1291, 25 burgesses, including Lawrence de Ludelawe himself, were prosecuted for selling cloth against the assize; the cloth trade was even then an adjunct to the wool trade and merchants could engage in both quite easily.[131]

Any town in sheep rearing country had a cost-advantage for a local industry supplying the needs of the locality. This advantage would not necessarily support an export trade or the luxury trade. Until about 1350 Ludlow's richest citizens were in the international wool trade; the cloth trade was very small by comparison.

There were many processes in cloth manufacture, not all of which needed to be carried out in the same place, although there is no evidence that Ludlow did not carry out every stage up to the production of usable dyed cloth within the borough. Whatever the magnitude of the trade, it was the most complex trade carried on there throughout. The wool had first to be collected, either from the merchants' own flocks, or bought by them from others. It had then to be sorted, graded, cleaned and beaten to produce 'washed wool'. As this work was often carried out on the sheep farms, we do not know how much went on in Ludlow.

The lack of early lists of inhabitants and their occupations prevents any exactitude in estimating the numbers engaged in various trades. For the 15th century an impression can be gained from the numbers of references to them which can be picked up from various records. These suggest, broadly, that 46 per cent of those engaged in the cloth trade were weavers, 20 per cent fullers, 21 per cent dyers and 13 per cent clothiers and drapers. The last category included those who controlled some manufacture, but whose chief business

41. Lower Broad Street, looking towards the site of the fulling mill. Dyers, fullers and weavers lived here before 1500.

42. The 'Great House' in Corve Street, where the Clungunwas family of weavers lived between 1439 and 1618.

was selling cloth, both manufactured and bought-in. The weavers were at the bottom of this economic hierarchy and were the first significant group in the manufacturing process.

Evidence for the preparatory stages of cloth manufacture in Ludlow is wanting. The work may have been done outside Ludlow or those engaged counted for little; only 'self-employed' people would appear in records. The wool was then carded or combed to make ready for spinning. Carding produced the wool for weft-yarn and combing wool for warp-yarn. Although we do not know of any carders or combers, for these may usually have been women or employees, in the 15th century Ludlow had several cardmakers, Thomas Bridewode being the earliest in 1421. Four others are known from the second half of the century.[132] Several cardmakers were in business around the year 1600; it was then a trade combined with ironmongery. The wool was then spun into yarn, using either distaff and spindle, as earlier in the period, or spinning-wheel, more common in the 16th century. These functions were capable of being carried out in the countryside, being tasks usually carried out by peasant women, along with their other tasks. Such work would not, however, commonly be done by the wool farmers, but would be 'put out' by the clothiers who had bought the wool where it could be done cheapest. Although it was possible to dye the yarn before weaving, it is likely that in Ludlow the normal sequence was for the yarn to be passed to the weavers.

Weavers appear regularly from the mid–14th century, Roger Wolvertone in 1355 and John Hunte in 1363, for instance.[133] Between the 1390s and 1600 considerable numbers of weavers are consistently recorded throughout. The paucity of references before the mid–14th century could, however, be due to the fact that it was less usual to record occupations in legal records then; nevertheless there are other reasons to suppose that Ludlow's cloth manufacture was becoming more important from this time. The type of loom in use by the 13th century, the flat-bed loom, was adaptable to the production of various sizes and types of cloth. Many weavers were also described as 'clothiers', indicating that, if they had ever operated a loom themselves, they had graduated beyond it and employed others to do the work. Many were merchants who bought and sold whatever would turn a profit, concentrating on putting out weaving work or employing others. Weavers, as such, even masters, would have found the long-distance business of selling cloth impossible to undertake. In the 16th century, however, much of the long-distance merchandising fell into the hands of citizens of other towns; Ludlow weavers were increasingly reduced to direct manufacture.

Once woven the cloth was re-washed and fulled (which thickened, felted and de-greased it), either by treading in a trough ('walkmill') or beating with mill-driven hammers, which was the method used for all or most cloth in Ludlow from early times. We do not know if, in general, the fullers bought cloth to full and sell on, or whether they fulled for fees, although in 1444 Simon Chaundler sued Griffith Boster of Ludlow, walker, for 100s. damages for not fulling his cloth properly.[134] Fullers usually required more capital than weavers if they were to lease mills from the Corporation or the Gild to drive hammers for the task, but some, usually called 'walkers', operated in a small way, treading or 'walking' the cloth in tubs. The weavers' output was processed by fewer than half as many fullers; we should, therefore, expect the fullers as a class to have higher incomes.

Fulling, as has been shown, existed from the early 13th century. In the 14th century the earliest fullers recorded were William Broctone in 1310, John Hereford in 1330 and Nicholas Stoke in 1344.[135] In the latter half of the century we know of eight; during 1400–1450, twenty-four. The numbers dwindle thereafter, perhaps a reason to suppose that the growing class of 'clothier' then included the fullers, although it is possible that unfulled cloth was being produced.

The cloth was then re-washed, dried and teased with teazels to raise a nap. Large shears

43. The shop on the corner of Drapers' Row, occupied in 1494 by Richard Sherman, Warden of the Palmers' Gild.

were then used to produce a smooth finish; there were grades of quality possible here. These stages were probably carried out by the 'shearmen', but we have no direct evidence of them earlier than 1429, when John Paty, a shearman, is recorded.[136] As the surname Sherman is found in Ludlow from the 13th century onwards, the trade it represents may be assumed to have existed that early, too. No instances have been found later than 1504, which may indicate that the trade had fallen in status to an employment by the clothiers.[137] Richard Hunt, a fuller, who left five pairs of shears and two tenters in his will, may have been typical in carrying out the related jobs of shearing and tentering.[138] That the well-to-do Sherman family of Ludlow in the late 16th century were calling themselves 'Shermound' suggests that the occupational surname had lost status. *Parmentarii* existed in the 1280s and in 1363, an imprecise term which may mean cloth-combers, but occasionally tailors, even furriers.[139]

The cloth was then stretched on tenterhooks before dying. Undyed cloth was exported from England, but Ludlow cloth seems to have been dyed in the town.[140] That cloth-stretching was carried out in Ludlow on a large scale is well evidenced by the existence of the 'tenteryards' in the suburbs of the town, those on the southern side of the town existing at least as early as 1392. [141]

The final stage was dying. This required the greatest capital to finance the plant – dye-vats, the purchase of dyes, usually from abroad, and to finance the stockholding of what by this stage were goods with high added value. William *de Lodelowe*, a 'teynturer', is recorded in 1317; the next is John Walshe in 1360.[142] So few early references suggest that dying was not an important trade then. Five dyers are known in the second half of the 14th century and 24 in the next half century. William Prestemde and other members of his family traded as dyers in the town between 1387 and 1428.[143] Nine are known in the second half of this century. John Braban, a dyer, who was sued for trespass in 1443, may have come from Brabant, judging by his name, whence he may have brought his skills. Was this a sign of an expanding trade? [144] In the 15th century seven dyers in the town bore the surname 'Dyer', often a sign of an immigrant from Wales where surnames were still rare. This, too, is evidence of expansion of the trade.

The dyestuffs were usually imported from overseas; by 1400 English middlemen controlled the supply to the dyers themselves. Dyes were expensive and the outlay considerable;

in 1402 William Dyer of Ludlow acknowledged a debt of £25 to Nicholas Wynde, also of Ludlow, for madder-wood and alum he had bought and not paid for. In 1443 Walter Codur bought 1 hundredweight of madder for 42s. and 2 hundredweight of alum for 45s. from Henry Braybroke of London.[145] Richard Selman (d.1539) had owned a dyehouse in St Mary's Lane with other property since about 1500; evidently quite well-off, he was described as 'armiger', not being an entrepreneur, but a landlord.[146]

In the 16th century the clothiers were dominant. Cloth manufacture naturally tends to division of labour and specialisation of skills; there was a countervailing tendency – the expansion of those who dominated one function in the process into other functions. The beginnings of this can be seen in the 15th century. The further away the market, the more capital was needed. The cloth trade was characterised by the ability of specialist traders to extend their businesses along the production and marketing chain. The more a process was concentrated in fewer hands the greater their bargaining power with their suppliers, so in Ludlow when a trader became successful and accumulated capital in one process he was often able to extend his interests into other processes. There was a constant incentive to try to control supplies in one direction and obtain access to the wider market in the other. There were impediments, too, harder to identify, but these effectively prevented the development of monopolies. The accumulation and maintenance of capital for more than a few decades was beyond the capacities of the provincial bourgeoisie who were without the legal and institutional protections which mortmain, primogeniture, uses and feudal rights gave to ecclesiastical corporations and the nobility. Nevertheless for short periods particular traders became rich until the hazards of chance and family dissipated their wealth.

There are, however, surprisingly few examples of men or trading families who did extend their interests along the production chain. The Hereford family were fullers in the period 1330–57; in the 1390s William Hereford was a rich 'clothier'.[147] Members of the Hoptone family were weavers, fullers and merchants between 1360 and 1396.[148] Walter Codur was described as a weaver in 1412 and as a merchant in 1444, having done well in business; he involved himself in dying, too.[149] The Cressett family, successful fullers in the 15th century, were also described as dyers, merchants and woolmongers.[150] John Simkins was a dyer and a merchant in the 1470s.[151] John Longeford was described as both weaver and fuller, 1432–41.[152] Some tradesmen, possibly in origin surnameless Welshmen, had occupational surnames, but were also noted as being in other trades, such as Hugh Walker, the dyer, in the late 15th century.[153]

Until the late 15th century the volume of Ludlow's cloth production is not known. Cloth manufactures bore the tax known as alnage, which was assessed on counties or groups of counties by alnagers, appointed by the king. These were often cloth merchants themselves. In 1365 Nicholas Prille of Ludlow, probably a cloth merchant, with another, obtained for 51 marks a year the lease of the cloth subsidy and a third of the alnage forfeitures (cloth forfeit for violating the regulations, or whose owners tried to avoid the dues) in Shropshire and three other counties. This was renewed to Prille and John Ray, a Coventry merchant, in 1366. In 1399 William Parys, the 'draper', was granted the Shropshire and March alnage; he was succeeded in 1402 by William Glovere, another Ludlow cloth merchant, who was in turn succeeded in 1408 by John Lawrence, also a draper, who paid £12 13s. 4d.[154] That Ludlow cloth merchants were of sufficient commercial and financial standing to obtain these grants and pay the large sums demanded demonstrates that the Ludlow cloth trade was prosperous, both relatively and absolutely. The town may well have survived the decline of the wool trade without too much hardship.

The 1461 charter exempted Ludlow from the royal alnage levied on the county and allowed the appointment of a town alnager who, by means of cloth searchers, checked the quality of the cloth sold in Ludlow, seizing that which failed the tests. Then the alnager, (or between 1566 and 1592 the annual alnager's permanent deputy, John Holland) levied the alnage at the rate (typically, although there were occasional variations), of 2d. a cloth presented by burgesses, 3d. for the cloths of chensers (non burgess residents) and 3½d. for foreigners' cloths. The last two categories were relatively unimportant, being recorded only between 1551 and 1607. The records are desultory and difficult to interpret exactly, because in some years the alnagers used 'long hundreds' (of six score) without making it clear; it is necessary to work backwards from the moneys raised. Nevertheless the figures show that from a level of about 525 long-cloths a year in 1475–83, Ludlow production fell (there is a long gap in the records) to under 300 cloths a year in 1522–3, rising again to 788 in 1554, falling again to 391 in 1565–6, rising to its highest recorded level of 827 in 1582. Thereafter it entered into an almost unbroken decline until 1610 when only 61 clothes were recorded. Through the period 1520 to 1582 we can discern three cycles of similar length, but each characterised by fluctuations of smaller amplitude and varying periodicity.

After 1582, however, Ludlow's cloth trade experienced, not trade cycles, but a progressive and permanent collapse. The cycles and trends shown by the Ludlow long-cloth alnage figures are closer to the national figures for exports of short-cloths in the earlier period to about 1570, but thereafter there is no similarity; national exports did not decline steeply after 1582. Despite the manufacture of 'medleys' in the 15th century and later, the basis of Ludlow's trade was in old-fashioned white long-cloth, which was badly hit from the 1570s onwards by the lighter and better quality 'New Draperies'. Even in 1534 the fine cloth for the Gild elders' robes had to be brought from London.[155] Ludlow seems not to have met the challenge by diversifying in the face of changing tastes and to have suffered catastrophically as a result, much earlier than the country as a whole. Even so, clothmaking carried on at a lower level of activity, usually serving local markets; the Foxe household at Bromfield, for instance, patronised Ludlow makers until the 1620s. In 1638 Thomas Taylor still traded as a dyer. In 1685 Richard Thomas was carrying out all the functions of clothmaker, shearman, fuller and dyer, a reversal of the normal tendency to specialisation, suggesting a shrunken local trade.[156]

Dominant though the cloth trade was in Ludlow's economy, it did not rank other than as a tiny centre of production, at no time as much as one per cent of national production, often a tenth of this.[157] By the mid-17th century the unimportance of the cloth trade was reflected in the conversion of fulling mills to corn grinding and in the relegation in status of the alnager's office from one place junior to high bailiff to being only the next office after churchwarden.

A little is known about the kind of cloth made in Ludlow and the manner in which it was marketed. In 1421, 15 Ludlow cloths of 'derkegrenemedle', that is, mixed green, were valued at £2 10s. each of London, while 16 wide cloths of 'blew medle' were valued at £2 6s. 8d. In the following year a Florentine merchant bought in London 39 Ludlow cloths of various colours for 50s. 9d. and a Genoese bought ten cloths for £4 each; Ludlow not only produced cloth of different values and, presumably, quality, as well as of different colours, implying that the dying trade was well-developed. The sellers in each case are not obviously recognisable as Ludlow men, so we may conclude that the export of Ludlow's cloth from London was in the hands of London merchants. It is likely that, unlike the earlier wool trade, Ludlow's cloth exports were never handled beyond London by Ludlow merchants.[158]

It is a long leap to 1554 when Walter Nichols of Burford 'made or caused to be made' in Ludlow a broad white cloth called 'long whites' like those commonly called 'Long Worcesters'; Oliver Truxton, a Ludlow common carrier, took this to Blackwell Hall in London to sell, but the searchers found that the cloth was only 28 yards long, instead of

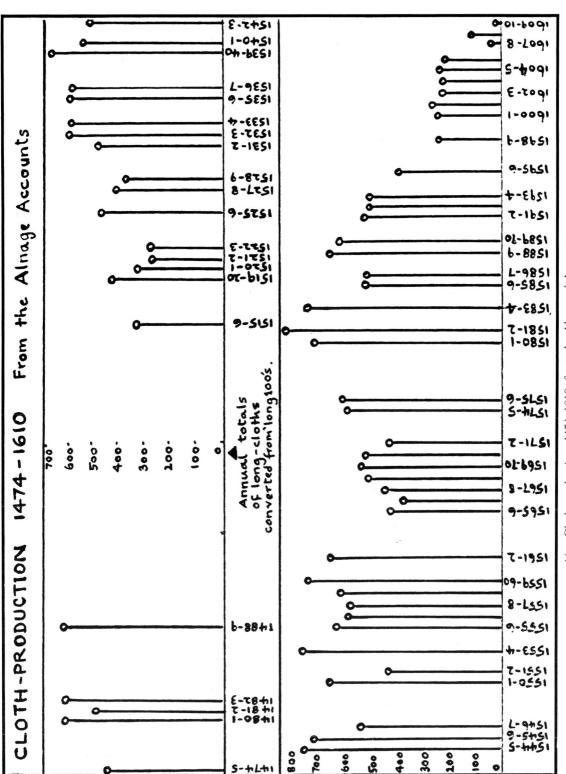

44. Cloth production, 1474–1610, from the Alnagers' Accounts.

the 29 to 31 yards required, and weighed 71 pounds rather than the standard 84 pounds; he had therefore to sell for less than Nichols wanted or would accept. This illuminates both the product and the organisation of the trade.[159] At about this time Roger Woore commissioned William Phillips, another Ludlow clothier, to sell in London nine long white cloths worth £34 4s. 4d.; at the same time he had seven other cloths in stock worth £23 10s.[160] In 1585 John Cupper, a clothier of London, but clearly of a Ludlow family, acted as a factor in London selling cloth on behalf of Ludlow traders, as well as buying other textiles to sell to Ludlow. Maintaining a London agency through a kinsman or local man was common at this time with Ludlow traders as with other towns' merchants; it was a middle stage between taking one's goods up oneself and selling them wholly at arm's length in a strange market.[161] In 1592 there was a dispute over what seems to have been a payment in advance by a London merchant to Thomas Hoke, a Ludlow clothier, for coarse cloth called 'Ludlow whytes'; it was this cloth which doubtless formed the bulk of Ludlow's late 16th-century trading.[162] Other Ludlow clothiers at this time owed money to Londoner customers; it seems that by this time some Ludlow clothiers were selling their wares before they had them, at any time a highly vulnerable business.

In the period 1550–1 to 1609–10, in which 29 years' detailed accounts have survived, 164 clothiers presented cloth to the alnagers for sealing. There are other years for which we have only the overall town totals.

It is apparent from these figures that a few individuals and their families dominated the business. Fourteen individuals accounted for 63 per cent of all the cloth presented, and their families 72 per cent; Thomas Blashfield 15 per cent of the total and his family nearly 25 per cent. Although they did well from the trade at its height, it was also these people who failed to meet the challenges of the 1580s and after. Many of the other 150 producers produced few cloths, some were weavers, and some of them did not normally work on their own account. As 17 were women it is possible that they were minor entrepreneurs who paid others to spin, weave and full small quantities of wool and cloth.

Clothmaking was not the only textile trade in Ludlow. Tailors existed early on, as we could expect in any town. We know of cappers from 1476, when Thomas Birgate appeared in the town court. In the mid-16th century one of the leading burgesses was Lewis Phillips who was a capper by trade and, like many Welsh immigrants to the town, was often known by his occupation.[163] John Brouderer, a 'brouderer' or embroiderer, along with John Breghenock, a 'webbe' or weaver, was sued for debt in 1424.[164] There were also hosiers, like John Hosyer, who provided the original endowments for the almshouse bearing his name. By the early 15th century at the latest Ludlow supported a wide range of textile trades directly producing consumer goods as well as materials for others to make up. We have no evidence, however, of the extent to which these goods were manufactured for a wider market than the Ludlow area, but textiles were certainly imported from London and other towns. The finer cloth was always imported; by the 17th century the gentry were beginning to acquire clothing and furnishings from elsewhere.

The Leather Trades

A town in the centre of grazing country inevitably became involved in the leather trades. John Scheremon was a tanner in Lower Galdeford in the late 13th century but it is likely that tanning went on from the town's earliest days. Sampson *de Ludelawe* was a shoemaker in the late 13th century and the row of shoemakers' shops existed in the 1280s. The earliest recorded skinner was John Lokare in 1350; the earliest saddler was John Bullesdone in 1415; the earliest glover was John Girrous in 1336.[165] There must have been many in these trades long before, whose occupations have not been recorded. Between 1300 and 1660 only a small number of skinners, saddlers and glovers are recorded, but at all times these were far outnumbered by the numbers of cordwainers or corvisers and tanners or barkers, in somewhat similar numbers. Cordwainers or corvisers included shoemakers and any skilled leather craftsmen. Although it took longer to tan leather than it took to produce, say, a pair of shoes, a tanner, depending upon the size of his premises, could produce more leather in a day than a shoemaker could produce shoes. It is probable that Ludlow had a large surplus of leather for sale to other towns and from the early 14th century at least Ludlow's tanning industry served markets well beyond the town.

Quantitative evidence for the tanning industry is lacking although it was in existence for a long time and supplied other markets with leather. Made-up leather goods were, however, made for the local market only. A level of prosperity was long maintained. It was in the early 17th century that the trade surpassed clothmaking to become the main trade of Ludlow.

The Craft Gilds

Although craft gilds, organisations of the masters in particular trades within a town, were developing in some towns during the late 13th century and became common in the early to mid–14th century, the earliest reference to the crafts of Ludlow, regarded as distinct entities, comes from 1368, when there was resolved a dispute between the crafts of Ludlow over the order of precedence to be observed in the annual Corpus Christi day procession.[166] The order was henceforth to be: milwards, bakers, butchers, barkers, sellers (that is, saddlers), glovers, dyers, weavers, fullers, corvisers, tailors, skinners, drapers and merchants. The more important trades came at the end, although the logic behind the precise order is difficult to discover. The precise social status of individual tradesmen may not have counted so much as the total wealth of the respective groups of fellow tradesmen. There were 14 recognised trades, although there were other (unlisted) crafts practised in Ludlow, including building and metalworking who at a later date were certainly organised in a gild. During the 14th century, and particularly after the Black Death in 1348–9, the observance of the feast of Corpus Christi became widespread and was often associated with craft gilds. The Ludlow craft gilds probably antedated the Black Death, for a Corpus Christi procession existed in 1331.[167] Many of the trades were practised in the 13th, perhaps even 12th, century and may have had some form of corporate existence then.

The 1368 dispute does not illuminate the organisation of the crafts concerned, but implicitly they were distinct. In many towns a man could not become a burgess unless he had first become a member of a craft gild; this condition may well have applied in Ludlow, too, for those candidates for burgess-ship who could not claim it on grounds of relationship. A gild protected its members' interests by regulating and restricting entry into the craft and maintaining work standards, so that the reputation of the town or the fortunes of tradesmen generally should not be harmed. Although outsiders normally prospered in the town, the gilds tried to maintain the particular fortunes of their leading members, and, in so doing, were no different from modern trades unions or professional associations. The 1368 dispute also demonstrates that the gilds were much involved in the conventional pieties of the age, which themselves conferred respectability and social status.

At a time when testamentary generosity towards the Church, the conventual houses, the Palmers' Gild and other good causes was common, it is surprising that there are only two recorded bequests to a craft gild, these being 3s. 4d. from Walter Codur to the 'steward or warden of the weavers' craft' in 1448 and 4s. from Robert Hill to the 'occupation or fellowship of bakers and myllers' in 1584.[168] The craft gilds became very workaday organisations with little sentimental appeal. By the late 16th century a good proportion of their funds was spent on entertaining themselves and others.

The tailors' craft gild paid for a window in the church in 1422 and in 1469–70 the

45.   Dinham, the house of the Langford family, 16th-century tanners and mercers.

46.   Lower Corve Street, centre of the tanning and leather trades in the 16th and 17th centuries. This, the western side, was within the Dinmore Fee, belonging to the Hospitallers of Dinmore, *c*.1185–1538.

stewards of the gilds each paid 6s. 8d. towards quarrying work for the church, no doubt sharing part of the refurbishment of the church; as there was a 'Shoemakers' Chancel' and a 'Weavers' Chancel' in the church in the late 16th and early 17th centuries, it is possible that each of the crafts had its own part.[169] The gilds contributing in 1469–70 were the corvisers, the drapers, the tailors, the smiths, the dyers and barbers, the bakers and the butchers. Missing from this list were the fullers and the tanners, who existed in 1368 and in 1542, and who may be assumed therefore to have existed in 1469, too. The merchants, glovers and skinners all existed in 1368, but may well have merged before 1469, the merchants with tailors, and the glovers and skinners perhaps with corvisers; the 'craft of the dyers and barbers' itself suggests an early merger of groups without any obvious community of interests, other than the possible need to create a larger due-paying member-ship to support administrative overheads. In 1475–6 actions for debt before the town court involved John Turner and Richard Hobold, stewards of the weavers' craft, the Six Men of each of the tailors', the corvisers' and the tanners' crafts or 'arts'.[170]

The basic structure of government of the craft gilds seems therefore to have been established by the mid-15th century; each had a steward or stewards and a group of Six Men with audit functions (like those of the Corporation's own Six Men after 1461) who were the real governors of the craft gild and who both chose the stewards and instructed them. The structure was the same for all the gilds – a consequence of their being under the control of the Corporation (as required by statute) and their forming part of the apparatus of government of the town, as the Palmers' Gild was not.[171] Despite this connec-tion with town government, the stewards of the craft gilds, while always well-to-do men, were not always aldermen or members of the common council. In 1575 four of the Six Men of the smiths' gild had held municipal office as churchwardens or above, but neither of the stewards, William Bradshawe or James Fennell, had or were to hold such offices. In 1603 the smiths' Six Men included Robert Saunders and Richard Benson, ironmongers, both former bailiffs, but the other four never held any municipal office. In 1618 none of the Six Men or the stewards had ever held such offices, nor were they to. Indeed, just as son followed father in municipal office, so kinsmen followed each other in gild office. In 1580 Lawrence Wellins was a steward of the smiths; in 1618 Thomas Wellins, his son, was one of their Six Men, while Cornelius Bould, also one of the Six Men, was followed in 1618 by his son, Andrew, in the office of steward. John Patchett became steward of the tailors, just as his father, Thomas, had been a steward of the smiths.[172]

The officers of the tailors' craft, unlike the smiths, seem also to have pursued municipal careers. In 1609 the craft was granted eight pews in the north side of the church, of which six were to be occupied by 20 former stewards. Eleven of these had already held the office of churchwarden or above and three were later to do so. Only six never held municipal office. Most of those listed who also held municipal office at some time were mercers (and all the listed mercers held such offices), which amply illustrates the economic and political dominance of mercers in early 17th-century Ludlow.[173]

During the 16th century the craft gilds continued to merge. In 1513 there were 10, according to the will of Thomas Cookes who left money to the ten 'crafts' to find four tapers each for his funeral.[174] By 1543 there were eight 'crafts' or 'societies': the walkers and shermen, the smiths, the corvisers, the tanners, the butchers, the bakers, the tailors and the weavers.[175] How the crafts of 1368 had merged is not apparent; indeed, it seems possible that some of the old trade groups were no longer organised at all. In 1541 the Gild paid for a gutter 'ad domum hatmakers', which may indicate another craft gild.[176] The Society of Hammermen, as the smiths were called by 1511, included smiths, ironmongers, saddlers, brasiers, pewterers, bucklemakers, armourers, masons, cordmakers and coopers.[177] The plasterers and slaters had merged with the smiths before 1575. As these were all very different crafts, whose sole characteristic in common was the use of hammers, any unanimity of view on how to promote trade would be impossible; such a body could only exist to restrict membership and to preserve the privileges of those who ran it. In 1511, at the time of the grant of a new charter by the Corporation, the craft included 12 smiths and 13 other tradesmen as masters. Between 1534 and 1583 124 men joined the Hammermen, including 34 carpenters and joiners, 16 tilers, 15 smiths and nine ironmongers.[178] In 1600 there were 65 masters in the smiths' gild.

The tailors' gild similarly merged with the skinners and the glovers between 1470 and 1542. Elaborate rules existed for defining the boundaries between the constituent trades; only skinners and tailors could measure and cut clothes and each had to keep off the other's preserves. No man could run more than two shops; journeymen could run shops only for wages; non-members could not trade in the town. These rules applied in 1669, but were almost certainly the rules of a century or more before.[179] For not practising his trade in the town for three years, John Evans, a carpenter, was discharged from the smiths' in 1594, while in 1617 William Lane was prosecuted by the tailors before the town court for working as a tailor in the town without having been admitted to the freedom of the tailors' gild.[180] In the long run it could only be an impediment to initiative, innovation and economic progress.

Supervision of trading practices was doubtless helped by the custom, still common in the Middle East and elsewhere, of trades grouping in particular streets. So the drapers congregated in Drapers' Row (now King Street and the Narrows), the cooks in Cooks' Row (the west side of the Bull Ring), the shoemakers in Shoemakers' Row (north side of High Street), butchers in Butchers' Row (between Church Street and High Street), locksmiths in Lockyers' Row (south side of High Street) and the tailors in Tailors' Yard (south side of Pepper Lane).[181] Other trades concentrated elsewhere; tanners in particular were numerous in Lower Corve Street, for they needed proximity to water.

Early in the 16th century the craft gilds had become integral parts of the government of the town, both through their control of their own membership and through the Corporation's power to control them. Amalgamations of gilds required Corporation approval, as did gild constitutions. In 1511 the Hammermen were governed by two stewards and six men, themselves former stewards. Biennial elections were held for the Six Men and the stewards. This was altered in 1539; thereafter one steward was elected by the Six Men and the other by the rest of the members. Then, after 1575, the stewards were to be elected by the majority of the members, a tendency away from oligarchy unusual for the times. In 1568 the Corporation approved the constitution of the tailors' gild, so that it had a steward and 30 members and was allowed to have possessions. Annual elections were held for the Six Men who chose the stewards to hold office under them for two years; implicitly the same system as the Hammermen seems to have existed. Little is known about the 'Mistery of Bakers and Milners', except that Thomas Houghton was its steward in 1637.[182]

In 1543 the craft gilds were taxed on their possessions. Then the walkers and shermen, the tailors and the weavers were assessed on goods of £5 each and the other gilds on lesser sums. Altogether the craft gilds bore 2½ per cent of the town's total charge (compared with the Palmers' Gild's burden of 9 per cent of the total). A year earlier Ludlow had been assessed under the so-called 'muster-review': milners and bakers for 16 items of armour and weapons, the smiths for 14, the tailors and mercers for 34, the walkers for 16, the corvisers for 14, the tanners for 17, the weavers for 30, the butchers for 14 and the barbers and dyers for 9. In each case the equipment was declared to be in the hands of the stewards of the 'occupation'.[183] The society of barbers and dyers is absent from the 1543 assessment, possibly because of comparative poverty, there being a *de minimis* limit for the tax.

The same craft gilds contributed to the 1558 subsidy for the Scottish war; the tailors and mercers paid most, followed by the weavers, then the smiths and the tanners, with the barbers and dyers paying the least. The gilds' income consisted chiefly of admission dues and fines for infringements. It was spent on relieving poor members (seldom), on mutual entertainment and on furnishing soldiers to the Crown, a curious objective, but probably a topical royal need at the time the rules were laid down.[184]

By 1568 the drapers had merged with the hatters, skinners, cappers, glovers and mercers in the 'tailors craft'. The minute books of the gild show that, between 1570 and 1659, 145 men were admitted, including 46 tailors, 33 glovers and 31 mercers and a few others of various trades, including apothecaries. Of 36 men who joined the tailors and mercers in the early 17th century, three had served apprenticeships in Ludlow with their own fathers, 14 with other masters in Ludlow, two had married freemen's daughters, one had been born in the town while 16 had no other connection with the town and so paid a fine of twice that paid by the others.[185]

The craft gilds remained in being into the 19th century and continued to exercise their privileges and to regulate their trades as they had always done, although with diminishing rigour after about 1750. The regulation of standards of skill was always a necessary function, but whether it was best done by a corporate body like this is an open question. Rigid demarcation of work between trades was a high price to pay for that benefit and it is doubtful if the craft gilds were an advantage to Ludlow in the tougher economic climate of the 17th century.

16th-century admission dues in the smiths' gild

	1511	1539	1575
Smiths, fletchers, bowyers, goldsmiths, ironmongers, cardmaker, saddlers, coopers, cutlers, etc.	6s. 8d. (13s. 4d.)	10s. 8d. (40s, 8d.)	10s. (40s.)
Masons, carpenters, tilers, plumbers, glaziers, etc.		7s. 4d. (14s. 9d.)	6s. 8d. (13s. 4d.)

Note: the figures in parentheses are the dues paid by those whose apprenticeships had not been served with Ludlow masters; the other figures applied to those who had.

The Carrying Trade

Ludlow sat astride the long-distance roads from Wales to Bewdley and Worcester, and the north-south road from Shrewsbury to Hereford. The nearest trading towns of any importance were Montgomery (26 miles), Shrewsbury (30 miles), Wenlock (20 miles), Bridgnorth (20 miles), Bewdley (20 miles), Worcester (30 miles), Leominster (12 miles) and Presteigne (16 miles). Crudely estimated, its markets would have served some 550 square miles, although some supplies and the main exports had to travel long distances to and from central Wales, Bristol, Coventry and London. The building accounts which have survived show cartage of fairly locally-based materials, such as stone, clay, sand and timber, to have formed a heavy expense. Those employed to cart such materials seem to have included both Ludlow carters and people from the villages which were the sources of supply.

For longer distances specialist carriers were employed. From Bristol came wine (chiefly from Gascony, and later sack from Spain), fish and dyestuffs; for these the River Severn, which was then navigable, was used as far as Bewdley, whence carts were used. The last stage cost the most. In 1424 a pipe of Bordeaux cost 15s. 6d. at Bristol; bringing it to Bewdley cost another 15d. and thence to Ludlow 30d. In 1428 this last lap of the journey cost 40d. for a pipe, and in 1447 bringing a hogshead from Bewdley cost 22d. By 1505 it cost 5s. to bring an unspecified quantity of wine from Bewdley.[186] Although there are sufficient indications that Ludlow relied on the river Severn for water transport, it is hard to quantify that use. In 1467 the Commons passed a bill to effect free passage of the Severn from Bristol to Shrewsbury by abolishing the tolls and fines which landowners were levying 'to the hurt of the people' of Ludlow and other places; it received the unhelpful response '*Le Roy sadvisera*'.[187] The late 16th- and early 17th-century port books contain few references to Ludlow. In 1570 the only one was a shipment of wax from Ludlow to Bristol, via Bewdley, by Hugh Salleway of Bewdley. In January and September 1612, the *Goodspeed* of Bewdley carried two cargoes to Bristol. The first, in the name of Robert Saunders, the Ludlow ironmonger, contained four cwt. of wax, six packs of lorimansware (harness, or small ironwork), 60 bags of nails and two packs of ropes. The second, in the name of John Dayos, a Ludlow tanner, contained 720 calfskins and three tons of metheglen.[188] This could not have been the extent of Ludlow's water-borne trade through Bristol at this time, so we must conclude that most of such trade was in the hands of merchants from other towns, who had already bought Ludlow goods to ship for their own account, very much a reversal of the position in the 15th century and earlier when Ludlow merchants normally traded for their own account as far as the cities or abroad. Ludlow suffered a considerable disadvantage compared with Shrewsbury and Bewdley in not being on a navigable river. In 1636 the Privy Council ordered the requisition of riverside properties to enable William Sandys of Fladbury to make passable a good part of the river Teme lying towards Ludlow, along with the river Avon, so that Worcestershire, Gloucestershire and Warwickshire could be better supplied with wood, iron and coals, evidence that the timber and iron mills in Bringewood and Mocktree needed a cheap outlet for their products.[189]

In all other directions the roads were used. William Blachod, who was wealthy enough to have property to sell, was described as a carter earlier than 1284.[190] No 14th-century references to carriers survive, but in 1433 David Lya, a common carrier, was sued for money he owed, very likely the proceeds of the goods he had carried and sold, this being one of the usual duties of carriers, a conclusion reinforced by a case 10 years later when John Stanburn, a merchant, sued William Jakkys, a carrier, to render account of Stanburn's money.[191] John Tranter was described as a 'weyner' in 1517, but the scale of his work is not known. Oliver Truxton worked as a 'common carrier' between Ludlow and London in 1553–5. In the mid–17th century Francis Ball and his wife, Rose, operated a comparatively large business. He died in 1652, leaving his business to his wife.[192] Other carriers at this time included John Hould and his son, Henry, both of whom died in 1654, and Richard Simons, who had dealings with Simon Bradshaw (d. 1638).[193] Bradshaw owned *The Star*, tenanted by Edward Miles, the son of Thomas Miles, for many years a common carrier of goods between Ludlow (and nearby towns) and London 'as his father had been before him . . . and by his own industry had acquired a good livelihood'. His father died in 1641, so Edward Miles managed to develop his business through the Civil War and Interregnum, which were in many respects damaging times for Ludlow. When he died in 1682 he left premises in Mill Street, 18 horses and waggons. His wife, Jane, a woman of character, carried on the business, eventually marrying her third husband, Richard Rogers of Leominster, after which they both conducted their own carrying businesses separately, with warehouses, teams and gangs in Ludlow, Leominster and London. The firm therefore lasted most of the 17th century in several hands.[194]. Around 1660 there was another carrier in Ludlow, Elisha Rogers, married to Margaret Miles. The carrying trade was very much a family business.[195]

At least one drovers' road from central Wales to London ran close to Ludlow. In November 1401, two Lancashire drovers acting for the king were driving a thousand cattle from North Wales to London. When they reached Ludlow they were attacked by an armed mob of over 200 men, led by Philip Lyngen, a former bailiff, Robert Barbour, soon to be bailiff, and other leading burgesses, who put the king's drovers to flight and themselves took the cattle into Ludlow market. This could cope with large numbers of beasts at one time and was apparently a participator in the long-distance cattle trade which the drovers' road served. The reason for the attack is not known; it is unlikely to have been a direct political act, arising from Mortimer affiliations, even less likely to have been a pro-Glyndwr act, but it is conceivable that the cattle had already been requisitioned by royal officers and the attackers were recovering their own. It may, however, have been a municipal attempt to control the drives or to levy tolls, legal or otherwise, upon them.[196]

External Contacts

Ludlow's contacts with the world beyond the Onny-Corve and middle Teme valleys were extensive. In the 13th century the borough was in competition with other hopeful boroughs, like Montgomery and Wigmore. Disputes with the former began with the grant of its charter when it tried to exclude Ludlow burgesses from trading there, as previously they had quite freely. Ludlow petitioned and Montgomery was ordered to desist.[197] The dispute revived in the mid-1270s when Montgomery petitioned the king to prevent Ludlow and Shrewsbury burgesses buying skins and hides or selling crops in Montgomery, because Gruffudd ap Gwenwynwyn, lord of Powys, at the request of Nicholas de Ludelawe and others, allowed Ludlow merchants to trade at a market at Welshpool. The extent of the *collecta* and the power of Ludlow's wool merchants is indicated here. Ludlow won and Montgomery remained unimportant in the wool trade.[198]

South of Ludlow there were other boroughs, Wigmore, Richard's Castle and the ephemeral Blithelow, two of which failed and none provided any competition for Ludlow. The older borough of Wigmore declined as the trade routes switched from Watling Street eastwards through Ludlow, but the final blow must have been the Mortimer succession to Ludlow.[199]

There is little evidence of competition or commercial contacts with Leominster, apart from the occasional affray. In 1283 Thomas Mynche of Ludlow had his goods seized in Leominster, and in 1349 Ludlow merchants were assaulted and maimed at Leominster and Ashford Jones. That no Ludlow man attended as a livestock trader at the Leominster market in 1556, which attracted people from towns many miles distant, implies that the Ludlow markets were themselves competitive.[200]

Ludlow maintained frequent commercial, social and political contacts with Shrewsbury, however. Borough accounts contain many references to official journeys there. The Ludelawe family were only the most notable of the Ludlow merchants with commercial contacts there. As these were the first and the second mercantile towns in the county, commercial rivalry could be expected, but evidence is surprisingly not to be found.

Generally, Ludlow's commercial contacts were to the west, north-west, east and southeast, but largely excluded the immediate south. In 1419 the executors of Thomas Mere, a vintner of Ludlow, sued tradesmen from Tutbury, Stafford, Coventry, Worcester, Bristol and Alton, Worcestershire, for debts totalling £52, a realisation exercise which demonstrates the breadth of Mere's trading connections.[201]

Ludlow received immigrants from Wales and the March, and Ludlow men emigrated eastwards. In the 13th century there were several men with the surname 'Ludelawe', living elsewhere, including Thomas *de Ludelawe* who was arrested in London in 1242, William *de Ludelawe* of Northampton, a late 13th-century wool merchant, and William, son of Robert Lodelowe of Coventry (1306). Thomas Typpere of Ludlow was living in Derby in 1397. John Ace had business in Southampton in the early 14th century. A later emigrant was Richard Newall, 'late of Ludlow, now of London' in 1608.[202]

Richard Sparchforde, a Ludlow mercer, conducted his business in Bristol, and died there in 1480.[203] William, son of Walter Codur, the 15th-century Ludlow bailiff and merchant, made his fortune in Bristol, becoming mayor there. William, son of John Lane of Ludlow, similarly made a commercial fortune in 15th-century Bristol. An even more remarkable merchant of Ludlow birth, Robert Sturmey, traded from Bristol to the Levant, losing his life in 1457 when his ship was attacked off Malta by the Genoese.[204]

Putting sons out to apprenticeships in other towns was often the way such emigration took place. So Robert, son of John Tailor, barker, of Ludlow was apprenticed in 1545 to William Tyndall, the great Bristol merchant; William, the son of William Huckisley of Ludlow, was apprenticed to Thomas Williams, a Bristol grocer, in 1548, and William, son of William Benson, cardmaker, was apprenticed to William Flecher, a Bristol draper, in 1551.[205] Seven Ludlow boys were apprenticed to London stationers between 1564 and 1597, the first, Thomas Butter, becoming the master of Richard Parkes, one of the later ones.[206]

Ludlow men sued and were sued by the people they dealt with in other towns. The records of the courts of Common Pleas, King's Bench and Chancery contain many scores of such cases, particularly involving other parties in London, Bristol and Coventry.

Direct contacts with foreigners took place both in England and abroad. Italians were met in England, where Roger Deighere of Ludlow sued Guglielmo, Bernardo and Dolfo Pucci of Florence in 1347 and 1350. Previously, in 1328, Gherardo Nerli, another Florentine, had sued Richard Agace of Ludlow for debt.[207] Such contacts would have diminished in the course of that century, as England gained control of its own export trade. In the early 15th century Ludlow shared in the increased contacts with France, for in 1420 John Revel obtained letters of protection to travel to Gascony.[208]

In the course of the 16th century Ludlow's economic horizons shrank rapidly. We hear of no more trading with the Levant or indeed with northern Europe. Ludlow's export trade, such as it was, fell into the hands of the great merchants of Bristol and, particularly, London. A growing proportion of the town's trade with these cities ceased to be in the hands of Ludlow men. As the largest proportion of added value in primary commodities and manufactured goods alike arose from getting them to their markets, there was less opportunity for Ludlow merchants to make fortunes like their predecessors'. Such profits went to the cities.

The Wealth of 16th-century Ludlow

The inventory valuations on which the Hereford diocesan courts based their probate fees give us some idea of the relative wealth of the residents of the town. Real property was not valued for this purpose, so this is not a measure of the wealth of those who were substantial landlords. The average valuation in each decade (excluding women, clergy and lawyers) was:

1540s	£7	1590s	£29
1550s	£20	1600s	£15
1560s	£27	1610s	£22
1570s	£37	1620s	£32
1580s	£29	1630s	£23

The largest valuation (with trade of testator) amongst these was:

1540s	£100	?	1590s	£101	?
1550s	£108	?	1600s	£20	fuller
1560s	£227	fuller	1610s	£41	clothier
1570s	£146	draper	1620s	£104	glover
1580s	£91	baker	1630s	£165	tanner

These figures are based on too few examples to be other than indicative, but they suggest that Ludlow's wealth may have kept pace with the rise in prices until about 1580, but afterwards declined relatively. This conclusion is consistent with other evidence which shows that cloth manufacture declined after 1580, the year in which it reached its peak. It is likely that profit margins were under pressure long before, and this may explain why the decline became a collapse after 1600.

Inheritance customs must also have played a part in the relative decline of the wealth of the town. Unlike the nobility, the urban bourgeoisie did not generally adopt the harsh dynastic policy of endowing one son at the expense of minimal support for other children. Family businesses were peculiarly vulnerable to the under-capitalisation which division of an inheritance brought about. Over 80 wills were proved in the prerogative court between 1500 and 1647 for Ludlow men, other than clerics. Of these at least 31 testators divided their estates in substantial ways, apart from minor legacies; while most of the property so divided was landed property, in Ludlow and elsewhere, in at least 25 cases there were money legacies substantial enough to constitute division of the estate. It was these which would have seriously disadvantaged family businesses. In an age when husbands were often wary of their wives' power to disinherit their heirs by remarriage, it is surprising that about a tenth left the bulk of their estates to their wives, thereby creating uncertainty for the future of their family businesses. This was not peculiar to Ludlow, but it was another reason why the town would not find it easy to recover from hard times when they came.

The same 80 wills include 35 in which the testator owned substantial estates outside Ludlow, in most cases agricultural land. Some of this was inherited, but some was acquired from the profits of trade. More study of the origin of the rest is necessary before firm conclusions can be reached. At least eight of the testators bequeathed livestock or crops in their wills; had the inventories survived it is likely that more chattels of this kind would come to light. It demonstrates that, in a rural town, even prominent traders also maintained strong agricultural interests, not always connected with their own trades, notwithstanding the numbers of butchers who owned livestock. Such widespread interests enabled them to hedge their commercial risks, but may well have blunted their entrepreneurial drive. Whether this was a new phenomenon we cannot know, but it would not have helped Ludlow to maintain its trading importance in the face of London, in particular.

The greatest clothier of mid- to late 16th-century Ludlow was Thomas Blashfield, who dominated cloth manufacture throughout his long life, to judge by the alnage accounts. When he died in 1593 he left £5 to the poor, £67 in minor legacies – a substantial sum – forgave three men their debts and left the rest of his fortune to his widow and his son, Thomas. This son was an official of the Council of the March, rather than a businessman, and when he died in 1597 he, too, was generous to the poor (£15) and left many minor legacies (£170). He left his property to his daughter, Susan, who later married a lawyer, and the rest of his fortune was divided amongst a host of brothers, sisters and aunts. The large Blashfield fortune was thus dissipated within a decade. The weaving trade seemed less likely to continue than other trades, like fulling and dying, where more fixed capital was necessary. Henry Ambler was for a while a leading clothier. When he died in 1587 he left his children, who were minors still, a loom each. His wife was his residuary beneficiary. His fortune did not last.

The leather trades, although not generally as likely as cloth manufacture to produce spectacular wealth in a short time, seem to have had a greater chance of continuity. The Powis family, tanners, exemplify the emergent bourgeoisie which replaced the clothiers. They, too, benefited at an early stage from inheritance of wealth derived from land from two marriages with the Padlands of Habberley. The importance of yeoman background as a basis for commercial fortunes can be seen again and again. Edward Powis (c.1553–1631) founded the tanning fortune; the probate-valuation of his chattels was the largest in the decade. The family continued in the leather trades for three generations into the late 17th century, representing what had become the most important industry.[209]

Another 16th-century phenomenon was the growth of large urban accumulations of property in the hands of gentry families. The Foxe family, with its acquisitions of conventual property, especially that of the Hospital, was the most notable. Other estates were in the hands of the Whittons, an old gentry family which had benefited from marriages with and inheritances from burgess families, the Townshends, a family of Council of the March officials who acquired the Austin friary and the Vernons, descendants of the Ludlows, who acquired the Carmelites' property.

In Old Street and Galdeford in 1626, clothiers, feltmakers and weavers numbered six, glovers and other leather trades six. The best evidence, however, comes from the muster roll for 1614, together with other sources, which enables us to reconstruct the occupational structure of Ludlow in that year. (This can be compared with the poll-tax return for 1667; see Appendix 6.) The decline of the cloth trade was already well under way by 1614; nevertheless the next 50 years witnessed its further decline. The leather trades were already important in 1614 and were not noticeably more so in 1667, except that the tanning industry was by then serving the growing glove manufacture of the town. The importance of the Council of the March in supporting trade in consumer goods, and inns is evident from the summaries.

Chapter Seven

The People of Ludlow

The People of Ludlow Before 1500

By the mid-13th century, when records begin to be plentiful, Ludlow was both prosperous and populous. We have no evidence which tells us when this happened, so we cannot know whether growth in population was a recent and rapid occurrence or whether it took place gradually over a long period. It is a commonplace that medieval towns could not naturally replace their populations, let alone increase them, without continual immigration. Ludlow is hardly likely to have been an exception. Where did this immigration come from?

The only evidence available is that of surnames, which has to be used carefully. Surnames were in use in Ludlow in the early and mid-13th century and it was at this time that hereditary surnames first appeared. We can, therefore, have some confidence that in 1250 a man with a surname which was also a place-name may well have come from that place. After about 1325 we cannot be certain that it was he rather than a forebear who came from there. Listings of inhabitants exist from this period in the form of rentals and we can see the proportion of them who bore 'locative' surnames. But, just as we cannot be certain that a locative surname indicates an immigrant, so we cannot know how many persons bearing occupational or patronymic surnames were themselves immigrants. Some people, like William de Atfretone *alias* le Cordewaner *alias* Kemp, were known by more than one name. Philip de Wyggemore was more often known as Philip Stevens, the surname borne by all his male descendants into the 15th century. Nevertheless the proportion of immigrants among the persons listed was probably not less than the proportion of locative surnames. A Palmers' Gild rental of about 1270 comprises 35 per cent locative surnames, 23 per cent occupational surnames, 10 per cent patronymics, two per cent Welsh names, and 30 per cent others or unclassified. On this evidence we might assume that a third of the population were recent immigrants.[1]

Welsh names were readily recognisable throughout the period, but people from Wales were more commonly known by Welsh patronymics after 1400 than before, which suggests a desire on the part of the earlier immigrant to merge with the population among which he had settled. This is not surprising for a time when there were legal disadvantages to being Welsh. Dulcia la Walesche is recorded in 1266[2] and the names 'Moile' and 'le Galeys' appear before 1300, both of which suggest Welshness, and Iorvard le Mercer of la Pole (Welshpool) held a tenement in Mill Street in 1385, but there were more obviously Welsh names among the leading inhabitants in the 15th century than hitherto.[3] So we find David ap Rees before 1424[4] and Morris ap Rys in 1502, as well as several families with Welsh surnames, some of whom rose to prominence in the town.[5]

Although some families can be seen to have lived in Ludlow for several generations, the Stevens, Ace, Piwau and Orletone families among them, and it is likely that there were others for whom records of the fact are now lacking, it is hard to avoid the conclusion that continuity of this kind was the exception rather than the rule. For this there may be several reasons: life in towns was more at risk of disease; commercial fortunes were more at risk than landed ones; there were also opportunities for the small number of continually successful urban families to move on and out of the town, some to other towns with which they had commercial links, such as London or Coventry or Bristol, some to landed estates which they had eventually acquired. Of the former we have more evidence of cadets from Ludlow,

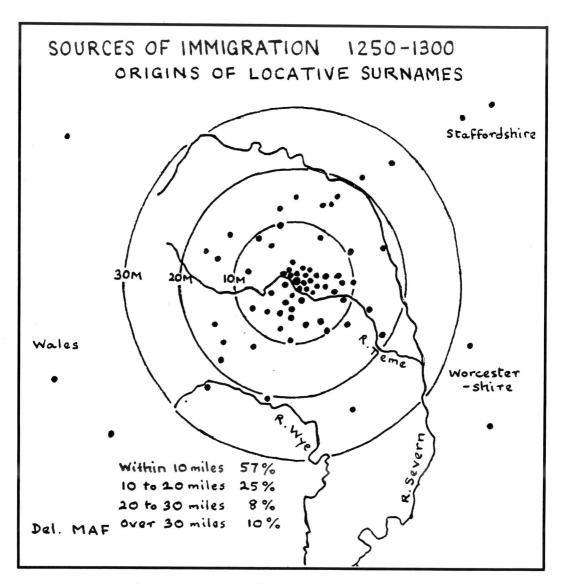

47.   Sources of immigration 1250–1300: origins of locative surnames.

like the Codurs of Bristol and the Dodmores of Northampton, than we have of a whole family migrating. Of the latter the Ludelawe family itself is the most obvious example which set itself up at Stokesay and elsewhere. The Foliots, too, became landed gentry in Worcestershire.

Several Ludlow notables had estates in the countryside; was this the reinvestment of commercial fortunes in land and status or were landed families moving to the town to engage in trade or service without severing their connection with the land? There is some reason to suppose that both were occurring. The Andrew family held their estates in Clee

St Margaret, Steventon and Stokesay concurrently with their prominent careers in Ludlow. The Eilrich family were prominent in both Ludlow and Stanton Lacy. Thomas Ry held land in Sheet, Steventon and Halton around 1400. The lords of Whitton, the Moneter (or *Monetarius*) family, long maintained themselves both in Ludlow and in the countryside; there is no evidence that they engaged directly in trade. In the 16th and 17th centuries it was not uncommon for gentry families, whose estates were outside Ludlow, to live in the town and to play significant parts in its government; was something similar happening in the 13th century?

Ludlow people often held land in the parishes immediately surrounding the town; to what extent they or their families worked this land themselves is not known, although it was common for them to rent out such holdings to others. The liberties of Ludlow extended into these parishes, but it is not known whether property-owning followed the jurisdiction or whether it was the other way round. As much of the land was to the south of the town in the townships of Huntington, Overton and Ashford, it seems more likely that it was the latter, since these places were not part of the original Lacy estate.

Ludlow had connections with Ireland which grew out of its lords' interests there. Ludlow names appear in Ireland. Even before 1200 the burgesses of Dublin included seven men from Ludlow, who either bore 'Ludelawe' as their surname or bore names very familiar in Ludlow itself.[6] Ludlow men frequently went to Ireland with the Mortimers or other magnates. There is also some evidence of people from Ireland settling in Ludlow, such as Henry de Irelond in 1268.[7]

In the period between 1200 and 1500 the population of Ludlow may have varied between about 750 and 2,000, and, even excluding women and children, say, about three quarters of the number, the majority of the adult males (between 200 and 500 in total) played no part in town government, did not feature in tax assessments, and did not transact the sort of business which would leave records to prove their existence as people. In short, Ludlow was dominated by a minority burgess class. While there were social classes, we know of no class conflict at any time before the 16th century. The attack on Roger Mortimer by a Ludlow mob in 1304, before he became lord of the town, was more likely to have been motivated by personal or local interests rather than class ones.[8] Indeed, although we have records of isolated riots, conspiracies and feuds at various times, it would be rash indeed to ascribe these to class-conflict, however one might suspect that sectional interests may have aligned themselves with the factions involved. There is no reason to suppose that the rich and powerful of medieval Ludlow were slower to exploit the rest of the people than the rich and powerful commonly are; Ludlow seems to have been organised to benefit the rich.

A clue may be found in the comparative lack of continuity in the leading families and their propensity to take their wealth elsewhere; the oligarchy was perforce not a closed one and it was possible for successful entrepreneurs of the middle rank, even immigrants, to join the ruling group, thus removing the potential leadership of outsider groups, dissent or 'have-not' movements. Ludlow was a market town for its district, but its fairs were rivalled by fairs and markets in many of the surrounding towns; for general agricultural produce and stock Leominster market was probably as important. In the early centuries the wealth of the leading merchants of Ludlow, many of whom were very rich men by any contemporary English urban standards, was derived from the wool trade, not from manufacture. The artisan class of Ludlow would have had different, but not necessarily conflicting, interests from those of the leading wool merchants. Indeed, it is possible that the prosperity of the former depended to some extent on the prosperity of the latter. Things changed when Ludlow took to making up its own cloth, when there would have been a large class of tradesmen who were economically controlled and perhaps exploited by the rich merchants.

Although the growth of cloth-manufacture can be discerned, class-conflict as its consequence cannot, but it may not have been absent. We have to look at secondary evidence;
the 1461 charter, as operated by the Corporation from at least as early as 1500, was
oligarchic in character and was increasingly interpreted so. The earlier constitution of the
borough may have been more open; since no charter exists (other than the Duke of York's
ample confirmation of 1449) and evidence is scarce, it cannot be proved.

One of the advantages of burgage tenure and burgess-ship was that a burgess of the
borough would have been recognised as a free man, particularly in relation to the lords of
Ludlow. Burgage tenure severed any legal connection between the individual and the
lord, substituting for it a relationship between the incorporated Community and the lord,
expressed in certain defined rights and obligations. In the 13th century this may not have
applied to non-burgess residents. In 1231 or earlier Walter de Lacy gave Stephen *Saponarius*,
his lands and his family to Crasswall Priory, which implies that the man was Lacy's serf;
in 1255 this gift may have been regarded as being represented by a burgage alone, but as
this was the last reference to Crasswall's interest, perhaps this had been merely a gift of a
serf, whose family may have been manumitted later.[9] It was never entirely clear what was
the relationship between an individual resident of Ludlow and other lords; this was common
elsewhere and in practice rarely became a problem unless the individual prospered and his
lord wished to exploit it to his own advantage. There is no such case known in Ludlow,
but there were individuals regarded as the *nativi* (bondmen) of other lords. In 1308 William
Abovethetowne, the *nativus* of Reginald Eylrich, was given to Thomas Foliot with lands in
Steventon.[10] In practice burgess-ship rapidly developed to be a right distinct from burgage-
tenure and was held by inheritance and grant from the Community, so that anyone of
substance could expect to attain it in due course. In the 16th century there is evidence of
a significant class of 'chensers', non-burgesses with restricted rights to trade and reside in
the town, many of whom eventually achieved burgess-ship, although rarely great prominence, perhaps because of the time it took to get onto the bottom rung of the ladder. Are
we entitled to see this relatively large class at this late date as evidence of greater exclusive-
ness in the oligarchy of the town than hitherto? In earlier centuries it may have been easier
to obtain the full rights of a burgess.

Of all social groupings kindred mattered most; this was true from the 12th century to
the early 17th century. There is abundant evidence of both explicit and inferential kinds
that families acted together and carried their actions to extreme lengths. As feuds between
families were common, concerted family policy was the rule in more mundane ways. The
history of the Ace family demonstrates how a family was likely to hitch its fortunes as a
whole to particular magnate patrons, to advance the careers of one another and to conspire
together in violent acts as well as to continue feuds through generations. The Orm family
and their friends came together to murder Thomas Marteley in what is now The Narrows
in 1331 and the affair was pursued ferociously through the courts by both families and
their connections.[11] At a lower social level there was the murder in 1399 by Richard Cook
of Jevan Bagh and his daughter Agnes, which was savagely avenged a year later by Jevan's
son, Lewis, who murdered Cook at the Oldfield (the present-day racecourse).[12] Presenting
a common front to non-kin, however, did not prevent bitter disputes within families, the
origins of which we might expect to have been inheritances. Members of the Ace family
sued each other and Nicholas Cressett and his brother Walter seem to have been continually
suing each other over debts and other matters.[13]

The People of Ludlow after 1500

Throughout the 16th century, as in the 15th, Ludlow was dominated by the cloth trade,
the dyers, the fullers, the weavers and, above all, the cloth manufacturers and cloth

merchants. Apart from those office-holders whose occupations are not definitely known, well over half the churchwardens and low bailiffs (offices likely to reflect current standing) in each *vicennium* from 1520 to 1600 were engaged in those trades. They were no longer dominant in 1601–20, were a smaller minority in 1621–40, and had almost wholly disappeared after 1640, being gradually replaced over the period by men engaged in the leather trades; the tanners, cordwainers, glovers and saddlers, who were dominant in 1621–40, wholly so after 1640. As the merchants among them in the early 16th century were often men who traded across the country, even abroad, while the mercers of the early 17th century were typically local retailers, the contrast is even greater than the figures suggest. Office-holding was confined to people of standing and so reflected the prosperity of particular groups. The economic groups represented by the chief officials were those whose interests were most carefully guarded by the Corporation.

Three or four generations of prominence were typical of the leading families. Their wealth was usually acquired by the first generation to come to the town; position came with it; thereafter the family's efforts were directed at exploiting and maintaining that position by ensuring that the family acquired its share of Corporation leases on favourable terms and making marriage-alliances with other leading families in the town. The circumstances of Ludlow in the second half of the 16th century, when the estates of the old Palmers' Gild had fallen into the hands of the Corporation, were especially conducive to the growth of oligarchy and its abuse of power. Mercantile wealth, however, has always been harder than landed wealth to consolidate and continue by inheritance. Primogeniture was less appropriate where all the sons acquired much the same skills and experience in their father's trade. Succession in trade had to be more gradual than in land ownership; the business may have relied on all the sons, whose co-operation might be withheld if they knew beforehand that their prospects of inheritance were tiny. Commercial fortunes tended to be split up; this was a severe handicap in trades requiring large fixed capital. Commercial families, therefore, either made it directly, or through their daughters, into the landed gentry or, more often, eventually they declined.

Whereas in the 15th century the neighbouring landed gentry had no great influence in the town, this changed in the next century, as the Foxes, enriched by commercial wealth inherited from the Downe family and by the estates plundered from the Church, acquired Corporation offices and, later, offices in the Council of the March. The Broughtons of Henley, landed gentry, on the other hand married their daughters into several leading Ludlow families, the Bradfords, Blashfields and Crowthers, without apparently acquiring any political influence in the town thereby. In the 17th century the Cressetts of Upton Cressett and the Townshends became connected by marriage to the Astons and, through them, the Fishers and Davieses, all leading burgess families. After 1660 the importance of gentry, like the Baldwins, Charltons and Herberts (descendants of the Foxes), increased, although these families rarely concerned themselves with municipal office, a measure of the decline in the importance of the Corporation.

Declining families are generally evidenced by their disappearance from records. The Langfords held municipal office between 1519 and 1628; the Crowthers from 1545 to 1647; the Blashfields from 1557 to 1623; the Powises from 1562 to 1676; the Heaths from 1565 to 1620 and the Colbatches from 1608 to 1660. Most other families' prominence was more short-lived. This was more apparent in the 17th century, which is to be expected in a period of economic decline, when fortunes were relatively small and more quickly lost.

In the conditions of the 16th century, where wealth created status and status led to office, sons often followed their fathers and grandfathers in Corporation office. Between 1490 and 1660 at least 33 low bailiffs were the sons, grandsons or brothers of earlier bailiffs or chamberlains. This may understate the position in the earlier decades, for which information is scarce, but by the early 17th century over a third of low bailiffs were closely related to earlier officials. More significant is the fact that in the period 1560–99 thirteen low bailiffs were, not sons, but the sons-in-law of earlier officials, for a man who married a daughter of a burgess became a burgess, thus ensuring the continuation of family businesses, where there were no sons, and the building of extended 'kindreds', where there were. In 1624 John Lythall, later to be chamberlain, was admitted as a burgess because his wife was the granddaughter of a burgess.[14] These kindreds, a normal social institution on the medieval March, were important in Ludlow even in the 17th century.

A small number of men obtained their entry into the town oligarchy by marrying the widows of former members. So Richard Swanson (low bailiff in 1575) married the widow of John Gwilliam; John Devawe (1593) married the widow of Maurice Phillips; John Patchett (1631) married Richard Nightingale's widow.

Families buttressed their social position through cultivating kindred; that is, the use of influence to advantage their cousins, relations by marriage, even their employees. It was a less formal and bourgeois version of the retaining and patronage by which the aristocracy maintained their social and political position. In Ludlow hints of its existence occur in the Middle Ages in the multiple conspiracies which were sometimes exposed in court and in the intercessions for pardons which noblemen made for their clients. In the 1590s the Ludlow 'charter disputes' exposed the working of 'kindred and affinity' in the government of Ludlow through the co-opting of councillors, the granting of favourable corporation leases and general laxness in accounting. In 1603 the Susan Blashfield affair provided a good example of how kindred and affinity was still strong enough to lead to conspiracy and riot, in which one faction was able to influence the town authorities to take its side. That the national authorities punished it severely suggests that the days of kindred and affinity were numbered, at least among small-town bourgeoisie.[15] Religious affinities proved to be stronger social bonds in the 17th century; the Townshend-Cressett-Aston connection, linking Catholics and Puritans, in the middle decades may have been but a notable exception.

From the mid-15th century immigration from central and north Wales became significant, probably more than at any time since the late 13th century. For many of them their probable places of origin can be deduced from their wills, like Edward Hughes of Felton, who came from Denbighshire, and Edmund Lloyd from Montgomeryshire.[16] Samuel Lloyd, low bailiff in 1628, came from Brecon. The prohibition on Welsh residence in towns like Ludlow, which followed the Glyndwr rebellions, seems to have been short-lived in its effect. Most Welshmen adopted either English surnames or their own patronymics as surnames and, in short, became Englishmen, although some, like the Hughes family, maintained their family and property connections with their places of origin, or even kept their Welsh names, as did Meredith ap Tudor of Galdeford, who joined the Palmers' Gild in 1488.[17] From this time Ludlow formed a stage in the westward transfer of population from Wales across England. Welshmen came to Ludlow; Ludlow men moved to the larger towns to the south and east, particularly Bristol, Coventry and London. There were five putative Welsh names appearing for the first time among the town officials between 1460 and 1480, nine between 1521 and 1540 and 17 between 1581 and 1600, coincidentally the high tide of oligarchy in the town. Thereafter the numbers of new Welsh names declined somewhat to 10 in 1601–20, nine 1621–40 and six 1641–60. Among the next rank of residents the proportion of Welsh names was greater; in 1543, 24 per cent of the men listed in the muster roll had Welsh names.[18] It is likely that, if the whole population could have been listed, the proportion would have been higher still. Nearly a third of those buried in the early 1590s bore Welsh names. There is no evidence that people of Welsh descent were regarded as inferior or were subjected to any disadvantages, notwithstanding the residence laws.

Notable Families

The Andrew Family

From the late 12th to the late 13th century the Andrew family was one of the most important families in Ludlow. Throughout the period this family had landed interests in Stokesay and Steventon, which may have represented mercantile wealth invested in land. It is possible that the family acquired its importance as burgesses of Ludlow from its landed status in nearby townships. So little is known of late 12th-century Ludlow that no evidence of personal wealth exists from the period.

The first of the family known is Andrew fitz Miles of Ludlow who acquired Stokesay mill from Elias de Say sometime between 1195 and 1221.[19] He had a brother Roger and possibly a second brother, Henry Miles.[20] A fine in 1203 for breach of the assize of cloth indicates that he was a cloth merchant.[21] In 1210 he granted a third of a messuage in Ludlow to Warin de Grendone, perhaps a grant of dower.[22]

Andrew fitz Miles's three sons, Nicholas, Geoffrey and James, all bore the surname Andrew. The first-named may have been the eldest, for he inherited Stokesay mill. In 1255 Nicholas Andrew held Clee St Margaret and half of Steventon of William Mauduit, lord of Holdgate, and these estates descended through his son John (d. before 1325) to, first, a grandson, Master William Andrew, and, secondly, to William's brother, Thomas Andrew, who died before 1347.[23] Nicholas Andrew's leading position in Ludlow is attested by his frequent appearances as a witness of charters and as one of the founder members and benefactor of the Palmers' Gild. It seems that another son, Andrew, (described as Andrew fitz Nicholas, son of Margery de Styvyntone) was killed in 1291 by Hugh Oweyn; in the same year Andrew's brother, William, murdered Hugh Sarote and then fled.[24] Nicholas's brother, Geoffrey, was the first warden or Gildalderman of the Gild.[25] Geoffrey died before 1284 and was succeeded only by a daughter, Yvette, who later married Geoffrey, lord of Greet, and she was, with Master William Andrew, a co-defendant in a disseisin claim in 1298.[26] The importance of the family as burgesses of Ludlow did not survive the century; their representatives were rural rather than borough notables.

The Ludelawe Family

Nicholas de Ludelawe accumulated a large mercantile fortune and a national reputation in his lifetime. With Lawrence his son he was licensed to export wool in 1272. He was appointed in 1276 to demand compensation from the count of Flanders for English merchants' losses during the war between Henry III and the countess. His personal claim for losses due to piracy, £1,920, was by far the largest in England. He died before 1283.[27] As Lawrence was probably at that time even richer than his father, it is likely that Nicholas died at an advanced age. It is curious that there is no earlier extant reference to him than 1272; it may be that hitherto he had been known by another surname and was a member of another prominent family. The surname 'de Ludelawe' would be an odd one for a man to be accorded in his own town, unless he had acquired it elsewhere, as a merchant trading internationally but based in Ludlow might well have. We can guess, therefore, that Nicholas, known by another name, built up a national and international business in which he became known as 'Nicholas of Ludlow', which name was adopted by him at home too. It may be significant that his son Lawrence was called simply 'Lawrence', without a surname, in the borough accounts for 1289.[28]

Lawrence established the family as landed gentry when he acquired Stokesay manor in 1281.[29] He died spectacularly – at sea on 24 November 1294, while commanding the English wool fleet to the Netherlands.[30] His wife may have been sister to the wife of Peter Gilemin, another Ludlow merchant.[31] Of Lawrence's brothers and sisters, Roger entered the Church,

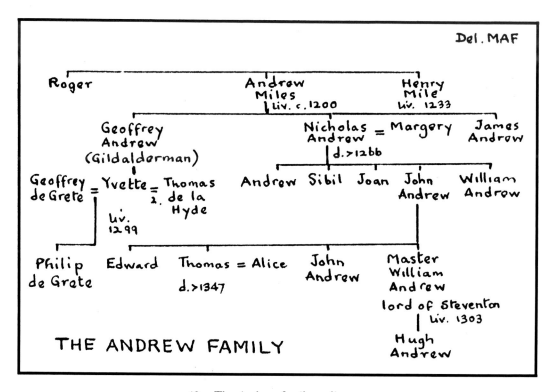

48.   The Andrew family pedigree

becoming rector of Chalgrove.[32] Thomas, who was knighted, had estates in Surrey; John, a Shrewsbury merchant, was lord of Coldweston. Agnes (who owned a house in Mill Street) remained a spinster. Cecily married John Adrien, a rich London draper.[33] The Ludelawe family were prosperous and prolific; Lawrence's descendants maintained their connections and property in Ludlow; his grandson, also Lawrence, founded the Carmelite priory to which he gave several burgages in Corve Street. This Lawrence and his brother William were each victims of homicide. Lawrence's Ludlow properties remained in his family until they descended, along with Stokesay, to the Vernons.

In 1344 William de Lodelowe was murdered by William Forde whom Sir John Bouldewas was accused of harbouring in Ludlow; Richard Esthame was charged with abetting the murder.[34] The most socially successful of the families of Ludlow, other than its lords, the Ludelawes, seem to have paid for their success by attracting lethal hostility; 10 years later William's uncle, Sir Lawrence de Lodelowe, was murdered by John Halghtone in Ludlow.[35]

While there were some families who remained prominent in the town over several generations, most of those who did so were landed families from an early stage. Commercial wealth, although important in the establishment of a family, was not sufficient for the survival of that family. With land went status and influence and the possibility of the rewards of office; commerce was precarious, being dependent upon current ability and luck. Few purely trading families lasted long.

The Ace Family

The Aces arrived in Ludlow before the mid-13th century. There were later connections between the Ludlow Aces and those of Southampton (who were resident there by 1250), but it is not known whether those of Ludlow came from Southampton.[36]

The first known Ace to own property in Ludlow was Richard, c.1272. That year his son, William, was killed in a brawl, the first of several homicides involving the Ludlow Aces. In 1304 William, son of Hugh Ace, killed Lawrence Harper, and this was echoed in 1360 when another William Ace killed William Harper.[37] They were a particularly litigious family, much given to suing each other over property. John Ace was engaged in the cloth trade, being prosecuted in 1292 for selling cloth against the assize.[38] Richard, dead by 1312, left his property to his daughter, Alice, and his son, John (c.1260–1321), who owned houses in Brand Lane, Galdeford, High Street and Corve Street, some by purchase, some by inheritance. He was connected with the Orletone and Routone families, conventionally pious in his gifts to the church, and considerate of the needs of his wife and sons and daughters.[39]

Several Aces entered the Church. John Ace had a son, Nicholas, a clergyman. In 1318 a Brother John Ace, a canon of Wigmore, was sent to St Augustine's, Bristol, for penitential discipline after misconduct.[40] The most successful of the clerical Aces was Hugh, son of William, (c.1330–93), who was presented to Sidbury by Philip Whitton, a curious circumstance, as four years later he was pardoned for the death of John Whitton, by which time he was a client of the Earl of Arundel. He later became treasurer of Hereford Cathedral.[41] Hugh's brother, Philip, was presented by Arundel to Hopesay in 1351, when he was about forty and still wholly unordained. Later he lost a case in the papal curia over Bullinghope prebend. He seems never to have progressed beyond deacon and probably spent his life as an Arundel clerk, a reversal of family loyalties.[42]

The most interesting member of the family was Thomas, son of John Ace (c.1280–1353), already an attorney in Roger Mortimer's service before 1309, when Mortimer charged Roger Foliot and William Sparcheford with assaulting him at Church Stretton and stealing deeds from him. In 1310 he acted as attorney for Ludlow men going to Ireland with Mortimer. In 1307 he may have been a juror at Kilmanagh, Ireland.[43] In that year he was parson of Middleton, Shropshire; if Middleton Scriven, it may have been a Mortimer presentation.[44] Thomas Ace of Newport was accused with others of the murder of Henry Salt at Stafford in 1320. Roger Mortimer owned the wardship of the lord of Newport, Nicholas Audley's heir; Ace was perhaps then engaged in this business.[45] In 1321 he was with Mortimer on the abortive expedition to Kingston upon Thames and also at the later seizure of Clun Castle, for which 'adherence' his property in Ludlow was temporarily forfeit.[46] He was by now heavily involved in the risks and opportunities of national politics, but he was sure-footed, for when Mortimer was a fugitive in France, Ace obtained the royal grant of Tilsop.[47] Yet in 1327 when Mortimer was returned, Ace was still his 'valett'.[48] At Easter 1327 he was appointed sheriff of Caernarvonshire, which he kept (apart from a brief gap in 1331–2) until 1337 when he was dismissed.[49] In 1328, described as 'king's yeoman', he obtained at the request of Edmund, Earl of Kent, the town of Nevyn, Caernarvonshire.[50] In 1328 he helped value the estates of Arundel and the Despensers, Mortimer's enemies.[51] He survived the fall and execution of Kent in 1329 and of Mortimer in 1330, and in that year was empowered to seize for the king all the Mortimer castles and estates in South Wales and the March. He remained as keeper of Cleobury and Wigmore.[52] His official career seems to have ceased in 1337; thereafter he engaged in law-suits and prosecutions over property and feuds in Ludlow and Shropshire, eventually being the prime mover in the murder of Richard Goldsmith of Ludlow at the Sheet in 1339.

In the middle decades of the 14th century there were two John Aces in Ludlow, who are impossible to distinguish. Between 1329 and 1331 a John Ace was king's bailiff itinerant in Hampshire.[53] He went to Gascony in 1324 and was the John 'of Lodelawe' who stole goods from ships in Southampton in 1327.[54] In 1332 a John Ace of Ludlow went on a pilgrimage to the shrine of St James of Compostela in Spain.[55] In 1343 John Ace was awarded the huge sum of £91 19s. 10d. for the appropriation by the king of his wool at Durdrecht in the Netherlands.[56] John, son of Thomas Ace, was involved in the murder of Richard Goldsmith but pardoned in 1346; the 1353 report of John Ace's escape from prison may be a very late report of him or relate to another John Ace. Was he the John Ace of Ludlow, murdered at Lyde in 1349, one of whose murderers was pardoned at the request of Roger Mortimer II? The Aces seem to have become the victims of the Mortimers, instead of their clients.[57]

In Ludlow it was William Ace who had clout. By 1340 he had added most of the family's property to his own purchases and owned houses in most streets. He was a senior member of the Palmers' Gild from 1330 until his death in 1361, a member of the Twelve of the town in 1339–40 and in 1332 was one of the representatives of the borough sent to the parliament *pro stapulis ordinandis*.[58] He sued and was sued often. His wool and cloth buying operations were extensive; in 1353 he was accused of not paying for wool bought in Newport.[59] He, too, sold wool in the Netherlands, being partially compensated in 1344 with 'Durdrecht bonds' for the king's appropriations.[60]

With the death of Hugh Ace in 1393 the Ace connection with Ludlow seems to have rested with Philip Ace's property ownership, which scarcely survived the century. The Aces had played an important part in town life for over 150 years, making for themselves commercial, official and clerical careers under a series of patrons, involved themselves in the fringes of violent politics, killed at least four people and lost three of their own to homicide. Personal wealth and patronage were the basis of bourgeois success, but, unlike land, these were not proof against the onslaughts of nature or of enemies. The family rose and disappeared, leaving no trace other than endowments for prayers for their dead. Their history suggests that those prayers were needed.

The Parys Family

The Parys family was prominent from about 1380 to 1449 and then disappeared. The first was John Parys, who became steward of the Palmers' Gild in 1383.[61] There were Parises in 1327 at Hodnet, a manor connected with Ludlow through the Ludelawe family. John Parys had trading connections with Coventry, for he, Agnes his wife and Hugh and Edith, the parents of one of them, were members of the Trinity Gild there.[62] He died by 1392.[63] His son, William Parys, a cloth merchant, was for many years the leading burgess of Ludlow, holding gild, borough and county offices. In 1399–1401 he was king's alnager in Shropshire, a subsidy commissioner for the county in 1404, warden of the Palmers' Gild in 1401–2 and 1422–40 and bailiff of Ludlow 1416–19.[64] He was not above criminality (false weights and affray). His son, John, was also bailiff of Ludlow and warden of the Gild, as well as subsidy collector. He, too, fell foul of the law and on one occasion was outlawed.[65] John had no children; his brother, Thomas, lived elsewhere and the Ludlow connection ended with John's death in 1449.[66]

The Langford Family

In the 16th century long-lasting families are harder to trace. Some families, such as the Langfords and Blashfields, lived in the town for 150 and 100 years respectively. William Langford or Longford owned property in Corve Street in 1528; he may have been one of the Langfords of Leintwardine, for a William Langford was executor of Roger Yryngmonger there in 1499.[67] His son, also William Langford, a mercer, was born in 1483.[68] His public

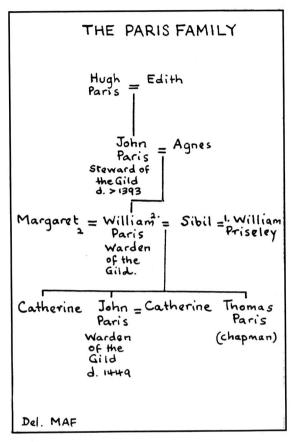

49. The Paris family pedigree.

career, which began with his joining the Gild in 1508, included the low bailiffship in 1519. He was high bailiff at least four times, coroner once, and the last warden of the Palmers' Gild 1547–51. His life ended in two calamities; in 1551 he was forced to surrender the Gild's properties and in 1552 he was subjected by his family to an enquiry into his sanity. Although he was declared sane, he died shortly afterwards and his heirs obtained his property notwithstanding.[69] William was the most prominent of the family, his descendants declining in the social scale. They had wide interests, but were chiefly tanners whose fortune began with the two Williams. Warden William's son, Richard, who inherited some of the wealth of his mother's family, the Downes, also held most borough offices, including rent collector (after holding the same position in the Gild), as well as being M.P. in 1562.[70] He died intestate in 1562 and his large estate was probably divided amongst his many children. His son, Thomas (1538–1610), was a tanner who held the post of rent collector in addition to the range of annual Corporation offices.[71] In the next generation Richard (d. 1630) was a baker and Walter (1565–1630) was an innkeeper; while Walter held all the offices, Richard went no further than low bailiff. They were the last of the family to live in Ludlow.

The Rascall Family

A family of similar longevity was the Rascalls, otherwise called Roscowe, Rosball and Rosegrove, who may have come from Presteigne in the mid-15th century. A cleric, Walter Rosegrove, is mentioned in Ludlow in 1475, but otherwise the first we know of is Thomas Rascall or Roscowe who obtained a lease of the Corporation mills in the late 15th century.[72] After his death in 1502 his successor as milward was his son, Thomas, who had interests in all the town mills (1480–1553).[73] In 1551 he was a Gild tenant.[74] He was succeeded by his son, Richard (1523–1607), a clothier, who was the first of the family to enter the ruling oligarchy of the town, being married twice, respectively to a Handley and to a Blashfield. He held all the important annual elective offices from churchwarden to high bailiff. He left his goods to a daughter. His son, William (1575–1633), proceeded no further than churchwarden and died leaving no surviving children. The other son, Richard, achieved no office, despite describing himself as 'gentleman' and died leaving only a daughter, Sarah, who married Cuthbert Hely with whom she moved to London.[75] That was the end of the Rascall family and fortune.

Class, Kindred and Crime

Crime was committed brazenly by all classes. Although crime rates cannot be calculated, theft and violence were undoubtedly prevalent, the latter, at least, much more so than in the late 20th century. Personal morality seems not to have improved over the period, but some improvement can be discerned in the incidence of crime.

In the 13th and 14th centuries, with the town never again so prosperous, there were a good many murders. Some were the consequence of drunken brawls, some accompanied robberies, but many were the result or cause of feuds. Most men carried weapons as a normal article of dress and, when roused over matters of honour or interest, did not hesitate to use them. Society generally approved of this. A man was far more likely to be hanged for robbery than for murder; execution was more likely if he were poor or a stranger than if he were well-off and locally well connected.

In the 12 months after October 1271, 16 people were tried for felonious killing in Ludlow, while in 1292 27 people were tried for murder or manslaughter. Even though some of them may have languished in prison for months or years while awaiting trial, this suggests that each year more than one inhabitant in a hundred might be involved in violent death as victim or perpetrator.[76] Drink was the cause of much mischief; in 1271 Roger Lyde was stabbed to death by Wyn Forester of Stanton Lacy after drinking in a Ludlow tavern and in the same year Thomas Gyllur knifed Elias Spark at Robert Dul's tavern in Broad Street. Richard Acton stabbed to death Richard Mideltone outside another tavern and Thomas Stoke similarly killed his own brother Roger.[77]

In the absence of effective police, private vengeance was often the only satisfaction left to a victim's family. So at the Oldfield in 1400 Lewis Bagh, with his friends, avenged himself on Richard Cooke, his father's and sister's murderer of ten months previously. Many other killings may have been acts of revenge whose motives were kept hidden.[78]

The juries of medieval Shropshire were often merciful, since they were appointed on the principle, not of impartiality, but of familiarity with the persons and events involved. There was no forensic evidence; everything depended on the credibility and standing of the witnesses, whom the juries could be expected to know. In a society in which kindred mattered, jurors were rarely likely to approach a trial impartially. Choosing the jury was crucial. To be the cause of a hanging would have brought a juror considerable opprobrium from the dead man's kindred and he would not choose to make new enemies in this way. In actions over property partial juries were often empanelled; so William Hurell of Ludlow claimed that the jury empanelled in 1358 to try Walter Cambray's case against him had been chosen to find for Cambray.[79] How much more likely it was that such embracery occurred in serious criminal cases. Most verdicts in murder cases were acquittals and many even declared the killing to have been self-defence. Of 48 men accused of felonious killing in Ludlow in the middle part of Edward I's reign, five only were hanged, 16 were acquitted without comment, three were found to have killed in self-defence, two claimed benefit of clergy and 22 fled to sanctuary or outlawry. Those who chose flight were either guilty or, more dangerous for them, friendless. The friendless would have included strangers to the town and poor men; they could not expect justice, so that they would be left with a choice between hanging and flight to join the swarms of robbers who preyed on travellers in the March.

Criminals could find sanctuary in any of the churches and chapels of Ludlow. In 1255 Nicholas *Cissor* (?Sherman) fled into Ludlow church when Roger Mortimer's men came from Wigmore to Ludlow to arrest him for theft; when they left the town, he emerged from the sanctuary they had respected.[80] In 1292 William Clyfford sought sanctuary in Ludlow church after killing Simon Wasgoch at Stokesay.[81] The Church usually upheld its rights in such cases, less from a sense of justice or mercy, than from a sense of its own privileges. A man who sought sanctuary had 'abjured the realm' and his goods were forfeit, a high price; many starved to death in sanctuary. Often someone seeking sanctuary was no more than putting himself beyond the reach of an enraged mob until such time as the authorities could sort things out. Offending clergy would do this until their claim to benefit of clergy could be upheld. John Berner of Cleobury was involved in a quarrel with Walter Wylyley of Ludlow in 1299; each stabbed the other, but Wylyley died. Berner claimed self-defence and fled to the Austin Friars' chapel with a mob on his heels which violated sanctuary by dragging him out. He was beaten, shackled and sent to Shrewsbury gaol. Bishop Swinfield protested to the king who restored Berner to the sanctuary. Nevertheless, Berner was later brought to trial when the assize jury found that he 'prowled in the night to do evil and is a common hooligan'.[82]

The clergy were no better behaved than the laity and could claim immunities not open to them, a privilege more conducive to bad than to good behaviour. Hugh Oweyn, found guilty in 1292 of killing Andrew Styvyntone with an axe, claimed benefit of clergy and was freed. Nicholas Wyke, a Carmelite friar, robbed his own prior in 1387, taking gold, silver and other goods; the prior sent a party to arrest him, but he went missing.[83] Benefit of clergy did not confer immunity in offences against the Church.

In 1413 William Parys, a leading merchant in the town, led an armed gang against the house of Thomas Kaynham at Wigley, wounding him and his wife Alice and stealing their stock. Parys, as unscrupulous as he was rich, was doubtless concerned to demonstrate that he could not be opposed in business matters with impunity. He was also charged with fraudulently using false weights, but his power and standing in the town suffered nothing from these prosecutions.[84] It was a friend of the Parys family, John Tylere, who broke into and ransacked John Werrewyke's house in 1366, not being tried for it until 1373 when there was a further charge of breaking into John Chabbenore's house and killing him as he lay in bed. As there is no record of a conviction, Tylere may have made good use of his connections. There is a sharp distinction between this case and that of David ap William alias David Llott who was hanged for burglary and murder in 1390; he had 'no goods' and no friends or influence either.[85]

The best documented crime in medieval Ludlow was the murder of Thomas Marteley on 5 December 1331, in what is now called The Narrows at the Fish Street corner. William, Nicholas and John Orm, and their friends, Richard Schrosbury and Roger Wynchecote, lay in wait for Marteley, whom they attacked with a sword, knives and sticks. The dead man's brother, Richard, raised the hue and cry, the only way of regularising the pursuit

50.   The Narrows and the Lane to Taylors' Gate.
In 1331 Thomas Marteley was murdered here by
the Orm brothers.

of criminals, there being no police force. At the subsequent trial Richard Marteley offered
to prove his accusation by judicial combat, which the court ordered in the belief (or hope)
that God would give victory to the side telling the truth. Nine months later the defendants
countered by claiming that their accusers had lied; each side assembled pledges. The truth
is not known, but a further defendant, Richard son of William Woder, was acquitted of
the murder. The numbers of people involved as defendants, accusers and pledges, suggests
that the killing was an incident in a wide-ranging kindred-feud.[86] Kindred could frustrate
even royal police measures; Roger Wyggeley of Ludlow, appointed by the king to arrest
several people for sedition, had to seek special royal protection, fearing personal danger
from the malefactors' friends.[87]

In 1203 a summary lynching followed Richard Falconer's theft from Adelina Ludelawe,
with whom he was lodging; the hue and cry was raised and the men of the town chased
and killed him.[88] Hue and cry was, however, open to abuse; in 1304 it was an earlier
William Orm and Richard Schrosbury who led the crowd which, after a quarrel, pursued
Roger Mortimer's servants back to Mortimer's lodgings, raised the hue and cry, and sent
for the common bells of the town to be rung, the normal procedure, then broke down the
doors. When Mortimer had failed to persuade them to go away the bailiffs were called and
the ringleaders were gaoled.[89]

The truth was often hard to discover, even if anyone were present with an interest in
finding out. Where there was not, *ex parte* explanations would be accepted to close down
cases. Did Rys ap David Lloyd really fall 100 ft. from the castle walls in April 1401, while,
as was claimed, escaping from Edmund Mortimer's prison?[90]

Many murders reaching the king's courts were committed by well-to-do people in the course of family feuds, often over property. Richard Goldsmyth, a rich Ludlow merchant, who owned the Sheet, was murdered in 1339 by John Ace and his father Thomas Ace or their agent, Simon Bigin. The case rumbled on for some years, with the Aces being gaoled and later escaping. No verdict has come to light.[91] John Ace, having been pardoned in 1346, was murdered in 1349 by Richard Wymond of Eyton, acting, it seems, for Master Henry Shipton, archdeacon of Shropshire. After the intercession of Roger Mortimer, Richard Wymond was pardoned in recognition of his service at sea against Spain.[92] Behind these events were surely complex conspiracies. Usually the links between crimes are hidden, but occasionally a hint survives. Five years before Richard Wymond *alias* Eyton killed John Ace, a Richard Heyton was involved with a Philip Wyht and others in the kidnapping of servants of the abbot of Wigmore at Cainham, and later Philip Wyht was charged with the murder of William Ace, for which he was pardoned in 1350 at the instance of Roger Mortimer, whose servant he clearly was.[93] These events suggest extensive 'affinities' in violent rivalry.

The well-connected were generally able to obtain royal pardons, even for murder, at the instance of powerful friends or patrons. In 1304 Roger Foliot and Reginald Eylrich obtained their pardons (for killing William Adam of Over Heyton) at the instance of Master John Kenles, archdeacon of Meath and chancellor of the Dublin exchequer, but an important king's clerk in England.[94] Then in 1346 John Ace obtained a pardon for various offences at the instance of Philip Whittone, a king's yeoman.[95]

Sudden death from disease, accident and crime was a banal occurrence. Few people avoided violence throughout their lives, so it was generally tolerated. It was property and honour which mattered and, for them, men would fight to the death, because the authorities and the courts offered imperfect and tardy protection for the former and none for the latter. Men looked for protection to their patrons, kindred and friends if they ran into trouble; those who had none were helpless.

Because statistical evidence is lacking, we cannot compare the crime rates of one period with another. Did crime diminish over the centuries or did it fluctuate according to circumstance, the incidence of famines, poor harvests, civil war or rising population? By the 16th century the power of the central government to enforce laws was very much stronger than it had been and it had a much stronger desire to suppress disorder, exemplified by Bishop Lee's letter to Thomas Cromwell from Ludlow in 1534, that he intended to go to Presteigne 'among the thickest of thieves and shall do the King such service as the strongest of them shall be afraid'.[96] The propensity of the well-off classes to kill their enemies was much diminished, although their quarrels were as bitter as ever they had been. Their terror of the poor however suggests that crime born of poverty was growing. The town court had the power to execute criminals and often did so; so common were public executions that it was only if something went wrong with procedures that we know of them.

A burglar's hanging was delayed in 1597 to allow Stephen Lesieur, a victim, a chance to travel from London to help in recovering the stolen goods. On that occasion Richard Benson, the bailiff, was not well and did not stay 'until all the malefactors were executed', that is, ' . . . for three quarters of an hour or more'.[97]

The parish register did not record executions and violent deaths unless otherwise noteworthy. Between 1578 and 1625 only one hanging, that of David ap Powell ap Thomas in 1578, was recorded. In 1607 John Powell – possibly the unhanged burglar – died in prison 'for murther'. Victims are more numerous and were recorded in 1584, 1607, 1613, 1616, 1619, 1621 and a double murder in 1625. There must have been in each case something unusual which led to its being noted; there were more killings and executions than this.

More mundane offences far outnumbered these dramatic crimes. The lowest level of justice was dispensed at the view of frankpledge. For the period 1547 to 1554 the records of this court for Lower Corve Street alone have survived and these include eight affrays, three cases of theft from St Leonard's chapel, four offences against the assizes of bread and ale, four failures to keep walls repaired, one common scold and several charges of nuisances (street dung heaps and throwing carcases into the River Corve). Alice Sankey and her son, William, were the chief offenders.[98] The 1654 view of frankpledge shows that Ludlow had still not greatly changed; there were eight charges of keeping dunghills in Corve Street, but fewer brawls.[99] Some offences filtered through to the Council of the March. In the 20 years 1616–37 Ludlow itself provided 33 affrays and assaults, 20 sexual offences (usually consenting offences), 16 breaches of the court's orders or failures of duty, seven cases of defamation and 15 other offences.[100]

The Poor

The town has always had its poor, although until the 17th century, when statutory provision was made for their relief and discipline, there are few records attesting their existence. Occasional charitable impulses towards the poor and, later, the establishment of almshouses, prove the existence of poor people but do not help us to estimate their numbers. For periods when estimating the total population is very difficult, estimating the number of poor is far harder.

Bad harvests, trade depressions and wars caused poverty throughout the Middle Ages, as did individual misfortune from age, sickness, injury and bereavement. Charity was more directed towards the sick; in 1309, for instance, the Community arranged a collection for lepers.[101] Bad harvests would bring desperate immigrants to the town, and poor trade might lead eventually to emigration. There were always poor people but their numbers probably fluctuated. Nevertheless, structural poverty, associated with capitalistic enterprises concentrated in a few hands employing a large class of workers, probably did not exist. The medieval borough was essentially a mechanism for controlling trade and industry against the threat of competition; it would have mitigated any tendency for the development of a large class of day-labourers competing for work. It would be from such a class that 'the poor' would have fallen. This phenomenon did not appear until the 16th century.

Fifty wills have survived from the period 1300 to 1500. All contain bequests to the church, but only nine leave money specifically to the poor (three of these in return for services at the funeral). One was John Hosyer's will, the most important single act in favour of the poor for centuries, in which he gave instructions in 1463 for the foundation of an almshouse, which still exists.[102] Almost all wills left money for masses and obits for the deceased's soul; in medieval Ludlow faith was a more esteemed virtue than charity. This does not, however, suggest that poverty normally existed on a considerable scale or that it was perceived as a pressing problem.

One of the objectives of the Gild was the relief of its own members in trouble. This was less a charitable than an insurance function and was aimed not at general poverty but at individual misfortune. In 1426 money was given to a Gild member, Reginald Draper of 'the Pole', 'who was lately plundered by false thieves'. The next year the Gild stewards distributed 10s. 2d. to various 'brothers and sisters of the Gild and other paupers' on the Friday after All Saints. In 1428 John Touer, clerk, was given 12d. by way of alms on Easter Saturday. 6d. was spent on burying Agnes Nyghtyngale, for the Gild was a 'burial club' for its members, providing suitable ceremony and, in cases of need, paying for the funeral itself. Nevertheless, this was not very munificent; in the period 1424–8 less than one per cent of the Gild's expenditure was laid out on this kind of individual relief.[103] When the Gild's property was handed over to the Corporation after 1551, part of the endowment was attached to Hosyer's almshouse, probably in substitution for previous Gild charity.

51.   Hosyer's Almshouse: an 18th-century building on the fondations of the earlier almshouse endowed by John Hosyer, a 15th-century merchant.

In the first half of the 16th century 22 Ludlow wills were proved in the prerogative court; of these only seven mentioned the poor. Between 1551 and 1600, however, 38 of the 57 proved mentioned them, with a growing stress on the 'honest' or deserving poor as proper objects of charity. Those whose wills were proved at Hereford were in general less well off; certainly they were less liberal. In the first half of the 16th century 19 per cent of all testators (prerogative court and Hereford together) remembered the poor, in the second half 33 per cent. Even allowing for changing perceptions of the objectives of charity, the inference must be that, after the Reformation removed conventual houses and prayers for the dead as destinations for surplus testamentary funds, the poor were present in sufficient numbers to provide an alternative. That it was proper to discriminate between the 'honest' poor and others suggests that there was now in existence a class of 'undeserving' poor, a term which implies vagrants but which (then as now) in the eyes of the cold-hearted included the unemployed (the 'idle' poor). William Foxe left £5 to the poor in 1553 which was to be given 'without making an open dole'.[104] The 'poor' as a class had come into being. For the next 300 years the administration of this class was to be a primary task of local government.

Contempt for the real poor was not the sole reason for this careful direction of relief; responsible citizens saw it as their duty to the town to help worthy young men to get started in business. So we see Richard Swanson in 1577 leaving £10 as loans for young beginners, smiths (his own trade) being exempt from interest, and Kenelm Shrawley in 1589 leaving money for £50 loans for two poor young men of good name to set them up in business.[105]

Between 1601 and 1645 there were 77 prerogative court wills, but only 31 of these and only 23 per cent of all prerogative court and Hereford court wills left anything to the poor. Possibly the level of generosity fell below what might have been expected because the 1601

Act now compulsorily rated residents for poor relief. Those who confidently claimed in their wills to be among the 'Lord's elect' were often conspicuous in their lack of liberality towards the poor. Good works, it may be assumed, were unnecessary for the salvation of the 'elect'. The larger the generosity the more likely was it to be directed towards the 'deserving', like 'such as are aged and impotent' (Thomas Hill, 1637) or 'poore yonge beginners being tradesmen' (Margaret Badie, 1611). 'Decayed tradesmen' were increasingly objects of charity. Particularity in the choice of objects of charity shows that the well-off thought there were now more poor people than could or should be subsidised. Although the poor as a class were now numerous, as a class they were increasingly ignored. Nevertheless, occasional bequests were still wide in their generosity, as was William Littleton's gift of £10 in 1655 which was disbursed to about 250 households, comprising some 320 adults together with an unknown number of children.[106] In that year it seems that the poor were not less than a fifth, and perhaps as many as a third, of the population.[107]

Some testators gave annuities for the benefit of the poor. Among them were Thomas Candland's bequest in 1617 of a rent charge on a shop to fund a weekly payment of 4d. to each resident of the almshouse with the balance to be divided by the bailiffs among other poor as they saw fit.[108] In 1624 James Walter gave a yearly rent of £20 from his lands in Stanton Lacy and Richard's Castle, half of which was to be used by the Corporation for the maintenance of the poor in the almshouse.[109] In 1629 Richard Gwillim left 20s. a year from his property in Leominster, effectively to be disbursed by the rector of Ludlow to 'the poor impotent people of Ludlow'.[110]

About this time Thomas Pingle gave £20 as a capital sum to be invested at eight per cent, half the interest being paid by the rector to the poor of the almshouse and the other half to 'the other poor and impotent people of the town'. How far this confident calculation of the income to accrue was borne out by events we do not know.[111] In 1634 Charles Sonnibank settled a rent of £13 6s. 8d. from Hopesay on the bailiffs and other notables of Ludlow to 'expend, pay and distribute' it among 10 poor widows at the rate of 6d. a week; the widows had to be 'of honest conversation and of good report fearing God and frequenting the church'. The practical administration of this was put in the hands of the rector for ever, for which good work he was to be paid as a first charge on the funds. Sonnibank decided to set the tone by naming the first 10 widows; none of them can be traced in the families of the notables of the town, so it seems that they were indeed poor.[112] The fee farm rent of the town became vested in the Corporation for the benefit of the poor after 1655.

Hosyer's almshouse was the most important of the almshouses. The rules provided that those admitted should be people of good character who had long lived in the town. In 1551 there were 33 'chambers' for as many poor people, each getting 4d. a week from the endowments.[113] It is unlikely that the small number of chambers available satisfied all needs and it is certain that nomination to vacancies became a matter of competition and influence. During the charter disputes of the 1590s it was laid down, doubtless after complaints, that only the aged impotent who had spent their youth in the town should be admitted. Many of the testamentary bequests to the poor specified that it should be the inmates of the almshouse who should benefit; this may have been a recognition that 16th-century inflation had eroded the value of the endowed dole there. Directing further charity to the almshouse, rather than more widely, may have been merely to avoid the trouble of selecting deserving recipients. In 1590 a second set of almshouses was built by Charles Foxe in the precincts of St Leonard's chapel in Corve Street, which he had acquired; he added an endowment to provide an income. Two houses were to be occupied by people from Bromfield, two from Ludlow; it is not recorded whether the Foxe family retained the nominations to these almshouses. The 18th- and 19th-century history of this foundation was a sordid tale of neglect and greed, lying beyond the scope of this book.

The abolition of the conventual houses of Ludlow may not have harmed the poor, apart from depriving them of minor employments, for the alms paid were not great.

The parish register scarcely noticed the poor and references to their burials were only to distinguish them from other people of the same name. Only in 1570, when the burials of seven poor people were registered, 1571 (four), and 1597 (nine), could there be another reason for indicating them as such. Among those in 1597 were the burials on 25 and 27 January of Gwen Corbett, a poor woman, and a poor stranger, both of whom 'died in the street'. There was little to hold off a cold winter for the poor.

Statutory provision of poor relief was in being from 1563, stiffened in 1572, and systematised in 1598 and 1601, but the Corporation continued with its own somewhat haphazard arrangements for helping particular people.[114] In 1594 Richard Heyton was granted 40s., having been crippled while on duty as a watchman. In 1596 Alice Brasier, widow, was granted 13s. 4d. twice-yearly to relieve her poverty; she had been the second wife of John Brasier, a former bailiff, and she herself died within the year, so did not constitute a long-term charge on Corporation funds. In 1603 a rate was levied for the relief of William Jones, a maimed soldier; discharged soldiers were often abandoned, so he was lucky. Anne Free's children received unspecified medical treatment in 1604 at public expense, but the reason is not known. Margaret, widow of a former bailiff, Richard Rascall, was granted a pension of 40s. a year in 1608; as she had well-to-do sons and Blashfield cousins, it is hard to see this as a case of special need, more a case of special clout. Henry Cleobury was given a donation in 1609 to relieve his poverty. His mother was granted 6d. a week for life in 1620 because of her old age and because her husband had been bailiff. William Gregory, the former bailiff, was himself a recipient of a hand-out in 1638, being 'an ancient alderman fallen into want'. Need could be relative and in 1615 Richard Bedowe, a student at Oxford, son of Ellis Bedowe, (who joined the Twenty Five at about that time) was given a bursary of £10 out of the Corporation rents.[115] Doles from the Corporation were generally directed less at poor people as such than at their own members, former members or their connections. Alice Gough's need was clear when she, her daughter and grandchild, were stricken with plague in 1604, but why she was singled out for relief in that year is not known. Nevertheless, in 1609 payments to plague victims became more general and orders had to be given for auditing the accounts of the fund. This was very much an early 17th-century development as haphazard charity from existing funds gave way to more general relief supported by collections and rates.

In the early 17th century poverty was a serious and continuing problem in Ludlow. Rating for poor relief began after the 1563 statute and the collection record for Castle and Broad Street wards of 1566 has survived. In those wards there were about thirty-eight recipients of relief. Of these 18 received relief in each quarter of the year and 12 in only one quarter, half of whom had died in the meantime. Seventy-five per cent of the poor at that time were therefore long-term or terminally poor. Nine were described as widows, but there were another nine women, perhaps also widows. The amounts paid to them varied, which probably reflects the numbers of their dependants. How the money was raised is not clear; only the better-off residents contributed, no more numerous than the recipients. Some names appear on the list without any amount against them, which may indicate a semi-voluntary collection rather than a compulsory rate. The amount collected in the two wards suggests a total of about £20 in the year from the whole town, which was a substantial sum and larger than the amount of the parliamentary subsidy raised from the town in 1571. Poor relief had already become a burden.[116] Evidence of poor relief is unfortunately either anecdotal or episodic. On Christmas Eve 1638, John Compton disbursed 3d. each to 22 poor people, probably in Corve Street ward, including 12 widows and six other women; this came from Corporation funds, having been given to Compton by Bailiff Wilks for the purpose. We do not know if this was a one-off 'Christmas box' or a typical weekly dole. In the period 1665–75 perhaps 30 per cent of the households of Ludlow were classified as too poor to pay taxes; a smaller proportion got poor relief. We have seen above that in 1655 the proportions were similar to this, but it would be risky to assume that the same proportions obtained before the Civil War.[117]

Chapter Eight

Population

Changes in Total Population 1200–1660

Estimating the size of the population of any town before the State census of 1801 is extremely difficult. Nothing short of a complete and accurate count of everyone present on a particular day can inspire confidence because the alternative is to rely on partial lists or counts, constructed for other purposes, to which have to be added estimates for those groups of the population left out, a difficult task. Nevertheless, this is what has to be done if we are to form any view.

Before 1377 only impressions of population are possible. We have to infer population size and trends from other evidence and the exercise is somewhat circular. If there were a semi-urban settlement outside the castle walls before the mid–12th century its population could hardly have exceeded a hundred or so. If Dinham formed a mid–12th century 'proto-borough' with laid-out streets, its population may have been 300 or more. The town was very prosperous by the mid-13th century and the present street pattern already existed; indeed, there seems to have been infilling of building where there had formerly been lanes, but whether this represented more or fewer houses and people we can only guess. By about 1270 or earlier the built-up area was very much what it was in 1800. Although that tells us nothing about the density of the population living there it does suggest that Ludlow's population may have been of the magnitude of 1,500 to 2,000, which may have exceeded 2,000 by 1300. The period 1150–1300, the first 150 years of the town's history, was a time of huge population increase in the country at large; Ludlow shared in that growth.

The town probably shared in those 14th-century disasters which reduced the national population by at least a third – the famines of 1315–25 and the Black Death of 1348–9, followed by at least two other plague epidemics. The Ludlow chronicle states that in the *'magna pestilentia'* of 1348 *'duas partes hominum'*, that is, two thirds of the population of Wales died; it seems unlikely that Ludlow would have fared much better. The same chronicler records later pestilences in 1361, 1370 and 1375.[1] So, by 1377, the town's population must have greatly declined from a much higher total in about 1300.

Only a 'snapshot' estimate of population is possible for 1377 for which the poll tax return states that there were 1,172 lay men and women over 14, excepting 'true beggars'. If we add on 30 per cent for children (the 1641 proportion was 38 per cent) and, say, 50 for clergy and mendicants, we arrive at 1,725 as the population of the town.[2] We cannot assume steady growth between the calculated 1,725 of 1377 and the calculated 2,500 of 1545, as both are 'by and large' figures and because a great deal happened in between. We do not know what were the effects of the Glyndwr wars or the sack after the battle of Ludford Bridge in 1459; nor do we know much about the state of trade during many of those 168 years. We do know, however, a little about relative mortality during the latter part of the period, from 1442 to 1545.[3] The probate acts for about half of these years have survived and may be regarded as providing an index of mortality among the propertied classes. If we take the average for the decade 1442–51 as 100, then for 1453–62 it is 67, 56 for 1463–72, 56 for 1473–82, 46 for 1483–92, 90 for 1493–1502, 120 for 1503–12, 71 for 1513–22, 66 for 1523–32 and 90 for 1533–42. If the average number of deaths over a period gave some indication of the base population, we would derive a picture of a slowly rising population in the century with probable temporary falls in the 1440s and at the turn of the century owing to epidemics. Such conclusions can be tentative only.

The muster return for 1543 purported to list able-bodied men between the ages of 18 and 60 but, as there were only 260 names on this, the business of adding on guessed figures for men over 60 and boys under 18 and all females, which could quadruple or octuple the base figures, make the results worthless.[4]

In 1545, when the confiscation of the endowments of chantries in the parish churches was contemplated, a survey was made both of those endowments and of the numbers of communicants in the respective parishes, whose spiritual needs might therefore be expected to be affected. For Ludlow a bare figure of 1,800 'housling people' (that is, communicants) was given.[5] At the time young people were generally confirmed at the age of 12, so this figure can be taken as a count of the numbers of men and women above that age. It has a suspiciously round number look to it; was it to the nearest 50 or 100, or was it merely a lazy and unreliable guess? We cannot know, but, while a healthy critical attitude should be maintained, we are not entitled to dismiss such contemporary evidence without good reason. What addition do we make for the unconfirmed children? Estimates of the age structure of the population in 1641 suggest that about 26.5 per cent of the population was aged under 12, so we might add 649 on this account to arrive at a total population of 2,449, not far short of the level of population in 1641.[6]

This conclusion, however, poses a problem when we consider the parish register which exists for 84 of the intervening 96 years.[7] This seems to show a rapid rise in the annual numbers of baptisms and burials and, indeed, in the cumulative net difference between the two. On this evidence alone we would imagine the population in about 1585 to have been about 320 greater than in 1557; thereafter the cumulative net difference fluctuated, but after 1625 burials exceeded baptisms, with the result that by 1641 the population could be supposed, on this evidence alone, to have been very much at the level of 1558. On the other hand, the number of baptisms is broadly a function of the numbers of fertile married couples resident at the time, so the average numbers of baptisms in a decade compared with the average in another might give a crude basis for comparison of the numbers of such couples. Ten-year rolling averages ending with these final years are shown below along with averages for burials.

These figures would suggest that the numbers of such parents remained stable until about 1580, peaked in the mid-1580s, fluctuated for 50 years and then rose rapidly in the mid-1630s to a new level 40 per cent above that of 80 years earlier. Two distinct factors may be involved: changes in mortality rates and migration. Rising numbers of deaths over a long period may reflect an earlier period of rising population or a current worsening of standards of health and nutrition; we do know that late in the 16th century there was a recrudescence of the plague in a cycle which did not subside until the 1660s. It is evident that Ludlow suffered severe epidemics of some sort in 1587, 1597, 1609, 1623, 1624, 1636 and in the early 1640s. These did not greatly alter infant mortality and may have been followed by falls in the numbers of births. It seems as if these took their toll as much among young adults as among the very old. It has long been an assumption that pre-industrial towns could only maintain or increase their populations by net immigration as they were unhealthy places to live. If that is so, then in Ludlow the period to 1587 must have seen considerable immigration to account for the surplus of births over deaths. After that point immigration continued, but probably at the same level as emigration. The declining fortunes of Ludlow's chief manufacture, the cloth trade, may have been the cause. Ten-year overlapping averages for burials on the same basis as the figures for baptisms given above are:

DATE	BAPTISMS	BURIALS
1567	57.5	45.5
1572	55.7	49.9
1577	57.4	55.4
1582	71.3	63.7
1587	75.5	85.2
1592	71.4	91.0
1597	66.9	87.6
1602	65.4	80.5
1607	71.1	68.7
1612	70.9	77.6
1617	69.7	83.2
1622	78.4	84.4
1627	79.3	109.7
1632	74.8	107.8
1637	82.6	96.2
1642	82.5	96.4

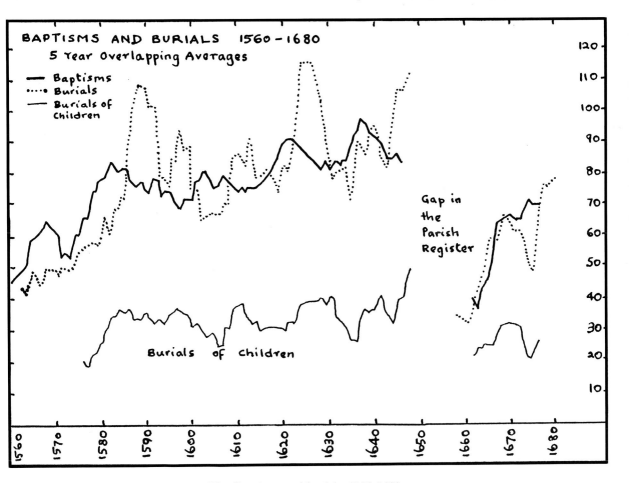

52.   Baptisms and burials, 1560–1680.

No firm conclusions can be reached except in broad terms. The population certainly increased between 1560 and 1587; we do not know whether in 1641 it maintained its 1587 level or had fallen back to its 1560 level, but may guess that it was somewhere between the two. We may not go far wrong in assuming about two thousand in 1560, about three thousand in 1587 and 2,600 in 1641.

The most reliable estimate which can be made is for 1641, using the poll tax return for that year along with the parish register. A similar estimate can be made for 1667, just outside the period covered by this book, and together the results illustrate the calamitous consequences of the Civil War for Ludlow, which I discuss in the next chapter. Even in this most reliable estimate, that for 1641, I have had to calculate an addition of 175 per cent to the counted figures of nine hundred and forty four.[8]

Just beyond our period, in 1667, another poll tax return enables a similar exercise to be undertaken. I calculate a population then of 1,559, which reflects the fall in population caused by the Civil War's disruption of the economy and destruction of the suburbs.[9]

Epidemic Disease

Epidemic disease could cause great havoc in a medieval town, particularly if it were associated with a period of bad harvests. Tracing either the incidence or the effects, however, is very difficult.

The first evidence of an epidemic which may have affected Ludlow comes from the so-called *Cronica Landavenses*, written no later than 1338, which records for the year 1149 '*mortalitas maxima pro totam Angliam*'. Then again in 1174 'the nation of the English suffered with a cough and many died of it in the month of January'. Ludlow is not mentioned but most of the events chronicled affected the area and the chronicler was clearly connected with Ludlow. In 1319 was recorded a cattle plague in the region, lasting two years. There are no other epidemics of any kind recorded in that part of the chronicle which was indubitably written by a Ludlow man, but the 'Llandaff section' includes references to the Black Death in 1348 and second, third and fourth pestilences in 1361, 1370 and 1375, the last three not being generally recognised as country-wide epidemics, but which were obviously serious in Wales and perhaps the Marches.[10]

Some comment is necessary on the impact of the Black Death. Here, too, the evidence is slight in the extreme, but we cannot assume from that that the impact was slight. Such evidence as we have from much of the country suggests quite the opposite; there is no reason to suppose that Ludlow was unaffected. Apart from the testimony of the *Cronica*,[11] the only evidence we have is that afforded by deeds of title. The Palmers Gild muniments of title which have survived include 27 for 1349, mostly gifts to the Gild. Four were gifts by persons acting as executors; four were gifts by heirs of deceased persons, one dying before signature; one was an executor acting for a deceased husband, his wife and their daughter. All this is evidence of an unusual level of both death and charitable impulse among the urban propertied class, and this may reasonably be put down to the incidence of an unusual and frightening epidemic, that is, the Black Death. Such evidence cannot however convey the devastation which that plague caused in most places, where between a third and a half of the population died.[12]

Evidence of later plague epidemics suggests that entire households were wiped out.[13] In rural society this would have a lesser impact, since replacement by remoter relatives or by other tenants whom the lord could find (if on better terms) could leave agricultural activity little changed. In a town, however, if a father and his sons died there would be no one to succeed to his trade; remoter relatives from the countryside without the relevant skills could not take over. We could, therefore, expect a town to be hit badly by such an epidemic. We do not know what measures the administration of the town took to protect and revive its trades; we can be sure that in such matters medieval boroughs were far from *laissez-faire*; protecting their own interests always came highest in their priorities. We might, therefore, expect Ludlow to have responded by making it easier for strangers to take up residence, even to apply for burgess-ships, so that with luck and good policy the town might substantially revive within a few decades. Unless, that is, its commercial rivals had been luckier. There can be no doubt that epidemics like the Black Death provided the supreme test for local government.

It is not until the mid-15th century that we have anything like a series of quantitative evidence which can be used to estimate the incidence of epidemic disease in Ludlow. The consistory court books of the bishops of Hereford survive from 1442 for about half of the subsequent years; these contain the probate and administration acts for all but the tiny minority which were granted at Canterbury. Although only the relatively prosperous made wills or left estates which were worth the court taking an interest, it is likely that their ability to withstand infectious disease was not much better than that of the poor, so records of their death rates may stand in for the death rates of the whole population.

It is worth tracing the figures which can be derived from the court books. This has already been done for the whole diocese of Hereford.[14] The figures for Ludlow, compared with those for the archdeaconry of Ludlow and the diocese, are shown in tabular and graphic form in Figure 53. The following are brief observations on particular years. 1442–3 was a bad year in Ludlow town and deanery, although of below average mortality in the diocese. 1445–6, a very bad year in the diocese, was a little less so in Ludlow, but in the town there died John, Thomas and Margaret Mordiford and their relatives, John and Richard Carpenter of Stanton Lacy and Bitterley, a group of family deaths which provides near-certain evidence of an epidemic. In 1455–6 Ludlow and its deanery again went against the diocesan trend in experiencing high levels of mortality. 1479–80 was for the diocese by far the worst year in the whole 'century' from 1442 to 1560, but only the sixteenth worst in Ludlow. But, possibly as a consequence, whereas the death rate in the diocese as a whole progressively fell to low levels in the next few years, it did not in Ludlow. 1486–7 was a bad year generally and in Ludlow; only Leominster had more deaths than Ludlow. In 1487–8 Ludlow town suffered much worse than the surrounding parishes. There followed a period of low mortality until a sudden rise began in 1499, increasing each year in Ludlow; in 1501–2 Ludlow had more deaths than any other place in the diocese. For both Ludlow and the diocese 1502–3 was the third worst of the 'century', and only Leominster had more deaths. 1508–9, the second worst year in the diocese, was ninth worst in Ludlow. On 24 June 1509 John Browne of Ludlow had to name a second executor in his will 'forasmoche as Margery my wife ys sore greved and vexed with infirmitie of Pestilence'.[15] This was a year in which Creighton noted both plague and the sweating sickness raging. In 1514–15 Ludlow's experience was very much the same. Generally the next decade suffered only average mortality and Ludlow reflected this, but in 1527–8 there was a general rise in mortality (possibly due to the sweating sickness, severe that year) which Ludlow did not experience. The northern part of the diocese, especially Leominster and Ludlow, exceeded the average in 1529–30, and again, after a space of mild years, in 1537–8, the fourth worst year of the 'century' for Ludlow. There were then two decades largely free of epidemics until 1556–7 and 1558–9 which were for Ludlow the two worst years of all.

After about 1560 the organisation of the court books is not helpful for this kind of analysis, but fortunately we have the burial register from 1558 onwards, which provides a more accurate picture of Ludlow, but, until a great many neighbouring parishes' burial registers are similarly analysed, it is not possible to make comparisons with the rest of the diocese.

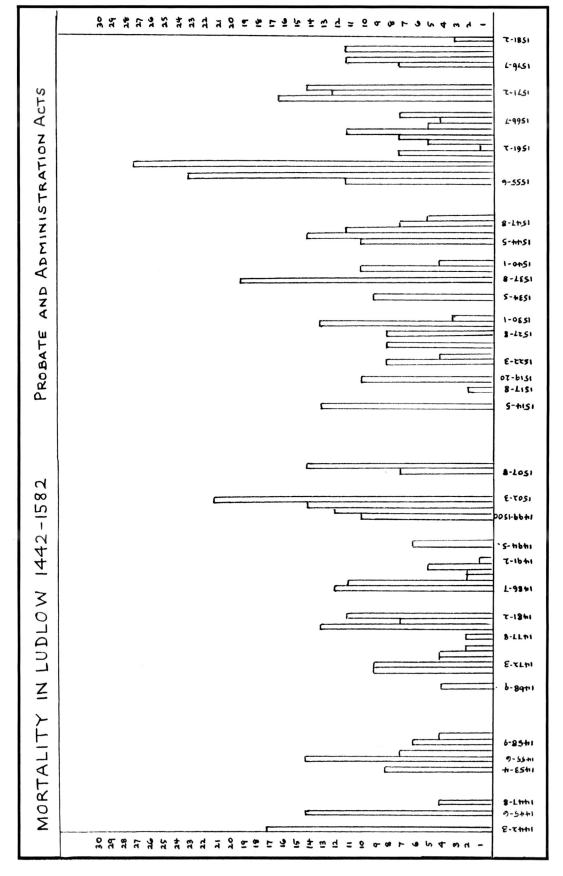

53. Mortality in Ludlow, 1442–1582: Probate and Administration Acts.

The registers indicate a steady rise in burials after 1560 which must be attributable to a rising population. Between November 1586, and February 1588 a huge increase occurred, peaking in the summer of 1587; doubtless this was plague. A smaller peak occurred in the summer of 1595 and the late summer and autumn of 1597. Plague struck again in spring to autumn 1609, (when plague deaths are marked as such in the register). Of the 158 burials between 1 December 1608, and 31 December 1609, 104 were marked as plague deaths, but from the names of the dead it seems likely that 127 were killed by plague. In each month between March and November plague deaths greatly exceeded deaths from other causes. Three out of five of those who died of plague were women or girls; while two out of five were described as sons or daughters, demonstrating that cyclical plague was particularly dangerous to the young, who may have been too young to have acquired any form of immunity from a previous cyclical outbreak. A characteristic of plague was that the high mortality resulted from a comparatively small number of households being severely affected. In 1609 seven members of the Shrawley family died, six each of the Hucke, Price and Evans families, five each of the Hampton and Griffiths families. Fourteen families accounted for half the deaths from plague that year. There was another peak in early 1620. The highest level of all was reached in autumn 1623 right through 1624, and 1636 was also very high. Quite high levels were suffered from 1643 to 1645. Thereafter, because of the Interregnum gap in the registers, there is no real evidence.

From 1593 the Corporation minutes show how much the plague concerned the town.[16] In that year 3s. 4d. was spent for digging plague-pits and carrying victims there for burying; the amount paid was doubtless small because only those desperate for work would have done it. By July 1593, common carriers were barred from travelling to London for a month lest they bring back infection, while carriers and goods from outside were not allowed in the town; the fair was suspended, too. In March the following year a pest-house was ordered to be built at public expense 'a bowshoot' from the town for lodging infected people. The town gates were guarded to bar entry to strangers. In August 1603, similar precautions were taken; eight wardens were appointed to search for and expel persons suspected of coming from London and other infected places, to stop all movements of common carriers and import of goods. In June 1604, another pest-house was ordered and, in October, St Catherine's Fair was suspended again. In early 1609 whole households were ordered to be kept indoors and to be 'watched and warded night and day' for a month. When the plague killed the whole Bulger household in their house in Dinham early in 1609, the bailiffs ordered the house to be used as a pest-house and they themselves escorted a small procession of sufferers to the house, when they were attacked by Richard Sherman and others, who presumably did not want plague victims brought into their part of the town.[17] Not all victims died; in April James Webb, Richard Dedicott and their wives were discharged from the pest-house. A rate was levied for the relief of those shut up in pest-houses and in their own homes; but the simultaneous order to send infected persons back to their places of birth or last abode was neither humane nor sensible. Later Samuel Parker's defence against a charge of opening a shop in Leintwardine was that he went there to escape plague in Ludlow, his neighbour's house being infected. John Lyngen, tenant of the Lord's Orchard, along the Teme, was compensated because his grass had been destroyed by the sick people walking to the pest-house built there. That different pest-houses are mentioned at different times suggests that they were insubstantial buildings, erected cheaply. In September 1609, the court-leet was adjourned owing to the increase in plague. Whatever the town had done about epidemic disease in earlier decades and centuries there can be no doubt that by the early 17th century outbreaks imposed a considerable administrative and financial strain on the town.

The Early 17th Century

For the period 1600 to 1645 there is material which, although far from comprehensive, gives us a good picture of the structure of the population and, particularly, of families.[18]

Seventeen marriages took place in Ludlow in 1600. Of these two were of non-residents who had no other connection with the town. Of the other 15 marriages, 10 appear to have been the only marriages entered into by either party; in one, the bride had been married before and in another she was to marry again; in two other cases the marriage was one of a sequence of three marriages, in the better documented of which the husband, John Clarke, later married, in 1615, a woman who had previously married in 1593. In this small sample there was one marriage which was in a sequence of four. William Rawlins, who had married Ales Wellyns in 1578, now married Edith Bowdler, who had in 1576 married William Partrich, who had previously had a wife, Julian.

The 15 marriages, therefore, 'represented' 25 marriages and of these the duration of five is unknown, three lasted six years each, three lasted about 14 years, three about 20 years, six about 24 years, while three lasted between 26 and 37 years. In this sample there are present both long marriages and 'serial' marriages, much as in 20th-century Britain, where divorce has taken the place of death.

A similar analysis centred on 1620 shows 10 out of 29 marriages involved non-residents, while of the rest five couples married only once, seven were part of two-marriage sequences, and seven of three-marriage sequences, in one of which John Harley, formerly married to Frances Bowdler, married Frances Mannering, who later married Edward Winwood. So these 19 marriages 'represented' 40 marriages. In almost all cases the death of a spouse was followed within weeks or even days by a remarriage.

Between 1560 and 1640 there were about 2,000 marriages, of which about 1,700 were of Ludlow residents. Among these we can detect a number of 'serial' marriage sequences, but the detected number and length of these sequences is limited by the fact that immigrants to and emigrants from the town often married outside the town. Thirty-five two-marriage sequences, 15 three-marriage sequences, and five four-marriage sequences can be detected. The longest was that which began with Jane Pinner's marriage in 1579 to Thomas Evans, who later married Margaret Waties, the widow of John Wynde, and she later, in 1611, married Thomas Watkins, a widower.

So much remarriage led to considerable complication of the system of kindred and alliance and to frequent disputes over property between stepchildren and stepparents, and between stepbrothers and sisters. A widower with young children would normally remarry quickly for the benefit of the children and typically would beget more children, who could grow up as either friends or rivals. Older men and women often remarried, perhaps for companionship, perhaps for other reasons.

In attempting to find some reasonably firm evidence for the size of the population of Ludlow in this period it is fortunate that among the borough records has survived the poll tax return for 1641.[19] This was the first of the 17th-century poll taxes. The rules for assessing the tax were set out in the statute: individuals were first charged according to their ranks and offices, then, those not so charged were assessed according to their disposable income on a crudely graduated scale with a minimum income and charge of £5 and 12d. respectively. Anyone not charged under these rules was charged a capitation or poll tax of 6d. provided he was over 16 years of age and not receiving poor relief. According to the statutory rules wives should have been subjected to a separate charge, but it seems that in Ludlow wives were deemed to have been covered by the 6d. or higher charge on their husbands.

As this list should represent everyone over 16 not receiving poor relief (also in practice excepting wives living with their husbands), it can, if used with other available evidence, help us towards an estimate of the total population of the borough when the return was taken, that is before 5 August 1641 (the day one of the spinsters listed married). By then Ludlow parish register had been kept for 82 years, long enough to cover all but the longest lives; in the more recent decades it had also recorded full details of the parentage of baptised children. The present exercise has been based for practical convenience on the volume published by the Shropshire Parish Register Society, which is in many respects inaccurately transcribed and indexed, but of great value if used carefully. Using the register it is possible to reconstruct the families of most of those whose names are listed in the poll tax return. The years of birth of those born in the town, the names of their wives, where married in the parish church, and their years of birth if born in Ludlow, and also the years of birth of their surviving children, can all be derived from the register. This detail can be supplemented from the wills of Ludlow people, proved at Hereford and in London. Anyone over 16, unless a married woman living with her husband, should appear by name, so we have only to find wives and younger children.

Table A sets out the arithmetic of the reconstruction of the population and describes the assumptions behind the exercise. It must be stressed that the records for Ludlow are not the best for such an exercise, but, given the records which exist, it represents a reasonable attempt. It can best be described as a structured estimate, where the categories into which the population would have been grouped have been defined and individually calculated.

The most difficult task of all is to estimate the numbers of those on poor relief. There are two contemporary lists of such people in Corve Street ward for 1639 and for another year, perhaps 1640. One gives the sums paid out per household; if the sums represent numbers of persons in a household we can form a view of the numbers of poor in the ward. For the town as a whole it is necessary to increase the numbers for the rest of the town proportionately to Corve Street's increase. I have arrived at 431 as a total number of the poor. Corve Street may have been untypical of the town, as trades congregated in different areas of it. 1639–40 may not have been like 1640. Nevertheless, there is no alternative, and some encouragement can be had from the fact that most of the poor were widows whose plight was likely to have been long-term and unrelated to the state of particular trades.[20] The result of the exercise is a total of 2,513; to avoid a spurious air of accuracy and to recognise that the methods used are more likely to have under- than over-estimated I prefer to adopt a figure of 2,600 as an estimate of the population of Ludlow in the summer of 1641.

The conclusions which may be drawn vary from the near-certain to the speculative. There seem to have been significantly more females than males living; this is not surprising for children, but is more so for adults. The evidence does, however, suggest a larger number of widows than of widowers, notwithstanding the childbirth risks to women's chances of survival. Half the population at least was born in Ludlow, although this may understate the proportion of adult women so born; for married women and widows we often do not know their maiden names, without which there can be no trace of their birth. Even so, the proportion of immigrants was clearly high. Estimates have been made in the appendix for immigrants, particularly for immigrant children. Only 75 per cent of children under 16 were born in Ludlow, which implies a substantial immigration of young adults, already with children, into the town in the years before 1641. For adult women we have to observe caution, for the reasons set out above. In addition to immigration of young families it seems that there was a significant immigration of adult women, probably in parallel with marriages of Ludlow men with girls from out-of-town. What we do not know is whether these were particular to the second quarter of the 17th century. If so, then we should be looking at a town whose population had either greatly increased or had remained stable by replacing, through immigration, population losses from emigration and disease. Perhaps a combination of the two is nearer reality. There had certainly been heavy losses through disease and it seems also that not all the children born in Ludlow who survived childhood lived in the town any longer. Some people migrated to London, which at this time was receiving immigrants in great numbers. It may be that Ludlow's young were moving to the capital, while the youth of rural Shropshire and surrounding counties were moving to small towns like Ludlow. It is therefore impossible to offer a view on whether Ludlow's population was able to replace itself.

For those inhabitants for whom we can find or guess at a year of birth we can attempt to describe the age structure of the population. Over a third of the population was aged under 16, while not more than four per cent were aged over sixty. Indeed, inspection of the 15-year age bands suggests that only about a tenth of the population was over 50, which may therefore be seen as the age which those who reached adulthood could hope to reach. That two persons are recorded as having reached the age of 100 does not alter this general conclusion.

The Ludlow parish register enables some tentative conclusions to be drawn concerning the structure of families. From 1621 the baptismal register gives both parents' names. Before that the mother's name has to be guessed, but sometimes can be done fairly certainly. After 1646 there are few entries of any sort until 1660; in the intervening period and to some extent back to about 1601 it is possible to use the information to obtain an interesting picture of family structure. Marriages can be connected with the baptisms of subsequent children, the deaths in infancy of some of those children, the deaths of either or both parents and sometimes remarriages of widowed parents. There are large numbers of marriages of persons who seem to have had no other connection with Ludlow; for these we must assume that they had no connection other than the wedding ceremony itself, since we know that Ludlow church was used in this way for a very long time (providing a useful increment to the earnings of its clergy at the expense of their rural fellows). If we can see some subsequent connection with Ludlow, either through a baptism or a burial then we can include the family in our survey. There were people who married in Ludlow and died in Ludlow but had no children; people who married and had children in Ludlow but did not die there; and people who had children in Ludlow and died there but were not married there. All of these can be included in the survey, but the best evidence is derived from those who married, had their children and died in Ludlow.

No less than 18 per cent of marriages produced no children; some were remarriages of middle-aged persons, it is certain, but most were young but infertile marriages. This suggests one cause of the very high rate of population mobility in the town at this time; families which did not perpetuate themselves would be replaced. To add to these unfortunates we have to add the nine per cent of marriages which produced children, all of whom died in infancy. An almost equal proportion, of marriages, 25 per cent, produced children, all of whom survived. This is perhaps a more surprising statistic. The most typical group was the eight per cent who had three children, of whom only one died in infancy. The survival of children to adulthood can be expressed in a tabular fashion (see opposite).

In addition to these, 29 per cent of the married couples in Ludlow who either had at least one child there or can be otherwise shown to have lived there were neither married there nor did at least one of the spouses die there. Leaving aside the distortion caused by the 1646–60 gap in the register, we may assume that most of these were temporary residents, so adding to the evidence for a geographically (if not socially) mobile rather than stable population. The next largest single group, about 28 per cent, were those who married in Ludlow and whose married lives were ended by death in Ludlow. The rest, about 43 per cent, were almost equally divided between, on the one hand, couples married in the town

Percentage of marriages	Surviving Children
27	0
19½	1
22½	2
12½	3
8½	4
4	5
2½	6
2	7
1	8
1½	10

but who did not die there and, on the other, who died there but were not married there. We must remember that some Ludlow people married elsewhere but maintained their continuous residence in the town, while the absence of burial records for 1646–60 may hide persons who died in the town. Extrapolating from the details we have for death rates, we could guess, therefore, that, if these distortions were removed, we would find, say, 36 per cent were 'Ludlow' married and buried, 21 per cent were 'Ludlow' married, 27½ per cent Ludlow buried, and 17½ per cent neither married nor buried. It has to be stressed that we are basing estimates upon estimates and the results can hardly be exact; the exercise is, however, justified by the need to recognise the deficiencies in our evidence. A picture does, nevertheless, emerge of a town in which perhaps a minority lived throughout their adult lives, where a significant number of families (not just the more rootless single people) moved in and out again, and, perhaps surprisingly at this time, there was still net immigration of families.

The same parish register analysis permits an estimate of the average duration of marriages: 17 years, although 35 per cent of marriages did not last five years. Within this average the fate of men and women differed, as the following table demonstrates:

Years Survival after Marriage

	Husbands	Wives
0 to 5 Years	14½ per cent	21 per cent
5 to 25 Years	64 per cent	45 per cent
Over 25 Years	23 per cent	34 per cent

These analyses demonstrate that the early 17th century in Ludlow, which was typical of many places, was a time of demographic and personal change. The formal class structure of society was superimposed on a population whose personal lives were always uncertain. Death and remarriage made family life unstable and gave most people limited horizons.

The Population in 1660

There is no precise means of estimating the population of the town in 1660, which has been chosen as the end of the period covered by this study. We do, however, have the evidence afforded by the poll tax of 1667, supplemented by the hearth tax roll of 1672 and the exemption certificates of the same year.[21]

Care, however, must be exercised in the use of this evidence from a very few years beyond our period. The Compton census of 1676 gave the number of conformists, nonconformists and Catholics in Ludlow over the age of 16 as 1,376, which suggests a total population of over two thousand.[22] Using the 1667 poll tax and other evidence, I have estimated the population to be about 1,460.[23] Was so great a change likely in the intervening decade? Much depends on the allowances for persons not counted, such as children or, in tax returns, certain categories of the poor; these give rise to problems in all population estimates before 1801. A comparison with the parish register suggests that the poll tax return did include the children of tax-paying households, but the number of exempt households and, particularly, the number of children they contained, is a greater problem. A re-calculation suggests that in 1667 more realistic figures should be:

	No. of Households	No. of Persons
In Poll Tax Return	409	1,330
Exempt children of Taxed adults		104
Living wives excluded		19
Exempt households	70	106
Total	479	1,559

Why was there such a change between 1667 and 1672? The number of persons calculated above for each household is 3.25, compared with over 4 in the census of 1801. Low density is, however, a sign of diminishing population, not a characteristic of the late 18th century, but certainly true of the period 1650–67. I shall refer to the ample evidence of the destruction of houses around the walls of the town and to the effects of the wars on the trade of the town.[24] Both circumstances would have led to depopulation, for which anecdotal evidence also exists. The parish register indicates that during the period 1662–6 the average number of baptisms each year was 56 and in the next five years 65.6, compared with a figure of 86.2 in the decade 1636–45. Burials in 1662–6 averaged 59.4 a year and, in 1667–71, 61 a year, compared with 101.5 a year in 1636–45. These figures suggest that the population in the 1660s was very much lower than it had been in 1641, but that it was beginning to recover. It was not, however, until the last quarter of the 18th century that the average annual number of baptisms reached pre-Civil War levels. We may conclude that the Civil War, following on the collapse of the cloth trade, had a calamitous effect on the population of the town.

TABLE A

POPULATION OF LUDLOW IN 1641

STATUS	MALES		FEMALES		TOTAL
	Born in Ludlow	Not Born in Ludlow	Born in Ludlow	Not Born in Ludlow	
Married					
In Ludlow	58 (a)	85 (c)	51 (e)	92 (g)	286
Not in Ludlow	67 (b)	164 (d)	72 (f)	159 (h)	462
Total Married	125	249	123	251	748
Widowed	35 (i)	27 (j)	110 (k)	158 (l)	330
Single	73 (m)	181 (n)	90 (o)	140 (p)	484
Total Adults	233	457	323	549	1562
Children	344 (q)	114 (r)	378 (s)	115 (t)	951
Total Population	577	571	701	664	2513
					say, 2600

(a) 48 listed in PTR (Poll Tax return) & PR (Parish Register) (marr.); 10 husbands in PR app. liv. in 1641 not in PTR.

(b) 62 listed in PTR not in PR (marr.) but in PR (bap.); 5 in PR app. liv. in 1641 not in PTR.

(c) 75 listed in PTR & PR (marr.); 10 in PR app. liv. 1641 not in PTR.

(d) 136 listed in PTR, not in PR (marr.); difficulty of finding origins of persons not in Ludlow; men likely to be realistic.

(e) 41 by reconstruction from PTR and PR; 10 wives in PR app. liv. in 1641 not in PTR.

(f) 66 estim. only for Ludlow born brides; 5 women after marr. in PR app. liv. in 1641 not in 1641; 1 reconstr. in PTR families marrying Ludlow men.

(g) 10 women after marr. app. liv. 1641 not in PTR; 82 by reconstr. from PTR & PR.

(h) 28 women after marr. app. liv. 1641 not in PTR; 131 by reconstr. from PTR & PR allowing for Ludlow born brides marrying ex-Ludlow.

(i) 15 listed in PTR ; 20 est. of aged widowed poor by extrapol. from Corve St. assume ½ b. Ludlow, ½ not.

(j) 7 listed in PTR; 20 aged widowed poor as (i).

(k) 5 women after marr. in PR app. liv. 1641 not in PTR; 10 listed in PTR; 95 est. of aged widowed poor by extrapol. from Corve St. Born Ludlow assume ½.

(l) 57 listed in PTR; 6 women marr. in PR app. liv. 1641 not in PTR; 95 est. of aged widowed poor by extrapol. from Corve St. where 20 men, 53 women, 21 children; pro-rated across town by ward population in PTR: men 92, women 243, (of whom 39 and 190 respect. widowed) children 96.

(m) Listed in PTR (185 men in PTR without wives in PR, but some may have immigr. with wives).

(n) Listed in PTR (see also (m))

(o) Listed in PTR

(p) Listed in PTR

(q) 274 children born Ludlow (PR) whose parents in PTR; 70 children bapt. Ludlow parents not in PTR

(r) 91 children of PTR families not b. Ludlow; 23 est. children not b. Ludlow to non-PTR families (same % as in PTR families: 25%)

(s) 304 children b. in Ludlow to PTR parents; 74 children b. Ludlow.

(t) 92 children of PTR families not b. Ludlow; 23 to non-PTR families (as in (r)).

TABLE B

AGE-DISTRIBUTION IN 1641						
	Total		Men		Women	
75 plus			0%	1	1%	4
61 to 75			4%	19	3%	12
46 to 60			20%	88	20%	91
31 to 45			47%	210	48%	224
16 to 30			29%	128	29%	136
Other Adults				244		407
Over 16	62%	1,562	60%	690	64%	872
Under 16	38%	951	40%	458	36%	493
Total	100%	2,513	100%	1,148	100%	1,365

Notes: a. The distribution into age-bands suggests that most of the other adults of unknown age fall into the 16–30 band (servants, unmarried adults, recent immigrants), the ones most likely to be missed in those records from which age may be inferred, say, 222 men and 240 women. There would also be a small number of widowers, say, 22, and probably more widows, to judge by the poor-lists, say, 40 in the 31–45 band, 50 in the 46–60 band and 77 in the 61–75 band. These reallocations would produce a credible distribution.

    b. While the ages of half of the males can be calculated from the parish register (PR) the approximate ages of the other half can be inferred from what is known about them from the parish register (PR) and other evidence. Similarly the ages of 29 per cent of the women can be determined and of 60 per cent can be inferred. Smaller numbers of men and women who are not in the poll tax return can be similarly allocated.

Chapter Nine

The Civil War and the Interregnum

The Approach of War

The Civil War and its aftermath had severe consequences for Ludlow. Between 1642 and 1660 the town's population fell substantially, from about 2,600 to about 1,500. Large parts of the suburbs were burnt by royalist defenders and the decline in population reduced the incentive to rebuild quickly. Ludlow showed the physical and social scars of 'the late unhappy troubles' for many years after the fighting stopped.[1]

Until late in 1640 there is little evidence that the Corporation or the inhabitants in general were passionately bound, by either interest or sentiment, to one national party or the other. This indifference reflected the mood of south Shropshire.[2]

Ludlow had its grievances, however. Prerogative taxation was as unpopular there as it was elsewhere. In 1636 the sheriff tried to shift some of Shrewsbury's shipmoney burden onto Ludlow, but the latter's protest was upheld.[3] In 1638 Ludlow was reported as having the worst record for payment in the county and in 1640 the town was short by £30 in its payment for coat and conduct, reflecting a reluctance to pay for local militia to be sent north for the Scottish war.[4] Resentment in the town at the king's grant of leases of the town mills to Alexander Gretton, a royal servant, was an additional irritant, but hardly enough to influence partisanship in the constitutional struggles of the time.[5]

The Laudian policies of the Church of England and the perceived undue power of the bishops were other grievances during the 1630s. There were influential Puritans in Ludlow, but at least one of them, Cuthbert Hely of the Bull Ring, is known to have fought for the king.[6] The continuing high status of the town's leading Catholic recusants, the Townshends, demonstrates Ludlow's ability to accommodate different religious loyalties without much strain.

The events of 1641, however, brought Ludlow a greater grievance against Parliament rather than the king. When the Long Parliament assembled in November 1640, an immediate objective was to abolish the court of Star Chamber, and the other courts of 'extraordinary jurisdiction', including the Council of the March. Notwithstanding repeated protests from the gentry of the border counties, the Council of the March had never attracted the same odium as Star Chamber, but it was proposed that it, too, should be abolished. A committee was set up to consider the Council's future and 'all through 1641 its position was precarious'.[7] Ludlow was represented in the Long Parliament by Ralph Goodwin, who held the lucrative office of deputy clerk of the Signet for 16 years, and by Charles Baldwin of Elsich (later described as 'a moderate royalist'). A letter from Baldwin to the bailiffs of Ludlow, written 13 March 1640/1, while the Council's future was being discussed in the Commons, reported only 'little determined yet in Parliament' and promised to do 'what I am able for your Corporation'.[8]

Popular feeling seems to have been against the Council and at least one riot occurred when a crowd of 40 people, armed with sticks, reaping hooks and other weapons, tried to prevent an arrested man from being brought before it.[9] The Corporation itself, however, was dominated by tradesmen who were more aware of the economic benefits which the presence of the Council's establishment brought to Ludlow. The bailiffs sent a petition to the king and Parliament claiming that if the jurisdiction of the Council were removed it would be 'to the utter undoing of a thousand poor souls', further pointing out that 'since the jurisdiction of the court hath been questioned there has been little resort to the said Town'.[10] The protest failed in its main purpose, for the Council's 'extra-ordinary jurisdiction' was abolished on 1 August 1641.[11]

Ludlow's more ambitious citizens had long aspired to the style and fashions of the lawyers and clerks connected with the Council. Such aspirations reinforced their natural conservatism, making them instinctively loyal to the king, despite discontentment over taxation and religion. The effective dismantling of the Council of the March added resentment on economic grounds to these sentiments. It is no coincidence that at least 10 of the 29 Ludlow residents known to have served the king as army officers had been officials of the Council, including six under-secretaries at the office of the Signet.[12] Most of the others were tradesmen, including two innkeepers, William Langton of the *Crown* and Adam Acton of the *Bull*, who must have lost heavily when 'a great conflux of people' ceased 'to resort to Ludlow to have justice administered'.[13]

The Council's long establishment at Ludlow had created links with many local families. By 1642 some of these were aligning themselves with king or Parliament and this affected relations in the town. The Herberts of Powis and Montgomery were committed Stuart supporters, and their cousin, Sir Henry Herbert of Ribbesford, was the king's master of Revels.[14] The Foxes, still the most important family in the neighbourhood, were also conspicuous royalists, Somerset Foxe the younger, of Caynham, being private secretary to Prince Rupert.[15] Local supporters of Parliament were fewer, but included Sir Robert Harley of Brampton Bryan, a zealous Puritan, active on Long Parliament committees before the war and notorious as the 'Iconoclast' during it.[16]

Locally, as well as nationally, tension increased during 1642. On 24 June Lady Brilliana Harley wrote of an incident involving William Littleton of The Moor, who thrashed a man who called him a 'roundhead'. Her final statement that 'they are now more quiet in Ludlow' implies some agitation earlier in the summer, although by 27 June she could write that 'Hereford is growing now worse than Ludlow'.[17] Three months later war broke out and families like the Littletons were then divided. William Littleton was a committed Parliamentarian and became a judge and recorder of Ludlow during the Interregnum, but his brothers were equally 'devoted royalists'.[18] Most Ludlow people aligned themselves politically as families, but humbler families than the Littletons found themselves divided. Avery Price of Holdgate Fee was a parliamentary soldier, while his brother, Robert, was an active royalist.[19] The most important influence was the early appearance of royalist armed forces, whose presence until 1646 determined the allegiance of the town.

Ludlow During the War

There was little military action in Shropshire during the early months of the war, although the king spent three weeks there recruiting soldiers and raising money. In late September a parliamentary army under the Earl of Essex advanced from the south but was checked at Worcester by a force under Prince Rupert. A contemporary pamphleteer claimed that Essex advanced to Ludlow with 20,000 horse and foot and took the town on 1 October after an action lasting 'from nine of the clock in the morning to foure in the afternoon'.[20] There is little corroboration available, but the validity of the report that a unit of Essex's army may have briefly seized Ludlow Castle after an engagement at Standard Oak, a mile south-east of Ashford Carbonel, at this time is not inconceivable.[21]

There was a more substantial threat of attack in May 1643 from Waller's army which briefly occupied Hereford after a victory near Gloucester.[22] Every inhabitant living outside the walls of Ludlow was ordered by Whitsun to build a fence or rampart 45 inches high and 36 inches thick as a defence for the town.[23] The bailiffs' accounts show that the walls and gates were repaired at this time, that musket loopholes were made through the gates and that coals, fires and candles were bought for the soldiers and residents serving as watchmen.[24] An undated paper in the town court papers, which belongs to this period, refers to the billetting of soldiers on civilians, the sequestration of horses and the compulsory building of defensive works on private property.[25]

The first military governor, Richard Herbert, was appointed in September 1643 and was soon succeeded by Sir Michael Woodhouse, a veteran soldier, knighted after the Battle of Newbury.[26]

The town defences, however, were organised by Thomas Fisher of Dodmore, who was granted a lease of 'The Hills', a 40-acre Corporation property near his home 'in consideration of his love and faithful preservation of this town in the tyme of hostilities'.[27] In 1643 he was described as 'governor'.[28] After his death it was alleged that he took ordnance from Bringewood Forge to defend Ludlow and also raised a company in Ludlow for the king.[29] The forge was operated by Francis Walker of Wooton, who cast nearly £1,000-worth of artillery in Shropshire for the royalist army in 1643 alone.[30]

A parliamentary committee for Warwickshire, Staffordshire and Shropshire was formed early in 1643 to co-ordinate local efforts, but its first success in Shropshire did not come until late in the year when Tong Castle was captured.[31] Brampton Bryan was besieged by the royalists in the summer of 1643, but successfully defended by Lady Brilliana Harley; it fell however in April 1644. Hopton Castle fell to royalist forces from Ludlow in 1644. The taking of the supposedly untakeable Montgomery Castle by parliamentary forces was of greater strategic significance.[32]

The conduct of the war was becoming more ferocious; at Hopton those who surrendered to the royalists were massacred. Henry Osborne, a royalist officer in Ludlow, observed that 'the malignancy which has been in many men's hearts has now burst forward to a manifest expression'.[33]

The burial records in the Ludlow parish register may indicate that sporadic fighting took place at Ludlow during the spring and autumn of 1644. Seventeen soldiers were buried in March 1643/4, three in April, four in May and another six in September. Three were officers. Only eight soldiers were buried during 1645. Elsewhere royalist reverses were substantial. Shrewsbury fell to parliament early in the year following an engagement at Stokesay. In September Robert Howard, a royalist, commented that Bridgnorth and Ludlow were the only places left in the county which were safe for meetings.[34] Nevertheless the parliamentary advantage was not yet pressed home.

Life in Ludlow went on as best it might under military government. Direction, inconvenience, confiscation and privation were certainly experienced, but, except when actually under siege, life went on as before. In 1645 billeting and fitting out troops had cost the town £850 17s. 10d., a very large sum.[35] This included the maintenance of 25 soldiers for a year at 6s. a week, together with housing itinerant companies for shorter periods. One group of soldiers had 'gunpowder, match, clothes, stockings, boots, shoes and other commodities' from several tradesmen for which they did not pay, at a total cost of £35 12s. 3d., while Prince Rupert's men failed to pay for horsemeat worth £15 10s. In June 1644, John Walker, a carpenter, claimed to have lost £13 10s. from quartering Woodhouse's soldiers and their confiscating his timber. Six months later turf from Mary Colbach's meadow in Broad Linney had been taken to the castle. An undated paper lists 28 empty houses regarded as available for billeting soldiers; all were within the walled town and include some of the more important buildings there, such as The Leaden Porch (now 16–18 Castle Street), the *Greyhound* Inn (now 49 Broad Street), Castle Lodge and the house now known as the *Feathers*.

The number of Ludlow men who fought in the war is not known. In the country as a whole no more than half the upper classes took any part in the war and an even smaller proportion of the rest; Ludlow manifested no greater enthusiasm. When the fighting was over 29 Ludlow people compounded for delinquency, that is, for actively supporting the king. Most of these had served as officers or ensigns within the town, and probably carried on their civilian concerns at the same time. Thirteen tradesmen can be identified; of these seven were in the leather trades, like William Colbach, the Broad Street corviser, who was 'in arms' at Stokesay in June 1645, and Roger and Thomas, sons of Edward Powis, the tanner, who took part in the capture of Brampton Bryan.[36] Less is known of the other ranks as individuals, but the town was required to raise 22 soldiers to serve under a Captain Baldwyn, presumably the former member of Parliament, and to furnish six of them with horses, clothes and arms. Ludlow was required to maintain soldiers for long periods.[37] Few exhibited any great professional commitment. Griffith Price was brought before the town court in October 1642. He had served under Essex at 'Edgdon Heath' (?Edgehill) and within a few days had come to Ludlow to bring linen to his sisters there from another sister in London; he rode into Ludlow armed, in soldier's dress and enjoying military pay and leave. The town authorities of Ludlow were, however, less complaisant than was his captain.[38]

Ludlow Castle still had military importance. Prince Rupert used it as his headquarters when recruiting in Wales.[39] Its defence was in the hands of 'foreign soldiers', including a detachment of Irish troops, commanded by John Davalier, a Florentine mercenary.[40] Prisoners were often kept at the castle; in June 1643, five were transferred there from Beaumaris for greater security.[41] They were often ill-treated; Lady Harley complained that her servant 'honest Peter . . . had been grevously treated in Ludlow . . . Turks would have used him no worse'. [42]

Life in the town preserved many characteristics of normality. The council continued to meet seven or eight times a year and between 1642 and 1645 eight new burgesses were elected.[43] The Gild of Stitchmen, however, held no meetings between 1642 and August 1646, immediately after the fall of the town.[44] Whether this gap had an ideological or a commercial origin, we do not know. Public opinion was hostile to those who openly professed 'roundhead' views, but this was to be expected while the town was under royalist control. Edward Cooke, a Corve Street tailor, was 'apprehended by divers soldiers and imprisoned and manacled' until he was able 'to steale away to London'.[45] Thomas Vaughan of Tewkesbury, who was 'well-affected to Parliament', was unable to visit Ludlow to collect rent from the King's Arms in the Bull Ring 'without great danger or hazard to life'.[46]

The presence of soldiers was often put to advantage in private matters. William Beddoe, one of the sons of Ellis Beddoe, alleged that when he tried to claim his inheritance his opponents had him arrested as a 'roundhead' by royalist soldiers and then a year later by parliamentary soldiers, presumably on some other pretext.[47] Avery Price, who fought for parliament, claimed that the title deeds of his land in Holdgate Fee were taken from his house 'in the late troublesome wars'.[48] Were other private scores settled with public force at this time?

Ludlow had lost the custom of the litigants and hangers-on at the Council of the March, but gained new visitors during the war. Some were refugees from areas by then controlled by parliament, presumably without their fortunes and purchasing power, however; one of them was John Warner, Bishop of Rochester. Others came on secret missions, like Lady Capel, who came with funds for the Ludlow royalists in 1645.[49] The mightier the visitor, however, the more likely he was to take rather than provide; the visits of Prince Rupert in 1642 and 1644 and of the king on 7 August 1645, would certainly have cost Ludlow a great deal, especially as the king arrived with 300 horse.

The Siege and Capture of Ludlow

When the king visited Ludlow the royalist cause was already lost. The final parliamentary offensive began to the south in December 1645, when Colonel John Birch attacked Ledbury and Hereford from Gloucester. Bridgnorth was taken on 26 April 1646, the occasion of 'scorched earth' tactics by the royalist garrison, the news of which terrified Ludlow – with some justification, as things turned out. In mid-April Birch had received orders to combine the forces of Radnorshire and Shropshire and take Ludlow. Artillery was sent for from Gloucester, although it was hoped that the Ludlow royalists would see sense and come to terms.[50] Birch took up position before Ludlow on 24 April. He had 450 infantry and 350 cavalry from Hereford and the Radnorshire and Shropshire forces added 160 infantry and 100 cavalry. Against him Woodhouse had 250 foot-soldiers and 100 horsemen.[51]

The first day of the siege was the most eventful. Birch's contingent forced the royalists into the walled town and saved parts, at least, of the suburbs from being incinerated. Nevertheless the devastation inflicted by the royalists both at this time and beforehand was considerable.

Some houses, probably those on the east side of Corve Street, had been demolished earlier, for on 31 October 1645, the bailiffs and surveyors were ordered to survey demolished houses in that street and set mean-stones between properties.[52] Others were destroyed on 24 April 1646, like that on the site of the present Smithfield Lodge in Lower Galdeford, later described as having been 'burnt down to the ground by the wicked command of Sir Michael Woodhouse'. By the evening of 24 April the royalists were confined within the walled town and Birch controlled the suburbs.

The conduct of besiegers and besieged over the next five weeks was more restrained than that at earlier Shropshire sieges. This was chiefly due to the moderation of Colonel Birch, probably the best commander on either side in the region.[53] Samuel More, colonel in command of the Shropshire contingent of the parliamentary forces, on the other hand, as sole survivor of Woodhouse's massacre at Hopton Castle and (until exchanged for Edward Cresset) a former prisoner of Woodhouse at Ludlow Castle, harboured an understandable personal enmity for Woodhouse.[54] On 4 May the Committee of Both Kingdoms ordered Birch to return to Hereford and to let the Committee for Shropshire take Ludlow with its own forces, but Birch delayed his leaving until surrender had been negotiated later in the month.

Birch had a formidable 'leaguer' or siege camp, either at Steventon (from which he wrote to London on 16 May) or at Cainham Camp, a mile to the north of Steventon. In preparation for bombardment of the castle Birch's men may have dug the long rows of trenches which still survive on Whitcliffe and which have traditionally been ascribed to this period.[55] Royalist units from Raglan, Goodrich and Madresfield tried to relieve Ludlow on 29 April, but were driven back.[56]

On 2 May Birch wrote to Woodhouse:

... it is far from my desire to be an occasion of shedding of blood or ruining the estates of any. And for that I conceive yourselves are sensible of the dangers of both ... it is yet in my power to prevent your own total ruine and in my power to grant you such terms as may be honourable to the military part and profitable to those who have other resolutions than to live by their swords ... there being neither any visible force in the field nor any garrison unbesieged which can yield you the least hopes of relief ... you need not send far to find those who have not only to their great dishonour destroyed utterly those under their protection, but have now thankfully within a few days embraced such terms as that their lives are at the Parliament's mercy; their own unadvisedness having been such that they had very near made the besiegers uncapable of granting them ... that which I now offer ... all kind of misery follow which the sword necessarily brings with it. Your loving friend, J. Birch. From my leaguer 2 April [sic]. Answer by tomorrow by 12 of the clock and in the meantime if you desire it all acts of hostility shall be forborne.[57]

Woodhouse, purporting to answer both for himself and for the Corporation, gave a short answer:

> ... in fulfilling this your advice I and the rest shall forfeit more than we can regain ... I cannot find any at all honour for me at this present without receiving His Majesty's command ... if extremity be made choice of I shall willingly condescend to what may avoid it as befits a soldier.

Both sides then played a waiting game. Birch sent 60 horse to escort the guns from Gloucester, but it is doubtful if the latter ever arrived in Ludlow, for on 4 May orders were given for them to be retained at Gloucester.[58] Royalist horse tried to get out of Ludlow but were forced back.[59] The suspension of the town court after 28 April indicates that conditions were abnormal, although the Corporation minutes on 4 May show that they could still devote time to electing new burgesses.[60]

London was informed on 20 May that negotiations for surrender had been successfully resumed before that date. The agreement was for the garrison to march out on 1 June. Why over 10 days should pass for the implementation of the surrender agreement is not clear. Birch's biographer later wrote that Birch had taken the town in 33 days, 'though not without envy from the Shropshire men', which implies 26 May. Perhaps the agreement to surrender was treated as the surrender itself. Since Birch was ordered elsewhere after the agreement (leading Woodhouse to refuse to surrender except to Birch himself, perhaps fearing More's revenge), credit for the victory may have depended upon the date on which the triumph should have been accepted as taking place. William Beddoe, driven from the town by royalist persecution, returned in May 1646, after the 'reducement' of the town.[61] It is most likely that the town was freed in May, but that the castle was still occupied by the royalists until the beginning of June. Woodhouse's refusal led to a resumption of fighting, during which seven besiegers were killed. Birch was sent for and Ludlow was surrendered to him personally.[62] The news reached London on 2 June and by 5 June Birch's forces were investing Goodrich. On 6 June Samuel More, commander of the Shropshire forces, which had remained, was appointed governor of the castle and garrison.[63]

The town records only hint at the effect of the siege on normal life. The parish register contains no baptisms after 14 May, no burials after 9 May and no weddings after 18 May. The weekly town court heard no cases between 28 April and 2 June. Ludlow had been under siege for six weeks. It had earlier been threatened at the time of the Stokesay engagement in 1645. At such times its trading activity may have been reduced to nothing. During much of the war Gloucester stayed in parliamentary hands and Ludlow's natural trading route was apparently blocked. Even though there were few 'front lines' in existence – for the most part the war consisted of small contingents of marauding troops – and civilians could often get across country, if at some risk, Ludlow's economy may have suffered badly from the disruptions of war.

Ludlow 1646–1660

After the capture Ludlow became a military backwater again under a series of parliamentary military governors, More being the first. As More combined the post with other appointments he may have made little personal impact on the town.

Twenty-nine Ludlow men were charged with delinquency, but not all were convicted. The M.P.s, Goodwin and Baldwin, were the foremost; others were John Cleobury, Edward Powis, Walter Stead, Samuel Weaver, William Colbach, Thomas Powis and Thomas Crump, who all again held office in the town before the Restoration. [64]

Although the forms of town government changed in nothing and its personnel little, life was very different for many. The war had brought to Ludlow a series of military garrisons, some local, some from further afield. Until late 1646, the influence of the military, from the governor down to the private soldiers, would have weighed heavily on the inhabitants. Where military concerns were involved, the council and the people did as they were told, whatever the cost to them. With about 350 in the town, most households would have had to provide billets. Even those who, like Richard Gough, were reputed to be committed royalists, resented the royalist taxes, the billeting and the confiscations.[65]

After the surrender, Ludlow was most affected by a series of county committees, whose membership changed frequently to reflect changing realities in London. The Corporation was adept at bending to the political mood, so there was no wholesale purge of the Corporation, as there had been in more overtly royalist boroughs. Of the eight bailiffs who had been in office between 1642 and 1645, two died shortly afterwards and the rest remained on the council, with two of them, Richard Davies and Edward Turford, serving as bailiffs. There were six new members of the Corporation in the autumn of 1646, but five merely replaced deceased members. The one expulsion, that of Richard Dewes, was for 'his evill carrydge towards this Corporation' rather than for political unreliability. The only other expulsion in 1646–47 was that of Roger Harries, 'a man of very idle and vile behaviour . . . chiefly towards his own wife'.[66] This political tolerance continued. Twenty-one men served as bailiff between 1646 and 1660; 14 had held Corporation office before or during the war. The exception was William Botterell, one of a handful of Ludlow men with clear parliamentary sympathies to achieve influence in the town during the Interregnum. He had been a captain in the parliamentary army and served as one of the governors of Ludlow Castle. He was three times bailiff and sat as a member of the 'Barebones' parliament in 1653. John Aston had been elected to the Corporation in 1631 and had been low bailiff before the war. He was high bailiff in 1650 and 1651, and M.P. for Ludlow in 1654–5 and 1656–8.[67] After the Restoration he lost all influence and moved to London. His will expressed a committed Puritanism even in such disadvantageous times; he may well have been an uncomfortable colleague for the more lukewarm councillors.[68]

Notwithstanding such lukewarm attitudes, the authorities ensured that positions of national political or military significance in the town were held by parliamentary partisans. The first members of Parliament for the town were Thomas Mackworth and Thomas More, meekly elected by the Corporation on 8 August 1646.[69] Mackworth, aged only 19, was the son of the governor of Shrewsbury, while More was the brother of the governor of Ludlow. In November 1646 William Braine, an officer in the parliamentary force which took Bridgnorth, was appointed town clerk of Ludlow, which he remained until he died in 1657. Braine was one of the republicans put on the Shropshire Committee in 1648–9 and was a witness against the king at his trial.[70] Little is known of the political or religious views of Paul Seeley, Moses Leigh and Ralph Fenton, presented to the Ludlow rectory in 1651, 1655 and 1658 respectively, but the last two were willing to subscribe to the Book of Common Prayer in 1662. At least two of the town preachers, however, Richard Steele (1648–51) and Richard Sadler (1651–60), were Puritans. William Whittall, reader and usher at the grammar school, was probably a Puritan too. When Thomas Holland, chief schoolmaster there since 1638, was forced out in 1648, Whittall took his place.[71] Clerical appointments in Ludlow came under the supervision of the county commissions set up for the purpose and which in Herefordshire and Shropshire included both Aston and Botterell.

In September 1646 it was ordained that, in Shropshire, only Shrewsbury and Ludlow should continue to have military garrisons. The Ludlow garrison played a part in suppressing the occasional royalist rising in the area. One of these was in the summer of 1648, when details of a plot to surprise Ludlow Castle were revealed by a soldier of the garrison, 'who is fled from thence'. Royalist gentry thereabouts remained a potential danger, but there is no evidence of support for risings within the town itself.

For reasons of economy, part of the Ludlow garrison was disbanded in 1655. Another troop had to be raised in 1659 during the confusion following Richard Cromwell's resignation from the Protectorate. Powder was sent from Shrewsbury and in August Captains Botterell and Groome were paid £100 by the war treasurer for forces 'lately engaged in the defence of Ludlow castle'.[72] We do not know what trouble was anticipated, but the Corporation voted the purchase of six muskets and eight halberks 'for the present occasion'.[73]

Corporation records show that the structure of borough government remained largely unchanged during the Interregnum. The county committee called the tune, especially on financial matters. In August 1649, for example, it was resolved 'that the tythes of this parish and the corn growing upon the glebe have to be disposed of according to the committee of Salop's order'. Some signs of conflict are discernible, particularly after 1650. In January 1652, the town's charters were required to be submitted for scrutiny by a parliamentary committee and perhaps as a result in December 1653 Ludlow, along with Bridgnorth, lost one of its parliamentary seats. This measure was reversed in 1659 when Ludlow once more had two seats. One was taken by a newcomer, Job Charlton, whose father, a London goldsmith, had suffered for his loyalty to Charles I, and the other was taken by Samuel Baldwyn, also a lawyer, son of Charles Baldwyn, the royalist member of the Long Parliament.

The parliamentary government's power was most felt through its taxation. In 1648 the council tried to get Ludlow's burden reduced, echoing pre-war protests against the burden of shipmoney. The tax assessments for Ludlow during the 1650s have mostly survived and show annual charges at a level thought scarcely acceptable for occasional taxation during shipmoney days. Moreover parliamentary taxes were collected with more success than was shipmoney in its later years.

The new order made itself felt in outward form, too. The royal arms in the parish church were erased. The pews formerly reserved for the lord president of the Council of the March were now occupied by the military governor and the aldermen of the borough. The organ pipes were melted down and the case dismantled. The church bells, as they had always been before the war, were rung to celebrate political events of importance to the authorities, like the appointment of Cromwell as lord protector.[74] Some of the town's finest houses were now occupied by people associated with the new regime.

The times favoured disorder in private matters; absentee landlords of small properties were particularly vulnerable. Cuthbert Hely moved to London and found that his possession of his houses at 4–7 Bull Ring had been disturbed by John Acton and others, including Francis Ball, a carrier, the mortgagee; his tulips had been replaced with onions, the privy doors had been barricaded and a tenant had been frightened off. Such events, even if not usually so farcical, occurred at all times, but were more common during this period.[75]

Destruction of the Suburbs

Throughout the Interregnum the ruins of burnt and demolished houses were a grim reminder of the 'late unhappy troubles' – the phrase common in contemporary records. Many building leases of Corporation properties were granted between 1646 and 1662. In a few cases the cause of destruction was explicit; for example, in 1647 the tenement over Corve Gate, 'ruined in these unnatural warres', was leased to Robert Berry, a corviser. In most cases, however, destruction is implicit in the description we have, as in the lease to Thomas Ward in August 1647 of 'the mese place where a house stood in Over Galdeford'. Occasionally the lease indicates that rebuilding had already taken place, as in the 1657 grant to Ralph Sharrett of 'a messuage without Galdeford Gate newly erected in consideration of his building'. In most cases rebuilding was a condition of the lease; in May 1652 John

Walbridge had to build and tile the decayed messuage at 76–9 Lower Galdeford. A barn replaced three former houses at 8 Corve Street.[76]

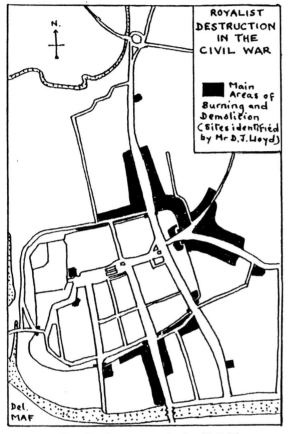

ROYALIST DESTRUCTION IN THE CIVIL WAR

■ Main Areas of Burning and Demolition (Sites identified by Mr D.J. Lloyd)

54.   Royalist Destruction in the Civil War.

Our knowledge of wartime destruction of freehold property is more fortuitous. Title deeds of such properties, or of bordering properties, and records of court proceedings provide the chief evidence. 40 Bull Ring was rebuilt, but this may not have been necessitated by wartime acts. The house on the north side of Castle Street, next to the Town Ditch, was 'pulled down' in the wars.[77] Edward Foxe's house on the west side of Lower Broad Street was 'lately demolished' in the war and Robert Townshend's large house, probably that built 50 years earlier from the buildings of the old Austin friary, was described in 1654 as 'burnt down'. Other houses, which cannot be located with certainty, include Edward Cooke's three houses, burnt to the ground when he fled to London.[78]

Richard Wilks claimed his house in Corve Street 'was put on fire and burnt down by the means and act of some ill-disposed soldiers who endeavoured the great ruin of himself and divers other persons in Ludlow'.[79] William Beddow had to pay out money to prevent his house, tenanted by John Compton, from being burned – which implies extortion.[80] John Price was forced to dismantle his house in Holdgate Fee as a later dispute over stored timber reveals.[81] There was also severe physical damage in the town perpetrated at the order of Sir Michael Woodhouse. Much of the planned destruction took place in the weeks before 4 April 1646, as it was on that day that the council minutes record that the bailiffs were to prepare a rent roll of demolished houses. On 23 September 1646, a lease was granted to Thomas Roe of a plot in Corve Street, where a 'house did lately stand'.

The Shambles was repaired at the end of 1649. A messuage on the east side of Corve Street was not let until 1664 owing to the great cost of building premises burnt in time of war. In 1669 Nicholas Payne was leased a void plot outside Broad Gate on the east side. In 1672 rent arrears had to be allowed on another void place in Corve Street burned in the war.

Comparison of the assessments of the 1650s, the hearth taxes of 1662 and 1672 and the poll tax of 1667 shows that a few of the identified destroyed houses were isolated examples with houses still standing on either side, but that most were in parts of the town where all or most of the buildings were razed. Most of this demolition was in the suburbs immediately outside the town walls, although there were small clusters of ruined buildings just inside

Old Gate and Galdeford Gate while others adjoined the Town Ditch in the Dinham-Castle Street area. The royalist garrison wanted to clear arcs of fire for their guns on the town walls and to deny to the besiegers shelter for tunnelling and sapping. The houses in Dinham and Castle Street, close to the castle gates, were perhaps demolished at the same time and for the same reason. The second phase of destruction, less justifiable on tactical grounds, was indiscriminate burning in the suburbs, probably on 23 April. All the known burnt houses were some distance from the town walls and it is recorded that one of these, 43 Lower Galdeford, 'was burnt down to the ground by the wicked command of Sir Michael Woodhouse'. At best this was scorched earth tactics by the royalists; at worst an excess committed by a demoralised soldiery running amuck in the face of imminent defeat; the latter is the more likely.

On 13 March 1647 it was resolved that future leases of burned down houses should be sealed only after a new house had been built, although this very strict policy was not continued, possibly because it gave the lessee no security whatever for his investment. Half the Corporation leases granted between 1646 and 1660 were building leases.[82] In 1652 Edward Turford committed himself to build and tile a dwelling house at 14 Corve Street within five years. Other incentives to rebuild were granted: in 1649 John Cleobury leased what is now the *Compasses* Inn outside Corve Gate without an entrance fine, provided he built there. In 1658 Edward Earsley was granted a property on the south side of Lower Galdeford at half the old rent. Rebuilding was nonetheless very slow; in 1655 Richard Scott's lease of 20–21 Lower Galdeford was resumed and granted to Edward Robinson when Scott refused to carry out a condition to rebuild, just as Thomas Price's lease of a property in the Town Ditch outside Broad Gate was cancelled and regranted in 1655 to William Woodall, nine years after the original grant, again upon a condition of rebuilding, which was not apparently carried out until 1668.[83] That these conditions and incentives did not succeed in accelerating the rebuilding process suggests strongly that Ludlow had become seriously impoverished; the catastrophic fall in the town's population at this time reinforces the conclusion.

At least one building lease was granted for each Corporation property during the 1650s, but no building occurred until after 1660. The 1662 hearth tax roll shows that only five buildings with hearths had been built in upper Corve Street (east side).[84] A later hearth tax roll, that of 1672, together with other assessments of the mid-1660s, show eight occupied houses here.[85] Even a century after the war the Corporation was still not satisfied with the rate of rebuilding. Leases between 1730 and 1761 still had a building condition for dwelling houses fronting the street.[86]

Although the forms of government of Ludlow survived the war and Interregnum, economically, demographically and architecturally the town suffered severely. It took a very long time to recover.

Ludlow Officials Before 1290

Herebert	1187	*prepositus* (Pipe Roll).
Adam de Kyvesac	1238	?bailiff of Walt. Lacy obt. Ludlow (CCR)
Robert *Monetarius*	*c.*1210–40	*pretor*; with Alan Owein; *prepositus* with Hen. Mile, Hen. *Fabro–*, Rog. FitzOsbert(MT.461, 721)
Alan Owein	*c.*1210–40	*pretor*; with Rob. *Monetarius* (MT.461)
Henry Mile	*c.*1210–40	*prepositus* with Rob. *Monetarius* (MT.721)
Henry *Faber*	*c.*1210–40	*prepositus* with Rob. *Monetarius* (MT.721)
Roger FitzOsbert	*c.*1210–40	*prepositus* with Rob. *Monetarius* (MT.721)
Roger Eilrich	*c.*1220–50	colman; with Wm Fenes and Walt. E. (MT.725)
Walter Eilrich	*c.*1220–50	with Wm Fenes & Rog. E.(MT.725)
Robert de Stantone	‹1241	constable; *temp.* Walt Lacy & Wm Condecoke stewrd (BL: Add.Ch.8343)
Richard de Chabbenovere	1255–6	*prepositus; ballivus;* son Hen. C. (MT.1; Shrops. Eyre Roll 1256)
Richard *Clericus als Ballivus*	1256	*prepositus; ballivus* (Shrops, Eyre Roll 1256)
Adam Cotele *als Clericus*	1257	*prepositus*; chaplain; *temp.* Ric. Cler. (MT1350)
William de Radenovere *als* **Pygin**	*c.*1261–72	*Elector* 1272 with Ric. Momele (PRO: Just.1/736m.24f);son Hen. P.; *with–* Ric. Momele 1272 (PRO: Just.1/737; MT.1,768); Verdun bailiff 1272 (Just.1/737m.35f)
Walter *Clericus als* **Heytone**	*c.*1261–66	precedes Ric. Momele; with Wm Radenovere (MT.731,759 (PRO: Just.1/737; MT.764)
Richard de Momele	1271–2	*capitalis ballivus* with Wm Radenovere 1272 (PRO: Just.1/736m.24f); bailiff *temp–*. Geoff. Andrew PG Warden *c.*1260s–1284; clerk (MT.11–2;CPR,1324); constable pre–1266 (BL: Add.Ch.8351; Eyton, v, 49; (MT.8,9); ?ident. with Sir Ric. de Aka farmer of Ludlow, in 1287 P. Genevile's attorney (CPR)
Roger Schermon *jun*	1272	*prepositus*; and *c.*1280s *temp.* Ric. Momele(MT.13)
Henry le Mercer	*c.* 1272	clerk (BL: Add.Ch.55535) *temp.* Ric. Momele (MT.499;) d.pre–1290 (Just.1/739,m.11d)
Thomas de Wulfreslaw	1274	*ballivus (Rot. Hund.)* ? Tho. de Ludelawe, G. Genevile's attorney 1277 (CCR)
John Esturmy	1274	constable *(Rot. Hund.)*
Robert *Clericus* **de Stantone**	1282	G. Genevile's attorney in Engd. 1280 (*CPR*)(MT.18)
Richard *Constabularius*	1284	d.*c.*1289–92 (PRO: Just.1/739,740; CP47/45/392) ?ident with Ric. de Lodelawe, G. Genevile's attorney 1278–80 (*CPR*)
Richard le Seneschal	1286	constable; ?ident. with Ric. Constab. (*CCR*)

Henry de Chabbenovere   ‹1288   *temp.* Ric. Momele

Note: in this, and the following appendices, shortage of space requires that references be kept to brief essentials. Pages, membrane numbers and years may be omitted as the information given will with diligence enable the authority to be found. Comprehensive referencing would have been at the cost of several lists. For similar reasons, the office-holder lists are not indexed.

Bailiffs Before 1461

Henry Chabbenovere:	25.1.1288–0.7.1294	PG co-fndr 1284; sn of Ric. C.; sn Ric. C. (MT.1036; PRO:C.47/45/392; SCRO 4032/1/1; MT.161–3, 278, 280–1)
Hugh Cleyburi:	1288	Farmer Genevile moiety 1291; PG elder; d.‹1335; (MT.761; PRO: C.47/45/392; CP40/301; SRO:356/419)
Thomas Eylrich:	29.12.1290	wool mercht; of Steventon; (CPR,1271; MT.278);
Henry Pygin *als* **Radenovere**	1291	Farmer Genevile moiety: 1291 PG Warden 1284–1314; sn of Wm P als R. (SRO: 356/419; MT.14, PRO: C.47/45/392)
Robert Broun:	25.3.1295–25.2.1298	Lo. of Wichcott; ?G. Genevile's attorney 1280 *CPR* (SRO: 4032/1/22; MT.29, 30, 507–9, 550–1, 628, 776; PRO: CP40/129; BL.Eg.Ch.5766)
Thomas Brid:	1.6.1297–0.3.1298	Verdun Bailiff (PRO: CP40/129)
John Tikelwardine:	25.3.1295–25.12.1298	d.c.1332 (PRO: Just.1/1432; MT.30, 32, 39, 164, 172, 340, 551, 628, 776)
William Routone:	25.12.1298	attorney; sn Jn R.; of Clungunford; (PRO: CP40/200; Just.1/1366; MT.164)
William Glovere *(le Ganter)*	2.2.1300	sn of Thos G.; sn Phil. G.; (Coll.Arms 468; PRO: Just.1/741; MT.31, 312)
Nicholas Eylrich:	2.2.1300–25.4.1300	Chf Bailiff Stanton Lacy 1292; co-parc. Steventon 1284; (Eyton,v,11; MT.36, 165, 312)
William Routone:	25.4.1300–12.3.1309	Coll.Arms Foliot 467, MT.31, 34, 38, 165, 782–3;
Geoffrey Helyoun:	29.9.1300	(MT.31)
John Tikelwardine:	6.5.1302–4.4.1304	(MT.32, 166)
John Clebury:	2.3.1305–0.3.1306	d.‹1314; (MT.38, 168, 467, 755; PRO: Just.1/744; CP40/205)
Robert Moneter *(Monetarius)*	6.1.1308	clerk; of Whitton; (MT.514, 629, 1029)
Matthew Agace:	20.7.1308	d.›1321; sn of Robt A.; (SRO: 356/419; MT. 164; 904)
John Tikelwardine	20.7.1308–2.3.1319	(SRO:356/419; MT.173, 554, 782)
John Clebury:	23.11.1310–25.5.1311	(MT.168, 552)
William Routone:	14.1.1313–26.5.1315	(SRO: 4032/1/23,29; MT.170, 313, 387, 4689)
Philip Glovere *(le Ganter)*	8.9.1315–14.4.1318	of XII 1317; son of Thos G; bro. of Wm G. (SRO: 356/419; 4032/1/6; MT. 340, 631, 788)
William Shermon *jun*:	5.4.1317–8.12.1320	(SRO: 4032/1/13; MT.555, 681, 789)
Henry Heytone:	8.12.1320	of XII 1317; d.?1349 (SRO; 4032/1/13)
John Tikelwardine:	12.3.1321–0.7.1324	?John de Lodelowe farmer of Verdun moiety (PRO SC6/1146/7; MT.174, 512–3, 557, 632)
Richard Corve:	12.3.1321–30.11.1324	wool mercht; farmer Mortimer moiety 1324; PG Warden 1334–49; (PRO: SC6/1148/7; MT.174, 512–3, 632, 6857, 1143)
Richard Chabbenore:	30.11.1324–11.11.1328	Of XII 1317; sn of Hen. C. (PRO: CP40/264; SCRO: 356/419)
John Tikelwardine:	30.8.1325–29.6.1332	MT. 46–7; 50, 52, 181, 562, 637, 685)
William Pirefeld:	11.11.1328	d.1348; sn Ric. P. (PRO: CP40/264; SRO: 356/520/6)

William Leinthalle: 29.9.1328–29.9.1330 — Lord's baker 1309–12; sn John L.; d.1341 (PRO: SC6/967/19;SCRO: 356/520/4)

William Buttere: 11.11.1328–15.10.1331 — (MT301,515; PRO: CP40/264; KB27/310; SC6/1236/2)

Hugh Westone: *c.*1332 — overseer of Mortimer moiety (SRO: 356/419)

Hugh Westone: 0.1.1337–23.3.1337 — SCRO: KB27/310; MT.571, 718)

William Buttere: 0.1.1337–19.4.1338 — (MT.301, 515)

Richard Dulverne: 0.7.1338–30.9.1338 — Dep. Kpr Mortimer estates 1331; King's Recvr for same 1331 (PRO: E.142/68/3; CCR 1331; SC6/1236/2; MT.301, 515, 565, 813

Hugh Westone: 1.4.1341 — (MT.571)

John Pywau: 7.5.1340–11.6.1346 — d.‹1367; sn of Rog. P.; wife Margt dr of Hugh de la Boure; involved in murder of Thos Marteley 1331 (PRO: Just.1/1347,1478; CP40/192; KB27/292;SRO: 4032/1/16, 26;MT.449, 643, 710)

John Schrosbury: 7.5.1340–4.4.1351 — wool mercht; sn of Wm S.; bro. of Ric. S.; wife Denise who re-m. Ric. Pywau (PRO: CP40/365, 387; KB27/294; C.260/43/37; SRO:4032/1/26; MT.560,710, 814)

William Orletone: 4.4.1351–18.10.1351 — wool mercht; b.1298 (*Cal.I.p.m.*, ix, 247; 83)

Richard Pauntleye: 28.10.1351–30.9.1372 — b.1298; elder of PG 1355–62; of Diddlebury (*Cal.I.p.m.* ix, 247; BL: Add.MS 24820 fo.99; PRO: SC6/1107/2,3; MT.81–3, 373, 520, 651)

John Cachepol: 2.10.1352–25.11.1369 — PG Stewd; sn of Thos C. (SRO: 356/325, 419; MT.61, 377, 652)

Richard Scot: 8.9.1378 — d.‹1402;(BL: Add.Ch.413264; MT.214,320, 528, 1402)

William Orletone: 8.9.1378–11.6.1392 — PG Warden 1372–1390; Subs. Collr 1377–9 (MT.522, 955; *CFR;* PRO: CP40/446, m.120v; 450, m.247v)

Philip Lingen: 27.11.1378 — draper; PG Stewd 1373–6 & 1388; PG Warden 1396–7 (MT.294, 698, 837, 1397; PRO C.47/45/392)

Richard Scot: 29.6.1381 — (MT.214)

Philip Lingen: 8.12.1382–23.11.1385 — (MT.216–7, 389, 684, 1354)

Richard Scot: 5.9.1387–29.12.1390 — (MT.88, 395, 397–8, 588, 590)

Richard Sibbetone: 11.7.1392–0.5.1399 — Living 1408; (BL: Eg. Ch.5763; Add.Ch.41324–5)

Thomas Stevenes: 11.11.1399–14.12.1401 — BL: Add.Ch.41327; MT.223, 408, 410, 659)

Philip Lingen: 18.10.1402–31.3.1404 — (MT.224, 410–2, 531, 694

Richard Dyer: 29.6.1404 — (MT.259)

John Girrous: 10.8.1406–30.11.1406 — draper; Commr 15th/10th 1401–2, 1416; d.‹1427; Drs Alce wife of 1. John Bradeford, 2. John Whitton; Elinor wife of John Marchamley; (SCRO 4032/1/27; *CPR; CFR; CPR;* PRO: KB27/893; Just.1/1504; CP40/666; BL: Add.Ch.41328; MT.262)

Richard Sibbetone: 23.3.1407–23.11.1407 — (MT.98–9)

Robert Barbor: 11.7.1408 — (MT.226)

Henry Herdeleye: 23.3.1409–14.2.1412 — draper; Commr 15th/10th 1413; (PRO: CP40/653; *CFR;* MT.413, 415, 591, 660, 851)

John Girrous: 11.6.1412–2.10.1412 — (MT.228, 853)

William Mersshetone: 23.4.1415–29.9.1418 — d.1436; wife Joan dr of Wm Conynge (PRO: KB27/694; SC6/967/21; MT.427; SRO: 356/520; MT.592, 1174–5)

William Parys:	6.1.1416–23.3.1419	draper; king's alnager, Salop 1399 1401; Commr Subs. 1404; PG Warden 1401, 1422–1440; sn of John Parys; wife Sibil wdw of Wm Pryseley; sn John P. (*CFR*; *CPR*; PRO: E.101/344/19; KB27/648; CP40/528 SC6/967/21; MT.93, 107, 230, 409,593, 594, 857, 965
William Moyle:	21.2.1424–24.6.1433	mbr Trin. Gild, Coventry; d.‹1435; wife Joan (CP40/640; SC6/419/764; SRO: 4032/1/20; MT.104, 232, 418, 598, 600, 661, 697–8, 860, 1180)
John Chapell:	0.9.1429	heir of Joan Ry (SRO: 356/321; MT.99).
William Mersshetone:	24.7.1434–29.6.1435	(MT.108–9, 421)
Walter Codur:	12.3.1437–12.2.1439	weaver/mercht; Commr for 15th/10th 1429; son Wm C. of Bristol; dr Agn. mother of Wm Colewall; d.1446 (PRO: CP40/723; 737; C.1/87/942; MT.110, 234 324, 425; *CFR*; Will, PCC).
John Parys:	18.10.1439–0.7.1440	Collr Subs. 1442; PG Warden 1443–9; son of Wm P. d.1449 (*CFR*; *CPR*; MT.863)
Walter Codur:	18.10.1440	(MT.110)
John Parys:	24.9.1443–29.9.1444	(MT.603, 865)
John Griffith:	10.2.1446–11.6.1447	hosier; PG Stewd 143640; PG warden 1451–62; mbr Stratford Gild 1433; d.1465–70 (MT.428, 604).
John Colewalle:	9.11.1448–11.7.1457	yeoman; d.1471 (PRO: KB27/667; CWAcc.1471; MT.305, 663).
Thomas Hoke:	25.7.1459–29.9.1459	dyer; of XII ‹1448(*CPR*; SRO: 356/2/1; MT.679, 703)

Wardens of The Palmers' Gild

Geoffrey Andrew	to *c.*1284	prob. 1st Gildalderneman or Warden; d.‹1284; son of Andr. Miles; bro. of Nic.A.; dr Yvette; juror 1256, 1271; liv 1275; (PRO:C.132/39/20; KB27/37; Just.1/734, 739, 784, 1230B; MT.11, 1132, 1350)
Henry Pygin *als Radenovere*	‹1284–1315›	2nd Gildalderneman, Rector or Warden; Bailiff 1291 q.v. (SRO:356/419; MT.23, 142, 627, 755, 783–4; PRO: C.47/45/392)
Richard Corve	‹17.11.1329–1349	?also pre–0.11.1329›; Bailiff 1321–4 q.v.
Richard Orletone	‹25.3.1359–15.10.1361›	PG elder ‹1330; wool mercht traded with Dordrecht and Bruges; son of Ric. O.; bro. of Wm O.; sons Wm & Thos O.; d.15.10.1361› (CCR1332, 1343; PRO: Just.1/1392; SCRO: 356/520; MT.51, 61, 68–70, 690)
John Hawkins	‹29.9.1365–24.3.1371›	chaplain; rector Whitchurch 1368–89; vicar S. Mich.,Coventry 1389–?1406; d.*c.*1406; prob. son of Rob. H. of L; bro. of Thos & Wm H. (*CPR* 1367, 1391; Reg. Stretton 61; Eyton, x, 27; SRO: 356/325, 520; MT.393, 521)
William Orletone	‹28.3.1372–21.9.1390›	Bailiff 1378–92 q.v.
William Hereford	20.9.1392	draper; PG elder 1383; liv. ‹1355–1396› (PRO: CP40/533, m.408r; MT.91, 392, 840)
William Broke	29.8.1393–24.3.1394	PG elder 1383; ?son of Adam Broke of Ashf. Carbonel; liv. ‹1377–1404› (MT.323, 392, 657, 717, 847, 921)
Philip Lingen	‹29.9.1396–29.9.1397›	Bailiff 1378 etc q.v.
William Parys	‹1401–1402›	Bailiff 1416–19 q.v.
William Broke	‹0.3.1404›	see above
John Leinthalle	‹25.3.1406–22.12.1408›	d.1409–3.5.1411; son of Wm L.
William Parys	‹1422–1440›	see above
John Parys	‹1443–1449›	Bailiff 1439–40 q.v.
John Griffith	‹1451–10.8.1462›	Bailiff 1446–7 q.v.
John Dodmore	‹12.3.1468–8.7.1471›	Bailiff 1464 q.v.
Richard Sherman	‹29.9.1472–20.12.1494›	of XII 1469; parker of Oakley 1478; Castlemeadow farmer 1481; son Edwd S. (*CPR* 1490; PRO: SC6/966/18. 19, 22; C.1/355/92; Duke MSS 1011/168; SRO: 356/420; MT.706, 873)
Walter Morton	‹20.3.1496–0.3.1509›	Bailiff 1476 q.v.
Richard Downe	‹21.4.1509–10.10.1531›	Bailiff 1499 q.v.
Walter Rogers	‹27.12.1535–4.5.1546›	Bailiff 1514 q.v.
William Langford	‹10.7.1547–1.7.1551	Stewd 1511–4, q.v.; Bailiff 1519 q.v.

Appendix 4

Other Palmers' Gild Officers

S: Steward; R: Renter; J: Janitor; C: Chaplain

Hugh Wystanstowe	R:1344–5	SRO: 356/322
John Cachepol	S:1364	Bailiff q.v.
John Munselowe	S:1364	cook; son of Wm M.; son Wm M. q.v. (SRO: PGColl.Ac 1359–64; MT369, 372, 377, 660, 834)
John Piers	R:1364–5	Exor of Edm. E. of March 1382; rector Kingsland 1384; rector Ludlow 1384–1404; d. 1404 (Reg. Gilbert; PRO: SC6/1304/17; PGReg; CPR 1405)
Hugh Ewyas	J:1364	(SRO: 356/325)
John Pusselowe	S:*c*.1371	(PRO: CP40/445 m.377r)
Richard Pirefeld	S:1373–8	merchant; ?son of Thos P.; son John P.; d.‹29.12.1389 (PRO: KB27/338, 346; SRO: 356/321; MT48, 589, 855, 1397)
Philip Lingen	S:1373–6	Warden q.v.
John Warewyk	J:1378	(SRO: 356/321)
Richard Borewey	S:1377–8	Commr 15th/10th 1383 (*CFR*); d.‹1403 (SRO:356/321; MT.91,225,841, 845)
Richard Chamburleyn	C:1377–8	(PG.Acc)
Richard Tranter	S:1389	PRO: C.47/45/392
John Parys	S:1383	Warden q.v.; (MT.392)
William Hawkynes	S:1383–5	(MT.392; MT.1165)
Richard Brugge	S:1385	chaplain; (MT.1165)
Philip Lingen	S:1389	PRO: C.47/45/392
William Munselowe	S:*c*.1406–8	*Temp.* Jn Leinthall warden
William Parsones	R:‹1424	chaplain (SRO: PGrental; MT.600)
John Lawrence	S:1423–8	draper; d.1472; son of Jn L. (PRO: KB27/661; SRO: PGAcc.; MT.598; AO1472;)
Mathew Grene	S:1423–8	clothier; of XII 1448; (PRO: KB27/661; SRO: PGAcc; RB; MT.228, 598)
Richard Kynstone	R:1424–8	d.‹1460; wife Joan (PGRental; MT.425, 621, 870)
Richard Ademond	J:1424–8	(PGAcc)
Thomas Dountone	S:1428–34	weaver; of XII 1448; d.1455; (SRO: PGAcc; RB; MT.229; AO 1455)
John Dodmore	S:1428–34	son of Jn D. bailiff q.v. (SRO: PGAcc.)
Thomas Bolesdone	S:*c*.1436	saddler; (PRO: CP40/678m.356r; SRO: PG Acc.)
John Griffith	S:1436–40	Warden q.v.
John Bowdeler	S:1436–40	mercht; of XII 1448; liv. 1454 (SRO: PG Acc.; RB)
Walter Russhe	R:1437–8	chaplain of college; deed witn. 1416–59; d.‹1470 (MT.236, 969, 1320)
John Hosyer	S:1440–2	hosier; of XII 1448; endowed Almshouse; d.1463 PCC1463; SRO: PGAcc; RB)
Richard Dylowe	S:1440–2	corviser; of XII 1448; keeper of prison 1423; d.1453; wife 1. Isab. dr of Jn Moyle, 2. Juliana,

		3. Joan; bro. or son David Dillow (*CPR* 1422; PRO: KB27/661; C.88/10/18; SRO: 356/520; RB)
Richard Knyghtone	S:1445–7	d.1466 funded re-building bell-tower church; ?b. Knighton (SRO: PGAcc. Will)
Richard Ryalle	S:1445–7	baker; d.1453› (PRO: KB27/640, 703; SRO: PGAcc)
Philip Gryme	J:1446–7	(PG Acc.)
William Knyghtone	S:c.1460	SRO: 356/316/8367
John Wroth	S:1461–3	Bailiff q.v. *ibid.*
John Dodmore	R:1461–2 S:1461–6	Warden q.v.
John Sherman	R:1461–2 S:1463–6	Bailiff q.v.
John Dale	R:1461–2 R:1471 S:1467	walker; PG S:1467renter 1471; d.1487 (SRO: PGAcc; PGRental; Bor. Acc; AO1486)
Walter Hobold	R:1469 R:1481–2 S:1469	Bailiff q.v. R:1469 (SRO: 356/325)
Richard Thornton	S:1469 R:1472	Bailiff q.v. (SRO: 356/325)
John Wylkes	S:1472–6	Bailiff q.v.
John Malmeshulle *als* Mercer	R:1488–9 S:1472–6	Bailiff q.v.
Walter Morton	S:1485–9	Warden q.v.
Thomas Teron	R:1499–1500 S:1485–9	Bailiff q.v.
John Eygnons	R:1485–6	Bailiff q.v.
William Parsones	R:1492–4	Bailiff q.v.
John Lane	R:1494–5	Bailiff q.v.
Richard Dyer	S:1497–1501	Bailiff q.v.
Richard Lane	R:1501–2 R:1516–7 S:1497–1501	Bailiff q.v.
William Cheyney	R:1497–8	Bailiff q.v.
John Brown	S:1505–9	draper; d.1509; son of Ric. B; wife Joan dr of Jn Pakynton; (SRO: PGAcc; PRO: PCC1509)
Richard Bragott	S:1505–9	weaver; ?son of Jn B.; d.1520 (SCRO: PGAc.; PGReg 1487; MT.272; AO 1507, 1520)
––Capper	S:c.1510–14	*TSAS*, vii
William Langford	S:c.1510–14	*Ibid.*; warden, q.v.
Richard Rog	J:‹1505	(PGAc)
John Shrawley	J:1506–37	(PGAc; MT.622)
Richard Bury	R:1524–5	Bailiff q.v.
Roger Bradshaw	S:1532–3	bro. of Jn B. bailiff q.v.; wife Eliz. wdw of Thos Crofton; d.1538 (SRO: PGAcc; PGReg1487; MT.272; AO1519)
Thomas Whelar	S:1532–3	Bailiff q.v.
William Phillips	S:1538–9	Bailiff q.v.
Richard Hoore	S:1538–9	(PGAc)
John Alsop	S:1548–51	perhaps Steward (PRO: E.321/30/14)
John Taylor *alias* Barker	S:1548–51	as Alsop; Bailiff q.v.
Richard Langford	R:1548–51	Bailiff q.v.(PGAcc.; 356/321, 324; PGrental; 356/325; PGReg SRO: 356/319; 356/2/1)

The Corporation Cursus Honorum *After 1461*

Abbreviations

AdB	Admitted Burgess
CW	Churchwarden
XXV	Joined XXV
Ch	Chamberlain
LB	Low Bailiff
Al	Alnager
HB	High Bailiff
Co	Coroner
CM	Capital Master
S	Sequestered
E	Expelled
P	Part-year
D	Died

Four lists of bailiffs after 1461 – Mytton's (Univ. Lib. Birm.), Wright's, Gough's and Baldwin's (q.v.) – were compiled in the 17th and 18th centuries. Wright, Gough and Baldwin, although a year out, accurate only from 1518. Mytton is wholly unreliable. Appendix 5 is based on documentary evidence.

NUM.	NAME.	AdB.	CW.	XXV.	Ch.	LB.	Al.	HB.	Co.	CM.	DIED
001.	John Sherman							1461			1468
002.	Philip Gryme				1461						1468›
003.	Nicholas Cressett				1462			1469			1482
004.	Robert Barbor				1462						
005.	William Sutton							1463			1469›
006.	John Waterfalle				1463						1481
007.	John Dodmore							1464			1472
008.	John Adams				1464			1471			1474c
009.	John Hosyer							?1465			
010.	Thomas Stevenes	1464				?1465		1473			
								1479		1484›	
011.	John Sparchford					1466					
						1474					
						1480					
								1485		1488	
012.	Henry Colewalle	1463				1466		?1472			1483–7
013.	William Griffith							1467			
								1472			1479
014.	David Stewe				1467						1473›
015.	John Wroth							1468			1477?
016.	Thomas Ludford					1468					
017.	William Bowier					1469		?1476			
						1474		?1487			
018.	Walter Hobold							1470			
								1475			
								1478			
								1482			
								?1490		1501	

NUM.	NAME.	AdB.	CW.	XXV.	Ch.	LB.	Al.	HB.	Co.	CM.	DIED
019.	Richard Thornton	1464				1470					
	als Barbor					1488					1490›
020.	John Wilkes	1469				1471		?1478			1487
021.	John Barbor	1469									
022.	William Shipston				1475						
023.	Geoffrey Baugh					1472		1489			1514
024.	Thomas Ferrour			‹1469		1473					
025.	Roger Morton					1475					1491‹
026.	John Lane	1469	1471			1478		1486			
								1494			
								1498			1500
027.	Thomas Teron		1471	1469		1479		1491			
								1496			
								1499			
								1510			1519
028.	John Typper					1480					?1490
029.	Walter Morton			‹1469		1476		1481			1511
030.	John Malmeshill										
	als Mercer		1464			1481					
031.	John Heywood					1482					1502c
032.	John Cheyney				1475						
033.	William Gery			‹1469		1485		1488			1500?
034.	John Tewe					1486		1493			
035.	Hugh Haseley	1468				1489					
036.	William Grene					1491		1504			1515?
037.	William Parsones					1493					1511?
038.	John Hoke	1469				1494		1501			
								1515			1523
039.	Thomas Cookes							1495			1513
040.	Richard Lane					1495		1509			
								1519			
								1524			1526
041.	Richard Dyer										
	als Bingham					?1496		1502			1549
042.	John Eynons		‹1469					1497			1500
043.	William Fern					1497					
044.	William Cheyney					1498					
							1501		1508			
045.	Richard Downe					1499		1506	?1511		
								?1516			1537
046.	John Clungunwas					1502	1519				
047.	John Pratte					1504					
048.	Thomas Clunton					1506		1514			
								?1523			
049.	William Clungunwas					1509		1521			
	als Clungunford					1511		1529			1544
050.	John Hare					1508		1517			
								1527			
								1532			1544
051.	Walter Rogers					1514		1518			
								1522			
								1525			
								1530			1546

NUM.	NAME.	AdB.	CW.	XXV.	Ch.	LB.	Al.	HB.	Co.	CM.	DIED
052.	Richard Smale					1515					
053.	John Cother					?1516		1520			
								1528			1535
054.	Richard Bury					1517					
055.	Henry Pickering					?1518	1521				
056.	William Langford					1519		1526			
								1533			
								1538			
								1542	1543		1553
056a.	Philip Penson						1526				
057.	John Stone					1520					
058.	Thomas Crofton					1521					1524
059.	John Bailey					1522					
060.	Richard Davies					?1523					
061.	William Foxe					1524		1531			
								1536			
								1544			
								1545	1546		
								1553			1554
061a.	Walter Codur				1520						
062.	Walter Phelips					1525	1520				1528
063.	John Taylor				1525	1526		1535			
	als Barker							1539	1546		
								1545	1554		1558
064.	John Hore						1525–32				
065.	Robert Bradocke				1526	1527					
066.	Roger Ferne				1527	1528	1537				
067.	William Evans					1529		1537			1547
068.	John Bradshaw					1530		1534	1541		
								1540			1567
069.	Thomas Lewis										
	als Draper				1526	1531	1536				
070.	John Tomlins				1530	1532	1533				1537
071.	John Lane				1529	1533	1545				1545
072.	Robert Hood										
	als Stayner				1528	1534					1549
072.	John Gwynne										
	als Baker		1528								
			1529								1557
073.	William Phelips	1525	1529p		1534	1535		1547			1559
074.	Thomas Cother				1533	1536		1543			1562
075.	Thomas Whelar	1527				1537		1541			
								1554			
								1565			1574
076.	Robert Harper		1529								
077.	John Passie	1529			1537	1538		1546	1547		
								1557	1558		
078.	Henry Young	1530	1532		1536						1538
079.	John Lloyd		1532								
080.	Philip Cupper		1536								1538
081.	John Lockyer		1528			1535	1539				1556
082.	Richard Bradford				1538	1540		1548			1556

NUM.	NAME.	AdB.	CW.	XXV.	Ch.	LB.	Al.	HB.	Co.	CM.	DIED
083.	Richard Handley				1539	1541	1550				1562
084.	John Alsap	1538		1541		1542		1552			
								1562			1569
085.	William Coxe				1531	1543					1544
086.	Richard Whittall	1526			1532		1529				1546
087.	Richard Langford		?1538		1540	1544		1549			
								1560			1562
088.	Thomas Lewis							1546			
089.	William Bradocke	1532	1537								1538
090.	Thomas Boyden	1532	1537								1548
091.	William Lacon	1534	?1538	1541							
092.	John Hoke			‹1541	1543	1545		1551	1552		1558
093.	Lewis Phillips										
	als Capper	1530		1541	1544	1546	1551	1556	1557		1561
094.	Thomas Blashfield	1538			1545	1547		1550	1551		
								1559	1591		
								1569			
								1579			
								1585			1593
095.	William Parterich	1528?	1539	1541	1546	1548	1552	1555	1556		1583
096.	Thomas Heyton			1541	1542	1549	1553				1558
097.	John Cocks										
	als Coxe	1539			1541	1550		1558	1559		1572
098.	Lewis Crowther	1542	1545		1549	1551	1554				1556
099.	Walter ap David										
	als Taylor		?1539	1541	1547	1552	1555				
100.	Edmund Sherman		1536	‹1541	1550	1553	1556				
101.	Lawrence Frensse		1540								
102.	John Draper		1540								
103.	Richard Water										
	als Watyes		1541								1558
104.	Robert Addes		1543								1544?
105.	John Season	1541	1544		1548						1562E
106.	Richard Lane	1532	1543								1545
107.	William Dedicott			‹1541	1551	1554	1557				1559
108.	Robert Mason	1540	1550		1553	1555	1558	1563			
								1571			1591
109.	William Poughnill	1539				1556		1561			
								1570			
								1575			1583
110.	Howell ap Rees										
	als Glover		1544								1560
111.	John Clee	1542	1544		1551						1552
112.	Thomas Coxe	1539	1547		1556	1557	1559				1579
113.	John Bell	1524	1546		1555	1558		1573			1581
114.	William Clunton		1546								1547
115.	William Chelmick	1532	1545	1561							1564
116.	Lawrence Beck	1549	1554		1557	1559	1561	1564			
								1572			1579
117.	William Hoke	1533	1547								
118.	William Benson	1536	1536	‹1561							1565
119.	Richard Stanwey	1534	1548								
120.	Antony Atkinson	1549	‹1561								

NUM.	NAME.	AdB.	CW.	XXV.	Ch.	LB.	Al.	HB.	Co.	CM.	DIED
121.	Edward Cupper	1535	1549		1552						1555
122.	Robert Mollinger	1540	1550	‹1561							1570
123.	Thomas Franke	1545	1551								1571
124.	Walter Symcockes		1552								
125.	William Beddow	1547	1552	‹1561							
126.	Thomas Beadow	1542	1553								
127.	Thomas Blackbache		1553								
128.	John Sherman	1557			1559	1560		1566			
								1576			1586
129.	Richard Farr	1551	1554		1560	1561		1568			
								1578			1586
130.	Robert Lewis										
	als Draper	1551	1555		1558	1562		1567			1571
131.	John Holland	1547	1551		1561	1563	1566				
132.	Richard Rascoll	1542	1555	‹1561		1564	1566	1574			
	als Rosgrove							1583			1607
133.	Richard Pooton		1556	‹1561							1562
134.	Richard Tomlins	1542	1556	‹1562							1562›
135.	Richard Blashfield	1548	1557		1564	1565	1567	1590	1591		1601
136.	William Bradshaw	1541	1557								1557
137.	William Pinner										
	als Yeomans	1554	1558	1561		1566	1568	1581			1590
138.	Edward Badger	1554	1558		1566	1567	1569				1576
139.	John Taylor		1559		1567	1568	1570				
140.	Simon Thornton	1557	1560								1588
141.	Richard Bailey	1562	1563		1568	1569	1571	1577			
								1582			
								1588			
								1602	1603		1613
142.	Morris Phillips	1539	1541		1554	1570					1578
143.	Richard Hoke	1557	1563		1569	1571		1589	1590		1591
144.	John Brasier	1553	1560	1561	1565	1572		1580			1592
145.	John Gwilliam		1562								1565
146.	William Powis	1532	1562		1570	1573					1577
147.	Thomas Deyos	1551	1564		1572	1574	1575				1589
148.	Richard Swanson	1550	1563		1573	1575					1578
149.	Thomas Ashbage	1564	1566		1577						
150.	George Sotherne	1563	1567								
151.	John Bell	1557	1567								
152.	William Browne		1568								
153.	Thomas Shrawley	1553	1568	‹1596							1609
154.	Simon Huddy	1562	1569								1588
155.	John Rawlins		1569								1594
156.	Richard Cupper	1553	1570		1585						1587
157.	Cadwallader ap										
	Edward		1570		1586						
158.	Thomas Candland	1568	1571			1576		1591	1592		
								1598	1599		
								1606	1607		1617
159.	John Clee										
	als Clungunwas										
	als Cleeton	1555	1564		1575	1577					1591
160.	Richard Heath	1553	1565		1571	1578					1585

NUM.	NAME.	AdB.	CW.	XXV.	Ch.	LB.	Al.	HB.	Co.	CM.	DIED
161.	Henry Cleobury	1561	1566		1576	1579					1604
162.	John Waties	1557	1565		1578	1580		1587			1598
163.	Roger Clerk		1572		1580	1581					1585
164.	Hugh ap Evan		1572								
165.	John Dalton		1573								1575
166.	Richard Grove		1573	‹1591							1614
167.	William Alsop	1569	1574								1596
168.	Robert Wright		1574								1597
169.	Edward Crowther		1578		1581	1582	1583	1586			
								1604	1605		
								1614	1615		1624
170.	John Blashfield	1569	1575		1579	1583					1612
171.	Richard Brasier	1567	1571		1582	1584	1585				1586
172.	Richard Hopton		1576								
173.	William Walle		1576	‹1596							
174.	Thomas Hunt		1577								1600
175.	Griffith Nawle		1577								1601
176.	John Crowther	1581	1582		1583	1585		1596	1597		
177.	Thomas Bower	1569	1581		1584	1586					1596
178.	Thomas Langford	1558	1559	1561		1587		1595	1596		1610
179.	Thomas Evans	1584	1584		1587	1588		1593			1603
180.	Robert Berry	1579		1585	1588	1589		1592			
								1601	1602		
								1613	1614		1618
181.	Roger Griffiths		1579								1599?
182.	John Parkes		1579								
183.	John Becke		1580								
184.	Philip Bradford		1580								1602
185.	Thomas Becke		1581								1594
186.	Henry Ambler	1578	1582								1587
187.	William Wogan	1581			1589	1590	1591	1594	1595		1597
188.	William Beddoe		1583								
189.	Robert Saunders		1583			1591	1592	1599	1600		
								1607	1608		1617
190.	William Becke	1567	1578			1592	1593	1597	1598		1613
191.	Thomas ap Robert		1584		1591						1613
192.	John Devawe	1578			1592	1593	1594				1599
193.	Edward Powis	1581	1587		1590	1594	1595	1600	1601		
								1610	1611	1630	1631
194.	William Cleobury	1553	1575		1591	1595	1596				
195.	John Bradford	1567	1585								
196.	Thomas Yerroth		1586	1591							1594
197.	William Bowdler		1586	1591							1594
198.	William Gwilliam		1587								
199.	Richard Baldwin		1588								1591
200.	Richard Benson	1580	1588		1593	1596	1597	1603	1604		1609
201.	Thomas Awbrey		1589	1591							1596
202.	Saunders Williams	1569	1590	1591							1595
203.	Edmund Lloyd		1594			1595	1597	1598			1607
204.	William Cooke		1590	1591	1596	1598	1599	1605	1606		1620
205.	Charles Wigley	1578	1585	1591	1594	1599	1600				1614?
206.	Rees ap Thomas		1591	1591							1598

NUM.	NAME.	AdB.	CW.	XXV.	Ch.	LB.	Al.	HB.	Co.	CM.	DIED
207.	Richard Nightingale	1582	1592	1593	1608						1618
208.	Richard Seare		1592	1593							1602
209.	William Hughes		1593	1596	1598	1600	1601				1639
210.	Richard Langford		1589		1597	1601	1602				1631
211.	John Candland	1597		1598	1599	1602	1603				1606?
212.	Simon Cupper		1596	1598	1601	1603	1604	1608	1609		
								1617	1618	1627	
								1620	1635	1638	
213.	Richard Fisher			1601	1602	1604	1605	1609	1610	1626	
								1618	1619	1628	
								1627		1631	
										1633	1634
214.	Samuel Parker		1600	1602	1603	1605	1606	1611	1612		1618
215.	Richard Edwards		1593	1598	1604	1606	1607	1612	1613		
								1626	1627	1628	1633
216.	Richard Wilson		1594								1595
217.	William Powis		1594								
218.	Andrew Sonnibank	1580	1595	1599	1600						1602
219.	John Blew		1595	1597							1598
220.	Roger Bebb		1596								1610
221.	John Deyos		1597	1599	1605	1607	1608	1615	1616		1621
222.	William Gregory		1597	1601	1606	1608	1609	1616	1617	1627	1646
223.	Thomas Bowdler		1598								1606
224.	Charles Amyas	1572	1599								1613
225.	James Greene		1599								1608
226.	Richard Whitcott		1600								
227.	Roger Cotton		1601	1603	1607	1609	1610	1619			1620
228.	George Barnes		1602								1629
229.	Thomas Wood		1602								1620
230.	Edward Harries		1603								1620
231.	Thomas Powell		1591	1603	1607	1610	1611				
232.	Thomas Hooke		1604								
233.	Walter Langford		1605	1606	1610	1611	1612	1620	1621		
								1628		1629	1630
234.	William Lane		1598	1606	1610	1612	1613				1621
235.	Richard Sherman		1604	1606	1609	1613	1614				1635
236.	Thomas Heath		1606	1607	1611	1614	1615	1621	1622	1630	
								1629		1637	
								1641		1644	
										1647	1648
237.	Henry Sherman		1607								
238.	Thomas Watkins		1607								
239.	Thomas Hill		1601	1604	1612	1615	1616	1623	1624		1638
240.	Thomas Blashfield		1608	1609	1613	1616	1617	1622	1623		1628
241.	Richard Wilkes		1609	1610	1617						1621
242.	Richard Nightingale		1609D								1610
243.	Henry Walker		1610								
244.	Richard Bowdler		1610								1640
245.	Henry Gough		1610								1620
246.	John Sanders		1611								
247.	Richard Pritchard		1605	1607	1614	1617	1618				1629

NUM.	NAME.	AdB.	CW.	XXV.	Ch.	LB.	Al.	HB.	Co.	CM.	DIED
248.	Ellis Beddoe		1611	1614	1616	1618	1619	1624 1635	1625	1629 1636 1639 1642	1645
249.	Richard Heath		1609	1610	1615	1619	1620				1654
250.	Thomas Edwards		1612	1613	1618	1620	1621	1634			1649
251.	John Clee		1613								1613
252.	Valentine Dawes		1614	1617	1619	1621	1622	1625	1626		1630
253.	Richard Baker		1612	1616		1622	1623	1632		1633 1636 1638	1644
254.	William Beck		1615								
255.	Henry Child		1616								1624
256.	Adam Acton		1617	1618	1620	1623	1624	1630 1636 1642		1631 1637 1640	1645
257.	John Crump		1617								1631
258.	William Reynolds		1618	1620	1623						1624
259.	Edward Colbatch		1606	1608	1617	1624	1625	1633		1634	1640
260.	Edward Jones		1620	1621	1624	1625	1626	1631 1637 1645		1632 1634 1638 1641–4 1646	1654
261.	Henry Blashfield		1620								1628
262.	John Ambler		1613	1617	1622	1626	1627				1644
263.	John Brasier		1621								1623
264.	John Gregory		1622								1623

NUM.	NAME.	AdB.	CW.	XXV.	Ch.	Al.	LB.	Co.	HB.	CM.	DIED
265.	William Lloyd		1615	1620	1624		1627	1628			1631
266.	Samuel Lloyd		1621	1622	1626		1628	1629	1638 1656	1639 1657	1660?
267.	Thomas Colerick		1616	1621	1626		1629	1630			1633
268.	Henry Pritchard		1622	1624	1627	1628	1630D				1631
269.	Edward Powis		1614	1619	1625		1631		1639	1640 1645 1648 1652 1654	1660
270.	John Patchett		1618	1621	1628	1629	1631	1632	1640	1641 1645	1645
271.	Thomas Crowther		1619	1623	1629	1630	1633	1634	1644	1647	1667
272.	William Powis		1619	1620	1630	1631	1632	1633	1643	1644 1646	1659
273.	William Rascoll		1623								1633
274.	Richard Blew		1623								1635
275.	Edward Gregory		1624	1629	1631	1632	1634	1635			1643
276.	William Evans		1624	1629	1632	1633					1635
277.	John Lythall	1624	1625	1631	1633	1634					1636
278.	Edward Edwyn		1625	1629	1632	1633	1635	1636			1647
279.	Ralph Hackluitt		1626	1630	1634	1635	1636	1637			1645
280.	Jonas Doe		1627								1631

NUM.	NAME.	AdB.	CW.	XXV.	Ch.	Al.	LB.	Co.	HB.	CM.	DIED
281.	Philip Clarke		1628	1631	1635	1636	1637	1638	1646		1668
282.	Richard Wilks		1626	1630	1636	1637	1638	1639	1647	1648	
									1666		1679
283.	Richard Cupper		1628								1633
284.	John Aston		1629	1631	1636	1637	1639	1640	1649	1650–1	
										1653	1665
285.	Walter Stead		1627	1630	1639		1640	1641	1648	1649	1650
286.	William Colbatch		1629	1632	1637	1638	1641	1642	1654	1655	
										1660–1	
287.	Edward Berry		1630								1641
288.	Richard Dewce		1631	1633	1641	1642					1645R
289.	Thomas Powton als Hitchcox		1631	1635	1638	1639	1642	1643			1644
290.	John Simons		1632								
291.	Richard Davies		1633	1636	1637	1638	1643	1644	1650	1651	
									1657	1653	1683
									1665	1655	
									1674	1658–60	
292.	John Bowier		1633								1636
293.	John Jones		1634								1636
294.	Richard Larkins		1634								
295.	Edward Turford		1635	1636	1640	1641	1644	1645	1655	1656	1674
296.	Thomas Aston		1636								
297.	Samuel Weaver		1636	1638	1642	1643	1645	1646	1660	1661	
									1668		1675
298.	Richard Munkland		1637								1663
299.	Thomas Hill		1638								
300.	Israel Lloyd	1639	1639	1640	1642	1643	1646	1647			1659
301.	Robert Cole	1630	1637	1640	1643		1647	1648	1653	1654	
									1658	1657	
									1660	1668?	
302.	William Botterell		1635	1638			1648		1651	1649–50	
									1659	1652	
										1656	
									1658	1661?	
303.	Richard Williams	1639	1639	1640	1643	1644	1649		1657		

NUM.	NAME.	AdB.	CW.	XXV.	Al.	LB.	Ch.	Co.	HB.	CM.	DIED
304.	Rowland Williams	1644	1638	1644	1646	1650	1651		1661		
									1667		1671
305.	William Skyrme		1640								1645
306.	Thomas Harford		1641–2								
307.	William Griffiths		1641	1646		1651	1649		1662		
			1642				1652		1670		
			1648						1675		1688
308.	Thomas Cleobury		1643–5	1643	1648		1645				1649S
309.	William Rawlins	1634	1643–5	1645	1649		1646				1650?
310.	John Reynolds	1638	1640	1643	1645	1652	1644				
							1653				
									1663		
									1671		1676
311.	Rowland Earsley		1632	1646		1653	1647				
							1654				1669

NUM.	NAME.	AdB.	CW.	XXV.	Al.	LB.	Ch.	Co.	HB.	CM.	DIED
312.	John Cleobury	1643	1647	1645	1650	1654	1662				1681
313.	Walter Jones		1650	1650		1655	1656				1662
314.	Richard Cole		1647	1646	1651	1656	1650		1672		
							1657				1690
315.	Roger Harris		1648	1646							1648
316.	John Rickards	1646	1649	1646	1652						1667
317.	Thomas Powis		1649	1646	1653	1657	1658		1676		1692
318.	Walter Lea		1646	1650	1655	1658	1659		1680		
			1651								1695?
319.	Edmund Jenks		1650								1661
320.	John Acton		1651	1650	1656	1659	1660				1661?
321.	Samuel Reynolds		1646	1644	1647		1645	1661	1664		
							1661				1676
322.	Richard Cupper		1652		1657	1664	1655		1677		1693
							1657				
323.	Humphrey Williams		1652								
324.	Tamberlaine Davies		1653				1668	1669		1682		1685
325.	William Reynolds		1653								1661
326.	Charles Baldwin			1640		1661					1674
327.	Richard Earsley		1654		1660						1680
328.	Ralph Sharrett		1654		1659	1663	1664				
329.	Thomas Turford		1655								
330.	Thomas Coates		1655								
331.	Edward Robinson		1656				1667	1668			
332.	John Powis		1656								
333.	William Rickards		1657								
334.	Robert Bond		1657								
335.	Samuel Bowdler		1658				1665	1666			1669
336.	John Cheshire		1658								
337.	John Pearks		1659								1667›
338.	Thomas Davies		1659								
339.	Richard Cole	1659	1660				1669	1670			
340.	John Bowdler	1659	1660			1670			1684		

Occupational Structure in 1614 and 1667[1]

		1614		1667
Gentry, Officials, Lawyers, Clergy		26		37
Innkeepers, victuallers & Distillers		19		19
Building and woodworking		20		21
Metalworkers:				
Ironmongers	4		4	
Cardmakers	3		0	
Smiths	11		5	
Cutlers, Nailors & Gunsmiths	2		5	
Others	3		0	
		23		14
Textiles:				
Clothiers	17		1	
Weavers	8		4	
Fullers	7		0	
Clothworkers & shearmen	4		0	
Dyers	4		7	
Feltmakers	0		5	
		40		17
Haberdashers, Hatters, Tailors & Upholsterers		20		17
Leather Trades:				
Tanners	12		10	
Cordwainers	25		20	
Glovers	10		16	
Saddlers & Bowstringmaker	4		1	
		51		47
Food Trades:				
Butchers	9		10	
Bakers	10		5	
Cooks	3		0	
Grocers & Apothecaries	2		0	
Maltsters	0		2	
		24		17
Mercers & Chapmen		15		4
Farmers		5		19
Barbers		3		1
Carriers		4		3
Bookseller		1		1
Labourers		3		44
Others		1		10
Not Known		68		87
TOTAL		263		356

Abbreviations and Key to Notes

Abb. Rot. Orig.	
Anc. D.	PRO: Ancient Deeds (cal. & uncal.)
AO	H.W.R.O., Acts of Office Books of the Bishops of Hereford,
APC	*Acts of the Privy Council*
Baldwin	BL: Add.MS.30317, f.174, Bailiffs of Ludlow *panes Caroli Baldwin de Aquilata*
BL	British Library
BRS	Bristol Record Society
Cal. Anq. Pet. Wales	
Cal. Chan. R.	*Calendar of Chancery Rolls*
Cal. Chart. R.	*Calendar of Charter Rolls*
Cal. Doc. Ire.	*Calendar of Documents Relating to Ireland*
Cal. Gascon R.	
Cal. Lib. R.	
Cal. Mem. R.	*Calendar of Memoranda Rolls*
Cal. Misc. Inq.	*Calendar of Miscellaneous Inquisitions*
Cal. Pap. Reg.	*Calendar of Papal Registers*
Cal Plea Mem. Rolls of London	
Cal. Priv. Seal	*Calendar of Warrants under the Privy Seal*
Cal. Rot. Orig.	*Rotulorum Originalium Abbrevatio*
Cal. Treaty R.	*Calendar of Treaty Rolls*
Cal. Var. Ch. R.	*Calendar of Various Chancery Rolls*
Camden Soc.	
CCAM	*Calendar of the Committee for the Advance of Money*
CCC	*Calendar of the Committee for Compounding*
CCR	*Calendar of Close Rolls*
CFR	*Calendar of Fine Rolls*
Chibnall	M. Chibnall, (articles in) *Victoria County History of Shropshire*, ii (1973)
C. Inq. a.q.d.	*Calendar of Inquisitions ad quod damnum*
C. Inq. p.m.	*Calendar of Inquisitions post mortem*
CMW	Council of the March of Wales
Comp. Peer.	*The Complete Peerage*, ed. G.E.C., rev. ed. Vicary Gibbs etc. (1910–59)
Corp. Min.	
CPR	*Calendar of Patent Rolls*
Cron. Land.	BL: Cotton Nero, A,iv, *Cronica Landavenses*
CSPD	*Calendar of State Papers Domestic*
CWAcc	Churchwardens' Accounts; T. Wright 'Churchwardens' Acc. of Ludlow, 1540–1600' (Camden Soc. 1869); Llewellyn Jones 'Churchwardens' Acc. of Ludlow 1468–1749', *TSAS*, 2 ser. i–lv.
DNB	*Dictionary of National Biography*
Eng. Hist. R.	
Eyton	R.W.Eyton, *The Antiquities of Shropshire*, London, 1853–60. 12 Vols.

Fasti ECC Anglic. Heref.	
Fasti Heref.	*Fasti Herefordenses*, ed. F.T.Havergal (1869)
Felton	W.Felton, *Copies of the Charters and Grants to the Town of Ludlow*, (Ludlow, 1821)
Gaydon	A.T.Gaydon, (articles in) *Victoria County History of Shropshire*, ii (1973)
Gough	Bodleian Lib.; Gough MS, Salop, i, ff.274–77 Ludlow Bailiffs
HWRO	Hereford and Worcester County Record Office (Hereford)
Hist. Parl.	*History of Parliament: (i) Reg. of Ministers and Members*, 1439–1509, ed. J.C.Wedgwood (1936, 1938); (ii) *House of Commons, 1509–1558*, ed. S.T.Bindoff (1982); (iii) *House of Commons, 1558-1603*, ed. P.W.Hasler (1981)
L.P.Hen.VIII	*Letters and Papers of Henry VIII*
NLW	National Library of Wales
Oxf. Dict. Christ Church	
PR	Ludlow Parish Register; *Shropshire Parish Register Society*, xiii (1912)
PRO	Public Record Office
RB	Red Book; SRO: 356/2/1
Reg. Swinfield	*Register of Bishop Swinfield*, Canterbury and York Society; (and other bishops' registers pub. in this series)
Rot. Hund.	*Rotuli Hundredorum*, Record Commission, 1812–8
R. S.	*Rolls Series, Chronicles and Memorials of Great Britain and Ireland*
Shopsh. Mag.	
SAS	Shropshire Archaeological Society
SRO	Shropshire Record Office
TRS	*Transactions of the Radnorshire Society*
TSAS	*Transactions of the Shropshire Archaeological Society*
TWNFC	*Transactions of the Woolhope Naturalists' Field Club*
Vis. Shropsh.	*Visitation of Shropshire 1623* (Harleian Soc. 1889)
VwFP	View of Frankpledge
Wright	T.Wright, *History of Ludlow* (1852)

Public Record Office collections:

C.1	Early Chancery Proceedings
C.2–3	Chancery Proceedings, Series I, II
C.5–10	Chancery Proceedings, Six Clerks
C.31	Chancery Affidavits
C.47	Chancery Miscellanea

C.66	Chancery, Patent Rolls
C.78	Chancery, Decree Rolls
C.132–135	Inquisitions *post mortem*
C.143	Inquisitions *ad quod damnum*
CP25	Common Pleas, Feet of Fines
CP40	Common Pleas, *De Banco* Rolls
E.36	Exchequer, Treasury of Receipt Books
E.101	Exchequer, Accounts Various
E.134	Exchequer, Depositions taken by Commission
E.142	Exchequer, Ancient Extents
E.150	Inquisitions *post mortem*, Series ii
E.163	Exchequer Miscellanea
E.178	Exchequer, Special Commissions
E.179	Exchequer, Subsidy Rolls
E.190	Exchequer, Port Books
E.301	Exchequer, Chantry Certificates
E.307	Exchequer, Fee Farm Rents Deeds
E.315	Exchequer, Augmentations, Miscellaneous Books
E.318	Exchequer, Augmentations, Particulars for Grants
E.321	Exchequer, Augmentations, Proceedings
E.322	Exchequer, Augmentations, Surrenders of Monasteries
E.359	Exchequer, Subsidy Accounts
E.368	Exchequer, Memoranda Rolls
Just.1	Justices Itinerant, Assize and Eyre Rolls
Just.2	Justices Itinerant, Coroners' Rolls
Just.3	Justices Itinerant, Gaol Delivery Rolls
KB9	King's Bench, Ancient Indictments
KB26	King's Bench, *Curia Regis* Rolls
KB27	King's Bench, *Coram Rege* Rolls
Prob.11	Prerogative Court of Canterbury, Registered Copy Wills
Req.2	Court of Requests, Proceedings
SC1	Special Collections, Ancient Correspondence
SC2	Special Collections, Court Rolls
SC6	Special Collections, Ministers' and Receivers' Accounts
SC8	Special Collections, Ancient Petitions
SC11	Special Collections, Rentals and Surveys
SP1–16, 46	State Papers
Stac.5, 8	Star Chamber, Proceedings
Wards.1	Court of Wards, Decrees

Ludlow Corporation archives, Shropshire Record Office:

356/1	Copies of charters
356/2	Minutes
356/165	Town court books
356/316–21	Palmers' Gild registers
356/322–7	Palmers' Gild accounts & early rentals
356/MT.	Palmers' Gild muniments of title (356/328, 347, 347B)
356/419–23	Corporation and lordship accounts

Notes

Introduction

1. Pipe Roll Soc. 1169, 139; 1177, 52; PRO: Just.1/736, m.40f; CP40/160, m.72d; HCRO: AO, 1442, f.29; 1445–6.

Chapter One: The Lordship (Pages 3–8)

1. Eyton, v, 235; space does not permit a detailed refutation of his argument, but it rests on a confusion of 'Lude' (Lyde in north-central Herefordshire) with Ludlow and a failure to recognize that Lude was grouped with places in the Teme valley only because of common ownership. Eyton seems to have wanted Ludlow to have had Saxon origins and looked for evidence to support his belief. It is one of the few errors in his fine work.
2. PRO: E.315/130, Ed. Croft 1542
3. W. E. Wightman, *The Lacy Family in England and Normandy 1066–1194* (Oxford, 1966), 124
4. This is based on the fact that Gilbert received most of the Lacy estates, suggesting that he had a stronger hereditary claim than his female cousins; Wightman, *op. cit.*, 185
5. Wightman, *op. cit.*, 175; *Comp. Peer.*, however, suggests that Sibil was the daughter of Geoffrey Talbot and his wife, Agnes, a supposed sister of Hugh Lacy. Unfortunately the two theories are not discussed together; the balance of probabilities favours the former view, *Comp. Peer.*, xii/1, 606
6. R.S., 58, *The Legend of Fulk Fitz Warin*
7. *See* p. 53
8. This hypothesis is largely dependent upon discussions I have had with Dr. M. E. Speight, whose considered views will be published in due course.
9. *DNB*
10. Wightman, *op. cit*, 240; M. Dolley, *Anglo-Norman Ireland* (Dublin, 1972), 70ff.
11. *Rot. Hund.*, ii, 69
12. Eyton, v, 270; J. Hillaby, 'Hereford Gold: Irish, Welsh and English Land', pt. 2, *TWNFC*, xlv, (1985) (1)
13. *CCR 1237–42*, 376
14. *Comp. Peer.*, v, 269; M. T. Clanchy, *England and Its Rulers, 1066–1273* (1983), 230ff.
15. *CPR 1232–47*, 421
16. *See* p. 77
17. The accepted spelling of the name in use in England
18. *Comp. Peer.*, v, 629–31
19. *Comp. Peer.*, xii (2), 246–52
20. *Comp. Peer.*, v, 630
21. PRO: *Coram Rege* Roll, no. 79, Mich.11 Ed.I
22. *CPR 1292–1301*, 75 & 415; *Comp. Peer.*, v, 632
23. PRO: E.315/55 f.21, Aconbury Cartulary
24. PRO: SC6/1107/5; SC6/Hen.VIII/7319, m.33
25. PRO: C.133/63/10
26. PRO: CP40/69, m.28r
27. *Comp. Peer.*, viii, 433
28. PRO: Just.1/745, m.3r
29. PRO: SC6/1148/7; *CCR 1318–23*, 415, 422 & 524; *1323–27* 50 & 151; *CPR 1324–7*, 326; *CFR 1319–27*, 93
30. *Comp. Peer.*, viii, 436; *Abb. Rot. Orig.*, v,i, 263
31. *Comp. Peer.*, viii, 438–42; *Cron. Land.*, 59
32. *CCR* (1330–3), 65, 111

33. PRO: C.134/72/10; C.135/133/28
34. There is no evidence that his father, Edmund, ever succeeded to Ludlow; the earldom was in abeyance (as it turned out) and he was allowed only his father's estates.
35. *C. Inq. p.m.*, ix, 247
36. *CPR 1354–8*, 87; PRO: C.143/316/4
37. *CPR 1358–61*, 40, 44 & 56; *CCR 1354–60*, 507
38. *CCR 1272–9*, 322 & 343; PRO: C.132/39/20
39. PRO: C.132/39/20
40. *C. Inq. p.m.*, ii, no. 78
41. *Comp. Peer.*, xii (2), 250–1
42. *CCR 1313–18*, 420; *Abb. Rot. Orig.*
43. *CPR 1313–17*, 672; *Comp. Peer.*, v, 583, ix, 81–2
44. PRO: C.134/72/10; *Cal. Mem. R. 1326–7*, no. 1929
45. *Comp. Peer.*, iv, 42–5
46. *CPR 1327–30*, 230
47. *Ibid.*, 273
48. *CPR 1330–3*, 152
49. *CCR 1330–3*, 451
50. *CCR 1343–6*, 203, 346
51. *CPR 1348–50*, 411; BL: Add.MS.6041, f.268
52. *CCR 1343–6*, 346
53. *CPR 1354–8*, 436
54. *See* p. 55
55. R. A. Griffith, *The Principality of Wales in the Late Middle Ages: The Structure and Personnel of Government: I, South Wales, 1277–1536*, 132–4 (Cardiff, 1972)
56. PRO: E.178/1900
57. *CPR 1358–61*, 267
58. *CCR 1360–4*, 114; *Comp. Peer.*, viii, 445
59. *CPR 1370–4*, 156
60. G. A. Holmes, *The Estates of the Higher Nobility in 14th Century England* (Cambridge, 1957), 45
61. *Comp. Peer.*, viii, 448
62. *CCR 1391–5*, 365
63. *Comp. Peer.*, viii, 448–50
64. *CPR 1401–5*, 140, 229, 231, 407, 414
65. *CPR 1405–8*, 394
66. P. A. Johnson, *Duke Richard of York, 1411–1460*, Oxford (1988) 14, 85, 104, 107, 210.;SRO: 356/2/1; *Comp. Peer.*, xii (2), 906
67. T. Wright, *History of Ludlow*, (Ludlow, 1852), 275
68. PRO: CP25/1/81/14
69. PRO: SC6/965/8; SC6/1107/2, 3, 5; SC6/Eliz./1913
70. PRO: C.143/316/4
71. PRO: C.143/15/32; Just.1 /737
72. PRO: C.143/256/7
73. PRO: C.143/268/14
74. PRO: C.143/295/4
75. PRO: C.143/295/1
76. PRO: C.143/318/20
77. PRO: C.143/326/16
78. PRO: Wards.1/3/14A/1
79. SRO: 356/419, Accounts 1288–9
80. SRO: 356/MT.768
81. PRO: C.132/39/20; C.133/63/10; C.134/14/19; C.134/72/10; C.135/7/14; *C. Inq. p.m.*, 2, 78; 3, 43; 5, 87
82. PRO: CP40/11, m.57r. Phil Burnel held Wootton of the Geneviles, providing a horseman at Ludlow in wartime (*Cal. Inq. p.m.*, Ed. I, ii, no. 194)

83. *Rot. Hund.*, ii, 69
84. PRO: SC6/Hen.VIII/7263, m.18d
85. PRO: SC6/1107/5
86. PRO: SC6/Hen.VIII/7319, m.33
87. PRO: C.143/15/32
88. PRO: C.143/268/14
89. PRO: KB27/397, Rex.31a
90. Eyton, v, 309
91. Is there a hint here of a pre-borough settlement with surviving obligations?
92. College of Arms, Foliot Deeds, 468
93. Eyton, iii, 300; PRO: KB26/193, m.16r
94. *Cron. Land.*, f.47d
95. Gerald died in 1287 and Joan 1292–4; *Cal. Doc. Ire.*, iii, 476
96. BL: Harl. MS.1240
97. *Cal. Doc. Ire.*, ii, 500; *CCR 1385–9*, 471; *Comp. Peer.* under Kerry, Kildare, Offaly and Pembroke
98. SRO: 356/325 Gild rent acc. 1364–5
99. SRO: 356/MT.845
100. PRO: C.143/412/5
101. SRO: 356/MT.841, 845
102. SRO: 356/325, Gild rental 1525 wrapping
103. SRO: 356/419, bailiffs acc. 1424
104. SRO: 356/325 Gild rent acc. 1481–2, 1490–1
105. SRO: C.1/1080/60
106. Sir M. Powicke, *The Thirteenth Century*, (2nd ed., 1962), 200
107. *Cron. Land.* ff. 39v–48v *passim*
108. *Cal. Chan. R.*, 314
109. SRO: 356/419 Comm. acc. 1330s
110. *CPR 1401–5*, 137
111. In 1466 Mulsho and others were outlawed after disturbances; by this time the House of York held the throne; PRO: SC.11/818; KB9/103/1–2; KB27/769, m.147d, 158d, 820, m.109d
112. PRO: KB27/768, m.98d
113. PRO: KB9/35, m.20, m.49
114. *CPR 1452–61*, 587
115. PRO: SC6/966/15, 17, 19
116. *See* p. 117
117. Kings stayed at Ludlow in 1223, 1231, 1278, 1322, 1328, 1332, 1452, 1461, and then not until 1645. (*CPR 1216–25*, 376; *CCR 1227–31*; *Itin. of Edw. I*, comp. E. W. Safford; *Itin. of Edw. II*, comp. E. M. Hallam; *Cron. Land.*, ff.59r, 60r; *supra* pp. 64, 174; C. Ross, *Edward IV* (1974) 49.)

Chapter Two: Government

1. M. Bateson, 'The Laws of Breteuil', *Eng. Hist. R*, 15 (1900), 73 *et seq.*
2. *Ibid.*
3. PRO: Just.1/733A, m.5d
4. *See* pp. 2, 14
5. Pipe Roll Soc., 15 Hen.II, 139
6. Pipe Roll Soc., 28 Hen.II, 14; 30 Hen.II, 27
7. Pipe Roll Soc., 33 Hen.II, 64, 66; 2 Ric.I, 125
8. *Cron. Land.*, f.42f
9. PRO: Just.1/733A, m.5d
10. PRO: Just.1/739, m.11f
11. PRO: Just.1/1278, m.8f
12. PRO: Just.1/1366, m.105d; 1413, m.38f
13. PRO: Just.1/1413, m.38d
14. PRO: Just.1/1478, m.25d

15. *R.S.*, 31, *Year-books of Edward I*, iii
16. PRO: KB26/146, m.2d
17. SRO: 356/419/218
18. PRO: KB27/193, m.6f
19. SRO: 356/419
20. *Ibid.*
21. *Ibid.*
22. SRO: 356/419/194
23. SRO: 356/419/218
24. SRO: 356/419
25. PRO: SC6/1148/7
26. *Cal. Mem. R.*, Returnable Writs, LTR, 1326–7, n.1929
27. SRO: 356/417
28. *Rot. Hund.*, ii, 80; A. L. Poole, *Domesday book to Magna Carta* (2nd ed., Oxford, 1955), 420
29. PRO: CP40/129, m.86f
30. PRO: Just.1/737, m.35f
31. SRO: 356/419
32. Who may well have been John Tikelwardyne by another name
33. The 'farmers' seem to have been the bailiffs; perhaps the issues of the town were frequently 'farmed' (that is, rented) by the bailiffs. There would have been an incentive to do this when the town's natural lords were in abeyance and strangers were enjoying the income; PRO: SC6/1148/7
34. SRO: 356/419
35. PRO: SC8/198/9852
36. For the growing financial responsibility of the bailiffs in the mid–14th century *see* p. 27
37. BL: Add.MS.30317
38. SRO 356/419; 356/2/1
39. SRO: 356/419, acc. 1317–20
40. SRO: 356/419
41. SRO: 356/2/1, f.33
42. SRO: 356/MT.354
43. SRO: 356/419, acc. 1308 and 1317
44. There are only two extant lists for this judgment however; SRO: 356/MT.354; 356/2/1
45. SRO: 356/419
46. SRO: 356/2/1
47. Rents paid by non-burgesses
48. SRO: 356/417
49. The claim of '*tres honourable service encountre le malice de voz rebeles de Gales*' permits the undated petition to be ascribed to this period; PRO: SC8/198/9852; C.66/372, m.12
50. *Shropshire Records 1952* (Shropshire County Council), 55
51. SRO: 356/2/1, f.33
52. *Comp. Peer.*, ii (2), 907–9; PRO: E.134/41–2 Eliz./Mich.20
53. *Copies of the Charters and Grants to the Town of Ludlow*, ed. W. Felton (Ludlow, 1821); SRO: 356/2/1; *Cal. Chart. R. 1427–1516*, 155
54. *CPR 1476–85*, 144
55. Felton, *op. cit.*
56. *Ibid.*
57. *Cal. Chart. R. 1427–1515*, 155
58. *CPR 1461–7*, 179
59. PRO: SC6/966/22
60. *CPR 1485–94*, 332; SCRO: 356/MT.443
61. *CPR 1485–94*, 333
62. PRO: C.10/44/145
63. *L.P.Hen.VIII*, i, n.1390, ii, n.500, iv, n.4124
64. R. H. Clive, *Documents of the History of Ludlow and the Lords Marchers* (London, 1841)
65. PRO: C2/Jas.I/E.6/1

66. *CPR 1551–3*, 345
67. PRO: E.134/14 Chas.I/East.34
68. H. T. Weyman, 'The Members of Parliament for Ludlow', *TSAS*, 2nd ser., vii (1), 20–24; PRO: C.10/44/145; *Report of the Charity Commissioners*, iii, 281 *et seq.*, House of Commons Sessional Papers (1820)
69. PRO: E.307/C.1/7
70. *Cal. Chart. R. 1427–1516*, 155; PRO: SC6/966/12; 966/16; 966/18
71. PRO: SC6/Edw.VI/392
72. SRO: 356/316/2/16
73. SRO: 356/2/1
74. Felton, *op. cit.*
75. SRO: 356/420
76. *Ibid.*
76a. SRO: 356/262 acc.1562
77. Penry Williams, 'Government and Politics in Ludlow, 1590–1642', *TSAS*, lvi, 282–94
78. *Acts of the Privy Council* (1588–93)
79. Corp. Min.
80. *Acts of the Privy Council* (1588–93)
81. Figure 13 shows the family connections of the protagonists
82. PRO: Stac.5/B.107/23 Th. Butler
83. PRO: E.134/39–40 Eliz./Mich.37
84. *See* Figure 13
85. PRO: Stac.5/B.107/23; Corp. Min.
86. SRO: 356/423, acc. 1475
87. PRO: SC6/967/21
88. PRO: SC11/818
89. SRO: 356/422/857 *et al.*
90. SRO: 356/262
91. M. A. Faraday, 'The Enticement of Susan Blashfield: A Ludlow Riot Brought to Star Chamber', *Shropsh. Mag.*, June 1979
92. PRO: C.260/158/22
93. BL: Harl.MS.4220
94. PRO: E.134/41–2 Eliz./ Mich.30; E.134/14 Chas.I/East.34
95. PRO: E.134/14 Chas.I/East.34; Ll.Jones, 'Churchwardens' Accounts of Ludlow', *TSAS*, 2nd ser., ii, 118; PR; Corp. Min.
96. HCRO: AO, 142, 1608–9
97. Ll. Jones, *op. cit.*, 112
98. HWRO: AA/20/A.275
99. PRO: E.36/153, f.71
100. PRO: E.134/39–40 Eliz./Mich.37
101. *Ibid.*
102. *Ibid.*; SRO: 356/14
103. PRO: C.2/Jas.I/E.6/1
104. SRO: 356/MT.291; 689
105. SRO: 356/MT.413
106. PRO: SC.11/818; and see p. 211 n.31
107. SRO: 356/422/858; 860; 862; 863; H. T. Weyman, 'Recorders of Ludlow', *TSAS*, 2nd ser. xi, 315
108. T. Wright, 'Churchwardens' Accounts of Ludlow', *Camden Soc.*, 1869; Corp. Min. *The Kyre Park Charters*, ed. J. Amphlett (1905), 348
109. Corp. Min.
110. Corp. Min.
111. PRO: Stac.5/B.52/29
112. Weyman, *Recorders*, 301–24
113. Penry Williams, *Government and Politics*, 285
114. PRO: SC8/198/9852

115. e.g. PRO: KB27/274, m.25
116. SRO: 356/419, acc.1332
117. Weyman, 'Members of Parliament'; *History of Parliament: Register of the Ministers and the Members of Both Houses, 1439 1509*, ed. J. C. Wedgwood (London, 1936, 1938); *History of Parliament; The House of Commons 1509–1558*, ed. S. T. Bindoff (London, 1982); *History of Parliament; The House of Commons, 1558–1603*, ed. P. W. Hasler, (London, 1981).
118. SRO: 356/2/1
119. *Hist. Parl.* is plainly wrong in identifying Rob. Mason, M.P., as two persons.
120. Penry Williams, *Government and Politics*, 288
121. J. E. Neale, *Elizabeth and Her Parliaments, 1584–1601* (Oxford 1957), 344
122. Penry Williams, *Government and Politics*, 287; PRO: Stac.5/B.107/23
123. J. K. Gruenfelder, *Influence in Early Stuart Elections, 1604–1640* (Columbus, Ohio, 1981), 37
124. *Ibid.*, 104
125. *CPR 1350*, 274
126. SRO: 356/419, acc.1317
127. Corp. Min.
128. Corp. Min.
129. SRO: 356/MT.720
130. Corp. Min.
131. SCRO: 356/262, acc. 1562
132. Pipe Roll Soc., 15 Hen.II, 139; 33 Hen.II, 66
133. PRO: E.368/K.ii, 21d; Kiii, 2d; Memoranda Rolls, LTR
134. *CPR 1266–72*, 439
135. S. Dowell, *A History of Taxation and Taxes in England*, (London, 1884), i
136. SRO: 356/419
137. 'Shropshire Lay Subsidy Roll of 1327', ed. W. G. D. Fletcher, *TSAS*, 2nd ser., 288; 3rd ser. vii, 364
138. M. Beresford, *New Towns of the Middle Ages* (London, 1967), 261
139. PRO: E.179/166/96
140. *Cal. Chart. R. 1427–1516*, 155, para. 17
141. Corp. Min.
142. *Statutes of the Realm*, 14 and 15 Hen.VIII, cap.16, S.27
143. *CPR 1232–47*, 35
144. *CPR 1258–66*, 83; *1266–72* 15, 612
145. *CPR 1272–81*, 367; *1281–92*, 347
146. *Cal. Anc. Pet. Wales*, ed. W. Rees, 524
147. *CPR 1292–1301*, 75, 415; *1301–7*, 230; *1307–13*, 183, 518; *1313–7*, 411; *1327–30*, 14
148. *CPR, 1350–4*, 274
149. SRO: 356/419, acc. 1317
150. PRO: E.179/167/50
151. PRO: E.179/168/218
152. *CSPD 1635*, 364; *1636–7* 405, 448, 506; *1638–9* 54
153. *CSPD*, passim; PRO: SP16/305/339; 337/49; 378/22; 400/36; 448/6; 473/103; 476/53
154. *CSPD 1640* 173

Chapter Three: The Church

1. BL: Eg.Ch.5762
2. *CPR 1330–4*, 275; *C. Inq. p.m.*, xv, 448; HCRO: AO (1468–9), f.63
3. T. Wright, *History*, 14; *Cron. Land.*, 42r
4. Eyton, v, 292
5. *Cron. Land.*, ff.48v, 50r; SCRO: 356/419/6
6. SRO: 356/419/8
7. SRO: 356/520/6
8. D. J. Lloyd, *The Parish Church of St Laurence* (Ludlow, 1980), 2
9. *Reg. Spofford*, 150

10. HWRO: AO (1453–4), f.58; SRO: 356/520
11. *Reg. Orleton*, ii, 253–4
12. *Cron. Land.*, f.48v; PRO: C.47/45/392
13. BL: Harl.MS, 273, n.1
14. *Rot. Hund*, ii, 98–100; BL: Add.Ch.19282
15. Wottenhulle was a senior naval administrator, Humberstane a Household clerk, Faryngton a Chancery clerk later involved in foreign diplomacy. *Reg. Myllyng*, 207
16. *CCR 1288–96*, 504
17. *Reg. Orleton*, 184; SRO: 356/520
18. PRO: CP40/460, m.271f
19. *Reg. Mascall*, 183 and 210; SRO: 356/520/25
20. SRO: 356/520
21. PRO: Prob.11/8, f.13; SRO: 356/520, R. Dodmore
22. PRO: Prob.11/11, f.25; Prob.11/13, f.10
23. HWRO: AA.20/9–11
24. SRO: 356/419, acc. 1299, 1330; Gaydon, 135
25. PRO: Prob.11/6, f.38; Prob.11/5, f.1; E.301/40–1; *CPR 1476–85*, 473, 510
26. *Signet Letters of Henry IV and Henry V*, n.220; *CPR 1401–5*, 478, 481; *Reg. Mascall*, 176
27. *Reg. Stanbury*, 47; PRO: E.315/130, E. Croft
28. *CPR 1327–30*, 343; PRO: C.143/316/4
29. PRO: SC6/967/21
30. PRO: E.315/130, E. Croft
31. *Reg. Myllyng*, 185
32. *TSAS*, v (1882), 260–1; SRO: 356/520/8
33. SRO: 356/520/14, 22
34. SRO: 356/491; 610; D. H. S. Cranage: An Architectural Account of the Churches of Shropshire, (Wellington, 1910) 999
35. *Reg. Mascall*, 190; *CPR 1408–13*, 217
36. *Reg. Stanbury*, 92
37. *Rot. Hund*, ii, 69
38. Inf. ex Dr. M. E. Speight
39. SRO: 356/MT.760
40. SRO: 356/520/5; *Reg. J. Gilbert*, 23–4
41. HWRO: AO, 1453–4, f.50
42. PRO: SC2/197/114; SC2/197/116
43. SRO: 356/400
44. PRO: C.66/1115, m.12
45. PRO: E.134/41–2 Eliz./Mich.30
46. PRO: Stac.8/269/27
47. PRO: C.31/363, pt.1
48. HWRO: AO (1445–6), 47, 49 & 50
49. *Ibid.* 47
50. *Ibid.*
51. HWRO: AO, 1501–2, 82
52. *Oxf. Dict. Christ. Church*, 109
53. *R.S.*,i, 157; Capgrave, *Chronicle of England*
54. *Cron. Land.* f.45v
55. D. Knowles, *The Religious Orders in England* (Cambridge, 1960), i, 201
56. Chibnall, 95
57. Over four-fifths of the Ludlow Carmelites 1350–99 were, however, apparently not of Ludlow families
58. Bishops' registers *passim*
59. *Reg. Bothe, passim*
60. CCR 1272–9, 476
61. Chibnall, 95
62. PRO: C.143/7/6; the interpretation I owe to Mr. D. J. Lloyd

63. *CCR 1296–1302*, 267; *Reg. Swinfield*, 359
64. PRO: C.143/184/18; *CPR 1324–7*, 257
65. Chibnall, 95
66. PRO: Prob.11/16, f.18
67. Ludlow PR, i, 374; HWRO: Glebe terriers
68. PRO: Prob.11/16, f.18
69. SRO: 356/MT.1387
70. *Reg. Trillek*, 21
71. PRO: CP40/585,m.242r; *Cal. Pap. Reg. 1431–47*, 310; SRO: 356/63
72. HWRO: AO, 1445–6, *passim*
73. *Reg. Bothe*, 353, 359
74. PRO: Prob.11/6, f.38
75. PRO: Prob.11/17, f.17; SRO: 356/421
76. *L.P.Hen.VIII*, 13, pt.2, n.171
77. *Ibid.*, n.171
78. Lambeth Palace Lib., Faculty Office Reg.
79. PRO: SC6/Hen.VIII/7444, m.30
80. PRO: SC6/Hen.VIII/7430; 7433; 7444, m.30; 7451; E.315/293, f.11v, f.75f
81. PRO: E.321/31/69
82. *CPR 1553–4*, 2 May 1554
83. A recent work, P. Klein (with A. Roe), *The Carmelite Friary, Corve Street, Ludlow Excavation, I: A History of the Carmelite Friary of Ludlow, 1358–1538* is comprehensive and excellent. It was published while the present book was in preparation and there has been some exchange between us of the results of documentary research. This chapter covers common ground and, where it does so, the treatment will be selective and summary to avoid mere repetition.
84. *CPR 1348–50*, 462; PRO: C.143/295/1
85. For a discussion of Sir Lawrence Ludlow's motives see Klein, *op. cit.*, 4–5
86. *CPR 1354–8*, 311; PRO: C.143/318/20; *Cal. Misc. Inq.*, iii, n.180
87. Klein, 6
88. *Reg. Gilbert*, 24
89. Chibnall, 93
90. *Cal. Pap. Reg. 1417–31*, 152
91. *Cal. Pap. Reg. 1458–71*, 425; Chibnall, 94
92. SRO: 356/520/12, 14, 16
93. PRO: Prob.11/4, f.9; Prob.11/16, f.18
94. PRO: Prob.11/12, f.2; Prob.11/17, f.17; Prob.11/21, f.40
95. PRO: Prob.11/5, f.1
96. *Reg. Charlton*, 61
97. PRO: Just.3/180, m.51f
98. *Reg. Trefnant*, 359; Chibnall, 94; Klein, 8
99. *Reg. Mascall*, 11
100. Klein persuasively suggests that this may have been a family response to the friars enticing a youth away from his family, a common practice at the time.
101. PRO: KB27/652, m.65f; 654, m.101f; 678, m.356f; 705, m.112f; CP40/678, m.165d; 683, m.161d; Klein, 9–10
102. *Fasti Ecclesiae: St David's Diocese*; DNB; *Handb. of British Chron.*, 317
103. PRO: KB27/708, m.66f
104. *Cal. Pap. Reg. 1471–84*, 729
105. Chibnall, 95
106. Klein, 73
107. *Ibid.*, 70–3
108. *Ibid.*
109. PRO: E.36/153, f.79
110. Klein, *passim*
111. R. A. Griffiths, *The Reign of King Henry VI* (London, 1981), 698; PRO: E.101/410/9, m.33d–34f. By

a curious chance this visit was exactly 120 years to the day after Edward III and Queen Philippa visited Ludlow; *Cron. Land.*, f.60r

112. *L.P.Hen.VIII*, xiii (i), 473
113. PRO: SC6/Hen.VIII/6445; 7451; Edw.VI/392
114. Klein, 28–33
115. BL: Add.Ch.41296
116. Eyton, v, 297–8; Gaydon, 102; *Reg. Bothe*, 185
117. *Cron. Land.*, f.43v
118. *Ibid.*, f.44r; Princeton Univ. Lib. W. T. Scheide Coll. 7718
119. PRO: E.163/1/10; J. Hillaby, 'Hereford Gold: Irish, Welsh and English Land: The Clients of the Jewish Community at Hereford, 1179–1253', pt. 2, *TWNFC* xlv (i), (1985), 238
120. CCR *1242–7*, 440; J. Hillaby, 234
121. CCR *1242–7*, 440; PRO: Just.1/739, m.19d
122. PRO: Just.1/1322, m.13d
123. *Rot. Hund*, ii, 69, 72 & 107; *R.S.*2, 65, 69, 72, 80 and 107; PRO: C.143/256/7; C.143/120/6; *CPR 1313–7*, 621
124. *CPR 1324–7*, 51; *CPR 1340–3*, 229, 234; *1348–50*, 464; PRO: C.143/256/7; 295/3–4
125. BL: Harl.MS.6690, ff.89–96; PRO: C.143/316/4; *CPR 1354–8*, 87
126. PRO: C.143/318/20; BL: Add.MS.6041, f.26B., n.11
127. PRO: C.143/352/11; *CPR 1361–4*, 495
128. *CPR 1461–7*, 542
129. *Reg. Stanbury*, 111
130. PRO: CP40/55, m.165d; Just.1/739, m.19d
131. PRO: Just.1/1322, m.13d
132. PRO: Just.1/1457, m.21f
133. PRO: CP40/418, m.89d
134. PRO: CP40/465, m.309f; 475, mm.200d, 344d
135. PRO: CP40/398, m.158d
136. PRO: CP40/549, m.19f
137. BL: Add.MS.248820, f.99d
138. SRO: 356/520/6
139. SR0: 356/ MT.848
140. PRO: Prob.11/19, f.22
141. SRO: 356/520; *Reg. Gilbert*, 24; PRO: Prob.11/6, f.38; Prob.11/14, f.9
142. *Reg. Mascall*, 191; *Reg. Lacy*, 21
143. Gaydon, 103; *Cron. Land.*, f.58v
144. PRO: Prob.11/14, f.9
145. *Reg. Gilbert*, 65
146. *Reg. Mayew*, 143
147. PRO: E.321/37/3
148. PRO: E.315/130; 131, ff.2–3; E.321/37/3
149. *Reg. Bothe*, 185
150. *Reg. T. Charlton*, 148; *Reg. Trillek*, 43
151. *CPR 1367–70*, 305
152. *Ibid.*, 338, 369
153. *CPR 1388–92*, 461
154. SRO: 356/MT.91; MT.94; MT.833; 356/321 Gild acc. 1377; 356/840; *Reg. L. Charlton*, 107, 109, 115
155. He may have been the son of Walt. and Amice Ferrour of Ludlow for the latter was unusual in asking in 1413 to be buried in the Hospital church; SCRO: 356/520
156. *Reg. Spofford*, 152, 185
157. PRO: CP40/549, m.19f; *Reg. Gilbert*, 131, 174–5, 178; *Reg. Spofford*, 204–5
158. *Reg. Mascall*, 139, 140, 143 and 189
159. *Reg. Spofford*, 204–5
160. *Ibid.*, 344–6; *Reg. Stanbury*, 38, 40, 42
161. PRO: E.315/130 E. Croft

162. HWRO: AO (1499–1500), f.105; 501–2, f.75
163. PRO: C.260/158/22
164. *Reg. Mayew*, 143
165. *Reg. Bothe*, 33
166. PRO: E.315/130
167. Leland claimed to have seen in Ludlow Church a monument to Dr. Denton 'master of St. John's Ludlow' and this has been elaborated upon in later works of reference; no reliable corroborative contemporary evidence of this exists however and the whole period 1501–37 can be accounted for without supposing that Princess Mary's chancellor, James Denton, although a notable clerical pluralist, also held this office; also descr. as 'dean of St John the Baptist's college' from about 1526 to his death in 1533. Leland's *Itineraries in England and Wales*, ed. L. Toulmin Smith, 2, 76–7; A. B. Emden, *Biographical Register of the University of Cambridge to 1500* (1963) 182–3; *DNB*
168. *L.P.Hen.VIII*, Add. pt. 1, 218; iv, 2709, no.20
169. *Reg. Bothe*, 344, n.7
170. 27 Hen.VIII, c.28; 31 Hen.VIII, c.13
171. PRO: E.315/30; Prob.11/36, f.29
172. In 1538 he had acquired the living at Eastham (being presented by Ralph Leighton) and was clerk of the King's Closet. In 1540 he was a royal commissioner in Calais to counter heresy (Gaydon, 104; *Reg. H. Coren*, 382; PRO: E.321/37/3; A. B. Emden *op. cit.*)
173. HWRO; AA,20/3
174. *Reg. Bothe*, 368; BL: Add.MS.6276, f.92r
175. Gaydon, 194
176. PRO: Prob.11/36/29; *Vis. Shropsh.*, 19, 325
177. BL: Add.Ch.41331; 1 Edw.VI, c.14; *CPR, 1547–8*, 253–6; PRO: C.143/235/111
178. *CPR 1405–8*, 352
179. HWRO: AO, 1529–30, 97
180. *Hist. Parl.*, i, 168, 482, 602 & 725
181. *CPR 1547–8*, 393
182. PRO: SC6/Hen.VIII/7263, m.18d; SC2/197/113–6; SC6/Edw.VI/392
183. PRO: C.66/931, m.6
184. PRO: SC6/Eliz.I/1907
185. PRO: SC6/1107/5
186. Churchwardens' Acc.
187. Lamb. Pal. Lib. Archb. Reg., Cranmer f.102v
188. HWRO: AA.20/20
189. HWRO: AA.20/8–9
190. HWRO: AA.20/18
191. PRO: Prob.11/57, f.26
192. HWRO: AA.20/17
193. HWRO: AA.20/3
194. HWRO: AA.20/3 Bamford; AA.20/9 Fletcher; AA.20/15 Mason; AA.20/57 Wilks; AA.20/1636/212 Twigge; PRO: Prob.11/112, f.79; Prob.11/92, f.59
195. PRO: Prob.11/164, f.108
196. F. C. and P. E. Morgan, 'Some Nuns, Ex-Religious and Former Chantry Priests', *TWNFC*, (1962), xxxvii (2)
197. *APC* (1575–7), 8
198. BL: Lansd.MS, 36, f.22
199. PRO: E.178/1900
200. HWRO: AO, 1599, 1601
201. HWRO, AO, 141, 138
202. *CSPD 1637–8*, 62
203. HWRO: AO 1563–4; AO 1570–1; AO 1581–3; AO (136)
204. HWRO: AO, 1595–6; AO, 1604–5 (141); 1606–7 (29); AO 1612–3 (131); AO, 1620 (136)
205. HWRO: AO 1529–9; AO, 1605–6 (128); AO, 1622 (138); AO, 1613 (132)

206. Six years later she was wrongly accused of maintaining a pregnant woman; it seems she had enemies; HWRO: AO, 1556–7, 1561 2
207. HWRO: AO, 1562–3; AO: AO, 1621 (137)
208. PRO: C.6/44/12
209. PRO: SP14/2, n.85
210. HWRO: AO, 1620 (136)
211. HWRO: AO *passim*
212. HWRO: AO, 1570–1; AO, 1574; 1579–80
213. HWRO: AO, 1576–7; 1613 (132)
214. HWRO: AO, 1566–7; 1577–8
215. HWRO: AO, 1576–7
216. HWRO: AO, 1544–5; AO, 1546–7; AO, 1548–9
217. HWRO: AO, 1546–7; 1548–9; 1564–5; 1574–6; 1579–80
218. HWRO: AO, 1604–5, AO
219. HWRO: AO, 1608 (130); 1608–9 (136); 1619
220. HWRO: AO, 1595–6; AO, 1620 (136)
221. HWRO: AO, 1612–3 (131).

Chapter Four: The Palmers' Gild

1. There is no evidence to suggest that he had had a predecessor and a great deal of circumstantial evidence which points to him as the first.
2. *Cron. Land.*, f.45r
3. SRO: 356/347B
4. L. Toulmin Smith, 'English Gilds', *Early English Text Soc. Pub.*, O.S., xl, (1870)
5. A. Hamilton Thompson, 'Certificate of Shropshire Chantries', *TSAS*, 4 ser., i, app., 155; W. C. Sparrow, 'The Palmers' Gild of Ludlow', *TSAS*, i, (1878), 355–7; Gaydon, 134; PRO: C.47/45/392
6. SRO: 356/325
7. *CPR 1281–92*, 492; PRO: C.143/15/32
8. Rent-charges on particular properties were the earliest form of gift received by the Gild; only later did the Gild acquire burgages and other real property.
9. My translation and punctuation.
10. W. C. Sparrow, *op. cit.*, 346–51
11. PRO: KB27/55, m.1r
12. PRO: Just.1/736, mm.8d, 47f; 737, m.45f
13. PRO: E.315/55, f.21
14. PRO: KB26/175, m.10v
15. PRO: KB26/166, m.14v
16. PRO: Just.1/736, m.22d
17. *Rot. Hund.*, ii, 74
18. SRO: 1996/16/1
19. I owe this suggestion to Murray and Janet Glover.
20. PRO: C.81/166/3070
21. SRO: 356/MT.638; 687; 769; 770
22. Gaydon, 134
23. SRO: 356/321
24. SRO: 356/MT.690
25. SRO: MT.392
26. SRO: 356/MT.655; 679
27. *Cal. Pap. Reg. 1396–1404* 309
28. SRO: 356/321
29. SRO: 356/520; MT.249; MT.1010
30. SRO: 356/324
31. SRO: 356/MT.236; 425; 621; 870; 969; 1320; Russhe was town court clerk in 1439 (PRO: KB27/718 m.64)

32. SRO: 356/321
33. SRO: 356/325
34. SRO; 356/MT.622
35. SRO: 356/MT.1387
36. PRO: E.322/141
37. *CPR 1327–30*, 459–60
38. Gaydon, 135
39. SRO: 356/MT.51; 859; 860; 862, *et al.*
40. SRO: 356/MT.328
41. SRO: 356/MT.545
42. SRO: 356/MT.154
43. SRO: 356/MT.857
44. SRO: 356/520
45. SRO: 356/520/9, 17
46. SRO: 356/325 Stewards' acc.
47. SRO: 356/520
48. Gaydon, 136
49. SRO: 356/322
50. SRO: 356/520/11
51. Gaydon, 135
52. SRO: 356/325
53. Gaydon, 139; SRO: 356/MT.656–7
54. SRO: 356/325 Stewards' acc; Gaydon, 136, n.66
55. *CPR 1367–70*, 14; *1388–92*, 420; *Reg. Stretton*, 61; SRO: 356/325; MT.393; 521
56. PRO: KB27/397, rex.31a
57. *CPR 1367–70*, 14
58. *cf.* Richard II's exercise of patronage over the mastership of St John's Hospital
59. SRO: 356/MT.848
60. PRO: CP40/445, m.277r
61. Gaydon, 136
62. SRO: 356/321
63. SRO: 356/322
64. Gaydon, 136–7
65. SRO: 356/321
66. PRO: E.318/31/1766; HCRO: AO, 1546–7; Churchwardens' Acc, 1597
67. SRO: 356/321
68. Gaydon, 147; D. J. Lloyd, *Country Grammar School* (Ludlow, 1977), 25–42. This is the standard work on the subject, which is still generally available, so the subject here has been dealt with summarily.
69. See p. 152
70. PRO: C.81/166/3071
71. SRO: 356/321 Stewards' acc.
72. SRO: 356/322, Gild rental 1525, the cover of which is a late 14th-century acc.
73. SRO: 356/321 Stewards' acc. 1425–7
74. SRO: 356/321
75. SRO: 356/316, n.8367
76. SRO: 356/323
77. SRO: 356/319, Gild register 1472
78. SRO: 356/319
79. SRO: 356/319 Gild register 1507
80. SRO: 356/319; 321
81. SRO: 356/321
82. SRO: 356/324, Stewards' acc. 1505
83. SRO: 356/321, Gild acc. 1533, 1539, 1540
84. SRO: 356/MT.220 Gaydon, 137; PRO: E.301/40; E.318/31/1766
85. Gaydon, 137

86. SRO: 356/321, Gild acc. 1521, 1538, 1540, 1544
87. Gaydon, 138; SRO: 356/321, Stewards' acc.
88. *Statutes of the Realm*, 1 Edward VI, c.14
89. PRO: E.318/31/1766; T. Wright, 366–76
90. SRO: 356/MT.1044
91. PRO: E.315/123, ff.278–80; E.321/30/13
92. SRO: 356/MT.1042
93. Comparisons cannot be certain, as the identities of all the early wardens may not be known, and, of those that are, their periods of office are not precisely known. This is also true of the bailiffs before 1514.
94. PRO: E.318/31/1766

Chapter Five: The Council of the March

1. Penry Williams, *The Council of the Marches of Wales under Elizabeth I* (Cardiff, 1958), 7–13
2. C.2/Eliz./P.9/35
3. Penry Williams, *op. cit.* 288
4. BL: Eg.MS.2882
5. *CSPD 1603–10*, 433; PRO: E.101/616/21
6. PRO: E.101/123/24
7. BL: Harl.MS.4220; *CSPD, 1611–8*, 380; *APC*, 1638–9, 15
8. Penry Williams, *op. cit.*, 289
9. M. A. Faraday, 'The Enticement of Susan Blashfield; a Ludlow Riot Brought to Star Chamber', *Shropsh. Mag.* (June, 1979)
10. PRO: E.101/123/20, 124/3, 533/26, 616/21
11. BL: Lansd.MS.32, f.97 *et seq.*
12. PRO: E.101/675/41
13. PRO: SC6/1236/9
14. PRO: SC6/Hen.VIII/2969, 2978, 2979; BL: Royal MS. xivB, xix
15. PRO: SC6/Hen.VIII/5656
16. *L. P. Hen.VIII*, vii, 1535, no.947
17. *History of the King's Works 1485–1660*, iii, ed. H. M. Colvin, D. R. Ransome and J. Summerson (London, 1975), 175ff
18. PRO: SP13/Case C/12
19. BL: Harl.Roll.N.8
20. PRO: SP46/164, ff.50–84
21. PRO: E.101/613/13
22. PRO: SP46/164 ff.50–84; E.101/613/13, 616/21, 675/41
23. BL: Collection of Pamphlets 1642, 6–8

Chapter Six: The Economy

1. *Rot. Hund.*, ii, 80.
2. Notwithstanding the formal status of Weobley as the Lacy *caput*
3. Professor Conzen has pointed out in a private discussion that such boundaries would have made Ludlow remarkable as one of the largest boroughs in Europe.
4. The name 'Linney' itself may indicate early flax cultivation.
5. PRO: E.134/39–40 Eliz./Mich.376.
6. SRO: 356/419, acc. 1288; PRO: SC6/967/19
7. BL: Add.MS.30317, ff.177, 216
8. PRO: Stac.5/B.107/23
9. PRO: E.134/41–2 Eliz./Mich.30
10. PRO: KB27/722, m.93d
11. PRO: C.8/17/68; Stac.5/B.50/32; B.55/31; B.57/18
12. SRO: 356/400
13. PRO: C.132/39/20; C.134/14/19; C.135/7/14

14. SRO: 356/417; 356/419/764
15. HWRO: AA.20/10; AA.20/3; PRO: Prob.11/36, f.46
16. Eyton, v, 213
17. SRO: 356/MT.720
18. PRO: Prob.11/61, f.43
19. SRO: 356/520; PRO: Prob.11/67, f.12
20. PRO: Prob.11/35, f.18
21. PRO: Prob.11/68, f.5; Prob.11/130, f.100
22. PRO: SC2/197/116
23. Inf. ex-D. J. Lloyd
24. PRO: Just.1/741, m.39
25. PRO: Prob.11/60, f.1
26. PRO: Prob.11/54, f.34
27. SRO: 356/417; 356/419/764
28. SRO: 356/MT.1363
29. G. Cocking, 'On the Remains of the Austin Friary at Ludlow', *Journ. Brit. Arch. Assoc.* (1868), 55
30. Parts of this paragraph are based on inf. ex-D. J. Lloyd
31. PRO: CP40/465, m.345f
32. SRO: 356/321, Gild acc. 1428
33. PRO: SC2/197/113–5
34. *Cron. Land.*, f.57r
35. Inf. ex-D. J. Lloyd
36. *Cal. Lib. R.*, ii, 16
37. PRO: CP25(1)/81/14
38. *Rot. Hund.*
39. *Cal. Chart. R., 1427–1516*, 155
40. PRO: E.315/55, f.21
41. PRO: SC6/Hen.VIII/7319, m.33; 7433; 1107/3; 1107/5; E.367/7123
42. PRO: SC6/Eliz./1913
43. SRO: 356/MT.364; MT.1143
44. PRO: C.132/39/20; C.135/7/14
45. Or 'Old Mill Street', as some later records have it, a misapprehension about the origin of the street name rather than an authoritative version of the name; it is used in pleadings only and not in rentals, e.g. PRO: E.134/14/Chas.I/East.34
46. PRO: SC6/1107/5; SC6/Hen.VIII/7319, m.33; SRO: 356/417, acc.1378
47. SRO: 356/417
48. SRO: 356/324
49. SRO: 356/322, Gild rental 1439
50. PRO; *Cat. Anc. Deeds*, iii, A.6109
51. SRO: 356/419, acc.1286, 1312
52. *Ibid.*, acc.1368
53. SRO: 356/417
54. SRO: 356/419, acc.1424; PRO: SC11/818
55. SRO: 356/420, acc.1427
56. Inf. ex-D. J. Lloyd
57. PRO: SC11/818; SRO: 356/400, rental 1540
58. SRO: 356/MT.254
59. SRO: 356/MT.255; PRO: SC6/Hen.VIII/7319, m.33; SC6/Edw.VI/392; SC6/Eliz./1907
60. PRO: E.134/14 Chas.I/East.34, S. Cupper, W. Hughes
61. PRO: E.134/8 Chas.I/Trin.13; C.2/Jas I/E.2/82
62. PRO: C.3/364/29
63. PRO: E.134/8 Chas. I/Trin.13
64. *CSPD, 1635–6*, 340
65. Corp. Min.
66. PRO: C.8/98/113

67. PRO: E.134/1655/East.10
68. PRO: C.10/175/121. His 99-year lease expired in 1755, when the Corporation obtained a Crown lease for £6 13s. 4d. annual rent, replaced by a 50-year lease in 1749, which barred any other mill being built; PRO: E.367/7123.
69. PRO: *Cat. Anc. Deeds*, iii, A.6022
70. SRO: 356/MT.1131–2
71. SRO: 356/MT.364; MT.658; MT.1141; MT.1143
72. BL: Add.Ch.41296
73. Eyton, v, 297
74. PRO: CP40/160, m.243f; C.143/120/6; SRO: 356/MT.1439
75. PRO: C.143/352/11
76. BL: Add.Ch.41315
77. PRO: E.134/14 Chas.I/East.34
78. PRO: E.134/8 Chas. I/Trin.13
79. PRO: E.134/43 Eliz./East.4; SRO: 356/MT.51; MT.160; 356/322 Gild rental 1462
80. PRO: E.134/14 Chas. I/East.34
81. For the latter see J. Bathurst and E. J. L. Cole, 'Leominster Fair, 1556', *TWNFC*, xlii (1976), i
82. SRO: 356/419 acc. 1287,1299, 1307
83. PRO: Just.1/734, m.23d
84. PRO: KB27/37, m.13
85. SRO: 356/417; BL: Add.MS.30317, f.206
86. PRO: C.260/186/51
87. *Rot. Hund.*, 98
88. BL: Add. Ch.19282
89. SRO: 356/MT.760
90. *Cal. Chart. R.*, 1327–41, 94
91. SRO: 356/418/4230; PRO: SC11/818
92. PRO: C.2/Jas. I/E.4/30
93. SRO: 356/322, rental 1462
94. PRO: Stac.5/B.107/23
95. Corp. Min.
96. SRO: 356/419, acc. 1287–9, 1308
97. PRO: SC11/818, acc. 1442
98. SRO: 356/417; BL: Add.MS.30317, f.206
99. PRO: SC6/966/22; SRO: 356/400; 356/422/857; 423/862
100. SRO: 356/63
101. PRO: E.134/39–40 Eliz./Mich.37
102. PRO: E.134/41–2 Eliz./Mich.30; Prob.11/109, f.28
103. PRO: C.1/1345/23–4
104. PRO: Stac.5/B.107/23
105. SRO: 356/2/1,ff.37–40
106. Corp. Min.
107. *CPR, 1266–72*, 555
108. *CPR, 1272–81*, 67
109. *R. S.*, 36, *Annales monastici, iv, Annales de Wigornia*, 518; *Cron. Land.*, f.48v
110. SRO: 356/419, acc.1287
111. *Cal. Var. Ch. R.*, 1
112. T. H. Lloyd, *The English Wool Trade in the Middle Ages*, Cambridge (1977), 51, 55, 67, 76, 78; M. B. Rowland, *The West Midlands from A.D.1000*, London (1987), 80
113. PRO: CP40/100, m.125f
114. *CCR, 1330–2*, 467; T. H. Lloyd, *op. cit.*, 120–1
115. SRO: 356/419, acc. 1332
116. *CPR, 1334–8*, 485
117. *Cal. Treaty R.*, ii, 48
118. *CCR, 1337–9*, 148

119. *CCR, 1337–9; 1338–41, passim*
120. rounded to the nearest pound
121. *CPR, 1348–50*, 405
122. PRO: CP40/361, mm.25d, 119f, 365
123. *Reg. Gilbert*, 24
124. T. H. Lloyd, *op.cit.*, 24
125. PRO: CP40/415, m.206f
126. *C. Inq. p.m.*, xv, n.448
127. PRO: Just.1/753, m.18d
128. Eyton, v, 287–8; J. Hillaby, 'Hereford Gold: Irish, Welsh and English Land', pt 2, *TWNFC*, xlv (1985) i
129. SCRO: 356/MT.1131–2
130. PRO: C.143/120/6
131. PRO: Just.1/741, m.40
132. PRO: CP40/640, m.56f; SCRO: 356/MT.431; MT.609
133. PRO: CP40/415, m.206f; SCRO: 356/MT.519
134. PRO: KB27/731, m.81r
135. SRO: 356/MT.345; MT. 539; MT.556
136. SRO: 356/MT.420
137. SRO: 356/MT.444
138. HWRO: AA.20/1607/A.314
139. SRO: 356/333; PRO: CP40/408, m.151f
140. J. L. Bolton, *The Medieval English Economy, 1150–1500*, London (1980), 153–5
141. SRO: 356/MT.841
142. PRO: KB27/230, m.105f; CP40/403, m.171d
143. PRO: CP40/506, m.30d; 559,m.19d; KB27/657, m.25d
144. PRO: KB27/731, m.7f
145. PRO: CP40/585, m.423f; C.1/19/204
146. PRO: C.1/1004/32–5; HWRO: AO, 1539–40, f.82
147. SRO: 356/MT.345; PRO: CP40/533, m.408f
148. SRO: 356/MT.199; MT.294; MT.488; PRO: CP40/390, m.80d; 415, m.206f
149. PRO: CP40/737, m.175f; KB27/613, m.48d
150. PRO: KB27/652, m.73d; 737, m.19d; 894, m.296
151. SRO: 356/MT.263; 356/63 court 1476
152. PRO: CP40/653, m.257f; 723, m.67f; KB27/682, m.22f
153. SRO: 356/MT.671; PRO: CP40/900
154. *CPR, 1346–7*, 130; *CFR, 1399–1400*, 90, 141, 183; *1405–13* , 98
155. SRO: 356/321, Gild acc. 1534
156. PRO: C.5/94/113
157. The alnage figures are scattered about Corporation minutes and accounts, inc. 356/400; 420; 422/819–60; 423/861–6; 424; 425; F. J. Fisher, 'Commercial Trends and Policy in 16th Century England', *Ec. Hist. R.*, x (1935) 2
158. *Cal. Plea. Mem. Rolls of London, 1423–37*, 88, 146
159. PRO: C.1/1387/55
160. HWRO: AA.20/4
161. PRO: Req.2/250/32
162. PRO: Req.2/273/19
163. PRO: E.321/30/14
164. PRO: CP40/653, m.19f
165. SRO: 1996/16/1;356/MT.13; MT.16; MT.482; MT.641; PRO: CP40/618, m.585f
166. In this section the words 'craft', 'art', 'occupation', 'society', 'brotherhood', 'fellowship' and 'mystery', contemporary terms, are used in addition to 'craft-gild', a modern term for an organised body of medieval craftsmen.
167. BL: Add.MS.24820, f.99v; SRO: 356/419 1331 acc.
168. PRO: Prob.11/1, f.13; HCRO: AA.20/11

169. Churchwardens' Acc. 1469–70, 237–8; 1610–1, 111; PRO: Prob.11/72, f.11; 107, f.49; 144, f.98; HWRO: AA.20/1604/06/107; AA.20/1617/62
170. SRO: 356/63
171. *Statutes of the Realm*, 15 Hen.VI, cap.6
172. Llewellyn Jones: 'The Antiente Company of Smiths and Others Commonly Called 'Hammermen' of Ludlow, *TSAS*, xi (1888), 297; Churchwardens' Acc., 2nd ser.,ii, 109.
173. Churchwardens' Acc, *TSAS*, 2nd ser.,ii, 109
174. PRO: Prob.11/17, f.17
175. PRO: E.179/166/155
176. SRO: 356/321
177. Llewellyn Jones, *op. cit.*, 291–324
178. inf. ex-D. J. Lloyd
179. G. M. Hills, 'On the Ancient Company of Stitchmen of Ludlow', *Journ. Brit. Arch. Assoc.* (1868), 327–334
180. Inf. ex-D. J. Lloyd
181. PRO: E.134/14 Chas.I.East.34
182. H. T. Weyman, *Ludlow in Byegone Days*, Craven Arms (1913), 8
183. PRO: E.36/48, f.42r *et seq.*
184. Churchwardens' Acc. 1558; Weyman *op. cit.*, 28
185. SRO: 353/1; G. M. Hills, *op. cit.*; Ll. Jones, op. cit.; inf. ex-D. J. Lloyd
186. SRO: 356/421, Gild acc. 1424; 356/321, acc.1447; 356/324, acc. 1505
187. *Rot. Parl.*, v, 570a
188. PRO: Port Books, E.190/1128/13; 1246/12
189. *CSPD, 1635–6*, 280
190. SRO: 356/MT.738
191. PRO: CP40/688, m.312f; 731, m.544f
192. PRO: C.5/26/81; 483/96; Prob.11/224, f.216
193. PRO: Prob.11/176, f.43; 236, f.169; 242, f.484
194. PRO: C.8/311/161; 626/9
195. PRO: E.179/255/37; Prob.11/450, f.62; PR
196. *Cal. Anc. Pet. Wales*, ed. W. Rees, 484, n.15103
197. Eyton, v,282; *CCR, 1252*; PRO: KB26/146, m.2v
198. *Welsh Assize Roll, 1274–84*, ed. J. Conway Davies , Cardiff (1940), 151–199. F. Noble, 'The Medieval Boroughs of West Herefordshire', *TWNFC*, xxxviii (1964) 65
200. PRO: CP40/46, m.63d; *CPR, 1348–50*, 319; Bathurst and Cole, *op. cit.*
201. PRO; CP40/635, m.429v
202. PRO: CP40/160, m.38d; 547, m.540d; HWRO: AO, 130, 1607–8
203. PRO; Prob.11/8, f.13
204. D. J. Lloyd, 'A Ludlow Merchant Killed for a Cargo of Spice and Green Pepper', *Ludl. Advertizer*, 23 Feb. 1978
205. *Cal. Bristol Apprentice Books, 1542–52*
206. *Reg. Comp. Stationers of London, 1554–1640*, (1875)
207. PRO: CP40/264, m.97d; 341, m.23f. 84d; 350, m.312f
208. *Cal. Gascon R.*, ii, 239
209. M. E. Speight, *The Great House*, Birmingham (1980).

Chapter Seven: The People of Ludlow

1. SRO: 356/322
2. PRO: Just.1/1199, m.6f, 8f
3. SRO: 356/MT.393
4. SRO: 356/MT.104
5. PRO: C.260/158/22
6. R.S.53, *Historical and Municipal Documents of Ireland, 1172 1320*, 7
7. PRO: CP25(1)/193/4

8. PRO: Just.1/745, m.3f
9. Eyton, v, 300
10. College of Arms, Foliot Deeds, 468
11. PRO: C.260/43/37; Just.1/752; Just.2/131; KB27/292, m.12a; KB27/294, mm. 155, 164
12. PRO: Just.1/752, m.26a; Just.2/145, m.2
13. PRO: Just.1/1413, m.38f; KB9/274, m.25; KB27/270, m.26a; 294, m.162a
14. Corp. Min.
15. M. A. Faraday, 'The Enticement of Susan Blashfield', *Shropsh. Mag.*, June 1979
16. PRO: Prob.11/64, f.43; 109, f.42
17. SRO: 356/319
18. PRO: E.36/48, f48r
19. *Cartulary of Haughmond Abbey*, ed. U. Rees (Cardiff, 1985), 1158
20. *Curia Regis Rolls*, xiv, 2357
21. Eyton, v, 70
22. PRO: CP25(1)/193/2, 57
23. PRO: CP40/257, m.107r; 353, m.242r
24. PRO: Just.1/739, m.44d; 741, m. 40
25. SRO: 356/MT.11 et al.
26. PRO: Just.1/739, m.19d; 743, m.6d
27. *CPR, 1266–72*, 692; *Cal. Doc. Ire.*, ii, 243; G. A. Williams, *Medieval London* (1963); PRO: CP40/53, m.10r
28. SRO: 356/419
29. Eyton, v, 36
30. *Cron. Land.*, f.48
31. PRO: C.143/15/32
32. SRO: 356/MT.336
33. G. A. Williams, *op. cit.*
34. PRO: KB27/377, rex.7a, 8a
35. PRO: KB27/377, rex.9b
36. C. Platt, *Medieval Southampton* (London, 1973) *passim*; *CPR, 1324–7*, 27 Dec. 1327; *Cal. Misc. Inq., 1307–49*, 1236
37. PRO: Just.1/744, m.18; 748, m.1
38. PRO: Just.1/741, m.40
39. SRO: 356/520, J.Ace
40. *Reg. Orleton*, 92
41. *Reg. Trillek*, 579; *Reg. Charlton*, 70, 85, 87; *CPR, 1370–4*, 364; PRO: CP.40/506, m.143d; SCRO: 356/520/17
42. See below; *Fasti Ecc. Anglic. Heref.*, 366/7; *Reg. Trillek*, 384, 396, 565, 579, 621
43. *Cal. Doc. Ire.*, 1307
44. PRO: KB27/188, m.22v
45. *Cal. Misc. Inq., 1307–49*, 458
46. PRO: E.163/4/48
47. *CCR, 1323–7*, 485
48. PRO: SC.1/36/148
49. PRO: *Lists and Indexes, Sheriffs; CFR, 1337–47*, 59
50. *CFR, 1327–37*, 92
51. *Abb. Rot. Orig.*, 1328; T. Rymer, *Foedera, Syllabus, i*
52. *Cal. Misc. Inq., 1307–49*, 1293
53. *Ibid.*, 1236
54. *CPR, 1321–4*, 321; *CPR, 1327–30*, 216
55. *CPR, 1330–4*, 275
56. *CCR, 1343–6*, 156
57. PRO: KB27/373, rex.7b; *CPR, 1345–8*, 480, 520; PRO: KB27/385, rex.11a
58. SRO: 356/MT.354 and *passim*; 356/419 Borough acc. 1332, 1339
59. PRO: CP40/375, m.149v

60. *CCR, 1337–9*, 430
61. SRO: 356/MT.392
62. *Register of Trinity Guild of Coventry*, ed. M. Dormer Harris, (1935)
63. PRO: CP40/525, m.428v
64. *CFR, 1399–1400*, 90, 285; PRO: E.101/344/19; KB27/648, m.8; SRO: 356/MT.107; 230; 409; 857; 965
65. *CFR, 1437–45*, 218; *CPR, 1416–22*, 368; SRO: 356/MT.863
66. SRO: 356/520/523
67. SRO: 356/MT.621; HCRO: AO, 1499–1500, 130a, 131
68. PRO: Req.2/7/87
69. PRO: E.150/868/5; Prob.11/36.f.27
70. *History of Parliament: The House of Commons 1558–1603*, ii, ed. P. W. Hasler, (London,1981) 437
71. PRO: Stac.5/B.52/29
72. HWRO: AO 1453–4, 29; 1475–6, 18, 45
73. HWRO: AO 1502–3, 66; AA20/65; PRO: E.315/115, f.23; SC6/Hen.VIII/7319, m.33
74. PRO: E.134/31/1766
75. HWRO: AA20, 1611/149; PRO: C.5/26/81
76. PRO: Just.1/739, *passim*
77. PRO: Just.1/737, m.32d, 35f, 44d, 45f
78. PRO: Just.1/745, m.2; 752, m.25
79. PRO: Just.1/1457, m.21d
80. PRO: Just.1/736, m.40f
81. PRO: Just.1/741,m.2f
82. PRO: *CCR, 1296–1302*, 267; PRO: C.260/12/13; Just.1/744, m.1f
83. PRO: Just.1/739, m.44d; Just.3/180, m.51f
84. PRO: Just.1/753,mm.13f, 18d
85. PRO: Just.3/161, m.9d; 180, m.49f
86. PRO: C.260/43/37; Just.3/131, m.1f; KB27/294, m.155, 164
87. *CPR, 1343–5*, 329
88. PRO: Just.1/732, m.3f
89. PRO: Just.1/745
90. PRO: Just.2/145,m.1
91. PRO: KB27/318, rex.17b; 373, rex.7b
92. PRO: KB27/385, rex.11a; *CPR, 1345–8*, 480
93. PRO: KB27/401, m.66b; Just.1/748, m.1; *CPR, 1348–50*, 566
94. PRO: *CPR, 1301–7*, 216
95. *CPR, 1345–8*, 480
96. *L.Hen.VIII*, vi, 1571
97. PRO: Stac.5/B.52/29
98. PRO: SC.2/197/113–5
99. SRO: 356/262
100. BL: Harl.MS.4220
101. SRO: 356/419, Comm.acc. 1309
102. PRO: Prob.11/5, f.1
103. SRO: 356/415/321, PG Stewards acc. 1424–8
104. PRO: Prob.11/36, f.29
105. PRO: Prob.11/60, f.1; Prob.11/74, f.71
106. SRO: 356/ W. Littleton's gift 1655
107. The numbers of the poor are also discussed in chapter 8 PRO: Prob.11 *passim*; HWRO: AA/20/211; SRO: 356/2/16
108. PRO: Prob.11/130, f.100
109. PRO: Prob.11/159, f.53
110. PRO: Prob.11/156, f.109
111. S. Bagshaw, *Directory of Shropshire* (Sheffield, 1851) 603
112. *SPRS*,xiii, 383–8; Bagshaw, 603

113. PRO: E.318/31/1766
114. J. B. Black, *The Reign of Elizabeth* (Oxford, 1959), 265
115. Corp. Min. *passim*
116. SRO: 356/472; PRO: E.179/167/50
117. M. A. Faraday, 'The Ludlow Poll Tax Return of 1667', *TSAS*, lix (ii), 1972

Chapter Eight: Population

 1. *Cron. Land.*, f.7f
 2. PRO: E.359/8c, m.3d, 5
 3. HWRO: Diocese of Hereford, Court Books, Acts of Office
 4. PRO: E.36/48, f.42r
 5. PRO: E.301/40
 6. See p. 168
 7. Shropshire Parish Register Society, 1912
 8. PRO: E.179/255/37
 9. See pp. 178–80
10. *Cron. Land.*, ff.7f, 39f, 40d, 53f
11. See p. 157
12. SRO: 356/MT.516 et al.
13. M. A. Faraday, 'Mortality in the Diocese of Hereford, 1442–1541', *TWNFC*, xlii, 1977 (2), 164–74
14. *Ibid.*
15. PRO: Prob.11/16, f.18
16. SRO: Corp. Min.
17. PRO: Stac.8/203/10
18. Ludlow Parish Register
19. SRO: 356/472
20. SRO: 356/501
21. M. A. Faraday, ed. 'The Ludlow Poll Tax Return of 1667', *TSAS*, lix (2), 1971–2; W. Watkins-Pitchford, ed. 'The Shropshire Hearth-Tax Roll of 1672', *SAS*, 1949; PRO: E.179/255/3; E.179/342
22. W. G. M. Fletcher, 'A Religious Census of Shropshire in 1676', *TSAS*, series 2, (i) (1889), 75–93
23. Faraday, Poll Tax Return
24. See pp. 174–5, 178–80

Chapter Nine: The Civil War and Interregnum

 1. PRO: C.6/272/63
 2. P. Zagorin, *The Court and the Country* (1969), 479
 3. *CSPD, 1637–7*, 405, 448
 4. *CSPD, 1638–9*, 54; *1640*, 173
 5. *CSPD, 1635–6*, 340
 6. *CCAM*, ii, 703
 7. C. A. J. Skeel, *The Council of the Marches of Wales* (1904), 158, 161
 8. Weyman, *TSAS* 1895, 24, 26–7
 9. Skeel, 161
10. BL: Coll. Pamph. 1642, .6–8
11. Stat. Realm., 17 Car. I, c.10
12. *CCAM*, *op. cit, passim*.
13. *CCC, 1484*
14. W. J. Smith, *Herbert Correspondence* (Univ. Wales Press, 1968), 5–6; *DNB*.
15. Weyman, 'The Foxe Family', *TSAS*, 2, xii, 1900, 177–8
16. *DNB*
17. *The Letters of Lady Brilliana Harley* (Camd. Soc., 1853), 172
18. E. Martin, 'The Littletons', *TSAS*, ser. 4, iii (1913), 308
19. PRO: C.6/9/130

20. BL: E.121 (12), *True Intelligence and Joyfull News from Ludlow Declaring a Battle fought by his Excellency the Earl of Essex against Prince Robert, Prince Maurice and the rest of the cavaliers neere Ludlow, Oct. 1, 1642*
21. J. Moxon, 'The Forgotten Battle of Standard Oak', *Ludl. Heritage News*, 10 Sept., (1988)
22. R. E. Sherwood, *Civil Strife in the Midlands, 1642–51* (1974), 64
23. SRO: 356/2/1, 11· May 1643
24. Weyman, 1913, 58
25. Corp. Min.
26. Bodl. L., Dugdale MS 19, f.30; Hutton, 65; *Docq.L.P.Charles I*, 77
27. SRO: 356/2/1, 11 May 1643.
28. Ll. Jones, *Churchwardens' Accounts of the Town of Ludlow.*
29. PRO: Prob.11/166 f. 102 Ric. Fisher; *CCC*, 1484
30. R. Hutton, *The Royalist Effort* (1982), 60
31. B. Trinder, 35
32. W. J. Farrow, *The Great Civil War in Shropshire 1642–49* (1926), 44
33. E. Warburton, *Memoir of Prince Rupert and the Cavaliers* (1849), 530
34. *CSPD 1645–7*, 143
35. SRO: 356/298
36. *CCC*, iii, 1474, 1484–5, 1544; iv, 2788, 2864; R. E. Auden, 'The War Services of some Shropshire officers in the King's Army' *TSAS*, ser.4, ii (1912), 224
37. SRO: 356/298
38. SRO: 356/120 (Town Court 1642)
39. P. Morrah, *Prince Rupert of the Rhine* (1976)
40. Ric. Symonds, *Diary of the Royal Army during the Civil War* (Camd. Soc. 1859), 255
41. P. Phillip, *op. cit.* 327
42. *The Letters of Lady Brilliana Harley*, 202
43. SRO: 356/2/1
44. SRO: 356/526 (Minute Book Gild of Stitchmen)
45. PRO: C.8/64/33
46. PRO: C.10/41/142
47. PRO: C.5/15/37
48. PRO: C.3/457/97
49. *CCAM*, 262, 1185
50. *CSPD 1645–7* 407
51. *Ibid.* 452; B. L. Burney 24a, *Perfect Diurnal of Some Passages in Parliament*, No. 143.;. *A Military Memoir of Col. John Birch by Roe his Secretary*, ed. J. and T. W. Webb, (Camd. Soc. 1873), 129; B. L. Burney 24a, *Perfect Occurrences of Both Houses of Parliament*
52. *SRO: 356/2/1*
53. *DNB*
54. *CSPD, 1645–7*, 431
55. O. Baker, *Ludlow Town and Neighbourhood* (1906), 72–3, 138
56. *Perfect Diurnal* etc
57. BL: 336 (13) *Thomason Tracts*
58. *CSPD 1645–7*, 431
59. *Perfect Occurrences* etc
60. Corp. Min.; *Perfect Diurnal, Moderate Intelligence; Military Memoir* etc
61. PRO: C.5/591/16
62. *Moderate Intelligence* etc
63. *CSPD 1645–7*, 440
64. CCC, ii, 1474. 1484. 1485. iv, 2788, 2864
65. PRO: C.5/15/37
66. Corp. Min.
67. *Hist. Parl.*
68. PRO: Prob.11/319., f.39
69. *Hist.Parl.*
70. Corp. Min.

71. D. J. Lloyd, *Country Grammar School*, (Ludlow, 1977)
72. *CSPD, Comm.*, xiii, 130
73. Corp. Min.
74. Churchwardens Acc.
75. PRO: C.5/26/81
76. SRO: 356/30 *passim*. These references are owed to Mr D. J. Lloyd and the Ludlow Historical Research Group.
77. PRO; C.5/453/96
78. PRO: C.6/9/130; C.8/64/33; C.10/30/74
79. PRO: C.5/6/80
80. PRO: C.5/591/16; C.6/117/17
81. PRO: C.6/9/130
82. SRO: 356/30; Corp. Min. 13.3.1647
83. SRO: 356/30
84. PRO: E.179/255/35
85. *The Shropshire Hearth-tax Roll of 1672*, ed. W. Watkins Pitchford (1949)
86. SRO: 356/30

Cursus Honorum: References and Notes

1. of XII (RB, Charter); PGRenter and Stewd q.v.; (Bor. Ct; MT.1314)
2. (Bor. Ct; MT.454, 780, 997)
3. walker; sn of Wm C.; (Bor. Ct.; Anc.D.8545; 356/420; MT.237, 239)
4. sn of Thos B. (MT.239; Bor. Ct)
5. dyer; b.‹1420; ? dr Agn. m. Wm Gery q.v. (Bor. Ct; MT.1372; PRO: KB27/719)
6. hosier; rel. to Wm W. (Bor. Ct, PGReg 1471; PRO: KB27/749)
7. draper; MP; PGStewd; PGWarden q.v.; witn deeds 1427–1471; wife Joan who re-m. Jn Aleyn; sons Jn, Walt (mercht tailor London), Ric. q.v.; drs Alice m. Ric. Lane q.v.; Maud m. Rog. Hervy of Shrewsb. (*Hist. Parl.*; MT 121–2,431 and various; PGReg 1487; AO,1472; PGAcc.
8. (MT.241, 431, 610, 873; 356/420; PRO: SC6/967/22)
9. (Wright: *Hist. Ludlow* – doubtful)
10. sn of Hugh S.; MP (*Hist. Parl.*; Bor. Ct; PRO: SC6/967/22; SRO: 356/420; MT.527)
11. MP; sn of Ric. S.; sn Ric. (*Hist. Parl.*; AO; Bor. Acc.; MT527, 1372; SRO: 4032/1/5; PRO: PCC 1480, 1486)
12. HB 1472 or 1473 acc. to Wright and Gough; only poss. if part year; poss 1476; sn of Jn C. q.v.; (Bor. Ct.; MT.1372)
13. mercht; sn Wm G. (AO; Bor. Ct; 356/420; MT.121, 125, 241, 609; Coll. Arms, Foliot 1174/1)
14. tailor; (MT.121, 125, 356/400; Bor. Rental 1470)
15. PGStewd q.v.(MT.263; SRO: 4032/1/3)
16. weaver; b.‹1420; acc. to Baldwin LB in 1470; acc. to Wright and Gough LB in 1472, HB in 1481; acc.to Wright HB in 1493; acc. to all three HB in 1488; some are poss. but others not.
17. (Wright; Gough; MT.237, 241–2, 1339; Anc. D.8545; PRO: SC6/966/17)
18. weaver; PGStewd q.v.; of XII 1469; ? son of Ric. H. als Browne (Bor. Ct; SRO: 356/420; MT.122, 126, 433, 610, 1327–8; AO; Wright; Gough; PRO: SC6/967/16, 19, 22)
19. barber; PGStewd q.v. (MT.122, 249, 433; SRO: 356/325, 420; PRO: SC6/966/12;)
20. PGStewd q.v.; acc. Wright HB 1482; (CWAcc; SRO: 356/420; PGAcc.; MT.241, 393, 873, 1357; PRO:SC6/967/22)
21. (CWAcc)
22.
23. tailor; (MT.124, 241, 250, 670; PRO: SC6/966/12; AO)
24. ? baker; (SRO: 356/420; MT.1000; PRO; SC6/967/22)
25. ? son of Thos M.; bro. Walt. M. (Bor. Ct.; PRO: SC6/966/16)
26. clothier; PGRenter q.v.; son Ric. q.v. (Bor. Ct; CWAcc; PRO: SC6/966/19; PCC; MT.126, 245, 612)
27. PGStewd q.v. (CWAcc; SRO: 356/420; Bor. Ct; MT.455, 539, 614, 1381; PGAcc; AO)

28. baker (SCRO: 356/400; MT.243, 264)
29. clothier; PGWarden q.v.; son of Thos M.; son Jn M. (MT.265, 617, 706, 875; PGReg 1487; PCCWill; PGReg 1508)
30. PGStewd q.v.; liv. 1496 (CWAcc; PRO: SC6/966/22; SRO: 356/420; 4032/1/5; Bor. Ct; PGReg; PGRent; MT.249)
31. ? corveser (Bor. Ct; MT.610)
32. (SCRO: 356/423)
33. Grocer of London; wife Agn. dr of Wm Sutton q.v. (MT.527, 668; SRO: 356/420; PCCWill)
34. draper; farmer of Castle meadow 1479 (MT.245, 437, 1117; Bor. Ct. 1476; PRO: SC6/966/18–9).
35. ? son of Hugh H.; sons Edwd, Ric., Hugh (Bor. Ct; MT.443, 703, 1285)
36. hosier; PGElder 1505–8; (MT.444, 455, 492, 671; PGAcc; AO)
37. PGElder 1505–8 (MT.437, 877, 1117; PGR; PGAcc)
38. walker; son Walt. H.; grandson Ric. H.; (MT.612, 716, 1015; Bor. Ct; PGReg; PCCWill; PRO: C.260/58/22)
39. b. Ilminster, Som.; dr Agn. m. Ric. Selman; (MT.440, 612; PCCWill)
40. PGStewd qv.; son of Jn L. q.v.; wife Alice dr of Jn Dodmore (PGReg; PGRental; PGAcc; MT.440, 612)
41. weaver; PGStewd q.v.; son of Ric. D; grandson Jn Bingham (MT.614, 616; PGReg 1502; PGAcc; PRO: SC2/197/114; AO)
42. PGRenter q.v.; m.1. Sibil wdw of Jn Preene; m.2. Alice (MT.535,537; PGReg 1487; SRO: 356/420)
43. (MT537)
44. PGbedell 1505–8; PGClerk ‹1517; son of Jn C. (PCCWill Prob.11/12f.2, 13f.28; PRO: C.260/58/33; BL: Add.MS 40930–1; PGRental; PGAcc; MT.127, 615, 1305)
45. weaver; PGWarden q.v.; dr Jane m. Wm Foxe q.v. (MT.347B, 579, 668, 876; SRO: 356/147B; PGAcc; PGReg.)
46. (MT.616)
47. MP; Recorder (MT.444; *Hist. Parl.*; Weyman)
48. son of Jn C.; son Walt. C.; (MT347B, 433, 673–5; PGReg 1502; AO)
49. (*KPC*.332; MT.540, 1381; Bor.Acc.; AO)
50. tanner (MT.445, 1374; BL: Add.MS 40930–1; Bor.Acc; Will Heref.)
51. mercer; Suprvsr Castle repairs 1525; PGWarden q.v.; son of Wm R.; drs Agn. m. Ric Langford q.v.; Cath. m. Edm. Sherman (Bor. Acc. 1514; MT.255, 673–5, 677, 1432; RB; AO,1546; PRO: SP1/36f.16; Anc.D.6009 ; Wright; Gough)
52. baker (MT.252, 1015)
53. MP; acc.Baldwin LB 1516 (Bor. Acc.1520; MT.1374; *Hist. Parl.*; AO)
54. PGRenter q.v.; of XII 1541; dr Agn. m. Ric. Lane (MT.1374; AO,1545)
55. (Wright and Baldwin)
56. draper, mercer; PGmbr 1508; PGWarden q.v.; b.1483 son of Wm L.; m. Margy wdw of Ric. Whittall; sons Ric., Jn, Owen, Edwd, drs Alice, Anne; inqu. into his sanity 1552 (Bor. Acc 1519; Wright, Baldwin; RB; MT.621, 1044; PRO: Req.2/7/87; E.150/868/5; WillPCC)
56a. (SCRO: 356/420/825)
57. (Bor. Acc)
58. wife Eliz. re-m. Rog. Bradshaw PGStewd q.v.; son Wm C. Recorder; (Bor. Acc; AO)
59. liv. 1528 (MT.255; Bor. Acc.)
60. (Wright and Baldwin)
61. MP; b. 1479; son of Edwd F. of Greete; m. Jane dr of Ric. Downe q.v.; son Chas F. q.v.; d. in off. 1553 (RB; Wright; Baldwin; *Hist. Parl.*)
61a. SRO: 356/420
62. (MT.494; Bor. Acc.)
63. 1547–50 kpr St Leon. graveyard; son Rob. (SRO: 356/420; RB; AO 1558; PRO: C.1/1080/60; SC2/197/114; Cal. Bristol. App. Bk, *BRS* xxxiii (ii); BL: Eg. MS 2882 f.200)
64.
65. (SRO: 356/420/825; MT.619)
66. (SRO: 356/420; PRO: C.3/102/47)
67. wife Burge; dr Ancret m.1. Wm Clunton, 2. Wm Beddoe (SRO: 356/420; AO)

68. mercht; MP; sheriff Rads 1542, 1553; b.c.1490; rel. to Bishop Lee; son of Rob. B.; bro. of Rog. B. q.v.; m. Margt dr of Ric. Chapman; son Jn B. (MT.619; RB; *Hist. Parl.*; E. J. L. Cole, 'Early Radnorshire Sheriffs', *T.R.S.*, 36, p.43)
69. draper; (Wright; Baldwin; RB)
70. (Bor. Acc.; AO)
71. baker; son Ric. L. q.v. (SRO: 356/420; RB; AO; PRO: C.1/869/18; Muster Roll 1541)
72. glass stainer; drs Joan m. Wm Bradshaw q.v.; Eliz. m. Ric. Stanwey q.v.(SRO: 356/420; Bor. Acc.; RB; Will Heref.; AO 1558)
72a. baker; dr m. Ric. Tomlins q.v. (Bor. Acc.; Will Heref.)
73. clothier; of XII 1541; PGStewd q.v.; b.1501; (SCRO: 356/423; RB; MT.257; PRO: C.1/1080/6; C.321/37/3; Muster Roll 1541)
74. mercer; of XII 1541; b.1499; wife Ales re-m. Wm Pope; dr Winif. m. Ric. Gwyn (SRO: Bor. Acc.; RB; MT.254, 620; PRO: E.321/30/14)
75. MP; PGStewd q.v.; b.1500; m.1. Jul. dr of Jn Passey; m.2. Anne dr of Wm Foxe; m3. Eliz. Barnaby re-m. Thos Butler; son Humf. Wheler (SCRO: Bor. Acc.; RB; Hist. Parl.; Vis. Worcs.; PRO: Req.2/207/3)
76.
77. mercer; MP (SRO: RB; 356/423; *Hist. Parl.*; MT.131, 878)
78. (SRO: 356/423)
80. victualler; son of Thos C.; (Will. Lamb. Pal. Lib.)
81. son Jn; dr Margt m. Walt. Jones (PRO: C.1/1080/60; C.78/25/24; SRO: 356/420; RB)
82. grandson of Jn Griffith q.v.; sons inc. Phil. B. q.v. (RB; Will Heref.; RB; C.260/158/22; 356/422/819)
83. fuller; wife Anne dr of Lew. Bedoe; drs Margt m. Ric.Rascoll q.v.; Jane m. Ric. Hoke q.v.; Alice m. Jn Jennings; Anne m. Jn Weaver; Margy m.1. Edw. Hunt, m.2. Thos Blashfield q.v.; Mary m. – Pateshull; Ancret m. Ric. Farr q.v.; (SRO: 356/422/818; RB; HCRO: AA/20/3)
84. TC 1545–55; MP 1554; Recorder 1569 (SRO: 356/422/20; RB; Weyman; AO 1569; PRO: SC2/197/116; BL: Add. MS 40831)
85. corviser (RB; MT446; AO)
86. wife Margy re-m. Wm Langford q.v. (SRO: 356/423; AO)
87. MP; PGRenter q.v.; Corp. Rent Collr 1562; son of Wm L. q.v.; son Chas (PRO: E.315/123 ff.278–80; SC2/197/116; *Hist. Parl.*; Bor. Acc.; CWAcc; SRO: 356/422/819; RB)
88. draper; (RB; Muster Roll)
89. (AO 1538; CWAcc; RB)
90. (RB; AO 1548)
91. (RB; CWAcc)
92. weaver; SM 1515, 1527 q.v.; son Jn H.; liv. Ledenporche (SRO:356/422/820–1; RB; PRO: Prob.11/35/18 Jn Cle; CWAcc; AO 1558
93. capper; b.1500 (Will Heref.; SRO: 356/422/816; PRO: E.315/122)
94. MP; 1583 superv. building Castle; m.2. Margy wdw of Edw. Hunt q.v.; son Thos B. q.v. (*Hist. Parl.*; PRO: SP13/Case C/12; Anc. D.C.7812; SRO: 356/381, 422/856, 858, 423/866; RB)
95. walker; wife Joan wdw of Ric. Bradford q.v.; ? son of Wm P.; comm. sergt. 1536 (PRO: E.179/167/50; SRO: 356/422/857, 859, 423/863; RB)
96. weaver (PRO: SC2/197/114;SRO: 356/422/820; RB; CWAcc; Will Heref.)
97. (SRO: 356/422/819; RB; AO 1572)
98. wife Eliz. Broughton re-m. Lawr. Becke q.v.; sons Jn C. q.v.; Edw. C. m. Anne dr of Lawr. Becke; dr Cath. m. Edw. Foxe (SRO; 356/423/861–2; RB; CWAcc; PRO: Prob.11/35/18 Jn Clee)
99. barker, tanner; expelled 1562 (PRO: E.179/167/9; SC2/197/116; Muster Roll; SRO: 356/422/857; RB; Bor. Rental; Bor. Acc; CWAcc)
100. wife Cath. dr of Walt. Rogers q.v.; son Jn S. q.v.(BL: Eg. MS.2882 f.200; SRO; 356/422/860, 423/862–3; RB; CWAcc; PRO: Muster Roll)
101. (CWAcc)
102. (CWAcc)
103. (CWAcc; AO)
104. liv. 1544 (PRO: E.179/362/11; CWAcc)
105. expelled 1562 (PRO: E.179/362/11; SRO: 356/422/857; RB)

106. son of Jn L. q.v.; d. in office (CWAcc; PRO: E.179/279/5; RB)
107. fuller (PRO: Muster Roll; RB; 356/422/861; AO 1559)
108. tanner; MP q.v.; b‹1527 (CWAcc; SRO: RB; 356/423/862–3, 347B)
109. MP 1559, 1563, 1571–2; Clk of Signet CMW to 1581; b.c.1510; wife Eliz. wdw of 1. Rog. Baldwin, 2. Ric. Rogers; base childr. Wm and Jane (SRO: 356/423/863–4; RB; *Hist. Parl.*; PRO: Req.2/207/3; Will PCC)
110. (CWAcc; AO)
111. cordwainer; son of Ric. C.; liv. The Angel (SRO: 356/422/860–1; RB; Will PCC)
112. dr Alice m. Rog. Clerk q.v. (CWAcc; SRO; 356/423/864–6; RB; PRO: C.1/1492/20; AO 1579)
113. (CWAcc; SRO: 356/423/863, 865; RB; AO 1581)
114. (CWAcc; AO 1547)
115. MP 1545 (*Hist. Parl.*; RB; CWAcc; AO)
116. mercer, weaver; b.c.1524; m.1. Cath.; m.2. Eliz. Broughton wdw of Lew. Crowther q.v.; sons Walt. B., Thos. B., drs Eliz. B., Anne B. m. Edw. Crowther q.v. (CWAcc; SRO: 356/423/864, 866; RB; PRO: Req.2/207/3; SP12/94/6; Will PCC; CPR 1572; Mon. Inscr.)
117. ? ident. with SM sergt at mace (RB; CWAcc)
118. cardmaker (CWAcc; SRO: 356/400; RB; PR)
119. m. dr of Rob. Hood als Steyner q.v.; CWAcc; RB)
120. (CWAcc; SRO:356/400; RB)
121. tanner; (SRO: 356/422/861; RB; AO 1555; CWAcc)
122. grocer; (SRO: 356/400; RB; PR)
123. draper (RB; CWAcc; AO 1571)
124. (CWAcc)
125. (SRO: 356/400; CWAcc; RB)
126. (SRO: 356/400; RB; CWAcc)
127. (CWAcc)
128. son of Edm. S.; many sons inc. Ric. S. q.v. (SRO: RB; 356/423/866; CWAcc; Will PCC; CPR 1566; BL: Add.MS 40831)
129. mercer; MP; wife Ancret dr of Ric. Handley q.v. (SRO: RB; 356/400, 423/876; *Hist. Parl.*; CWAcc; PCC Will Jn Bedows 1575; PR)
130. ? son of Thos L. als D.; exor Jn L. als D. (BL: Add. Ch 40831; SRO: RB; 356/423/866; CWAcc; Will PCC)
131. Dep. Aln. 1566 etc; wife Elinor dr of Wm Hibbins (CWAcc; SRO: RB; Corp. Min)
132. clothier; miller; son of Thos R.; b.c.1523; wife Margt Blashfield; sons Wm R. q.v., Ric.R. (SRO: RB; CWAcc; PR; PRO: E.134/39–40 Eliz./Mich.37; HWRO: Wills AA/20/1611/149; 1553/65 Th.R.)
133. (CWAcc; SRO: 356/400; AO 1572)
134. (CWAcc; SRO: RB; 356/400)
135. clothier; b.c. 1539; sons inc. Jn B. q.v., Sim. q.v. (CWAcc; SCRO: RB; 356/400; PRO: Req.2/207/3; Will Heref.)
136. wife Joan dr of Rob. Hood als Steyner q.v. (SRO: RB; CWAcc; PR)
137. mercer; wife Margt dr of Ric. Langford; dr Jane m. Thos Evans q.v. (CPR 1566; SRO: RB; BL: Add. MS 40831; CWAcc; Will PCC; HWRO: AA/20/1601/132)
138. tanner; affeerer at Vw of FP 1550–1 (PRO: C.260/158/22; SC2/197/114–5; CWAcc; SRO: 356/424/838; RB; PR)
139. wife ? Eliz. dr of Jn Passey q.v. (CWAcc; SRO: RB; 356/424/855; *CPR* 1569)
140. schoolmaster (APC 1576; SRO: RB; CWAcc; Will Heref.)
141. mercer; b.1532; wives 1. Jane Langford dr of Ric.L q.v.; 2. Margt Powys wdw of Ric.Heath q.v.; dr Mary m. Thos S. son of Saunders Williams q.v. (SRO: RB; 356/423; 424/840; CWAcc; PR; PRO: Stac.5/B.107/23; E.134/39–40 Eliz./Mich.37)
142. organist for life; ? ident. with Maurice *Cantator* fl.1546; wife Anne re-m. Jn Devawe q.v.; dr Cath. m. Wm Wogan q.v. (CWAcc; SRO: RB; 356/423/862; PRO: E.318/31/1766; C.2/James I/P7/60; Will Heref.; PR)
143. clothier; b.c.1539; wife Jane dr of Ric. Handley q.v.; son Thos. H. q.v. (PRO: E.134/39–40 Eliz./Mich.37; Req.2/165/115, 207/3; PR; SRO: RB; 356/263, 347B; Corp. Min.; CWAcc)

144. cordwainer; wives 1. Jane dr of Ric. Blashfield q.v.; 2. Alice (SRO: RB; 356/424/854; *CPR* 1572; PRO: SP12/94/6; Will Heref.)
145. wife Emme re-m. Ric. Swanson q.v. (CWAcc; AO 1565; PR)
146. barker; SM q.v.; affeerer VwFP 1545; wife Margt re-m. Ric. Padland; sons Edw., Wm, Jn, Thos, Ric. (SRO: RB; 356/425/857, 425a; PRO: SC2/197/114–5; Will PCC)
147. tanner; son Jn D. q.v. (SRO: RB; AO 1589)
148. ironmonger; cous. of Rob. Saunders; wife Emme or Anne wdw of Jn Gwilliam q.v. (SRO: RB; 356/423, 425A; Will PCC; PR)
149. wineseller (*CPR* 1555; SRO: 356/425A; RB; CWAcc)
150. baker (SRO: RB; CWAcc)
151. (SRO: RB; CWAcc)
152. (CWAcc)
153. weaver, clothier; son of Jn S.; wife Mary ? dr of Jn Whitton (PRO: Req.2/207/3; SRO: 11/9; RB)
154. (CWAcc; PR)
155. saddler (CWAcc; Will Heref.)
156. ? son of Jn C. of Steventon; sons inc. Sim. C. q.v. (CWAcc; SRO: RB; 356/425A; Will PCC)
157. (CWAcc; SRO: 356/425A; PR)
158. mercer; MP; b.c.1540; wives 1. Eliz. Beck; 2. Mary dr of Lawr. Becke q.v.; bro. Ric. C. q.v.; son Jn C. q.v. (SRO: RB; 356/423, 425A; *Hist. Parl.*; PRO: Req.2/207/3; E.134/39–40 Eliz./Mich.37; Mon.Inscr.; *CSPD* 1584; Will PCC)
159. smith (SRO: 356/423; RB; CWAcc; Will Heref.)
160. baker; grandson of Ric. Bangam SM; wives 1. Elinor; 2. Margt Powis sr of Edw. P. q.v. re-m. Ric. Bailey q.v.; sons Ric. H. Thos H. q.v. (SRO: RB; 356/425A; CWAcc; HWRO: AA20/3; PRO: C.2/James I/H5/38)
161. cordwainer; b.c. 1531; wives 1. Margy Beck; 2. Jane Cupper; sons inc. Thos C. and Wm C. q.v. (SRO: RB; CWAcc; 356/425A; Will Heref.; PRO: Stac.5/B.107/23)
162. dyer; drs inc. Anne m. Jn Saunders q.v.; Margy m. Wm Powis q.v.; Margt m. Thos Evans q.v.sons inc. Edward W. the judge (SRO: RB; 356/425A; PRO: E.134/39–40 Eliz./Mich.37; Prob.11/72f.11 H. Amler; CWAcc; Will PCC; *Vis. Shropsh.*)
163. ? from Radnorshire; wife Alice dr of Thos Cox q.v. (CWAcc; SRO: RB; 356/425A; *CPR* 1560; Will PCC)
164. (CWAcc)
165. bookbinder; SM; b.c.1530 (SRO: 356/423/864, 866; RB; PR; PRO: Req.2/207/3)
166. cutler (PR)
167. (PR; RB)
168. (PR)
169. mercer; mbr Stitchmen's gild 1616; mbr of Bradford faction; b.1547; wife Anne dr of Lawr. Becke q.v.; bro. Jn C. q.v. (SRO: RB; 356/425A; PRO: Stac.5/B.107/23; PR)
170. clothier (SRO: RB; 356/425A; PR)
171. cordwainer; wife Sibil sr of Wm Beck q.v.; son Jn B. m. Jane dr of Ric. Blashfield q.v. (SRO: RB; 356/425A; PR; *CSPD* 1584)
172. (PR).
173. saddler (PR; Felton; PCCWill Jn Sherman 1586)
174. walker (PR)
175. weaver; formerly chenser; b.c.1540 (PR; PRO: Req.2/207/3)
176. mercer; b.c.1557; of Bradford faction; displ. 1601; liv. Rose and Crown, Church St. (SRO: RB; 356/425A; Corp. Min.; PRO: Stac.5/B.20/13, B.63/19; E.134/41–2 Eliz./Mich.3; Anc.D.C.7812)
177. wife Anne Gwilliam sr in law of Ric. Swanson q.v.; drs inc. Anne m. Ric. Heyton q.v. (SRO: 356/425A; RB; PR)
178. corviser, tanner, mercer; b.c. 1538 Ludlow son of Ric. L. q.v.; Corp. renter to 1598; prosec. under penal laws at CMW (PRO: E.101/533/22; Stac.5/B.52/29, B.107/23; Req.2/207/3; Prob.11/72f.11 H. Ambler; E.134/39–40 Eliz./Mich.37)
179. attorney to CMW 1581ʰ; wife Jane dr of Wm Pinner *als* Yeomans q.v. (SRO: RB; 356/425A; PR; PRO: E.101/123/24; E.134/39–40 Eliz./Mich.37)

180. b.*c.* 1542 son of Jn B. of Devon; MP (SRO: RB; 356/263, 425A; PRO: E.134/39–40 Eliz./Mich.37; Stac.5/B.107/23; Will PCC; *Hist. Parl.*)
181. (PR; Will Heref.)
182. (PR)
183. ? son of Wm B. q.v. (PR)
184. stationer; son of Ric. B. q.v. and Joan; wives 1. Jul. Thornton; 2. Anne dr of Ric. Broughton and wdw of Jn Clungunwas q.v.; expelled 1593–5; led anti-oligarchy faction (SRO: Corp. Min.; RB; PR; Will PCC)
185. son of Lawr. B. q.v. (PR)
186. weaver; son Jn A. q.v. (SRO: RB; PR; Will PCC)
187. wife Cath. dr of Morris Phillips q.v. (SRO: RB; 356/425A/526; PRO: E.134/39–40 Eliz./Mich.37)
188. (PR)
189. ironmonger; cardmaker; mbr Co. of Hammermen 1578; wife Elinor ? dr of Ric. Bailey (SRO: RB; 356/347B; Min.Bk; AO)
190. b.*c.*1533; ? son of Wm B. (SRO: RB; PR; PRO: E.134/39–40 Eliz./Mich.37; E.134/41–2 Eliz./-Mich.30; Stac.5/B.107/23)
191. (PR; SRO; 356/425A)
192. Sergeant at Arms CMW; b.*c.*1529; wife Anne wdw of Morris P. q.v. (SRO: RB; Fenton; PRO: E.134/39–40 Eliz./Mich.37; C.2/Eliz./P9/35)
193. tanner; b.*c.*1552; wife Elinor dr of Ric. Padland; sons Wm, Edw. q.v., Jos., Jerem. (SRO: RB; PR; PRO: E.134/39–40 Eliz./Mich.37; Will Heref.)
194. (PRO: E.134/39–40 Eliz./Mich.37; SRO: RB; PR)
195. weaver (SRO: RB; PR)
196. (PR)
197. (PR)
198. (PR)
199. son in law Edw. Jones bro. of Rol. J. Sgt at Arms CMW (PR; Will PCC; *Vis. Shropsh.*)
200. ironmonger, cardmaker; mbr Hammermen 1580; b.*c.*1556; MP; wife Ann dr of Ric. Rascoll q.v.; dr Anne m. Thos Hooke q.v.; Will PCC (SRO: RB; PRO: E.134/41–2 Eliz./Mich.3; Stac.5/B.20/13; Will PCC)
201. (PR)
202. (SRO: RB; PR; Felton)
203. b.*c.*1549; connect. Worthen and Montgom.; Corp. Renter 1598⟩ (Corp. Min.; E.134/39–40 Eliz./-Mich.37; Will PCC)
204. cordwainer (RB; PRO: E.134/41–2 Eliz. Mich.3; Stac.5/B.107/23; Corp. Min.; PR)
205. clothier (SRO: RB; 356/347B; PR)
206. hatter (PR; Felton)
207. glover; son Ric. N. q.v. (SRO: RB; PR)
208. (PR; Felton)
209. baker; b.1554 (SRO: RB; PR; PRO: E.134/8 Chas. I/Trin.13, 14 Chas I/East.34)
210. baker; son of Ric. L. q.v.; dr m. Jn Ambler q.v. (SRO: RB; Will Heref.; PRO: Stac.5/B.107/23)
211. neph. of Thos C. q.v.; prosec. at CMW under penal laws (SRO: Corp. Min.; PR; PRO: E.101/533/22)
212. innholder; b.1564 son of Ric. C. q.v.; of Bradford faction (SRO: Corp. Min.; PR)
213. apothecary; childr. inc. Jud. m. Ric. Davies q.v.; Martha m. an Aston (SRO: 356/502; Corp. Min.; CWAcc; PR)
214. mercer (Corp. Min.; PR; Will PCC)
215. Corp. renter 1608⟩; of Bradford faction; reversion of Castle portership for life 1616; bro. of Thos. E. (*CSPD* 1616; PRO: C.2/James I/E.6/1; SRO: Corp. Min.; PR)
216. (CWAcc; PR)
217. clothier (CWAcc)
218. goldsmith; supplied silver for church 1556; pardon for accid. killing 1569 (RB; Corp. Min. CWAcc; PR; Will Heref.)
219. son Ric. B. q.v. (Will Heref.)
220. butcher (CWAcc; Will Heref.)
221. tanner; of Bradford faction; b.1568 ? son of Thos. D. q.v. (SRO: Corp. Min.; PR)

222. corn-miller; b.c.1551 son of Jn G.; wife Jane Hoke; son Edw. G. q.v. (SRO: Corp. Min.; PR; PRO: E.134/14 Car.I/East.34)
223. clothier (Will PCC)
224. (RB; CWAcc; PR)
225. (CWAcc; PR)
226. (CWAcc)
227. mercer; of Bradford faction (Corp. Min.; PR)
228. (PR)
229. (PR)
230. baker (CWAcc; Will Heref.)
231. (CWAcc; Corp. Min.)
232. (CWAcc)
233. innkeeper (PR; Corp. Min.)
234. weaver; clothier; of Bradford faction; wife Jane Becke (PR; Corp. Min.)
235. son of Jn S. q.v.; wife Audrey wdw of Jn Hartgill, castle porter (Corp. Min.; PR) 236. clothier; son of Ric. H. q.v.; bro. of Ric. H. q.v. (Corp. Min.; PR; PRO: C.2/James I/H.5/38)
237. (PR)
238. mercer; Corp. renter 1638; b.c.1575 (PRO: E.134/14 Car. I/E.34; PR)
239. tanner; of Bradford faction (Corp. Min.; PR)
240. clothier; of Bradford faction; b.c.1564 son of Ric. B. q.v. (AO; Corp. Min.)
241. glover (AO; Corp. Min.)
242. glover; son of Ric. N q.v. (PR)
243. (PR)
244. walker (PR)
245. mercer (PR)
246. ironmonger (PR)
247. shoemaker; of Bradford faction; son Hen. P. q.v. (PR; Corp. Min.; Will Heref.)
248. attorney; childr. incl. Wm B.; Mary m. Edw. Gregory q.v.; Margt m. Wm Wade; Ric. B. (PRO: C.5/377/30; BL: Eg. MS.2882 f.149; PR; Corp. Min.)
249. clothier; son of Ric. H. q.v.; b.1577 (Corp. Min.; PR)
250. innkeeper (AO; Corp. Min.)
251. (PR)
252. mercer (Corp. Min.; Admon.PCC; PR)
253. cordwainer; b.1580 (Corp. Min.; PR)
254. (PR)
255. (PR)
256. innkeeper; son of Ric. A. of Acton Scott; wife Margt Edwin sr of Edw. E. q.v. (Corp. Min.; AO; PR)
257. (PR)
258. corviser; (Corp. Min.; Will PCC)
259. corviser; dr Margt m. Sam. Pritchard son of Ric. P. q.v.; Wm C. q.v. (PR; Corp. Min.)
260. bro. of Ric. J. Sgt at Arms CMW to 1619; royalist (Corp. Min.; *CCC*, ii,p.1484; *CSPD* 1616; Corp. rental 1619; PR)
261. clothier; b.1587; son of Ric. B. q.v. (PR; Corp. Min; AO)
262. clothier; sequ. 1633, 1634; b.1580 son of Hen. A.; Corp. Min.; PR)
263. (PR)
264. (PR)
265. son Israel L. q.v. wife Alice re-m. Rob. Horne, rector, q.v. (SRO: 356/502; PR; Corp. Min.; Will PCC)
266. mercer; son of Evan L. of Brecon; wife Winifred Baldwin dr of Ric. B. q.v.; bro. in law of Jn Holland, Thos Crump, Edw. Jones q.v. (SRO: Corp. Min.; PR)
267. miller; wife Audrey re-m. Thos Aldwell (SRO: Corp. Min.; PR; Will PCC)
268. b.1596 son of Ric. P. q.v. (Corp. Min.; PR; Will PCC; Mon. Inscr.)
269. tanner; son of Edw. P. q.v.; son Thos P. q.v.; royalist; removed 1654 (Corp. Min.; PR; *CCC*, ii, 1484; Will PCC)

270. glover; wives 1. Mary; 2. Dorothy wdw of Ric. Nightingale q.v. (Corp. Min.; PR) 271. son of Edw. C. q.v. (Corp. Min.; PR)
272. son of Edw. P. q.v. (Corp. Min.; PR)
273. (PR)
274. son of Jn B. q.v. (PR)
275. miller; son of Wm G. q.v.; wife Mary dr of Ellis Beddoe q.v. (HWRO: AA/20/1645/5; PR; Corp. Min.)
276. dyer (PR; Corp. Min.)
277. (Corp. Min.; PR)
278. cordwainer; b. 1584; ? son of Jn E. CS (SRO: 356/241; Will PCC; PR)
279. ? butcher (Corp. Min.; PR)
280. (PR; Will PCC)
281. bookseller; b.1584 son of Jn C. bookseller (Corp. Min.; PR)
282. kinsman of Ric. W. q.v.; glover; royalist (Corp. Min.; *CCC*, ii,1484; PR)
283. CS 1609 (Will PCC; PR)
284. mercer; tutor of Townshend childr. in Interregn.; son of Wm A. and Eliz. Cressett (Corp. Min.; RB; PR; *Vis. Shropsh.*; PRO: C.6/44/12)
285. mbr of S. family of Pembridge; dr Jane m. Wm Griffiths q.v., dr Anne m. Rowl. Williams q.v.; 1626 petty constable Old St.Wd; royalist captain (SRO: 356/421; Corp. Min.; PR; Will PCC; *CCC*, ii, 1484)
286. b.1600 son of Edw. C. q.v.; wives 1. Joan; 2. Cath. Blashfield; royalist (Corp. Min.; PR; *CCC*, ii, 1484)
287. mercer (PR; Will PCC)
288. disfr. 7 Jun. 1646; baker (Corp. Min.; PR; PCC Will Wm Reynolds 1624)
289. cordwainer; 1634 lic. to sell tobacco; wife Eliz. Dyke re-m. Ric. Scott q.v. (PR; Corp. Min.; Will Heref.; *Cal. Priv. Seal* 1634)
290. (PR)
291. apothecary; b. Halton; wives 1. Judith Fisher dr of Ric. F. q.v.; 2. Mary dr of Rees Jones; son Edw. D. q.v.; drs Isab. m. Rowl. Earsley q.v.; Mary m. Ric. Cole q.v. (Corp. Min.; PR; Will Heref.)
292. innholder (PR)
293. innholder (PR)
294. (PR)
295. glover; b.1597 Ludlow; (PR; Corp. Min.)
296. b.1594 (PR)
297. haberdasher; hatter; connect. with Disserth; wife Jane dr of Jn Powis; royalist ensign; (Corp. Min.; Town Court 1645; PR; *CCC*, ii, 1484; PRO: Prob.11/298 f.88 Edw. Powis) 298. Dyer (PR; Will PCC R. Vaughan 1635)
299. (PR)
300. son of Wm L. q.v. (Corp. Min.; PR; Will PCC)
301. saddler; b. 1601 son of Ric. Cole bro . of Ric. C. q.v.; son Ric. C. q.v. (Corp. Min.; P);
302. (PR; Corp. Min.)
303. ? son of Wm Griffiths and Jane (Stead) (PR; Corp. Min.)
304. mercer; wife Anne dr of Wal. Stead q.v. (Corp. Min.; PR)
305. (PR)
306. (PR)
307. (Corp. Min.; PR)
308. corviser; ? b.1606 son of Thos C. q.v.; sequ. 1649 for evil fame (Corp. Min.; PR)
309. ironmonger (Corp. Min.; PR; Will PCC)
310. ? son of Wm R. q.v. (PRO: Prob.11/290 f.215 Isr. Lloyd; Corp. Min.; PR)
311. tanner; son Ric. E. q.v., ? Rowl. E., bailiff (Corp. Min.; PR)
312. corviser; b.1612 son of Thos C. q.v.; royalist (Will Heref.; RB; Corp. Min.; PR; *CCC*, ii, 1484)
313. mercer (PR: Corp. Min.)
314. saddler; b.1604 son of Ric. Cole (Corp. Min.; PR)
315. (PR)
316. Town Clerk q.v. (Corp. Min.)

317. tanner; ? son of Edw.P. q.v.; royalist at siege of Brampton Br. (Corp. Min.)
318. yeoman (Corp. Min.; PR)
319. (RB; PR)
320. glover (Will PCC; PR; Corp. Min.)
321. b.1617 son of Wm R. q.v.; royalist officer (*CCC*, ii, 1485, 2788; PR; Corp. Min.)
322. (Corp. Min.; PR)
323. (PR)
324. mercer (PR; Corp. Min.; Will Heref.)
325. glover (PR)
326. gent. (Corp. Min.)
327. tanner (PR)
328. baker (Corp. Min.; PR)
329. (PR)
330. (PR)
331. bookseller (Corp. Min.; PR)
332. (PR)
333. (PR)
334. tailor (PR)
335. (RB; Corp. Min.; PR; Will PCC)
336. joiner liv. *Rose and Crown*, Corve St. (PR)
337. corviser (PR)
338. glover (PR)
339. saddler (PR; Corp. Min.)
340. mercer (PR; Corp. Min.)

Appendix 6

1. The 1614 figures are largely the work of Mr D. J. Lloyd, who identified the names in the muster book (SCRO: 356/298) using the Quarter Sessions records (SRO: 356/239), The Churchwardens' Accounts, Wills, the minute books of the Gilds of Hammermen and Stitchmen, other records at Shrewsbury (356/21; 45; 84; 91; 104; 163; 166; 170), augmented by my own researches in the State records (PRO: E.101/675/41; 533/22; 26; E.134/41–42 Eliz./Mich.30; SP46/163; 164; Stac.5/B.107/23; Stac.8/269/27. The 1667 figures come (after adjustments based on similar sources) from M. A. Faraday, 'The Ludlow Poll-Tax Return of 1667', *T.S.A.S.*, LIX (2) 1971–2, 104–123.

Index

The words 'Burgesses', 'Corporation', 'Ludlow', and 'Shropshire' have not been included in the Index. Some detail is given to identify or 'date' individuals: 'd.' = 'died'; 'E14' = 'Early 14th century'; 'L' = 'Late century'; 'M' = 'Mid-century'; '1292' = 'living in 1292'; '⟨1308–40⟩' = 'known to be active in both years'.